Sociolinguistics and th

MM Textbooks

Advisory Board:
Professor Colin Baker, *University of Wales, Bangor, UK*
Professor Viv Edwards, *University of Reading, Reading, UK*
Professor Ofelia García, *Columbia University, New York, USA*
Dr Aneta Pavlenko, *Temple University, Philadelphia, USA*
Professor David Singleton, *Trinity College, Dublin, Ireland*
Professor Terrence G. Wiley, *Arizona State University, Tempe, USA*

MM Textbooks bring the subjects covered in our successful range of academic monographs to a student audience. The books in this series explore education and all aspects of language learning and use, as well as other topics of interest to students of these subjects. Written by experts in the field, the books are supervised by a team of world-leading scholars and evaluated by instructors before publication. Each text is student-focused, with suggestions for further reading and study questions leading to a deeper understanding of the subject.

Full details of all the books in this series and of all our other publications can be found on http://www.multilingual-matters.com, or by writing to Multilingual Matters, St Nicholas House, 31-34 High Street, Bristol BS1 2AW, UK.

MM Textbooks
Consulting Editor: Professor Viv Edwards

Sociolinguistics and the Legal Process

Diana Eades

MULTILINGUAL MATTERS
Bristol • Buffalo • Toronto

Library of Congress Cataloging in Publication Data
A catalog record for this book is available from the Library of Congress.

Eades, Diana
Sociolinguistics and the Legal Process/Diana Eades.
MM Textbooks: 5
Includes bibliographical references and index.
1. Sociolinguistics. 2. Law--Language. I. Title.
P40.E13 2010
340'.14–dc22 2010005052

British Library Cataloguing in Publication Data
A catalogue entry for this book is available from the British Library.

ISBN-13: 978-1-84769-254-2 (hbk)
ISBN-13: 978-1-84769-253-5 (pbk)

Multilingual Matters
UK: St Nicholas House, 31-34 High Street, Bristol BS1 2AW, UK.
USA: UTP, 2250 Military Road, Tonawanda, NY 14150, USA.
Canada: UTP, 5201 Dufferin Street, North York, Ontario M3H 5T8, Canada.

The policy of Multilingual Matters/Channel View Publications is to use papers that are natural, renewable and recyclable products, made from wood grown in sustainable forests. In the manufacturing process of our books, and to further support our policy, preference is given to printers that have FSC and PEFC Chain of Custody certification. The FSC and/or PEFC logos will appear on those books where full certification has been granted to the printer concerned.

Typeset by Saxon Graphics Ltd, Derby
Printed and bound in Great Britain by the MPG Books Group

This book is dedicated to my parents:
my mother Pam Kelloway and my late father Paul Kelloway

Contents

List of Figures   xi

Transcript conventions and abbreviations   xii

Acknowledgements   xiv

PART 1: INTRODUCTION

1:   **Using sociolinguistics to study the legal process**   3

    1. What is sociolinguistics?   4
    2. What is meant by 'the legal process'?   4
    3. Some basic sociolinguistic principles   5
    4. Introducing spoken language in the legal process   8
    5. What can sociolinguistics contribute to the study of the legal process?   11
    6. The impact of written legal language on spoken legal language   12
    7. Different kinds of sociolinguistic analysis   14
    8. Transcription   16
    9. Different legal systems around the world   18
    10. Outline of the book   19
    11. How to use this book   20
    12. Notes on terminology   21
    13. Anglocentric orientation of this book   21
    Assignments and further research   23

PART 2: COURTROOM HEARINGS

2:   **Researching courtroom talk**   27

    1. Introduction   28
    2. Who are the participants?   31
    3. Constraints on courtroom talk   32
    4. Rules of evidence   34
    5. Access to data for researching courtroom talk   35
    Assignments and further research   38

3:   **Focus on trials**   39

    1. Introduction   40
    2. Jury selection   40
    3. Opening statements   42
    4. Witness examination   42
       4.1. Lawyers' questions   42

4.2. Witnesses' answers 47
4.3. The power of words 49
4.4. Strategies in cross-examination 50
4.5. Summarising the power imbalance in witness examination 52
5. Closing arguments 52
6. Judges' summaries and instructions to the jury 54
7. Unidirectional dimensions of courtroom talk 57
Assignments and further research 60

4: **Second language speakers and interpreters** 63

1. Introduction 64
2. Assessing and understanding the need for an interpreter 66
3. Arguments against the need for an interpreter 69
4. Understanding the role of the interpreter 70
5. Linguistic challenges in courtroom interpreting 72
    5.1. Semantic challenges 72
    5.2. Grammatical challenges 72
    5.3. Pragmatic challenges 73
    5.4. Cultural challenges 76
    5.5. Additional challenges for creole speakers 77
6. Second language speakers without interpreters 77
7. Deaf sign language users 78
Assignments and further research 81

5: **Vulnerable witnesses** 83

1. Introduction 84
2. Children 84
    2.1. Unclear and confusing questions 85
    2.2. *Do you remember* questions 86
    2.3. Suggestibility and credibility 87
    2.4. Provisions for child witnesses 88
3. Second dialect speakers 88
4. Cultural differences impacting courtroom talk 92
    4.1. Cultural presuppositions about language use in court 92
    4.2. Cultural presuppositions about actions outside of court 93
    4.3. Cultural presuppositions and courtroom discourse structure 95
5. Legislative protection for vulnerable witnesses 99
Assignments and further research 102

6: **Courtroom talk and societal power relations** 105

1. Introduction 106
2. Courtroom power revisited 106
3. Courtroom talk and the liberty of the individual 108
4. Courtroom talk and patriarchal power 112
5. Courtroom talk and neocolonial power 115

6. The power of courtroom talk   122
Assignments and further research   127

PART 3: POLICE INTERVIEWS

7: **Police interviews**   131

    1. Introduction   132
    2. Communicating the suspect's rights   132
        2.1 Police caution/Miranda rights   132
        2.2 Rewriting the rights: a linguistic approach   134
        2.3 A sociolinguistic approach   135
        2.4 *Do you understand that?*   137
        2.5 Scripted cautions: for and against   141
        2.6 'Perilously easy to waive ... nearly impossible to invoke' 142
    3. Putting the Miranda rights in context   143
    4. Truth or proof?   145
    5. Cognitive interviewing and conversation management   147
    6. Suspect resistance   149
    7. From interview to written report   153
        7.1 Fabricated confessions and policespeak   153
        7.2 The blurring of source distinctions   156
    Assignments and further research   158

8: **Police interviews with members of minority groups**   161

    1. Introduction   162
    2. Second language speakers   162
        2.1 Interpreters in police interviews   162
        2.2 Linguistic challenges in interpreting suspects' rights 165
        2.3 Second language speakers without interpreters   167
    3. Deaf sign language users   170
    4. Speakers of creole languages and second dialects   172
        4.1 Creole speakers   172
        4.2 Second dialect speakers   172
    5. Children   176
    6. Intellectually disabled people   180
    7. The politics of police questioning   180
    Assignments and further research   184

PART 4: OTHER LEGAL CONTEXTS

9: **Lawyer–client interactions**   187

    1. Introduction   188
    2. Legal rules, emotions and personalities   189
    3. Linguistic features associated with power, control and gender 191
    4. The interweaving of text and talk   194

5. From interview to affidavit   196
6. Learning to bracket emotion, morality and social context   201
Assignments and further research   204

10: Informal and alternative legal processes   205

1. Introduction   206
2. Informal courts   207
    2.1 Telling your story in informal courts   207
    2.2 Talking about social problems in informal legal processes   209
    2.3 Small claims courts and arbitration   212
3. The microdynamics of mediation talk   213
    3.1 Disputing in a different way   213
    3.2 Mediator impartiality   216
    3.3 An inherent paradox of power?   219
4. Alternative criminal justice practices   220
    4.1 Restorative justice practices   220
    4.2 Therapeutic courts   224
    4.3 Indigenous sentencing courts   225
Assignments and further research   229

PART 5: CONCLUSION

11 : What (else) can sociolinguistics do?   233

1. Introduction   234
2. Expert evidence   234
3. Legal education   239
4. Investigating inequality   240
    4.1. Language ideologies and inequality   241
    4.2. Language and understanding   243
    4.3. Storytelling and retelling   247
    4.4. Linguistic and cultural difference   251
5. Conclusion   256
Assignments and further research   257

Notes   259

Legal glossary   265

Sociolinguistic glossary   269

References   273

Subject index   295

Author index   301

Teachers' notes: http://www.mmtextbooks.com/eades/

List of Figures

Figure 2.1   Structure of New Zealand courts   29

Figure 2.2   A typical Crown courtroom in England and Wales   33

Figure 3.1   Question types in courtroom talk   44

Figure 6.1   Structure of the spoken guilty plea   109

Figure 7.1   Temporal *then* in the Bentley case   154

Transcription conventions and abbreviations

underlining	indicates emphatic stress
SMALL CAPITALS	indicate raised volume
° before and after an utterance°	indicates that it is spoken in a very low volume
°° before and after an utterance°°	indicates that it is in an extremely low volume
=	indicates latched utterances, i.e. no pause between the end of one utterance and the start of the next
[	indicates talk overlapping with that of another speaker, marked at the point in each utterance where overlap begins
-	a hyphen indicates a pause within a turn of less than 0.5 of a second
a number in parentheses	indicates the length of a pause in seconds e.g. (3.2)
parentheses	around a word or phrase indicates transcriber doubt
(xxxxxx)	indicates an inaudible utterance
double parentheses	are used to enclose transcriber's description of paralinguistic or other activity by the speaker e.g. ((laughs)), or others e.g. ((laughter))
:	a colon within a word indicates lengthened sound
...	omitted talk
C	client
Ch	child
D	defendant
DC	defence counsel
Int	interpreter

Iv	interviewer
J	judge
L	lawyer
(Lx)	indicates an assignment topic most suited to students with a linguistics background
M	magistrate
PL	paralegal
PO	police officer
Pros	prosecutor
Sus	suspect
W	witness
Bold type	indicates particular segments of the transcript being highlighted in my analysis. It is used only in extracts where one particular utterance pertains to the discussion more than the rest of the utterances in that extract
Regular English spelling	is used throughout, except for a few places where a word or phrase is pronounced in a clearly abbreviated or non-standard way
All names in examples	are pseudonyms
i, ii, iii	Roman numeral superscripts refer teachers to the teacher notes

Acknowledgements

This book would never have been possible without many valuable discussions with and publications by colleagues in the language and law/forensic linguistic community around the world over the last two decades or so. It also owes a great deal to the students in my language and law classes at University of Hawai'i and Victoria University of Wellington. I am particularly grateful to Jeff Siegel and John Conley for their careful reading of the draft, and for their helpful comments and suggestions. Ron Butters, Michael Cooke, Susan Ehrlich, Justice Peter Gray, Audrey Guinchard, Chris Heffer, David McKee, Jim Martin, Ikuko Nakane, Jemina Napier, Mack O'Barr, Matt Prior, Andrea Schalley, Michael Walsh and Michele Zappavigna provided feedback and/or information on specific sections. All errors are of course entirely my responsibility.

I would also like to thank Viv Edwards for the invitation to write this book, and for her continuing support through all stages, and Anna Roderick and Sarah Williams at Multilingual Matters for their encouragement and excellent editorial and production work which has transformed my manuscript. Vicki Knox has once again provided meticulous assistance with proofreading.

Special thanks go to friends and family for patience and encouragement. My greatest debt of gratitude is to my husband Jeff Siegel, for always supporting me – materially, emotionally and intellectually.

I am grateful for permission from the following authors and publishers:
Figure 2.1 is reproduced with permission from New Zealand Ministry of Justice, copyrighted 2009 to New Zealand Crown; Figures 2.2 and the jury direction quoted in Section 7 of Chapter 3 from *The Language of Jury Trial: A Corpus-Aided Analysis of Legal–Lay Discourse* by Chris Heffer published in 2005 by Palgrave Macmillan; The sample jury directions in Exercise 3.7 are from Beyond 'reasonable doubt': The criminal standard of proof instruction as communicative act, by Chris Heffer, published in *International Journal of Speech, Language and the Law* 13 (2), 159–188, © Equinox Publishing Ltd 2006; Extract 5–iv and the related discussion are from 'I don't think it's an answer to the question': Silencing Aboriginal witnesses in court, by Diana Eades, published in 2000 *Language in Society* 29 (2), 161–196, © Cambridge University Press; Figure 6.1 and Extracts 6–ii and 6–iii are from *Ideology in the Language of Judges: How Judges Practice Law, Politics and Courtroom Control* by Susan U. Philips, published in 1998 by permission of Oxford University Press Inc.; Extracts 6–vi, 6–vii, 6–viii, 6–ix, 6–x and 6–xi and the related discussion are from *Courtroom Talk and Neocolonial Control* by Diana Eades, published in 2008 by Mouton de Gruyter; Extracts 9–i, 9–ii and 9–iii are from *Latinas' Narratives of Domestic Abuse: Discrepant Versions of Violence* by Shonna Trinch, published in 2003 with kind permission by John Benjamins Publishing Company Amsterdam/Philadelphia; Extracts 10–i and 10–ii are from *Rules versus Relationships* by John M. Conley and William M. O'Barr, published in 1990 by University of Chicago Press; The sociolinguistic glossary draws with permission on *A Dictionary of Sociolinguistics* by Joan Swann, Ana Deumert, Theresa Lillis and Rajend Mesthrie, published in 2004 by Edinburgh

Press (www.euppublishing.com); The legal glossary draws with permission on *Butterworth's Concise Australian Legal Dictionary* (3rd edition) published in 2004 by Reed International Books Australia Pty Ltd trading as LexisNexis.

Part 1

Introduction

1

Using sociolinguistics to study the legal process

1. What is sociolinguistics?	4
2. What is meant by 'the legal process'?	4
3. Some basic sociolinguistic principles	5
4. Introducing spoken language in the legal process	8
5. What can sociolinguistics contribute to the study of the legal process?	11
6. The impact of written legal language on spoken legal language	12
7. Different kinds of sociolinguistic analysis	14
8. Transcription	16
9. Different legal systems around the world	18
10. Outline of the book	19
11. How to use this book	20
12. Notes on terminology	21
13. Anglocentric orientation of this book	21
Assignments and further research	*23*

Using sociolinguistics to study the legal process

Language is central to the legal process: written laws, judicial decisions, police interviews, competing claims in a dispute, courtroom evidence, legal argument, mediation hearings, all of these events or products of the legal process are carried out through language, whether written or spoken or both. Lawyers have to be 'good with language' to succeed in their profession. Indeed, some might argue that success in any legal process depends to a considerable degree on the linguistic dexterity of participants, including witnesses, litigants and legal professionals.

This book is intended as a textbook for a university or college postgraduate or advanced undergraduate course in which sociolinguistics is used in an examination of the legal process. Some students will know nothing about the legal process, and some will know nothing about sociolinguistics. This chapter aims to address these two gaps at a fairly introductory level, so students from both backgrounds can go on to use the substantive chapters as part of the same course. Further background about sociolinguistics and law will be provided as necessary throughout the text.

1. What is sociolinguistics?

In the simplest terms, sociolinguistics is the study of language use in its social contexts. While linguistics primarily analyses the structure of language, sociolinguistics analyses language function and use. Modern sociolinguistics has developed since the 1960s, and most of the founders of various sub-disciplines within sociolinguistics are still alive today. Sociolinguistics often requires an understanding of principles and methods from linguistics, and there is often no hard and fast boundary between sociolinguistics and linguistics. Strictly speaking, some of the approaches, studies and publications discussed in this book would be described as '(socio)linguistic', or 'linguistic and sociolinguistic'. But to avoid repeated clumsiness, I will use sociolinguistics to refer to the analysis of language function and use, with the understanding that this often also incorporates some study of language structure. If you do not have a background in sociolinguistics, you are recommended to read Holmes (2008).

2. What is meant by 'the legal process'?

All societies have systems of law which govern acceptable behaviour and which comprise social mechanisms for dealing with disputes. It is common to distinguish between formal and informal legal systems, just as between formal and informal education. This book is concerned with language in formal legal systems. For reasons explained in Section 9 below, the primary legal focus will be the common law legal system found in countries such as Australia, England, New Zealand, the United States and most of Canada. Legal anthropology mainly examines informal legal systems (sometimes referred to as 'customary law'), and readers interested in pursuing this area should start with Conley and O'Barr's (2005: Chapter 6) introduction to the area. The terms 'legal system' and 'legal process' can often be used interchangeably. I will mainly refer to the legal process because the interest of sociolinguists is in what happens in the process, specifically what people do in interactions that take place within the legal system.

3. Some basic sociolinguistic principles

Sociolinguistics is concerned with the complex relationship between language and society. There are three main ways in which this relationship can be conceptualised. First, much sociolinguistics in the 1960s–1990s proceeded from the axiomatic assumption that language reflects society. Such an assumption would view the hierarchical ways of addressing people in the courtroom – such as calling the judge *your honour* – as a reflection of the hierarchical authority structure of courtrooms. Second, an influential axiomatic assumption reverses the direction of the relationship between language and society, so that the hierarchical authority structure in courtrooms would be seen partly as the effect of such language usage as calling the judge *your honour*. This view that language determines aspects of society, or culture, or even thought, is associated with the work of early 20th century American linguistic anthropologists Benjamin Lee Whorf and his teacher Edward Sapir, and is often referred to as 'the Whorfian hypothesis'.

Like so many other earlier dichotomies in the social sciences, these two opposite ways of thinking about the relationship between language and society have been deconstructed in the later part of the 20th century. Twenty-first century sociolinguistics assumes a dynamic and reciprocal relationship between language and society, so that language usage at the same time both reflects and shapes society. This third view can be seen as part of the wider approach in the social sciences, in which the earlier dichotomy between social structure and agency is also rejected, in favour of an understanding that the two are inseparable: it is the agency of individuals in social groups which creates, shapes, maintains, reinforces and changes social structures, which in turn limit and enable the agency of individuals. This axiomatic understanding of society underpins the best sociolinguistic work on language in the legal process. Indeed, the legal process is an ideal institutional site for the examination of this dynamic interrelationship between social structure and agency, as we will see. To understand language usage in any specific legal context is impossible without an examination of structural institutional aspects of the legal system. On the other hand, sociolegal studies of the law can be greatly enriched by an examination of situated language practices in specific legal contexts.

The social contexts of language use are of central importance in any sociolinguistic study. This book is organised according to the overarching legal contexts of courtrooms in Part 2, police interviews in Part 3, and then in Part 4, the lesser researched legal contexts of lawyer–client interviews followed by informal and alternative legal processes. In all of these contexts, the main focus will be on spoken language.

One of the basic investigative methods in the descriptive phase of sociolinguistic research is to look for patterns in language use. We constantly ask what happens in what contexts, with what people, and what results. We also pay attention to unusual occurrences, as they can be as illustrative of language use as regular patterned behaviour. At the analytical phase of research we ask why people use language in these ways in these contexts, and at the interpretative phase, we ask whether and how these patterns of language use matter.

Spoken language is characterised by variation. This variation is studied by linguists and sociolinguists along two dimensions: diachronic and synchronic. Diachronic variation is best summed up by saying that all languages change over time. You don't have to do linguistic analysis to observe that English has changed since Shakespeare's time. Even within three generations of your own family, you can probably observe some of this diachronic variation. It's often easiest to notice in terms of vocabulary change, but linguists also observe changes in grammar, accent, meaning and language use. In my family, some members of the generation born in the 1920s pronounce the first sound in *where* or *white* differently from the first sound in *were* or *wide*. No one in the younger generations of our family does this.

Synchronic variation refers to differences in the ways in which language is used in the same time period, and is best summed up by saying that people speak differently in different contexts. If you have never observed this variation, try paying close attention to, or audiorecording, a friend in two quite different contexts (with their permission, of course). The variation is easiest to observe where these contexts differ considerably in terms of formality, for example in a bar and in a formal interview.

It is undeniable that all languages are constantly in a state of change – although there is no consistency in the extent to which such change in different languages is observable to the untrained analyst. Analogous in some ways to the situation with living organisms, when a language ceases to change, this is a fairly good indication that it is dying. But the popular view, especially among educators in some societies, is that language change can be prevented, and that it is a sign of slipping standards, or even moral decline. Linguists such as Lippi-Green (1997) have written about the problems which arise from such myths about the nature of language.

It is not just spoken language which is always in the process of change. The same is true of written language, although the rate of change and the extent of synchronic variation can be much less significant than with spoken language. But nevertheless, we can still see synchronic variation, for example depending on the formality of the written text. Letters between family members differ in grammatical structure and word choice from legal statutes. And examination of either of these types of writing over a few generations will provide evidence of diachronic change in written language.

Lack of understanding about differences between spoken and written language, and about variation in language use can be important in the legal process, as we will see in Section 2 of Chapter 7 and Section 4 of Chapter 8, respectively. There is a widespread popular view that the way in which language is written, especially after being carefully checked and edited, is 'correct'. In this view, any ways in which spoken language deviates from such written norms amount to errors. Such a prescriptive view – how language should be written or spoken – reflects beliefs and value judgements about how people should act. But (socio)linguistics, for the most part, avoids prescriptive views and concentrates on description – describing the way that language is actually written or spoken. I say that this is what (socio)linguistics does for the most part, because there are some areas in which our discipline does venture into prescriptivism. These occasions on which we argue that language should or should not be spoken or written in a certain way arise from descriptive work on the social consequences of particular ways of using language. The best-known example comes from the area of language and gender, where sociolinguists have contributed greatly in the last three decades to the development of practical guidelines about how to avoid sexist and other forms of discriminatory language. Similarly, sociolinguists who examine and describe the impact on disadvantaged social groups of specific aspects of language use in the legal process, sometimes also advocate changes to language practices, such as to the ways in which interpreting works in court (e.g. Mikkelson 1998).

It is very common for people to speak differently from the way they write. There are many reasons for this: some are cognitive, relating to the greater opportunity for planning and revision with most types of writing than with most types of speaking. Other reasons are interactional: any kind of feedback that we receive from interlocutors while we are speaking can affect what we say. This feedback may be as minimal as non-verbal feedback from students during a lecture, or it may involve a friend overlapping or interrupting during a dyadic conversation. Within the single legal context of a courtroom trial, we may observe a continuum from formal written texts (such as a written affidavit, resulting from many earlier drafts), to formal spoken texts (such as a judgment being read from a prepared written text), to less formal written texts (such as contemporaneous notes in a police officer's notebook), to formulaic scripted spoken texts (such as the oath to tell the truth), to formal spoken legal talk (such as legal argument between lawyers), to less formal spoken talk (such as a police officer's oral evidence about *the male person observed to be travelling in a northerly direction when apprehended in the said motor vehicle*), to informal spoken talk (such as may be found in many interactions between witnesses and those who are questioning them, whether lawyers or judges). At the more formal end of such a continuum, there are less likely to be incomplete sentences than at the less formal end. Such a difference in the grammatical structure of language does not reflect the intelligence of the speaker or their educational level, as is commonly believed. Just as learned judges may well swear just as much as anyone else in the company of friends over a few drinks, so too grammatical informality can be observed by any of these participants at the less formal end of the spectrum of language variation in the courtroom.

Having established that language variation is ubiquitous and that it is related to social factors, rather than personal attributes such as intelligence, let us consider a key sociolinguistic term, namely 'dialect'. Sociolinguists use this term in a neutral way, unlike the popular usage, where the word is often collocated with the word *only*, as in *she only speaks a dialect*. The word 'dialect' in popular usage tends to be derogatory, and indicates something less than a language, but it does not have this meaning in (socio)linguistics. Finding it easier to define in terms of the plural form 'dialects', we use this term to refer to forms of a language which are generally mutually intelligible, and which differ from each other in systematic ways, such as in accent, grammar, words and their meaning, and communication patterns. The notion of mutual intelligibility is not necessarily as simple as it might sound, and the distinction in some parts of the world between related languages and related dialects can be a tricky one, so linguists find the cover term 'variety' useful for referring to languages and/or dialects. Differences between social groups based on ethnicity or geographical and/or political space often correspond to the use of different language varieties. However, the variety that a person speaks is not determined by their ethnicity or geographical/political origin, but by the language variety/varieties that they were socialised in – that is the language variety/varieties they learned, mainly implicitly, from the people they interacted with. While the ability to acquire language is innate in all humans, the particular language variety which any individual acquires is one which is spoken to them and around them in their social environment as part of their socialisation. Primary socialisation occurs from birth and is the stimulus for learning your first language, but later socialisation in different social environments can result in learning additional languages (and note that some children learn more than one language as their 'first languages', if they are socialised in a multilingual environment).

4. Introducing spoken language in the legal process

So what is spoken language like in the legal process? Before you read some introductory comments, do Exercise 1.1 (in small groups or individually).

Exercise 1.1[i]

Examples (a)–(d) below come from the author's observations of courtroom hearings. Example (e) comes from an audiorecorded police interview. Consider the brief contextual information given, and for each example
1) give an ordinary English translation of the utterance.
2) think of possible reasons why such an ordinary English utterance was not used.
3) discuss whether it matters that ordinary English was not used in this instance.

(a) Lawyer to judge during a trial:
I wonder if I could uplift from your honour the documentation.

(b) Lawyer to a police officer giving evidence during a trial:
In relation to the accused John Frederick Smith you prepared a two page antecedent form?

(c) Lawyer to judge during trial:
Your honour I'm sure my learned friend will concede that it was in fact the eighth of May.

(d) Lawyer during examination-in-chief in trial, asking defendant about his sister:
She's got three girls? I withdraw that, three children?

(e) Police officer to 18-year-old suspect in a recorded interview in the police station:
As I already informed you Jane, I'm making inquiries in relation to an amount of green vegetable matter which was located in the glove box of a motor vehicle today searched by myself and Detective Sergeant John Miller.

There are several observations we can make about the data in these examples. The most striking feature of the language in these examples are the words and phrases (= lexical items) in the legal register. The term 'register' refers to a language variety used in a particular context, or by a particular group of people, usually sharing the same occupation or the same interests. In (a) above, the lawyer could just as easily have said to the judge *I wonder if I could take that paperwork back from you,* and in (c), the lawyer could have said *agree* instead of *concede.* But legal professionals – lawyers, magistrates and judges – often use this legal register in their written and spoken communication with each other. The utterance given as (b) above shows that it is also used with police officers, in this instance when the police officer was giving evidence. Why is such complex legal language used in such instances of spoken communication?

To answer this question, we need to consider a number of factors. First, much of the training and day-to-day work of lawyers requires them to examine and study written law, which is very complex. (We will briefly discuss this in Section 6 below.) It is possible that some lawyers are not very good at switching from this complex legal register to everyday talk. And lawyers may become so used to saying *in relation to* instead of *about* that they don't even notice that it sounds stilted to non-lawyers. There also appears to be a pervasive assumption in the legal process that written communication is more important than spoken communication. For example, in preparing an appeal to a higher court about a decision in a lower court, most lawyers will pore over the transcript of the lower court hearing. Even when this hearing has been officially audiorecorded and the lawyer could listen to what is said, it is the official typed transcript of this hearing which is counted as evidence, and which is the basis of the appeal lawyer's work. It is hardly surprising then, that in court lawyers often speak in a way that addresses the transcript and future readers of it, as much as it does the people in the court that day, if not more. This is why in the utterance given as (d) above, the lawyer says *I withdraw that,* meaning something like *Ignore that question* or even *Delete that question.* It is not at all clear whether the witness understood what the lawyer meant, but the judge in court that day, and any legal professional reading the transcript later, would understand that he thought that the witness's sister had three daughters, but realised as soon as he said it that maybe not all of her children were girls.

We also see within the legal process the workings of a more widespread societal assumption that formality indicates respect. From my observations of the lawyer who said the utterance given as (a) above, I formed the view that he is quite good at switching between such formal talk to the judge and quite informal talk to the witness, with questions such as *Where does your brother Kim live?* His use in (a) of the legal register involving formal sentence structure and two stilted lexical items (*uplift* and *documentation*) was possibly a part of his enactment of deferential respect to the judge. Such a stance is an integral part of the workings of the authority structure in court, and might also result in the judge extending patience to this lawyer and his witness. Thus such bizarre sounding spoken interaction in court that day may have been part of the intricate work being carried out by this lawyer. For example, he may have been thinking something like this: *my next witness may be rather long-winded, and this might risk making the judge feel impatient. I'll do all I can this morning to be particularly respectful to the judge.*

There are other reasons why legal professionals use legal register (= legalese). Like any other profession, law has its own register, its 'terms of art' – words which have a specific technical meaning. To 'translate' such terms into ordinary English would often make lawyers' legal talk more wordy. And when they are talking to other legal professionals this would be unnecessary and somewhat clumsy. For a lawyer to avoid using the term *antecedent form* to a police officer about the official list of previous convictions of the witness, would be like one computer technician asking another about a problematic computer without using specialised terms such as *boot* and *USB port*. Another reason why lawyers might sometimes use complex legal language to another lawyer or to a judicial officer during a courtroom hearing is explained by Tiersma (1999: 154). He says that lawyers may sometimes deliberately do this 'to discourage their clients from interfering in the process and slowing it down'.

If you ask a lawyer about why they use complicated legal language, they will often say it is because they need to be precise, and this might also explain the use of the term *antecedent form* in (b) above. Precision is central to all dimensions of the legal process. A good example of the need for precision is found in (e) above. There are a number of lexical items in this example which seem more like the language between legal professionals than I typically hear addressed to laypeople in other legal contexts. Thus the use of *informed* rather than *told*, *in relation to* rather than *about*, and the placement of the time adverb *today* all make this a rather stilted thing to say to an 18-year-old. Does this formal and stilted way of talking to a suspect matter? Might it be hard for Jane to understand? Or, on the other hand, might it serve a useful purpose in signalling to her that this interview is serious business? What about *green vegetable matter*? Does anybody refer to marijuana as *green vegetable matter* apart from legal professionals? But there is probably a legal reason for this lexical choice: the police officer cannot legally assume that this *vegetable matter* is marijuana, until this has been proven by laboratory testing. This is a good example of the occasional need for technical stilted language in order to be precise, although a more common expression could probably have been used, such as *green plants* or *green leaves* or *plant stuff*. In Section 7.1 of Chapter 7, we will take up this issue in the discussion of 'policespeak'.

But much of the language addressed to laypeople in the legal process – such as people being interviewed by the police, or witnesses (including defendants and complainants) in court – does not contain any special legal language. It can be much more straightforward, as in the examples in Extract 1–i from lawyers questioning a defendant in a criminal trial:

Extract 1–i Eades' unpublished transcription of official audiorecording
1. (in examination-in-chief): *And whereabouts were those chairs being thrown around?*
2. (in cross-examination): *Would you agree with me that you told the police on that night that 'he threw me up against the china cabinet and smashed the glass'?*

Most of the examples of legal register occur in talk between legal professionals, as in Examples (a), (b) and (c) in Exercise 1.1 above. In my experience, much of the language addressed to laypeople in the Australian legal system contains little, if any, of this specialised legal language (and Heffer (2005) makes the same report about trials in England and Wales). But many people who go through a formal legal proceeding end up feeling alienated by the way that language is used. While I've heard people complain about the *big words* used by lawyers, this is not a particularly accurate label. Much of what they are referring to appears to be the linguistic dexterity which lawyers have in using language to suit their legal purposes, and to present their version of events and situations. This involves such linguistic strategies as subtle word choice, embedding of presuppositions in questions, double negative questions and passive constructions, as we will see in Chapters 3 and 6. Lawyers are often skilled at language manipulation, and this skill, combined with the constraints on witnesses – for example being restricted to providing an answer to the most recently asked question – often leaves witnesses feeling confused, silenced, overwhelmed or contradicted.

The examples we have seen have given us a tiny glimpse at some of the workings of language in the legal process. With its focus on language function, sociolinguistics can investigate how language works in legal contexts. This investigation often entails examination of aspects of the form or structure of language as well, the traditional domain of linguistics (as contrasted to sociolinguistics). Our brief discussion of the aspects of legal register above mainly examined lexical examples, although you will have noticed unusual word order in (a) above with the object (*the documentation*) of the verb phrase (*could uplift*) coming after the prepositional phrase (*from your honour*) instead of immediately after the verb phrase. As we will see throughout this book, all levels of language are of interest in sociolinguistic studies of language in the legal process: phonological (or sound systems), morpho-syntax (or grammar), lexical (or word choice), semantic (or meaning) and pragmatic (or contextual usage).

5. What can sociolinguistics contribute to the study of the legal process?

Sociolinguistics can be a valuable tool in the examination of the workings of the legal process, contributing insights on a wide range of questions, such as these:

- How can witnesses present themselves in the best light?

- How can a lawyer destroy a witness's version of events?

- How can a lawyer subtly manipulate a witness's story?

- How can police officers ask questions in a way which presents a suspect in the most legally damaging light?

- Can we tell whether a second language speaker of English understood the questions she was asked in a police interview?

- What communication issues affect deaf sign language users in the legal process?

- What impact does cultural difference have on a person's participation in the legal process?

- Is it fair to subject children to questioning in police interviews or courtroom hearings?

- How do lawyers explain the law to their clients and explain their clients to the law?

- How does language use in informal courts differ from language use in formal courts?

- When mediation is used as an alternative to court, are disputing parties given more equal opportunities to argue their case than if they had taken their dispute to court?

- How do indigenous courts work differently from other courts?

This textbook will address many questions of this nature. But, as we will see throughout this book, sociolinguistics can go further, making a valuable contribution to bigger issues of justice. A central concern of much of the recent and contemporary work in sociolegal studies is the failure of the law to deliver justice. In an important book which calls on sociolinguists to make a contribution to sociolegal studies, Conley and O'Barr (2005) lament the tendency of sociolinguistic studies to avoid examining the social consequences of the language patterns they have been finding in the legal process. They argue for a sociolinguistic approach which goes beyond description of language patterns to analysis of the role of such language patterns in the workings of the legal process. It is this approach which is taken in this book. Like Conley and O'Barr, I believe that rigorous sociolinguistic analysis can help us to understand the workings of the law and to see its shortcomings as well as its strengths. We will see that sociolinguistics can make important contributions to the central question about how social inequality is reproduced both in the legal system and through the legal system.

As this book draws on a wide range of sociolinguistic studies, I will introduce a number of sociolinguistic approaches and methods in Section 7 below. It should be pointed out, however, that not all scholars feel the need to label their particular type of sociolinguistics, and there are no hard and fast boundaries between several of the different approaches. My own theoretical orientation, which underpins this book, is critical sociolinguistics. But the book is by no means restricted to this approach in its consideration of sociolinguistic and related approaches to the study of language use in the legal process. Further, typical of much contemporary social science research, there is no canonical formulation of what counts as critical sociolinguistics. In my discussion in Eades (2008a), I explain that critical sociolinguistics is part of the wider critical turn in the social sciences. While there is a range of critical approaches, they all share a major aim, expressed by Blommaert (2005: 6) as 'performing analyses that ... expose and critique existing wrongs in one's society'. Critical sociolinguistic analysis of language in the legal process enables us to expose and critique how and why the legal system fails to deliver justice, as we will see throughout this book, especially in Chapter 6 and Chapter 11.

6. The impact of written legal language on spoken legal language

Written legal language has a reputation for being wordy and hard to understand. This topic is outside of the scope of this book, which focuses mainly on spoken language in legal contexts, but readers are referred to Mellinkoff (1963) and Tiersma (1999). (See also Coulthard and Johnson (2007) and Gibbons (2003).)

We have already considered some of the reasons why spoken language in legal contexts such as police interviews and courtroom hearings can be hard for non-legal professionals to understand. But in addition to the reasons discussed in Section 4 above, we need to consider the particularly close relationship between written language and some spoken language in legal contexts. Police officers, lawyers and judicial officers are often very mindful of provisions of a particular written statute (or law) which is relevant to particular spoken legal contexts. Thus, they may talk about a particular issue to a layperson in terms of this statute. The obvious question is 'why can't they talk about it in ordinary language?' to such a person. Even if they are aware that the layperson may find it hard to understand, as we will see in Sections 6 and 7 of Chapter 3, the legal professional may be concerned that their explanation in ordinary English may leave open the possibility for some error or grounds of appeal. All the more reason for laws and contracts to be written in ordinary English in the first place!

A good example occurred in an Australian magistrate's repeated advice to a 13-year-old witness about his self-incrimination privilege.[1] This privilege, extended to anyone being questioned in a police interview or courtroom hearing, gives them the right to refuse to answer any question which might incriminate them, i.e. provide evidence of their guilt. This is consistent with the right to silence, and the fundamental principle that it is up to the state to prove a person's guilt. (This is like the 5th Amendment to the Bill of Rights in the US which applies in any situation in which the state attempts to get incriminating evidence: hence the expression often heard on American television police or courtroom dramas *I plead the 5th*).

In this Australian case (to be discussed in Section 5 of Chapter 6), the child was a prosecution witness in a case against six police officers charged with abducting him and two of his friends. The witness was not under investigation for any criminal act of his own. But the defence lawyers questioned him at length about his criminal record – more about this than about the incident in which police told him and his friends to get into police cars, and then drove them out of town and abandoned them. When the lawyers asked questions like *Have you ever thrown rocks at a light?*, the magistrate was obliged to advise the witness of his self-incrimination privilege, as an answer could involve him talking about an incident for which he had not been 'caught'. The magistrate constantly referred to this not as advice, but as a *warning*, which he usually gave with the formulaic expression *I warn you that you are not obliged to answer any question which will incriminate you in relation to the commission of a criminal offence.* He sometimes delivered it somewhat indirectly, by replacing the second person pronoun *you* with a third person form, such as *the witness* (and on two occasions with the erroneous third person form *the defendant*, erroneous because the child was not the defendant in this case, but the witness). On one occasion the magistrate asked this child witness if he knew *what the words claim privilege mean?* When the witness replied *No*, the magistrate said *It means you can refuse to answer questions which might incriminate you- you follow- all you have to say is- I refuse to answer because the answer might incriminate me.* It seems hardly likely to have helped this boy's comprehension of what *claim privilege* means, by defining it in terms of *questions which might incriminate you*, which is itself a complex notion.

While this example shows the influence of written legal language on spoken legal language, this influence is not apparent in much of the talk addressed to laypeople.

Exercise 1.2[ii]

Imagine that you are a magistrate needing to explain the self-incrimination privilege to a teenager. How would you explain it? Use the magistrate's formula above, as a point of departure, that is:

I warn you that you are not obliged to answer any question which will incriminate you in relation to the commission of a criminal offence.

You may want to consult Section 15 of the Queensland Evidence Act in order to clarify exactly what the privilege involves:

http://www.austlii.edu.au/au/legis/qld/consol_act/ea197780/

If you are a fluent speaker of a language other than English, try translating this advice into this other language.

Discuss the legal and linguistic issues involved in providing an explanation of this privilege in ordinary English (and in another language, if possible).

---

7. Different kinds of sociolinguistic analysis

Regardless of the particular approach or methodology undertaken, all sociolinguistic analysis has an empirical basis. We do not make claims about the relationship between language and society on the basis of introspection, philosophy or intuition. We gather evidence of actual language use – a person or people saying or writing something – and examine this language use in its social context. Depending on the nature of the particular research question(s) we are pursuing, certain approaches will be more suitable than others. This is not the place to catalogue sociolinguistic approaches with any depth. The following list introduces sociolinguistic approaches most commonly found in studies of language and the law (see Swann *et al.* 2004 for further information and introductory references). You will see that researchers often use more than one of these approaches in addressing their research question(s). There has been a tradition within sociolinguistics to distinguish between microanalysis, such as discourse analysis, and macroanalysis, such as survey studies of language choice in multilingual contexts. However, increasingly, the macro/micro divide is becoming harder to sustain, as many (but not all) scholars engaged in microanalysis, for example of courtroom talk, find that this is impossible to understand without examining the wider societal context (see Eades 2008a). Similarly, researchers find that understanding language use at the societal level is impossible without examining in detail actual instances of language use.

Ethnography of speaking/ethnography of communication studies the ways of speaking (or more broadly ways of communicating) in a speech community. It can be characterised as the study of who can talk to whom about what, where, when and how. It uses the anthropological approach of ethnography, in which researchers are interested in how members of a social group live, and in learning about their beliefs, values and practices from careful observation (rather than for example, interviews).

Discourse analysis studies language use beyond the sentence level, whether in face-to-face interactions such as conversations or interviews or public speeches, or written

---

communication such as newspaper articles or codified laws. Analysis in this approach examines the details of actual talk, and is a type of microanalysis. It often uses audio- or videorecorded data, although it can use written data. The term 'discourse analysis' is used quite widely in the social sciences to refer to a range of approaches to the analysis of discourse. Sociolinguistic discourse analysis pays attention not just to the content of what is said but how it is said, examining linguistic dimensions, such as grammar, accent, word choice, turn-taking and context. Within sociolinguistic discourse analysis, there are several more focused traditions:

- Conversation Analysis (CA) is a particular type of analysis of discourse, which has concentrated mostly on everyday conversations, but is increasingly being used also in the study of institutional talk, such as in courtrooms. Originating in the sociological tradition of ethnomethodology, CA has a primary focus on the structure of conversations, and on how this is cooperatively managed by participants.

- Interactional sociolinguistics is another particular type of analysis of discourse, which, in contrast to CA, highlights contextual and cultural dimensions of language and interaction.

- Critical Discourse Analysis (CDA) is discourse analysis which examines the ways in which language use (or discourse practices) reproduce and/or transform power relations within society.

Variationist sociolinguistics studies patterns and structures of language variation, often using quantitative analysis, e.g. to examine different ways of pronouncing the same word by a large number of speakers. Initially this approach correlated social variables such as age, gender and socioeconomic class with language variation. Increasingly this is being broadened to examine dynamic interactions between variations in ways of using language and ways in which speakers can actively fine-tune a wide range of aspects of their social identity.

Sociology of language focuses on society-level issues involving language. Topics include language choice and language planning in multilingual contexts. Traditionally this kind of analysis has used macroanalysis.

Critical sociolinguistics typically uses a range of sociolinguistic approaches (both macro and micro) in combination with social theoretical analysis to examine the role of language in power relationships.

Descriptive linguistics studies the structure of language and it complements and accompanies much sociolinguistic analysis. It uses a number of analytical approaches: phonetics and phonology encompass the study of speech sounds and sound systems, morphology and syntax make up the study of the structure of words and sentences (and is sometimes referred to with the term 'grammar'); and semantics refers to the study of the meaning of words and expressions.

8. Transcription

As the section above has outlined, sociolinguistics often involves the study of what individual people say in specified contexts. Transcripts of recorded talk are central to analysis and reporting in this kind of sociolinguistic study. It might seem that transcription is straightforward – you just write down what is said. However, all transcription involves choices, both in what is written down and what is left out, as well as in how talk is represented. For example, do you write down all the sounds which are not recognisable words? What do you do when two people are talking at once and it is hard to make out what they are saying? How should non-standard words be represented – in the closest relevant Standard English spelling, or in phonetic symbols, or in eye dialect, that is using non-standard spelling conventions to convey the way the talk sounds, as in *D'ya see the turdles?* A number of scholars have addressed these issues, pointing out that there is no such thing as a neutral transcription and that researchers tend to make choices about transcription that best suit their audience and their theory. There is also a trade-off between the level of transcription detail and the amount which can be transcribed. Rough estimates from a number of researchers suggest that it takes at least six hours to transcribe the propositional content of one hour of talk, where the sound quality is excellent, the transcriber knows the speakers and the language and was present during the recording, and there is minimal overlapping of speech. It takes much longer if you include interactional and prosodic features such as overlapping talk, pauses, and changes in volume and pitch. Matoesian (1993: 52) reports that his detailed CA transcription of courtroom talk took approximately 50–60 hours of work for one hour of recording. So, depending on the quality of the recording, and the interactional detail to be transcribed, it can take between about six and 60 hours to transcribe one hour of talk. Students who plan to undertake research involving transcription are strongly encouraged to read Bucholtz (2000, 2007, 2009) and Edwards (2001). A comprehensive listing and explanation of some commonly used transcription conventions is found in Schiffrin (1994).

There is some inevitable variation in the transcription conventions used by authors whose data I quote from in extracts throughout this book. In the interests of clarity and readability, I have standardised transcriptions to some extent, using the conventions listed below. Some authors provide more transcript detail than others. Thus for example scholars who use official court transcripts are not able to provide information about pauses, overlapping talk, repairs and a range of prosodic detail, such as tone and volume. But quite a bit of this kind of detail is provided in some other studies, where the basis for analysis has been recorded talk. In some cases, I have simplified the original transcription, in order to maximise readability (see Conley & O'Barr 2005: xv) and to minimise errors in transcription reproduction (see O'Connell & Kowal 2000). The following transcription conventions and abbreviations are used in this book:

underlining	indicates emphatic stress
SMALL CAPITALS	indicates raised volume
° before and after an utterance°	indicates that it is spoken in a very low volume
°° before and after an utterance°°	indicates that it is in an extremely low volume

=	indicates latched utterances, i.e. no pause between the end of one utterance and the start of the next
[	indicates talk overlapping with that of another speaker, marked at the point in each utterance where overlap begins
-	a hyphen indicates a pause within a turn of less than 0.5 of a second
a number in parentheses	indicates the length of a pause in seconds, e.g. (3.2)
parentheses	around a word or phrase indicates transcriber doubt
(xxxxxx)	indicates an inaudible utterance
double parentheses	are used to enclose transcriber's description of paralinguistic or other activity by the speaker, e.g. ((laughs)) or others, e.g. ((laughter))
:	a colon within a word indicates lengthened sound
...	omitted talk
C	client
Ch	child
D	defendant
DC	defence counsel
Int	interpreter
Iv	interviewer
J	judge
L	lawyer
M	magistrate
PL	paralegal
PO	police officer
Pros	prosecutor
Sus	suspect
W	witness
Bold type	indicates particular segments of the transcript being highlighted in my analysis. It is used only in extracts where one particular utterance pertains to the discussion more than the rest of the utterances in that extract
Regular English spelling	is used throughout, except for a few places where a word or phrase is pronounced in a clearly abbreviated or non-standard way
All names in examples	are pseudonyms.

9. Different legal systems around the world[2]

There are two major formal legal systems: the common law system originated in England and is also found in the countries it colonised. The civil (or continental) law system originated in continental Europe and is also found in the countries colonised by continental European powers. The common law system began with judges resolving disputes, with the decisions of judges forming the law to be applied in future cases. In common law countries today judges still examine previous relevant cases to extract decisions and principles relevant to the current case, and lawyers do the same thing in arguing their case. But within common law countries there is now also a large body of written statutes (written law/legislation) which play an important role in any legal proceedings.

In contrast to the common law system is the civil or continental system (also known as the Romano-Germanic system). This legal system has its origins in the Roman legal system, which was formalised in the 6th century on the extensive writings of Emperor Justinian. Starting in the 11th and 12th centuries, a number of European universities revived interest in Roman law and began to formalise it on the basis of the 6th century writings. The 19th and 20th centuries brought a vast movement of codification in these continental legal systems. Thus, while the common law system privileges previous judicial decisions or case law (also referred to as 'judge-made law'), in continental law it is the codified principles of law which are most important. However, continental law judges do not ignore previous cases, just as common law judges apply codified legislation.

Another important difference between the two legal systems lies in the nature of courtroom proceedings: in the common law they are predominantly adversarial, with two sides arguing their case in front of a judge or jury, while in the continental law they are predominantly inquisitorial, with the judge conducting an investigation, determining who to question on what topics, and whether to do this orally or in writing. A number of countries combine these two approaches, such as the Netherlands in its criminal proceedings (see Komter 1998).

In addition to these two main formal legal systems – common law and continental law – are a number of other formal systems, many of which draw for their sources of law on religious texts rather than judicial decisions or legislation. The best known of these are Islamic Shari'a law, based primarily on the Koran; Hindu law, based primarily on Sastras; and Jewish law, based primarily on the Torah and the Talmud.

It is common for countries or states to combine elements of different legal systems. Papua New Guinea, for example, inherited the common law system from Australia. But it also uses customary (informal) law at the level of village courts, for example in disputes over land usage or occupation, but not ownership. The complex social, political and colonial histories of many countries and states is reflected in their mixed legal systems. Thus, combinations of civil and common law are found in Cyprus, Malta, the Philippines, Scotland, South Africa, the US state of Louisiana and the Canadian province of Quebec. Israel combines elements of common law, civil law and Jewish law, while Nigeria combines common law, customary law and Muslim law.

There are significant changes happening in legal systems in many countries around the world, for example in many of the former communist countries of Eastern Europe which are applying for membership to the European Union. One dimension of change is in the participation of lay adjudicators as decision-makers in some legal processes, particularly in criminal matters. There is a range of models of lay adjudication, many of which are similar to juries in the common law system (see Jackson & Kovalev 2006/2007).

While my aim in this textbook is to introduce students to a wide range of sociolinguistic research about language and the law, I believe it is important to anchor any investigation of talk within the specific legal practices in which it occurs. This means that no study of language will be discussed without some explanation of its legal context. It is impossible to do justice (so to speak!), even in summary form, to the differences between and within legal systems around the world. Thus, this book will primarily focus on one system, namely the common law system. There are two obvious reasons for choosing the common law system as the focus: most of the research about sociolinguistics and law which is written in English is about the common law system, and this is the legal system with which I am most familiar.

However, this book can be used by students in countries with other legal systems, who are encouraged to use it as a basis for pursuing questions relevant to their own legal systems. Before carrying out any sociolinguistic study of language in the legal process, you need to have an understanding of the legal system you will be studying – and you can't rely on television drama as an accurate source of information! Assignment topics 1 and 2 at the end of this chapter will provide some guidance as you begin to learn about the specific legal system in which your study will be situated. Sociolinguists have much to learn from legal scholars and professionals in this ongoing endeavour.

10. Outline of the book

The book is organised according to the main legal contexts in which sociolinguists investigate language use in common law countries. As some aspects of language use are similar in different contexts, there will be some inevitable overlap in coverage between some sections of some chapters. So for example, issues affecting second dialect speakers in the courtroom are similar to those in police interviews. Cross-referencing will be used to minimise unnecessary repetition.

Part 2 deals with the legal context for which it is easiest to gain access to data for research purposes, namely the courtroom. Because of this research advantage, it is hardly surprising that this is the legal context which is most researched by sociolinguists to date. Part 2 starts with a short chapter (Chapter 2) which introduces students to issues involved in researching courtroom talk. Chapter 3 focuses on talk in courtroom trials, the legal context for which there is the greatest body of sociolinguistic research. The following two chapters deal with particular social groups in court: second language speakers and sign language users (in Chapter 4); and vulnerable witnesses – children, second dialect speakers, and people who do not share culture with the mainstream – in Chapter 5. The last chapter in Part 2 specifically examines the relationship between language and power, investigating the way that talk in the courtroom is a part of wider social power relations and struggles.

In Part 3, we turn to police interviews. Chapter 7 deals with the two main areas of sociolinguistic research interest, namely the ways that police advise suspects of their rights, and the ways that police interviews (with suspects or witnesses) are summarised in written reports. It also introduces the main approaches used by police in investigative interviewing. In Chapter 8, we turn the spotlight to police interviews with members of minority groups, including second language speakers, deaf sign language users, speakers of creole languages and second dialects, and children.

Part 4 investigates language use in other legal contexts, starting with lawyer–client interactions in Chapter 9. Chapter 10 turns to informal and alternative legal processes, starting with informal courts (such as small claims courts), then moving to mediation, and finally to alternative criminal justice processes, namely restorative justice practices, therapeutic courts and indigenous courts. These alternative legal processes are relatively recent developments and there is little sociolinguistic research. After being introduced to these processes in this book, some students will hopefully pursue future research that can contribute to the understanding of how language works in such legal contexts as victim–offender mediation and therapeutic courts.

Part 5 concludes the book by answering the practical question about what sociolinguistics can do. Thus, Chapter 11 introduces sociolinguistic expert evidence, the application of sociolinguistics to legal education, and the ways in which sociolinguistic research can contribute to the understanding of fairness and equality.

11. How to use this book

This book has been written primarily as a textbook for graduate or upper undergraduate courses on Sociolinguistics and Law. The first 10 chapters include exercises and topics for class discussion and debate, all aimed at facilitating active student learning in relation to the issues, research findings and questions being discussed. Class discussion topics are best suited to whole group discussion facilitated by the teacher and enhanced by contributions from the teacher. Exercises, on the other hand, can be done by small groups of students before some whole class summary discussion. Teachers need to consider for each exercise and class discussion what preparation students should be directed to undertake. In some instances no preparation is required, while in other cases students may need to do some preparatory research for homework (for example in preparation for the class discussion in Section 3.2 of Chapter 10, students will need to read a journal article and a report on standards for alternative dispute resolution, both of which are easily accessible online). Some discussion of most of the exercises and a few of the class discussions can be found in the Teachers notes, which can be downloaded from the *Multilingual Matters* website http://www.mmtextbooks. com/eades/. Please note that I use the generic term 'teacher' to refer to the person teaching this course, who would be called 'lecturer' or 'course coordinator' in England and Australia, and 'professor' in the US.

All textual material is authentic, and comes from my observations and/or recordings of language use in legal contexts, unless otherwise acknowledged. My recommendation is that students read aloud all spoken data quoted in this book (following the transcription conventions explained in Section 8 of this chapter).

At the end of each chapter, I provide topics for 'Assignments and further research' which can be used in various ways, depending on the level of class knowledge, the amount of time to be invested in an essay or project, and students' access to data and relevant publications. Some of these topics or questions would also be suitable for class work, provided that students have done the preparation required. Some others are better suited to essay or term paper work, while others might provide the basis for a thesis/dissertation. Course teachers should assess the suitability of topics provided for the level of their students, and may choose to adapt some of these Assignments and further research questions, depending also on the time allocated to the task, and access to suitable data and literature. I use the abbreviation **(Lx)** to indicate that a particular question is best suited for students with a background in linguistics.

As this textbook is written for graduate or upper undergraduate courses, I have given many references to relevant work. Thus, I expect that readers – both students and their teachers – will read widely beyond this book, using references provided here as a starting point for their bibliographic searching. But I must apologise to any scholars who feel I have not referred adequately to their work: it would be impossible to refer exhaustively to all the published work on all the topics covered here.

12. Notes on terminology

Despite the fundamental similarities and common historical origins of the common law legal system in countries such as Australia, Canada, New Zealand, the UK and the US, there are many differences both in the details of the legal process and in legal terminology. It is impossible to account for, detail or explain most of these differences in this textbook (but see for example the discussion of *voir dire* in Section 2 of Chapter 3). You are strongly recommended to refer to textbooks, legal dictionaries and relevant websites before undertaking any research in your legal system – the law librarian in your university should be able to help you find suitable resources.

Throughout this book I use the third person plural pronoun (*they, them, their*) in the generic sense, to avoid the clumsiness of such expressions as *he or she, him or her* and *his or her*.

13. Anglocentric orientation of this book

From the outset, I apologise for the Anglocentric orientation of the discussion, examples and topics for assignments and further research. As discussed in Section 9 above, this book focuses mostly on the common law legal system, which originated in England, and which is the focus of most of the anglophone research on language in the legal process. Further, the book will deal more with criminal law contexts than other legal proceedings, owing to that imbalance in this research to date.

In a few instances I will also be able to refer to research published in English which deals with relevant aspects of other legal systems in other countries. I hope that students with interests in language in the legal process in diverse societies around the world may find this book useful as a starting point. It should also be pointed out that there is a great deal of variation within common law systems in anglophone countries. For example, Vidmar (2000a) reveals the extent of differences in the operation of jury trials. It would be impossible for this textbook to recount all of these differences. My general principle is to focus on published sociolinguistic research, delving also into relevant sociolegal work where possible. It will also become apparent that the legal systems with which I have the greatest familiarity are Australian, particularly in the states of New South Wales and Queensland. I recommend that as you work through this book, you constantly ask yourself how the particular research being discussed compares with language use in your own legal system. Thus it is important to start this course with some understandings about your own legal system (see Assignment topic 1 below) in which to situate your thinking and discussion of the research presented throughout this book.

Class discussion

Discuss the meanings of the terms 'law' and 'justice'. It might be helpful to start with dictionary definitions and/or corpus-based studies of the use of these terms. To what extent do these terms overlap in meaning, and how are they different? Think about the translation of these terms into any other language which you or your classmates speak. How do these translations in other languages shed light on similarities to and differences from the English concepts of 'law' and 'justice'?

Assignments and further research

1. What kind of legal system(s) is/are used in your country? Check official government websites (such as the Justice Department), encyclopedias or other research material in a law library, or talk to someone who teaches or studies the legal process. You might also find useful introductory material in the references cited in footnote 2 in Section 9 above. Then find out what are some of the structures and processes which characterise this legal system or combination of systems. At this stage an introductory law textbook may be helpful. If you are not in one of the common law countries on which most of the sociolinguistic research published in English has been focused (e.g. England, Australia, US and Canada), try to find out some of the main ways in which the legal system(s) in your country differ(s) from the common law legal system.

2. Spend a few hours visiting a courthouse while hearings open to the public are being conducted. Check in advance if you need permission to make notes for the purposes of your study in a course on language in the legal process. Pay attention to the kind of language being used, and note any specialised legal register, including who uses it and who they use it with. Discuss your observations with other class members in the light of the issues raised in this chapter about the use of specialised legal register.

3. **(Lx)** Should legal language be considered a specialised register, or a dialect, or a separate language? In addressing this question, consider definitions of language, dialect and register, as well as examples of spoken and written language. Consult Danet (1985) and Tiersma (1999, especially Chapter 8) in working on this topic.

Part 2
Courtroom hearings

Part 2

Courtroom hearings

2

Researching courtroom talk

1. Introduction   28

2. Who are the participants?   31

3. Constraints on courtroom talk   32

4. Rules of evidence   34

5. Access to data for researching courtroom talk   35

   Assignments and further research   *38*

Researching courtroom talk

1. Introduction

Before we look at how language is used in court, we need to understand how courts operate, and how we can access courtroom talk for purposes of sociolinguistic research. As explained in Section 9 of Chapter 1, this book is focusing on common law legal systems, in which the courtroom hearings are adversarial. Thus it is not able to investigate the way that talk works in courtrooms in other legal systems. However, students in countries which have an inquisitorial approach to courtroom hearings, or a combination of approaches, are encouraged to use the chapters in Part 2 as a point of departure for investigation of courtroom talk in their own legal process.

In the common law system, there is a fundamental distinction between criminal law and civil law (not to be confused with the term 'civil law' often used to refer to the overarching legal system used in much of Europe, for which I am using the synonymous term 'continental law' as explained in Section 9 of Chapter 1). The criminal law system involves the state prosecuting someone charged with an offence, known as the defendant. The offences are defined in statutes (written laws enacted by legislature) and it is the task of the judge (and jury) to apply the relevant statute to the particular facts which have been established through the evidence in the case.

In contrast to criminal law, civil law in the common law system deals with claims that a wrong (sometimes referred to as a 'civil injury') has been done to someone who turns to the law for compensation (sometimes referred to as a 'remedy'). In contrast to criminal law, where it is the state which takes action against an individual, in civil law action is taken by an individual (or party), known as the plaintiff, and the state is often not officially involved. In both criminal and civil law, the person against whom the action is taken is referred to as the defendant. Most successful civil law cases result in either monetary compensation, or decisions which restrict or mandate certain actions to be carried out by the defendant. In contrast, criminal law revolves around prosecutions which typically result from police investigations. The same event can sometimes lead to both criminal and civil action, as in the famous US cases against O.J. Simpson relating to the death of his former wife (Nicole Brown Simpson) and her partner (Ron Goldman) in 1994. Simpson was charged with murder by the state of California, and he was therefore the defendant in the 1995 murder trial, which was decided by a jury. Although the jury found Simpson not guilty of the two murders, a jury in the civil case decided in 1997 that he was liable for the death of Goldman and for the 'battery against Nicole Brown Simpson' which led to her death, and he was ordered to pay compensation. How can the same legal system allow two such apparently contradictory decisions to stand?

 The answer lies in the different 'standards of proof' required in criminal and civil cases. In a criminal trial a jury (or judge, if it is not a jury trial) must be satisfied that the defendant is guilty beyond reasonable doubt of the crime(s) they are charged with. If the jury (or judge) is not convinced of the defendant's guilt beyond reasonable doubt, then the defendant is acquitted of the charges (although never technically found to be 'innocent'). But in a civil trial the 'burden of proof' is not nearly so stringent. The decision-maker (sometimes a jury, sometimes a judge) must be satisfied that the defendant is liable 'on the balance of probabilities', sometimes expressed as 'more likely than not' or 'by a preponderance of the evidence'. There is considerable debate about how to define 'beyond reasonable doubt' (an issue we will examine in Section 6 of Chapter 3). One guide to law explains it as 'a standard of certainty rather than likelihood', meaning 'virtual or practical certainty rather than absolute certainty' (Colvin *et al.* 2005: 13).

Most legal systems have a tiered system of courts, which differ according to the seriousness of the matters to be decided. Figure 2.1 provides an overview of the structure of a relatively straightforward courts system, that of New Zealand, a small country which has no states or provinces.

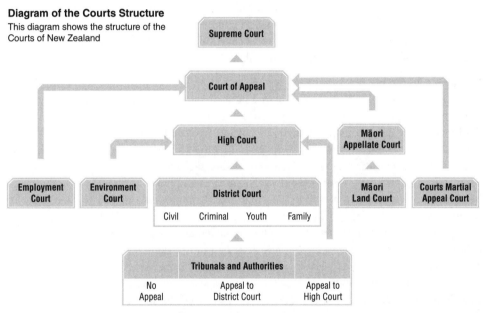

Figure 2.1 Structure of New Zealand courts
http://www.courtsofnz.govt.nz/about/system/structure/diagram.html (accessed 19/11/07)

As with other former British colonies, the New Zealand courts system is based on that of England. At the lowest level in New Zealand, most of the work of courts is done in one of four types of District Courts: civil, criminal, youth and family. While District Courts are often presided over by a judge, minor matters in these courts may instead be dealt with by Disputes Tribunal Referees or by one of the 400 Justices of the Peace. There are more than 60 District Courts at locations throughout the country. Appeals against decisions in any of these District Courts are heard by the High Court, which can also hear appeals against decisions from a number of tribunals and authorities (such as the Human Rights Review Tribunal and the Liquor Licensing Authority). The High Court also deals with serious criminal and civil cases, and all criminal cases in which the defendant chooses to be tried by jury. Appeals against High Court decisions go to the Court of Appeal, which is located in the capital city, Wellington. This court also hears appeals against decisions in the [military] Courts Martial Appeal Court and the Māori Appellate Court, which is the first court of appeal against decisions of the Māori Land Court. (The Māori Land Court hears cases dealing with land management and entitlement of indigenous New Zealanders, the Māori people.) The final appeal court in New Zealand, the highest court in the country, is the Supreme Court. Until its establishment in 2004, the highest level of appeal for New Zealand cases was the Judicial Committee of the Privy Council in London (which was also the highest appeal court for Australia until the 1980s).

You will notice some similarities between the names of courts in New Zealand and those in other common law countries. As in New Zealand, the highest appeal court in the US is also the Supreme Court. But in Australia, while the Supreme Court is the highest court in the states, appeals against any of these courts can be heard in the national High Court. If you intend to study courtroom language, you should start by making sure that you understand how the courts system is organised in the state or country you are studying. The term 'District Court', for example, refers to the lowest level of courts in New Zealand, but to the intermediate level in the Australian state of New South Wales.

In addition to the main courts discussed so far, common law countries have a number of specialised courts and tribunals, which are established with a specific function, such as the Waitangi Tribunal in New Zealand and the Refugee Review Tribunal in Australia. While the first of these deals with claims by Māori people relating to government breaches of the promises made in the historic Treaty of Waitangi, the second hears appeals on decisions made by the immigration department about asylum seekers' claims to refugee status. The adjudicator in a tribunal is not generally referred to as a judge, although their function can be similar to the judge in a civil or criminal trial. But tribunals generally have more in common with the inquisitorial approach of the continental system. Thus, the head of the tribunal takes a more active role than judges in adversarial courts, and the proceedings of tribunals are more similar to an investigation or inquiry than a trial. However, there is considerable variation, even within a single country, in the structure, organisation and workings of tribunals. If you are researching language use in a tribunal, make sure that you start with careful research on the particular tribunal itself, finding out how, why and when it was established, what its functions are and what procedural rules guide its hearings. Most of the sociolinguistic research discussed in this part of the book on courtroom talk has been carried out in criminal courts. But you will see that some work has also been done in civil courts (e.g. small claims courts, see Section 2 of Chapter 10), a coronial inquiry[3] (see Sections 5.4 of Chapter 4 and 4.2 of chapter 5), and in Australian land claims hearings, held before an adjudicator called the Aboriginal Land Commissioner (see Sections 3 and 4.2 of Chapter 5).

There is considerable variation in the steps involved in the processing of a case through either a criminal or civil proceeding. Our main focus will necessarily be on those courtroom events which have been subject to sociolinguistic research. Typically in criminal proceedings a person first goes to court to formally hear the charges against them. In some jurisdictions, bail is determined in this initial court hearing, while in others it is done in the police station.

Minor charges are heard in a lower court. As explained above, the name of this court varies – in New South Wales (Australia) it is the local court, and it is presided over by a magistrate. With more serious crimes, there is a process by which the evidence against the accused is tested, so that a determination can be made about whether there is sufficient evidence for the case to go to a higher court for trial. In many of the states in the US, this testing of evidence is done by a grand jury in a closed hearing, while in Australia, it is typically done by a magistrate in an open committal hearing. The term 'hearing' refers to any formal event within a court or tribunal, and includes arraignments, guilty pleas, committal hearings, trials and sentencing hearings.

There are other areas of law which have received much less attention in the sociolinguistics literature, and mostly they will not be covered in this book. These differ from country to country and can be classified in many different ways. So, in Australia for example, in addition to common law – comprising criminal and civil law – some of the other areas of law include:

- Family law: we will see in Section 3 of Chapter 10 that much of the sociolinguistic research on mediation sessions involves divorce mediation, which is part of family law.

- Public law includes constitutional law (dealing with the constitutions of the country and the state) and administrative law (dealing with the accountability of public officials).

Chisholm and Nettheim (2007: 42) point out that 'many important areas of law, such as public health, social welfare, taxation, local government and family law, depend largely or virtually entirely on the detailed provisions of the governing legislation'.

2. Who are the participants?

Central to any sociolinguistic study of how a person or people use language is the consideration of who they are talking to. In the case of courtroom talk, this is often a fascinating and multilayered dimension. The bulk of any courtroom hearing involves evidence, that is witnesses (including defendants, complainants or plaintiffs) give their side of the story, primarily in answer to questions asked by their lawyer and by the lawyer(s) on the opposing side. Thus, it might seem that the witnesses and lawyers are talking in a series of interviews. But there are other important addressees for this seemingly dyadic talk.

First, both lawyers and witnesses are talking as much for the legal decision-makers – that is, the jury or judge(s) – as they are for each other. And judges can and sometimes do engage in direct questioning of witnesses, although to a much lesser degree than the lawyers do. Generally, members of the jury are not allowed to ask any questions, or to talk to anyone in the courtroom hearing, but they are central participants. In Drew's (1985: 134) terms, jurors are generally 'non-speaking recipients of courtroom discourse'.[4]

Second, an important addressee function is played by what is generally termed 'the record', namely the official record of the proceedings. While the courtroom hearing takes place in present time, lawyers and judges are always conscious of the possibility of future appeals against the decision made in the case. In the event of an appeal, the official transcript and/or audiorecording of the hearing plays a crucial role in legal argument (as discussed in Section 4 of Chapter 1). Thus, lawyers in a courtroom hearing are always partially oriented to the record as an addressee, and some of their utterances only make sense in that light. Do you remember the example of a lawyer's utterance made for the record in Chapter 1?[iii] Other common lawyer or judge utterances which fulfil this function are found when a witness gives a non-verbal answer, which is then verbalised for the record by the judge or lawyer, such as *witness is indicating his right forearm* (for example in answer to a question such as *where did he hit you?*)

Third, there are a number of people present in the courtroom, who are the audience, rather than the participants, in a courtroom hearing. These people do not talk in the hearing and do not play any role in the decision-making in the case. This audience includes people in the public gallery – typically family members of witnesses, as well as 'courtwatchers', journalists and, occasionally, students of sociolinguistics or law. Other secondary addressees are members of the public who follow particular cases through media reports of them. Depending on public interest in any particular case, these secondary addressees may play an important, although silent, role in what people say in a courtroom hearing and how they say it. In referring to courtroom participants, I will use the following terms:

- 'Decision-maker' refers to the person(s) making a decision in a legal case. Depending on the case, this may be a magistrate, a jury, a judge or a panel of judges.

- 'Judicial officer' refers to the judge(s) or magistrate presiding in a case (sometimes also referred to as the 'presiding officer', and also sometimes referred to as the 'court').

- 'Legal professional' refers to any person with legal training carrying out a legal function, and includes lawyers, judges and magistrates.

- 'Witness' refers to any person giving evidence in a courtroom hearing and includes defendants, complainants and plaintiffs.

3. Constraints on courtroom talk

The most striking aspect of courtroom talk is its highly constrained nature. As with other formal institutional contexts, such as a parliamentary debate or a meeting of a board of directors, turns at talk are regulated within a hierarchical rule-governed participation structure. And as with parliament, people in the visitors' gallery have no right to participate verbally in proceedings at all, although they may whisper in a private conversation with the person sitting beside them. But courtroom talk is arguably even more constrained than other formal institutional talk, with the possible penalty of imprisonment for anyone charged with contempt of court, for such actions as refusing to stop talking when told to, refusing to answer a specific question or talking in a manner judged unacceptable by the presiding judicial officer. While such contempt charges appear to be rare, witnesses are threatened with contempt more often, in tangible reminders of the strict rules about who can say what, where, when, how and to whom in court. And I have seen a judge threatening a lawyer with contempt during an argument between them over timetabling of a case and the time the judge was willing to wait for a certain document. The actual action which led to the contempt threat was the lawyer slamming the door, as he stormed out to try to fulfil the judge's demand to expedite the delivery of the document (which the lawyer had argued was an unreasonable demand). I have also seen a witness threatened with contempt by a cross-examining lawyer for refusing to answer a question, and a visitor threatened with contempt by a judge for his angry outburst during the evidence of a particular witness.

Not only is courtroom talk highly constrained, but courtroom organisation is hierarchical. The presiding judicial officer controls proceedings, and indeed the issue of how successful they are in controlling their court appears to be a common topic of discussion among magistrates and judges. This control relates to various aspects of 'order in court', such as compliance with rules of evidence, as well as controlling potentially unruly members of the public. The extent to which individual judicial officers control the freedom of lawyers can vary, but I have seen male prosecutors and defence lawyers formally ask permission from the judge to remove their suit coat.

The hierarchical nature of courtroom organisation and relations is frequently reinforced by the physical arrangement of the courtroom, with the bench (where the judicial officer sits) elevated above the rest of the courtroom. Figure 2.2 shows a typical courtroom layout for a Crown Court in England and Wales.

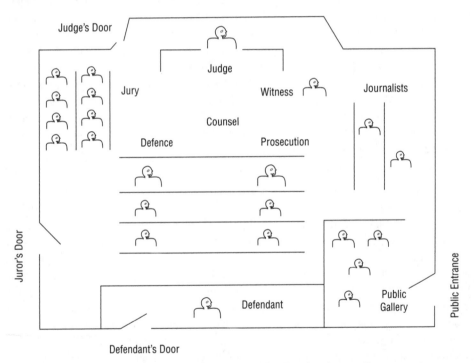

Figure 2.2 A typical Crown courtroom in England and Wales (Heffer 2005: 37)

There are a number of local variations in courtroom design – you might like to observe courts at different levels in your area. How is the hierarchical relationship between participants represented and reinforced in the physical layout? To what extent do courtroom participants move around during a hearing, and how do these shifts relate to shifts in communicative behaviour? (See Philips 1986.)

4. Rules of evidence

There are many different events which take place in courtrooms, such as arraignments, guilty plea hearings, trials, sentencing hearings and appeals. Despite having different legal purposes, these events are mostly consistent in their ways of speaking, including the use of routinised formalities. The trial is the central event in courtrooms, and the other events are preliminary to a trial, or they result from a trial. The main purpose of a trial is for each side in a case to present evidence to support their case so that the decision-maker can decide the 'facts' and apply the law. In criminal matters the case being argued is that the accused is guilty or not guilty of the charge. In civil matters it is that the defendant is liable or not liable for some wrong suffered by the complainant. The legal concept of 'fact' is central to the court process, and it is often distinguished from the law. Thus juries make decisions of fact, but not of law. In jury trials judges make decisions of law, but not of fact. In judge-only trials judges make decisions of both fact and law. The word 'fact' (often used in the plural) has a particular legal meaning which is not quite the same as its ordinary English meaning. In ordinary English, we can't usually say that something is a fact without being able to produce some kind of evidence if required. But a legal fact has to be established legally, according to rules of evidence. As Mertz (2007: 67) explains, the claim that something is a legal fact 'is not a strong assertion that [it] actually occurred. Rather, the claim is that this version of what occurred is to be accepted as true, based on the legal status of the case'. In making findings of fact, legal decision-makers are restricted to the rules of evidence, some of which we will see in Exercise 2.1 below (see also Section 4.1 of Chapter 3). In restricting the ways in which knowledge can be produced and accepted in court, rules of evidence can be seen as a set of epistemological rules. In Chapter 11, we will examine some of the assumptions about language which underlie the legal approach to what counts as reliable knowledge and information, and we will see how different these can be from assumptions used in everyday storytelling.

To take a simple case: if Jane Smith is accused of murder, the prosecutor must prove to the jury beyond reasonable doubt that she intentionally killed the victim. In different jurisdictions, the law defines murder in slightly different ways (and in some jurisdictions, the case might be determined solely by a judge, rather than by a jury). Typically, in making the case that Jane is guilty of murder, the prosecution would have to establish two basic facts: that she killed the victim and that she did this intending the victim to die. Evidence that she killed the victim may come from the testimony of an eyewitness, or from an accumulation of circumstantial evidence, such as finding her fingerprints on the murder weapon, and testimony of someone who saw her entering the victim's office around the time of the killing. Evidence about her state of mind may be deduced from facts about her actions relevant to the action which resulted in the victim's death. For example, did she go into the kitchen and sharpen a knife before taking it with her into the victim's office while saying *I'm going to kill you*? All of this evidence must be presented in court, within the constraints of rules of evidence, in order for the decision-maker(s) to make findings of fact and then apply the relevant law. In contrast to the ways we use in ordinary conversations to work out what happened, in court witnesses cannot normally report anything that another person has said (see Section 4.1 of Chapter 3), and any earlier criminal convictions of an accused person cannot be made known to the jury or taken into account by the judge in determining guilt or innocence.

Central to the conduct of any interaction in courtroom hearings are the rules of evidence, generally based on a statute enacted by the legislature (e.g. *Evidence Act 1995* (Commonwealth) for Federal Courts in Australia). The rules specify what evidence can be given and how, as well as restrictions on types of evidence and ways of giving evidence. Not all evidence is given linguistically: for example, photographs and material objects (such as weapons used in an assault), may be given (or 'tendered') to a court as evidence. But a great deal of evidence in court is given through language, as answers to questions or as written statements. Thus rules of evidence have a lot to say about talking in court, for example:

(a) the linguistic ritual to be undertaken by a witness before beginning to answer questions;

(b) inferences that can be drawn from a person refusing to answer a question;

(c) restrictions on the kinds of questions asked of witnesses;

(d) who has to answer questions and who is not allowed to answer questions, under what circumstances;

(e) restrictions on what witnesses can talk about in their answers.

Exercise 2.1[iv]

Examine the following extracts from the Australian *Evidence Act 1995* (Commonwealth). Match each extract, numbered (i)–(vi) with the corresponding description from the list (a)–(e) above. (Short extracts only are provided here. You may want to read more about how these and related rules of evidence proscribe ways of talking in court: *http://www.austlii.edu.au/au/legis/cth/consol_act/ea199580/*)

(i) 17(2) A defendant is not competent to give evidence as a witness for the prosecution.

(ii) 21(1) A witness in a proceeding must either take an oath, or make an affirmation, before giving evidence.

(iii) 42(1) A party may put a leading question to a witness in cross-examination unless the court disallows the question or directs the witness not to answer it.

(iv) 55(1) The evidence that is relevant in a proceeding is evidence that, if it were accepted, could rationally affect (directly or indirectly) the assessment of the probability of the existence of a fact in issue in the proceeding.

(v) 76 Evidence of an opinion is not admissible to prove the existence of a fact about the existence of which the fact was expressed. [generally referred to as the opinion rule]

(vi) 89(1)a In a criminal proceeding, an inference unfavourable to a party must not be drawn from evidence that the party or another person failed or refused to answer one or more questions.[5]

---

5. Access to data for researching courtroom talk

One of the factors which attracts sociolinguistic researchers to the courtroom is that it is typically a relatively easy place to conduct research, at least in the initial stages. With some exceptions (such as childrens courts, or hearings involving sexual assault), court hearings, in the common law countries at least, are open to the public. It is considered a right of citizenship to be able to observe the work of the courts. Thus, in courthouses around the world, you can see – in addition to journalists with notebooks, and relatives of people giving evidence – researchers with notebooks. In many courts it is considered polite for researchers to inform the judge, through one of the court officials, why they will be taking notes during the hearing, and it is of course imperative to observe the rules of the court. In some places in Australia, this still includes politely bowing to the presiding judge or magistrate when you enter or leave the courtroom.

Having started your research by spending time observing some court proceedings and taking some notes on what is happening, your appetite may be whetted to undertake a research project. It is impossible to do a serious sociolinguistic study of language in the courtroom without access to a recording of exactly what was said. Handwritten notes will not suffice, unless you have learned shorthand and have the proficiency level of a court reporter. Most studies of courtroom language are based on audiorecordings and/or official transcripts of hearings.[6] Recordings are preferable, as they allow the researcher to make repeated listenings to what was said, without having to rely on someone else's transcription. As mentioned in Section 8 of Chapter 1, the process of transcription by anyone, including researchers, is a selective process. It is impossible to capture in a transcription every detail of the spoken interaction. And the focus of official transcriptions is generally on recording the words said, without other details which are often very important to sociolinguistic considerations, such as silences, overlapping talk and changes in volume. On the basis of many years of observing courtroom hearings and reading official court transcripts, as well as a small empirical study, I concluded in Eades (1996b) that there is a fundamental difference between transcriptions for sociolinguistic research and transcriptions for official court records. The former represent interaction between participants, while the aim of the latter is to represent 'facts' or information which have been given in evidence.

Being official records of information, not interaction, official transcripts do not record such features as pauses and overlapping talk, and they only sometimes record prosodic features, such as raised volume and increased or decreased speed of utterance. Non-verbal features, such as averting the gaze, and paralinguistic features, such as trembling voice or laughter, are also generally not recorded. This does not mean that official court transcripts are of no use as data for sociolinguistic research. It all depends on the research question(s) being addressed. In my work on Aboriginal English, an important issue relates to pauses or silences (see Eades 2000, 2008a), so official transcripts are not suitable. Luckily, in some jurisdictions, including many in Australia, courtroom proceedings are officially audiorecorded. I have been granted permission to purchase copies of the official audiorecordings of court hearings, from which I make my own transcripts (in addition to observing these hearings and making notes). Depending on the jurisdiction, permission to purchase official court recordings for the purpose of research may come from the Chief Justice, or the Attorney-General, or the Courts Administrator. Typically, such permission will only be granted in relation to proceedings in cases which are finished and are not subject to possible appeals. In some courts, scholars have gained permission to make their own recordings for the purposes of research. On the other hand, Heffer (2005) was able to use official trial transcripts for a study which examines features of grammar, lexis and discourse structure (to be discussed in Sections 6 and 7 of Chapter 3).

What about using televised courtroom hearings as research data? There is a difference between high profile cases that are televised (such as the Louise Woodward and O.J. Simpson cases in the US) and reality television court TV shows (such as *Judge Judy* in the US). In the former cases, the recording occurs because of the huge public interest in a serious case. Cotterill's (2003) study of the O.J. Simpson criminal trial shows that such televised trials can provide rich data for sociolinguistic analysis. While the TV crews, and through them, a potentially large public audience, create an added audience for the participants in the case, participants are arguably not nearly so attuned to this viewing audience as are those in the reality TV court shows. These cases are 'private' dispute resolution proceedings produced for television. That is, they are not official legal proceedings, and the judges who preside have no legal jurisdiction over the televised matters, although they have judicial experience. In these court TV shows, courtroom rules of evidence are not followed, but participants enter into a legal contract when they sign an agreement at the end of their hearing.

Whatever approach you use to obtain data from courtroom hearings, unless they have been televised, you will need time to gain appropriate permissions and funding to pay for copies of recordings and/or transcripts (which are typically quite expensive, e.g. $15 for a 30-minute CD, or $5 per page of official transcript). You will also need to negotiate with the authority which gives permission, the confidentiality agreements pertaining to publication of data.

You may be tempted to use fictionalised courtroom dramas as research data. Never assume that such performances accurately represent authentic courtroom hearings. But you could use such fictional data or reality court TV data for a class exercise or assignment in assessing the ways in which it is similar to and different from authentic courtroom talk, as discussed in research literature to be introduced in the next four chapters.

An important development in some recent studies has been corpus linguistics, in which analysis of linguistic features can be carried out on a sizeable corpus, with the aid of computer tools, such as concordance programs. For example, Heffer's (2005) study of language in jury trials analyses official transcripts from 229 criminal trials in England and Wales. In his examination of language use in these trials, Heffer draws for comparison on three well-known reference corpora: the British National Corpus (100 million words of British English), the Cobuild Direct Online Corpus (56 million words international corpus of English) and Early Modern Trial texts in the Helsinki Corpus of Historical English.

Assignments and further research

1. Choose one or more studies of courtroom talk (from those to be discussed in Chapters 3–6) and examine the data collection involved. What data was used? How was it collected? What difficulties were involved? How were these difficulties dealt with? In what ways do you think the practical issues involved in data collection in the study limit the research – for example, in relation to theoretical approach, analysis, findings?

2. How are the courts in your state or country structured? Check with online information of the justice department or a similar government department. If possible, make a flow chart which shows the possible progress of a case through the courts system (similar to the New Zealand example in Figure 2.1 above). For each court, note who makes the decision: e.g. single judge, group of (how many?) judges, jury. Find out how the court keeps records of the proceedings for each court: e.g. official transcript, audiorecording. Also find out what a researcher needs to do to access such records for the purposes of research. What costs are involved?

3. (This assignment follows on from Assignment topic 2 in Chapter 1.) Spend a few hours observing language use in a local courtroom. Prepare for this field trip by learning about the function of this court in the wider justice system. Is it a civil court or criminal court? Is it a lower, intermediate or higher court? Are decisions made by a judicial officer (e.g. magistrate or judge) or jury?

    During your observation of proceedings, pay attention to the following aspects of language use, making notes where possible:

    -   What evidence do you find that participants are speaking for the transcript?

    -   Is there any language that appears to exclude any participants?

    -   What evidence do you find for the hierarchical structure of the courtroom from its physical design and the spatial arrangements?

    -   What linguistic evidence do you find for the hierarchical structure of the courtroom?

4. (Lx) Compare language use in a small claims court in which you can do direct observations with that in a televised private dispute resolution hearing, such as *Judge Judy*. Ideally this assignment would be based on comparison of recordings from the court you observe and videorecordings of the television show. To what extent is language use in these two hearings similar, and in what ways does it differ? Some possible features to examine might include: length of turns, amount of overlap, choice of address terms, paralinguistic features, prosodic features. You may also want to consider the ethnographic research on small claims courts to be discussed in Section 2 of Chapter 10. How does the fact that *Judge Judy* and similar hearings are reality television productions relate to your findings about how language use in these shows differs from those in a regular small claims court? (Note that this last question requires some attention to research on language use in reality television productions.)

3
Focus on trials

1. Introduction   40

2. Jury selection   40

3. Opening statements   42

4. Witness examination   42

    4.1. Lawyers' questions   42

    4.2. Witnesses' answers   47

    4.3. The power of words   49

    4.4. Strategies in cross-examination   50

    4.5. Summarising the power imbalance in witness examination   52

5. Closing arguments   52

6. Judges' summaries and instructions to the jury   54

7. Unidirectional dimensions of courtroom talk   57

    Assignments and further research   60

Focus on trials

1. Introduction

Courtroom trials have been considered from a variety of perspectives, including ritual, drama, debate and game (see Danet & Bogoch 1980; Heffer 2005). Tiersma (1999: 4) says 'the courtroom drama is best understood in terms of a story or narrative'. Trial textbooks and manuals also place storytelling as the central activity, as you can see in this Australian example, which instructs lawyers in the five 'principles of effective trial preparation' (Mauet & McCrimmon 2001: 9–13):

1. Develop your theory of the case, that is 'a logical, persuasive story of "what really happened"'
2. Develop themes and labels
3. Use storytelling techniques
4. Focus on the key disputed facts and issues
5. Prepare from the jury's point of view

As we will see in this chapter, as well as Chapter 6 and Chapter 11, the ways in which stories are told and retold in court has some very strange characteristics.

Exercise 3.1

Collect a sample of media reports on trials. Examine the reports in terms of the perspectives on trials presented in Danet and Bogoch (1980) and Heffer (2005). You could also examine law textbooks, particularly trial manuals. In what ways are the perspectives outlined in the two cited sources found in discussions about how to conduct trials? Pay particular attention to metaphoric language.

One of the most comprehensive sociolinguistic treatments of courtroom talk is by Heffer (2005) who argues that trials are a 'complex genre'. Within this complex genre are a series of events[7] (sometimes themselves also referred to as genres). The initial events of jury selection, swearing-in and indictment are procedural in nature, and involve a considerable amount of ritualistic language. These events are followed by opening speeches from the lawyer for each side, witness examinations and closing addresses, again by the lawyer from each side. Each of these events is adversarial in nature, and the language is characterised by its strategic orientation. Most sociolinguistic research has focused on these adversarial events within courtroom talk. Finally, the judicial officer's summing-up, jury deliberation (in cases involving a jury) and sentencing are adjudicative in nature, and the language is correspondingly deliberative. In this chapter we will examine some of these main courtroom events, and some of them will be taken up again in Chapter 6.

2. Jury selection

The first event in a jury trial involves selecting members of the jury. There is a range of ways in which this is done in common law countries and in countries which use juries within continental law or which combine elements of both systems (see Vidmar 2000a for a collection of chapters dealing with a number of countries). Potential jurors are typically chosen from a public listing of citizens, such as the electoral role. Before a case begins, members of the jury pool who are required to perform jury duty for that day are called into court. Then follows a process of random selection of names from this pool of potential jurors (like drawing winners in a lottery). The prosecution and the defence have the opportunity to reject any particular juror, up to a specified limit. This rejection of a potential juror is known as a 'challenge', and there are typically limits on the number of 'challenges for cause' and 'peremptory challenges' which can be made by each side. 'Challenges for cause' are those for which the challenging lawyer provides a reason, while 'peremptory challenges' do not require a reason. In Australia, the decision to reject a potential juror is typically made on the basis of the demographic or social information available to the lawyers, and evaluated by them in terms of the likely usefulness of particular people to the legal strategy in the case. This information is available from the electoral role, namely the person's home address and occupation. Combining these social characteristics with the person's gender, and their demeanour in court during the jury selection process, provides the only basis in some Australian states, such as New South Wales, for lawyers to assess whether or not to challenge any particular juror. Thus, the assessment tends to be made on the basis of generalisations, such as, *as my defendant is charged with rape, I'll make sure there are more men than women on the jury*; or *my defendant is facing charges relating to marijuana, so I'll try to have more young people on the jury*. In South Australia, both prosecution and defence must be provided in advance with a list of people called for jury duty for the date of the case, and this enables each side to do some research into the backgrounds of potential jurors in order to inform their decisions about challenges (Chesterman 2000).

In the US, there is another important speech event used in the jury selection process, namely the 'voir dire'. In this part of the pre-trial process, jurors selected from the jury pool are asked questions, in some places by the judge as well as both prosecution and defence lawyers, and in other places by the judge alone. Typically these questions are about life experiences and beliefs that might make it difficult for a person to make a fair and impartial decision. Thus for example, in a case in which crucial evidence is to come from a police officer, these prospective jurors might be asked if they have any relatives who are police officers, or if they have ever had any dealings with police officers. Anyone who answers positively to such questions might then be interviewed about their experiences or their relative, and about their feelings about police officers, with questions that seek to establish possibilities of bias. This voir dire process provides lawyers for each side with an opportunity to determine whether to make any challenges for cause. It also provides prospective jurors with an opportunity to interact with the lawyers, and to actually speak in the courtroom, although this is often very brief.[8] In Canada, the authority to decide a potential juror's partiality rests not with the trial judge, but with two layperson 'triers' selected from the jury pool (see Vidmar 2000b).

Uehara and Candlin (1989) show some of the ways in which the voir dire differs from ordinary conversation, particularly in terms of the asymmetrical organisation of talk (see also Stygall 1994: 45–80). And Shuy's (1995) analysis of one voir dire conducted by a judge in a death penalty case shows how such questions can influence answers in a number of ways. Given that this is the only opportunity that jurors have to talk in the courtroom, and given also that jurors are the final decision-makers in a case, it would be interesting to examine interaction between lawyers/judges and jurors in this speech event. What light can such an examination shed on the ways in which lawyers and judges conceive of, talk about and investigate attitudes, biases and stereotypes?

Note that in Australia and Britain, the term 'voir dire' refers to a different trial-within-a-trial speech event, namely where certain parts of the evidence are heard by the judge in the absence of the jury, in order for the judge to determine if this evidence is to be presented to the jury. (In the US, there can also be voir dires of this type.)

3. Opening statements

Opening statements are supposed to be a neutral summary of the case, a 'road map' by which the lawyer for the prosecution and the lawyer for the defence explain to the jury how they will organise the evidence to be presented. But Cotterill argues that since '*overt* evaluation and persuasion are banned in opening statements, lawyers must achieve a persuasive effect in their opening statements through the subtle use of language' (2003: 64, emphasis in original). So, for example, in the famous O.J. Simpson case in the US, the defence counsel used the word *incident* to refer to violent actions by Simpson over several years leading up to his wife's death, saying:

[The prosecutor] talked in his opening statement about the April 1985 **incident** in which some damage was done to a vehicle, and as I understand it, the testimony will be that there was not any **incident** in 1985 because Miss Nicole was pregnant ... They did have some discussion apparently maybe in '86 or '84, some damage done to a car and she was not in that car. She was not struck on that occasion, so I think you will find that **incident** is not a great consequence. (Cotterill 2003: 80)

Cotterill found that in the Cobuild Bank of English corpus, the word *incident* 'collocates strongly with a series of words which convey singularity and randomness' (p. 81). And, as incidents often occur with the intransitive verb *occur*, the use of this word *incident* enables the defence to talk about the alleged domestic violence pre-dating the murders, without attributing agency to the defendant (or to anyone else). This avoidance of the attribution of agency or responsibility through the use of the word *incident* is compounded with the use of agentless passive on three occasions in this short extract: *some damage was done to a vehicle*, and *some damage done to a car* and *she was not struck*. In Section 4 of Chapter 6, we will discuss such linguistic devices in terms of Ehrlich's (2001) concept of the 'grammar of non-agency'.

4. Witness examination

4.1. Lawyers' questions

Much of the sociolinguistic interest in language in the legal process has centred on lawyers' questions in court. Before we examine some of the findings of this research, we need to clarify some legal and linguistic terms. In adversarial courtroom hearings witnesses present their story to the court in answers to questions asked by their lawyer. This is known as examination-in-chief [= direct examination]. Witnesses for the prosecution answer examination-in-chief questions from the prosecutor (referred to in some countries as 'the Crown'), while defendants and witnesses for the defence answer examination-in-chief questions from the defence counsel. Then they can be questioned by the other side, and this is the cross-examination phase. A major aim of cross-examination is to show weaknesses and/or inconsistencies in the witness's story. This is often combined with strategies to show that the witness is unreliable, or lacks credibility, or is untruthful. Witnesses for the prosecution answer cross-examination questions from the defence counsel, while defendants and witnesses for the defence answer cross-examination questions from the prosecutor. For each witness, the cross-examination phase is optionally followed by re-examination, in which they answer further examination-in-chief type questions, and this is occasionally also followed by recross-examination.

Rules of evidence restrict courtroom talk in a number of ways. The two most widely known restrictions relate to leading questions and hearsay evidence. The rule about hearsay evidence generally prohibits a witness from reporting in court anything which another person has said. However, hearsay evidence is a complex issue, and the 'task of finding a universally accepted definition of what does constitute hearsay has proved to be a difficult one for jurists, academics and legal practitioners' (Arenson & Bagaric 2007: 408). Leading questions are defined in legal terms, not grammatically, although they most commonly have the syntactic form of Yes/No questions (see below). A leading question is one which suggests a particular answer, or assumes the existence of a fact which is in dispute (*Butterworth's Concise Australian Legal Dictionary* 2004). Thus, a question like *You were there, weren't you?* suggests a particular answer. And the question *About what time was it when you saw the red car?* assumes two particular facts, namely that the witness saw a car and that it was red. If either of these two assumed facts is in dispute, then this is also a leading question. But if both of these two assumed facts have been agreed upon, then it is not a leading question.

Generally speaking, lawyers are not allowed to use leading questions in examination-in-chief, except in relation to background details that are undisputed, such as the witness's age and address. But leading questions are a major tool of cross-examination, allowing the lawyer to suggest a version of events or situations. The assumption which underlies this practice is that leading questions in cross-examination test a witness's truthfulness and the consistency of their story.

While leading questions are important to lawyers, to understand the linguistic analysis of courtroom talk we need to explain the terms Yes/No-questions and WH-questions. Yes/No-questions are questions that can logically be answered with *yes* or *no*, although they do not have to be answered in this way. Such questions are often referred to in training manuals for lawyers and other professionals, such as teachers and counsellors, as 'closed' questions. WH-questions are those that ask where, who, when, what, why and how, and that are often referred to as 'open' questions.

The difference between Yes/No-questions and WH-questions has been important in the studies of lawyer questions, which began some three decades ago. The major concern of these studies has been the ways in which the structure of questions in examination-in-chief and cross-examination exercises power and control over witnesses. Examining question–answer pairs, several studies have focused on the way in which the syntactic structure of the question serves to constrain the type of answer (e.g. Danet *el al.* 1980; Harris 1984; Walker 1987; Woodbury 1984). These empirical studies found that lawyers follow the advice given during their training in asking more open questions in examination-in-chief and more closed questions in cross-examination. It seems logical that examination-in-chief would comprise more open or WH-questions, because this is where the lawyer is questioning their own witness and providing the chance to present them in their best light. And the restriction on leading questions in examination-in-chief reduces the scope for Yes/No-questions.

The imbalance between witness and lawyer in control over the content and form of talk has been discussed in terms of conduciveness, control, coerciveness or manipulation, and a number of scholars have produced hierarchical typologies of question form, based on the syntactic structure of the question. These studies all found that the most controlling or coercive questions are Yes/No-questions with tags (such as *You were there, weren't you?*), while the least controlling or coercive questions are broad WH-questions (e.g. *What happened then?*). Figure 3.1 provides one such hierarchy, based largely on the work of Woodbury (1984). It is ordered on a continuum of control from least controlling questions to most controlling ones. Woodbury (p. 199) defines control as 'the degree to which the questioner can impose his (sic) own interpretations on the evidence'.

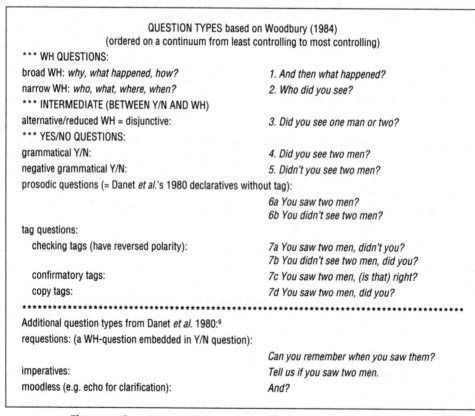

QUESTION TYPES based on Woodbury (1984)
(ordered on a continuum from least controlling to most controlling)

*** WH QUESTIONS:

broad WH: *why, what happened, how?*	*1. And then what happened?*
narrow WH: *who, what, where, when?*	*2. Who did you see?*

*** INTERMEDIATE (BETWEEN Y/N AND WH)

alternative/reduced WH = disjunctive:	*3. Did you see one man or two?*

*** YES/NO QUESTIONS:

grammatical Y/N:	*4. Did you see two men?*
negative grammatical Y/N:	*5. Didn't you see two men?*
prosodic questions (= Danet *et al.*'s 1980 declaratives without tag):	
	6a You saw two men?
	6b You didn't see two men?
tag questions:	
checking tags (have reversed polarity):	*7a You saw two men, didn't you?*
	7b You didn't see two men, did you?
confirmatory tags:	*7c You saw two men, (is that) right?*
copy tags:	*7d You saw two men, did you?*

****

Additional question types from Danet *et al.* 1980:[9]

requestions: (a WH-question embedded in Y/N question):	
	Can you remember when you saw them?
imperatives:	*Tell us if you saw two men.*
moodless (e.g. echo for clarification):	*And?*

Figure 3.1 Question types in courtroom talk (based on Woodbury 1984)

Exercise 3.2ᵛ

Extracts 3–i and 3–ii are excerpted from the evidence of a defendant in an assault case. Examine the structure of the questions and decide for each question which type it exemplifies in the hierarchy given in Figure 3.1. Read the transcript with a classmate, allocating the role of lawyer to one person and of witness to another. Discuss which of these extracts is examination-in-chief and which is cross-examination, giving reasons for your decision.

Extract 3–i Eades' unpublished transcription of official audiorecording

1. L: Now if you cast your mind back to Saturday 10 May 1999- I think you were having a birthday barbecue at your home?
2. W: Yeah.

3. L: And I think around about eleven o'clock in the evening two people arrived?
4. W: Yep.

5. L: And who were they?
6. W: Jenny and Reggie Jones.

7. L: And when they arrived there what condition were they in?
8. W: Sober when they arrived.

9. L: And when they- after they arrived there did certain things happen?
10. W: Oh yeah- later on through the night- yeah.

11. L: And what did you notice about them later on through the night?
12. W: Oh chairs getting chucked around and that.

13. L: And whereabouts were those chairs being thrown around?
14. W: Kitchen.

15. L: Was that your kitchen?
16. W: Yeah- my wife's house.

17. L: And at that time did you say anything to Mr Reggie Jones or Jenny Alberts?
18. W: No- it's my uncle- he's a bit mad when he has a few drinks- they just started pushing each other around and I said- 'not inside the house'.

19. L: And what happened then?
20. W: Oh it just started to break out then.

21. L: What do you mean?
22. W: Started to break out- started fighting.

Extract 3–ii Eades' unpublished transcription of official audiorecording

1. L: So you pushed him- is that correct?
2. W: After he'd pushed me around- yeah- and pushed my uncle around.

3. L: Yes- all right- well after his- and that's what caused the cabinet to break- is that what you say?
4. W: Yeah- when we landed on it.

5. L: Would you have a look at your statement at paragraph four?
6. W: Yeah.

7. L: Would you agree with me that you told the police- on that night- that 'he threw me up against the china cabinet and smashed the glass'?

8. W: We both hit the china cabinet.

9. L: Would you agree with me that you told the police ...?

10. W: Yeah- all right- yeah.

11. L: Today you gave evidence of the fight continuing on the lawn?

12. W: Yeah- out the front.

13. L: Right- would you agree with me that when you told the police what occurred- on that night- that it happened on the roadway?

14. W: Yeah- right near a pine tree.

15. L: The event- the party which you were having on that particular night was a party- I think- to celebrate a birthday- wasn't it? I think Katie Miller?

16. W: Yep.

17. L: And in that birthday party alcohol had been consumed?

18. W: Yes.

19. L: And alcohol had been consumed by you?

20. W: Yep.

21. L: And you had started consuming alcohol in the morning?

22. W: No- about eleven o'clock I started drinking.

23. L: Eleven o'clock in the morning?

24. W: Oh well- if you call it morning- yeah.

...

25. L: And at that stage- if I put this to you- you started throwing punches at him- that's Mr Robinson?

26. W: No- not at all.

27. L: And- in fact Katie was trying to hold him?

28. W: Not at all.

29. L: And it was at that stage when you split his head open?

30. W: Not at all.

Critics of the studies of question form in courtroom talk have shown that restricting courtroom linguistic analysis to syntactic structure ignores the ways in which such features as propositional content, context, intonation and the sequential placement of the question can intensify or mitigate the control exercised by questions (e.g. Dunstan 1980; Eades 2000; Harris 1984; Lane 1990). And in my (Eades 2000) study, I pointed out the problematic assumption of a one-to-one relationship between the linguistic form of questions and the extent to which they function to control the witness's answers. That study shows how lawyers' use of the question forms which had been analysed as most controlling is sometimes taken by witnesses as an open invitation for an explanation, and thus such question forms can actually function in the least controlling way. Can you see an example of this in Extract 3–i above?[vi]

Further, it has become clear that questions in examination-in-chief and cross-examination are multifunctional (see Harris 1984). On the one hand many questions in Extract 3–i above appear to be aimed at eliciting information, such as what condition Jenny and Reggie Jones were in when they arrived at the party (Extract 3–i Turn 7). But this is not information required by the questioner, who already knows the answer. So more accurately, questions like this serve to structure the way in which the witness's story is presented to the judge/jury. But other questions, such as Extract 3–ii Turn 5 *Would you have a look at your statement at paragraph four?* do not serve any information function, but rather function as directives. And cross-examination questions often serve as challenges to the witness's story, as in Extract 3–ii Turn 13 above. Other questions can serve control functions, such as accusation, punishment or rebuke. For example, Eades (2008a) discusses three young teenage witnesses giving prosecution evidence against police officers who had allegedly abducted them. In their work to discredit the three witnesses, the two cross-examining lawyers asked a large number of questions about the children's criminal records. These questions served to present the witnesses to the court as untrustworthy. And questions such as *What do you think gives you the right to go and destroy people's property?* clearly functioned to rebuke, humiliate and punish the witness, rather than to seek information. While such questions are not necessarily found in all hearings in the Anglo system, Chang (2004) says that they play a central role in criminal trials in China, where questions addressed to defendants are used to obtain confessions, and at the same time as a form of punishment, which invokes the cultural notion of shame.

4.2. Witnesses' answers

At the same time as the studies examining the structure of lawyer's questions and its relationships to courtroom control, early studies of witnesses' answers also foregrounded the importance of power. The Duke University Law and Language Program (hereafter the Duke study), co-directed by law professor Conley and linguistic anthropologist O'Barr, undertook a major empirical study of variations in witness speech style, and the impact of this variation on jury decision-making (Conley *et al.* 1978; O'Barr 1982; O'Barr & Atkins 1980). An important influence on this study was Lakoff's (1975) book *Language and Woman's Place*, which set the scene for subsequent empirical studies on gendered differences in language use. Lakoff's view was that women's language is characterised by such features as:[10]

hedges, e.g.	*It's sort of hot in here, I'd kind of like to go*
intensifiers,[11] e.g.	emphatic *so* or *very*
(super)polite forms, e.g.	*I'd really appreciate it if ...*
empty adjectives, e.g.	*divine, charming, adorable, lovely*
use of tag questions, e.g.	*It's hot today, isn't it?*

The Duke study used these 'women's language' features as a baseline for their investigation of answers of witnesses to courtroom questions. But of course, they could not include tag questions in their study, as it is rare for witnesses to ask any question, and even rarer to ask a tag question.

An important finding of the Duke study is that gender is not the distinguishing social variable: it is situated social power. Thus, some of the features attributed by Lakoff as characteristics of women's speech – such as hedges and intensifiers – were found in the evidence of some male witnesses. Conversely, they were rarely found in the evidence of women with powerful status in the courtroom context, namely those giving expert evidence. This led Conley and O'Barr and their colleagues to coin the terms 'powerful' and 'powerless' speech, to indicate that these ways of speaking, in their courtroom study at least, are not primarily linked to gender, but to the witness's 'social standing in the larger society and/or status accorded by the court' O'Barr (1982: 70). Thus, a powerful witness is defined in terms of socioeconomic status and/or their situational status of being an expert witness.

This investigation of features of witnesses' speaking style, correlated with aspects of their social identity, is consistent with the approach of variationist sociolinguistics. Most such research has examined phonetic or syntactic features, and has not been undertaken in legal contexts. The Duke study of language in court examined discourse and lexical features, such as hedges, intensifiers and hesitations. But this study did not stop with the descriptive account of variations in the ways in which witnesses give their evidence. It went on to investigate the likely effects of these variations in form, particularly on decision-making. To do this, it employed a well-known experimental approach developed for the investigation of attitudes to different languages, dialects or speakers. Known as the matched guise technique, this experimental approach, developed by social psychologists in the late 1950s, is a clever way of finding out how a particular way of speaking can influence the way that a person reacts to a speaker. In a matched guise experiment, subjects listen to a recording with a number of extracts of individuals speaking, and rate the speaker in each extract on a number of characteristics. In the Duke study, university students participated as subjects in the role of 'mock jurors' or 'experimental jurors'. These subjects heard actors who had recorded a segment of powerless-style testimony based on the original study. They also heard the same actors presenting an edited version of this testimony in which the powerless features, such as the hedges and hesitations, had been removed, thus resulting in powerful witness style. Matched guise experiments are delicately planned, so that subjects think that each individual extract is presented by a different speaker – they don't realise that some speakers present more than one extract (see Erickson et al. 1978; Giles & Powlesland 1975).

Following each recording, the subjects were asked to rate the witness they had heard in terms of this person's convincingness, truthfulness, competence, intelligence and trustworthiness. The results of this experiment showed that subjects rated speakers using a powerless style as less convincing, truthful, competent, intelligent and trustworthy than they rated the same speakers using the powerful style. So, it is clear that the details of the ways in which witnesses present their evidence can be important to the outcome of a case.

The Duke study also examined some other characteristics of witness speech style, finding that sample jurors reacted more favourably to witnesses giving narrative answers, than to those whose stories were fragmented by lawyer questions. It also found that sample jurors reacted more favourably to witnesses who did not use overly formal expressions – such as *72 hours*, when the expression *three days* would suffice.

Exercise 3.3[vii]

In this example from the Duke study, Extract 3–iii is from the evidence of a witness to a car accident in which her neighbour died. Extract 3–iv comprises the rewritten version of the original evidence, with the powerless features removed. Compare the two extracts and underline all the features of powerless language in Extract 3–iii. You should be able to find examples of intensifiers, hedges and hesitations.

Extract 3–iii O'Barr's (1982: 65–66) transcription of audiorecording

1. L: State whether or not, Mrs A, you were acquainted with or knew the late Mrs X.
2. W: Quite well.
3. L: What was the nature of your acquaintance with her?
4. W: Well, we were, uh, very close friends. Uh, she was even sort of like a mother to me.

Extract 3–iv O'Barr's (1982: 66) transcription of text for experiment

1. L: State whether or not, Mrs A, you were acquainted with or knew the late Mrs X.
2. W: Yes, I did.
3. L: What was the nature of your acquaintance with her?
4. W: We were close friends. She was like a mother to me.

4.3. The power of words

Many people involved in the legal process are aware of the power of words. The choice of lexical items (that is, words or phrases) to refer to events, people or situations can play an important role in influencing people's memories, perceptions, reactions and evaluations. The groundbreaking work in this area was carried out in the late 1970s by psychologist Elizabeth Loftus and her colleagues. In one of their experiments (Loftus 1979: 77–78), subjects were asked questions about a car accident they had seen on film. Asked to estimate how fast the cars where going, those who were asked ... *when they smashed into each other* gave higher estimates of speed than those asked ... *when they hit each other*. Lawyers have taken good note of such findings, which are explicitly referred to in some legal training literature. Thus, for example Mauet's trial textbook, which prepares lawyers for their prosecution and defence work in court, tells lawyers to 'condense' their theory of the case 'into themes and labels' (Mauet 2000: 25). These themes and labels thus become the 'psychological anchors [which lawyers] want the jurors to accept and adopt as their own during the trial'. In linguistic terms, these themes and labels are lexical items, and they create and represent versions of the events, situations, people and 'facts' being contested in court. Danet (1980) discusses this legal awareness of the power of words in her analysis of the terms used by lawyers in a high-profile US abortion case to refer to the object of the abortion. No fewer than 40 lexical items are used with this reference in the case (ranging from *fetus* to *loved one*, and including such terms as *baby boy, the deceased* and *victim*). Danet examines the 'remarkably fine-grained patterning' (p. 210) in the use of terms by different parties, as they strove to define the opposing reality in this case.

But it is not just lawyers who use word choice in their definition of reality. Several studies have showed how lawyers and witnesses sometimes negotiate or struggle over the choice of words to describe a person or a situation.[12] An example which has been frequently cited in the sociolinguistic literature comes from Drew's (1985) analysis of a rape trial. In Extract 3–v, you can see how the complainant produced several 'alternative competing descriptions' (Drew 1985: 138) in answer to the lawyer's characterisation of the circumstances in which she had met the defendant, one evening a few months before the alleged rape.

Extract 3–v Simplified version of Drew's (1985: 138) transcription of audiorecording

1. DC: And you went to a ba:r in Boston- is that correct?
2. W: It's a clu:b.
3. DC: It's where girls and fellas meet, isn't it?
4. W: People go: there.
5. DC: And during that evening didn't mister Jones come over to sit with you?
6. W: Sat at our table.

You can see how the lawyer is presenting that meeting as a kind of dating or pick-up situation, that the witness had gone to a *bar* where *girls and fellas meet*, and that during the evening the defendant *came over to sit with* her. The witness however, rejects any implication that she might have had any forewarning of the defendant's intentions, in her rejection of several aspects of the lawyers' characterisation of that particular occasion. Thus her alternative characterisation of the venue is a *club* where *people go*. And she rejects any particular connection between the defendant and herself, interpreting the lawyers' *you* in Turn 5 as having plural reference, when she says that he *sat at our table*.

This example highlights one of the important ways in which lawyers try to control witnesses' stories, namely through the choice of lexical items or labels to describe or refer to significant people, events or situations in witnesses' stories. It also shows that these attempts may not always be successful, as some witnesses have sufficient linguistic dexterity to challenge this control. In Section 5 of Chapter 6 we will see that not all witnesses are able to do this.

4.4. Strategies in cross-examination

In contrast to the studies which focus on questions or answers or word choice, a few scholars have taken a more discourse-based approach, examining cross-examination strategies. Atkinson and Drew's (1979) book *Order in Court* focuses on the structure of courtroom talk, using a Conversation Analysis approach. For example, they examine the structure of the attribution and negotiation of blame in accusation sequences, in the cross-examination of police witnesses involved in Belfast disturbances in the late 1960s. They show how the lawyer in one of these hearings used complex blame sequences, avoiding outright accusation. In response, the police witness used a number of strategies, such as descriptions of other parties' actions, as well as rebuttals and accounts, which aim to mitigate projected blamings.

Since that early work, Drew has published several accounts of strategies used by lawyers and witnesses in the production of 'contrasting versions' of the story being presented to the court. We saw one of these strategies in Section 4.3 above, in which witness and lawyer negotiated 'alternative competing descriptions' of the place where the complainant and defendant had met up, and the circumstances of their meeting.

Drew (1992) also discusses a more complex strategy used by lawyers in cross-examination, which he describes as a contrast device. Basically, this involves the lawyer asking the witness to confirm two or more facts which are juxtaposed in such a way as to generate a puzzle for the jury. Some of these facts might be taken from earlier evidence from the witness. The lawyer does not give the witness the chance to solve the puzzle: it is left for the jury to puzzle over. This puzzling discrepancy implies what might be termed an *unless* clause, which damages the witness's story. That is, what is implied is something like *You've told us such-and-such, and you've told us so-and-so. But this doesn't make sense, unless* ... However, this *unless* clause is not stated by the lawyer, because it would have to be done in the form of a question, which the witness could then challenge or deny. But the lawyer has led the jury to that point, and then leaves a pause for them to work out the puzzle, before moving on to the next topic.

Exercise 3.4[viii]

Analyse the extract below from the cross-examination of a complainant in a rape case, according to Drew's contrast device. What were the conflicting facts? What was the puzzle? What was the implied *unless* clause? How did the timing before the lawyer's questions in this extract work in this contrast device strategy?

Extract 3–vi Simplified version of Drew's (1992: 510) transcription of audiorecording

1. DC: Now subsequent to this uh (0.6) uh you say you received uh (0.8) a number of phone ca:lls?
2. W: (0.7) Yei:s.
3. DC: (0.4) From the defendant?
4. W: (1.2) Yei:s.
5. DC: (0.8) And isn't it a fa:ct uh Miss Brown that you have an unlisted telephone number?
6. W: (0.3) Yei:s.
7. DC: (1.2) An' you ga::ve the defendant your telephone number didn't you?
8. W: No: I didn't.
9. DC: (0.3) You didn't give it to [him
10. W: [No:.
11. DC: (10.2) Du:ring the:se uh ...

Another cross-examination strategy is what Matoesian (2005b: 735) calls 'nailing down an answer' (following Philips 1998: 97), in which a lawyer attempts to 'control a witness's testimony, overcome their steadfast resistance to questioning, and obtain confirmation of a specific version of "the facts"'.

Komter (e.g. 1994, 1998) studies strategies used by judges and defendants in criminal trials in the Netherlands, which combine the adversarial and inquisitorial approaches. (Her study examined 31 audiorecorded criminal trials, mostly of 1–2 hours duration.) With the judge doing most of the questioning as part of the court's investigation, there does not appear to be the same finetuning of linguistic manipulation as we find in adversarial courts. However, Komter shows that both judges and defendants face interactional dilemmas, which they have to solve through talk. Thus, for example, she finds that defendants presented themselves as cooperative by making partial admissions, while at the same time defending themselves against more serious aspects of the accusations by making partial denials (Komter 1994: 173).

Assignment topic 10 at the end of this chapter provides an opportunity for you to explore this work in more depth.

4.5. Summarising the power imbalance in witness examination

The concern in early sociolinguistic studies with the power imbalance between witnesses on the one hand, and lawyers and judges on the other, has remained central to most of the more recent studies. Here are some of the linguistic ways in which this imbalance works:

- In examination-in-chief, the lawyer's questions organise, control and limit the witness's story.

- In cross-examination, the lawyer's questions aim to challenge, distort, and contradict the witness's story.

- In both examination-in-chief and cross-examination most questions require a minimal response.

- The majority of questions put to witnesses in cross-examination contain already completed propositions.

- Witnesses say very little compared to those questioning them.

- Witnesses can only speak in answer to the most recently asked question – they cannot introduce new topics or go back to an earlier topic.

- Witnesses have no power over interruptions to their talk.

In addition to these characteristics of the discourse structure of courtroom talk, a number of linguistic mechanisms in cross-examination intensify the power imbalance between lawyer and witness, as we will see in Chapter 6. These linguistic mechanisms include:

- lawyer reformulation of a witness's descriptions of events or people;

- lawyer manipulation of silence, for example with the use of strategic pauses;

- incorporation of damaging presuppositions in questions;

- metalinguistic directives given to the witness (such as *You must answer this question*);

- lawyer management of topics in order to convey a particular impression to the jury;

- lawyer use of strategies such as the contrast device.

With such findings, sociolinguists have provided empirical evidence to support the widespread feeling that witnesses are not really given the chance in court to tell their story 'in their own words'.

5. Closing arguments

In this event (also known as 'closing statement', 'closing address' or 'summation' in different jurisdictions), lawyers summarise their argument, with the intention of persuading the decision-maker – whether jury, judge or magistrate – that their version of the facts is the true one, or at least that their case is stronger than that of their adversary. In their closing arguments, lawyers have the chance to 'summarize and comment on the evidence and the credibility and demeanour of parties, witnesses and opposing counsel, and to employ a wide range of rhetorical devices to persuade jurors to adopt [their] version of the facts' (Hobbs 2003a: 278).

Cotterill's (2003: 199) examination of the closing arguments in the O.J. Simpson trial, as well as collections of published closing arguments leads her to the observation that closings have 'an undeniably theatrical quality'. Walter (1988) observed 66 summations in jury trials in an American city, interviewed 34 lawyers and administered a questionnaire to more than 200 jurors after their deliberation. Interestingly, she concludes from these interviews and questionnaires (p. 233) that 'jurors respond to [summations] as ... performance, but that it is not usually vital to their decision in the case'. Walter's descriptive account lists and exemplifies features found in the summations, which include rhetorical questions and complimenting the jurors. The lawyer interviews and juror questionnaires elicited self-report on such questions to jurors as 'Did you change your opinion after hearing the Defense Attorney's closing speech' (p. 230) and to lawyers as 'Do you respond positively or negatively to the concept of audience?'

The dramatic and persuasive nature of closing arguments is investigated by Hobbs (2003a) in a detailed analysis of just three minutes of the closing argument made by an African American lawyer in a televised trial. In this trial, the judge, both lawyers, the defendant and 10 of the 12 jurors were African American. Much of the courtroom talk was in Standard English, and both Hobbs (2003a) and Fuller (1993) have shown the strategic switch by lawyers in this case to AAVE (African American Vernacular English) to achieve a number of purposes in the trial (such as to make an accusation of the plaintiff during her cross-examination). Hobb's analysis of the short segment of the prosecutor's rebuttal argument shows how she used AAVE oratorical style to construct a shared identity with the jurors, to urge them to affiliate with her point of view (p. 281). These features include personalisation, proverbial statements, cultural references, phonological variants and a 'high spirited style of delivery marked by rhythmic evocative repetition' (p. 285).

In comparison to the studies by Walter, Cotterill and Hobbs of closing arguments in jury trials in adversarial courts, Carranza (2003: 45) found that closing statements in Argentinean cases, which are typically addressed to a panel of three judges, 'tend not to be overly emotional or dramatized'. But Carranza found a number of features of these closing arguments that are consistent with their performance as 'considerably ritualized events' (p. 49). These performance features include:

- rhetorical questions;
- triplets, that is series of three words (occasionally four words) that have a very similar meaning;
- direct speech animating the witness;
- historical present tense, which places the addressee at the scene of the story.

Stygall (1994) and (Tiersma 1999) also find some of the same features in their analyses of closing arguments in two different US trials.

Exercise 3.5[ix]

Examine the extracts below from Argentinean closing addresses to the panel of three judges. What linguistic features from Carranza's analysis (as summarised above) can you find in these examples (from Carranza 2003: 49, 51)?

1. *La reconstrucción de los hechos y los argumentos de la fiscalía se sentian, se sustenan, se fundan en una [prueba] testimonial parcial viciada de animosidad, de bronca, de resentimiento.* The reconstruction of the events and the arguments put forward by the prosecution are based on, are supported by, are built on a witness' testimony which is partial, vitiated with animosity, anger, resentment.

2. *Huguito que todavía estaba más próximo de Lucas Cravero según sus palabras, dice '¿Qué te pasa con mi hermano?' intenta acercase donde estaba Rundie y es cuando ve que Rundie le apunta ...* Huguita who was still closer to Lucas Cravero, according to his own words, says 'what's your problem with my brother?', he tries to get closer to Randazo and it is then when he sees that Randazo aims the gun to him ...

Felton Rosulek (2008, 2009) has examined contrasting ways in which defence and prosecution lawyers talk about defendants, victims and witnesses in closing arguments in five US criminal cases. Focusing on the work which the lawyers do in this monologic speech event to create opposing representations of reality, she shows that they do not do this by making contradictory statements. Rather, they refer to the people involved in the case in different ways. One part of Felton Rosulek's (2009) discourse analysis of this set of closing arguments examines the linguistic choices made by the opposing lawyers in terms of how they referred to the victims and the defendants. Thus, defence lawyers personalised the defendant, using their name, while prosecutors ignored any identity that this person had outside of the courtroom, instead mostly using the term 'the defendant'. While both prosecution and defence lawyers referred to victims by name, the prosecution used a higher proportion of first names or nicknames, compared to the defence who used more formal titles (such as first name plus last name, or Ms/Mr plus last name).

To date, there has been no sociolinguistic examination of the effect of linguistic strategies in closing arguments. In witness examination, we can get some indications of the effects of particular questions from looking at witness answers. But closing arguments are monologic, and sociolinguists to date have not had research access to jury rooms, where jurors discuss everything that has been said during the course of a case. Thus, apart from the self-reports of jurors in Walter's (1988) study, the question of the impact of particular linguistic choices in closing argument remains so far unresearched.

6. Judges' summaries and instructions to the jury[13]

After the evidence has been presented (mainly in the form of witness testimony, but also with any other material or written evidence), the judge talks to the jury before they leave the court to deliberate on their verdict. In this event, the judge summarises the evidence and instructs (or directs) the jury on relevant points of law. These jury instructions (= directions) often rely to a considerable extent on the way in which the law defines elements of the offence or offences of which the defendant has been accused. Thus, the judge's directions often consist of definitions from written statutes, or explanations in terms of written statutes (similar to the magistrate's 'explanation' of the self-incrimination privilege to a witness, which we saw in Section 6 of Chapter 1). The syntactic and lexical complexity of jury instructions have been analysed by a number of scholars, starting with Charrow and Charrow's (1979) study. Although these instructions are delivered in spoken form, they are often written instructions read aloud in the court (sometimes referred to as 'pattern instructions' or 'standard instructions'). Heffer (2008: 51) points out that judges in England and Wales have more legal latitude to give jury instructions in their own words, than judges in the US. And Tiersma (1999: 193–196) explains why judges in the US take the reading approach rather than the explaining one: in that country some appellate decisions have given judges reason to be concerned that any small or subtle way in which their explanation might deviate from the statute could become grounds for appeal.

A particular focus of linguistic study of jury instructions concerns the standard of proof in criminal trials, namely that the defendant can only be convicted if found guilty *beyond reasonable doubt* (e.g. Dumas 2000; Heffer 2006, 2007, 2008; Tiersma 1993, 1999: 193–198, 2001b; Wierzbicka 2003; see also Wood 2007). Judges are often reluctant to explain what *beyond reasonable doubt* means, presumably for the same reasons that they are reluctant to explain written instructions which they read aloud. I have heard juries ask for clarification on what this means (through a written question submitted to the judge from the jury foreperson). One response to a jury which I heard a judge give in an Australian court was something like this: *It means what the words mean: beyond (pause) reasonable (pause) doubt.* A more wordy explanation was given by the judge in the O.J. Simpson case, who used the standard (pattern) jury instructions current in California at the time, saying:

Reasonable doubt is defined as follows. It is not a mere possible doubt because everything relating to human affairs is open to some possible or imaginary doubt. It is that state of the case which, after the entire comparison and consideration of all the evidence, leaves the minds of the jurors in that condition that they cannot say they feel an abiding conviction of the truth of the charge. (Tiersma 1999: 194–195)

Exercise 3.6ˣ
(a) Decide which of the two explanations given directly above you would prefer if you were a juror, and why?
(b) Identify any parts of the Californian instruction which seem unclear.
(c) **(Lx)** Specify the linguistic structures (such as passive) involved in these unclear parts.
(d) Rewrite this instruction in clearer English, making a note of difficulties involved in this task.

Heffer is one of several linguists who has discussed this Californian instruction. He argues (2006: 162) that it is 'stylistically archaic and thoroughly impersonal', in addition to comprising 'lexical and syntactic features which have been identified as impeding instruction' (by Charrow & Charrow 1979). But rather than rewording either the phrase 'beyond reasonable doubt' or rewriting this jury instruction in plain English (see for example

Tiersma 2006), Heffer examines ways in which a better explanation might be provided to the jury. This includes his consideration of a number of different approaches which have been used or suggestions which have been made. He argues (in both his 2006 and 2008 articles) that the problem is not so much in the specific wording of this three-word phrase. He sees the problem in the approach taken to instructing the jury, namely an approach which seeks to transmit a (written) legal text. He advocates that courts should see the instruction of juries on the standard of proof (and any other matters on which they need instruction) as a communicative act. This would involve explaining *beyond reasonable doubt* not as a legal text, but as part of the principles of proof in a criminal trial: the presumption of innocence until proven guilty, the burden of proof on the prosecution, and the standard of this proof, explaining *beyond reasonable doubt*. Heffer recommends a number of communication strategies, which include the use of hypothetical examples, rhetorical questions and reiteration.

Exercise 3.7[xi]

Heffer (2006: 183–184) provides the following sample directions (= instructions) to the jury on the principles of proof in a criminal trial – the presumption of innocence, the burden of proof and the standard of proof.

Now, before I go on to remind you of the specific charges against Ms Jones and the evidence relating to those charges, I need to remind you how you must decide the case. I told you this in my talk to you at the start of the trial, and I am sure that you have kept this in mind while you have been hearing the evidence. It is so crucial, though, that I am going to repeat it to you again now. In a criminal trial like this, the prosecution have to *prove* that the defendant is guilty. Ms Jones *doesn't* have to prove she is innocent. People often think that defendants must be guilty if they are on trial, but that's quite wrong. Imagine if you were mistaken for somebody else and were identified by an eyewitness as having robbed a bank. If you went to trial you would hope, wouldn't you, that the jurors would keep an open mind and not simply presume that you were guilty. For this reason, we always presume that defendants are innocent when they come to court. It is the job of the prosecution to prove to you that Ms Jones is guilty.

How, then, does the prosecution succeed in proving to you that a defendant is guilty? Well, they have to *convince* you through the *evidence* so that you are *sure* of the defendant's guilt. Now, you have probably all heard the expression "beyond reasonable doubt" – it's used on TV and in the movies and it was used by Mrs Hobsbawn and Mr Bishop in their speeches. That's just the traditional legal way of saying the same thing. When lawyers say that the prosecution have to prove the case "beyond reasonable doubt" they simply mean that the prosecution have to *convince* you through the *evidence* so that you are *sure* of the defendant's guilt. When you are in the jury room deciding the case, you need to ask for each of the charges: "Have the prosecution *convinced* us so that we are *sure* that Ms Jones is guilty of this charge or should we give her the benefit of the doubt?" Of course, there are very few things in life that we can know with absolute or mathematical certainty, and the prosecution are not expected to overcome every conceivable doubt that you might have. But they do need to convince you so that you are sure, and they need to convince you on the basis of the evidence. You also need to take into account the defence evidence to the extent that it shows weaknesses in the prosecution case. But remember that the defence are not obliged to raise doubts or an alternative version of events. So, if, after considering all the evidence for a given charge, you are convinced as a group that the defendant is guilty of that charge, you must return a verdict of "Guilty". If you are not convinced, your verdict must be "Not Guilty" for that charge.

Examine these sample directions. Analyse the ways in which this example aims to explain
the principles of proof as a communicative act rather than through transmitting a legal
text. Discuss your views on any advantages and disadvantages of such an approach.
The italics indicate Heffer's suggestions for 'marked stress in delivery', although he does
not intend this text to be read out – it is intended to provide a kind of template which
should be modified according to specific details of a particular case.
(You will notice the use of *sure* in the explanation of *beyond reasonable doubt* here. Heffer
explains (2006: 173–174) that this has been common practice in courts in England and
Wales for more than 50 years. See also Heffer 2005: 165, 2007.)

7. Unidirectional dimensions of courtroom talk

Heffer's work on the ways in which judges communicate with jurors is part of a larger study
(Heffer 2005) of what he terms the unidirectional dimensions of courtroom talk. By this he
means the ways in which the main focus for lawyers' and judges' talk is the jury, who never
reply. In contrast, most sociolinguistic studies of courtroom talk have examined interaction,
typically between lawyers and witnesses. But, as we saw in Section 2 of Chapter 2, this
seemingly dyadic talk actually has many intended audiences. As Heffer points out, talk with
witnesses serves primarily for the lawyer on each side to structure their version for the jury
(or judge/magistrate in cases with no jury). Heffer's interest then is not so much in strategies
that lawyers use in arguing or cooperating with witnesses. He examines how lawyers present
their version of the story to the jury (mainly through the questions they ask the witnesses,
rather than what the witnesses say in reply), and how lawyers try to persuade the jury of their
view of the case. The other dimension of this legal–lay discourse – or language that is 'received
by' the jury – comprises judges' talk, particularly their explanations to the jury of the legal
framework in which they should view the case (which we have glimpsed in Section 6 above),
as well as their own summary of the case for the jury.

Heffer points out a number of strange features of interaction between witnesses and lawyers.
Referring to these features as 'apparent discoursal oddities', Heffer (p. 209) says they are due
to the fundamentally unidirectional nature (lawyer to jury) of the superficially dyadic talk in
trials (between lawyers and witnesses):

- Witnesses are asked to look at the jury rather than their addressee [lawyer, or judge]
  when they answer questions.

- Lawyers' turns are longer than witnesses, even in examination-in-chief.

- Most 'questions' in cross-examination are effectively declarations rather than requests for
  information.

- Cross-examiners can virtually narrate to the jury ignoring the witness altogether and can
  focus on creating solidarity with the jury rather than eliciting information from the witness.

So these rather 'weird' features of interaction in courtrooms can be explained by reference to
the fact that much of what happens in court is not primarily interactional in purpose, even if

it is in form. Heffer further shows that this legal–lay discourse is characterised by a tension between two different ways of viewing trials. In everyday conversation, we talk about incidents of crime in a narrative fashion, based on subjective reconstructions of personal experience. This is the approach that lay participants, that is jury members, bring to court. But lawyers are trained to use a 'paradigmatic approach', based on detached analysis using logical reasoning, rules and definitions to apply law to a particular situation.

In his exploration and explanation of the paradigmatic approach to courtroom talk, Heffer's work helps us to understand what makes legal language different. Before his work, the important contributions to this question were about the morpho-syntactic and lexical complexity of written legal language (especially Mellinkoff 1963; Tiersma 1999). And while popular notions may suggest that lawyers use *big words* or complex grammar in the courtroom, this seems to be rare in talk addressed to witnesses, or intended for jurors (although it does occur in legal argument in court). Heffer's work shows us how lawyers and judges actually talk in court (using a paradigmatic approach), and how and why this can often be at odds with ordinary talk (using a narrative approach).

Heffer's analysis is that jury trials work by 'bringing together the paradigmatic skills of the legal professionals with the narrative skills of the jury' (2005: 214). For Heffer, this is not a contradiction, but a necessary combination in the deliberations required in criminal trials: jurors need to understand human actions in terms of actions, experiences and contexts (the narrative mode), but they also need to apply the law logically and view the events dispassionately (the paradigmatic mode) (pp. 23 and 35). So, a major role of judges is in bringing together the two modes – narrative and paradigmatic.

Following Heffer's example (p. 177–179) about applying the legal definition of 'handling stolen goods' enables us to see the challenges involved in balancing the narrative and paradigmatic ways of thinking and talking about a crime. The statute (written law) defines this offence in typical paradigmatic fashion, using hypothetical language, in a long and complex sentence involving both subordination and coordination. You might like to represent this sentence diagrammatically to uncover its complex structure.[xii]

A person handles stolen goods, if (otherwise than in the course of the stealing) knowing or believing them to be stolen, he dishonestly receives the goods or dishonestly undertakes or assists in their retention, removal, disposal or realization by or for the benefit of another person, or if he arranges to do so. (Section 22 of the Theft Act, England 1968)

If the judge just reads this section of the Theft Act to the jurors, what is the likelihood of them understanding it, and being able to apply it accurately to the particular case in which they must make the decision: *did the accused handle stolen goods?* Let's see how one judge explained this law to the jurors, as well as how they should apply it to the evidence they had heard. (Following Heffer (2005: 177–179), I have italicised the parts of this jury direction which are in narrative mode, the plain font being in paradigmatic mode. Note that the use of italics here does not indicate emphasis as it did in Exercise 3.7.)

Let me just move on then to the offence of handling, because *you need to consider* the definition of that. That is *a bit more complicated* and *I will go through rather more slowly with you* ...

I have to find the right page. A person handles stolen goods, if (otherwise than in the course of stealing) knowing or believing them to be stolen, he dishonestly receives them. *Now* that is the offence which is handling *here.* ...

What *you* would have to be *satisfied in this case* – and in *each of these cases* if *you are considering* the handling counts – *was* that *the defendant received* them, *took* them into *his* control *as it were.* And that *at the time that* he *took* them into *his* control (he *received* them) *he knew* they were stolen or *believed* they were stolen ...

You can appreciate the difference between knowledge and belief. When it comes to knowledge *of course that means* you have direct knowledge of the actual theft and therefore for that reason you know they are stolen.

If for example *you were standing in Marks and Spencers and you watched a shoplifter steal and then ten minutes later you took the goods from the shoplifter* you would receive them knowing that they were stolen. If on the other hand *you were* not *in Marks and Spencers when the shoplifter stole that elegant hat and you were outside in the Crown and Robe and someone came up to you and said "Look what I have just nicked from Marks and Spencers",* you do not have direct knowledge of it but you have the belief based on what you have been told. *So that is the distinction if I can put it that way.*

Exercise 3.8[xiii]
Use the extract above to work out some of the linguistic characteristics of the paradigmatic and the narrative modes used in legal–lay discourse.

Exercise 3.9
Go back to the discussion of the self-incrimination privilege in Section 6 of Chapter 1. Develop an explanation of the privilege to the witness in the case discussed there, based on Heffer's approach introduced above.

Assignments and further research

1. In their recent book, Conley and O'Barr (2005: 65–66) revisit the classic Duke study discussed in Section 4.1 above, reanalysing this early work as evidence of the patriarchy of the law. Critically examine this reanalysis, taking care to read some publications from the original study, such as Conley et al. (1978), O'Barr (1982) and O'Barr and Atkins (1980).

2a. **(Lx)** Carefully research the design and analysis used in the matched guise technique, such as used in the Duke study. Outline what you see as the advantages and disadvantages of such a study.

2b. **(Lx)** Write a research proposal for a matched guise study to investigate a topic relevant to this course, such as attitudes to the use of AAVE or Jamaican or Jamaican English by witnesses.

    Make sure you address all of the following questions:

    - What research question will be addressed in the study?

    - What is the relevance of this question?

    - How does it relate to any published work on language and the law?

    - Where will this study be conducted and who will the subjects be?

    - What permissions will be required to carry out the study?

    - How will the taped guises be prepared?

    - How many speech samples will be on the tape, and how many subjects will be asked to do the experiment?

    - What characteristics will subjects be asked to rate the speakers on? Why these characteristics?

    - What statistical methods will be used in the data analysis?

    - What problems do you envisage in carrying out this research, and how will you address them?

3. **(Lx)** Examine the linguistic features of closing arguments in a court to which you can have access to courtroom data. A small project could take a small number of closing arguments and examine the features discussed in Section 5 above. A larger project would involve going to the studies discussed in that section, and examining your own data, to see how it provides support for the analyses already published or extends them. Make sure to consider differences and similarities between closing arguments by defence and prosecution. Pay particular attention to how the linguistic strategies used might be part of the speaker's persuasive work in addressing the judicial decision-maker(s) – whether jury or judge(s).

4. **(Lx)** If you are in the US or any other jurisdiction that uses a voir dire process during jury selection (see Section 2 above), observe a number of voir dire sessions and write a report about the ways in which language is used. You could use Stygall (1994: 45–80), Uehara and Candlin (1989) and Shuy (1995) as starting points for your investigation. It may not be permissible to record voir dire sessions, so your report will probably be based on your careful notes. (If this assignment is undertaken without access to recordings for repeated listening, it could not form the basis of a major study at graduate level, see Section 5 of Chapter 2.)

5. **(Lx)** Class field trip to court. (This assignment follows on from Assignment topic 2 in Chapter 1 and Assignment topic 3 in Chapter 2.)

   - In preparation, the class should draw up a checklist of characteristics of courtroom talk, based on this chapter and additional reading. Different features should then be allocated to different students. Another important part of the preparation is for the teacher to liaise with court officials to find out the most suitable courtroom(s) in which to have class members observing.

   - Spend a day or half-day observing court proceedings in a local courthouse, with each student paying particular attention to the feature(s) allocated to you. Make notes about these features, and any others you observe. Also make notes about the following:
     ○ the physical layout of the courtroom (prepare a sketch for later comparison with Figure 2.2 in Chapter 2);
     ○ ritualistic language.

   - Following the field trip, devote a class session to discussion of the court observations, paying attention to:
     ○ connections to linguistic and sociolinguistic research on courtroom talk;
     ○ possible further research topics.

6. **(Lx)** Spend a few days observing language use in a local courtroom, and prepare an ethnography of communication account of one genre, such as trials, guilty pleas or sentencing hearings. (This assignment can be undertaken following Assignment topic 2 in Chapter 1 and Assignment topic 3 in Chapter 2, and in conjunction with Assignment topic 5 above).

7. **(Lx)** Hobbs' (2003a) study of an African American lawyer's use of AAVE oratorical style could be a starting point for students who have a good understanding of the analysis both of this language variety and of code-switching. Examine the use of AAVE by lawyers and/or judges, paying particular attention to code-switching between AAVE and Standard English. What contribution can be made by different theoretical approaches to the analysis of code-switching? Some references on approaches to code-switching to get you started are Auer (1998, 1999), Muysken (2000), Wei (2005), Woolard (2004).

8. **(Lx)** Matoesian (2001: 7) says that the legal institutional identity of expert witness is not a static identity but one that 'emerges in and through discursive interaction between attorneys and witnesses'. Explain and exemplify this claim, drawing on Cotterill (2003:

Chapter 6), Hobbs (2003b), Matoesian (2001: Chapters 6 and 7), Stygall (2001) and Winiecki (2008).

9. **(Lx)** Critically review sociolinguistic research on discourse strategies in cross-examination, paying particular attention to Atkinson and Drew (1979), Drew (1985, 1990, 1992), Eades (2008a), Heffer (2005) and Matoesian (2001, 2005b).

10. How is courtroom interaction different in the Netherlands' criminal courts from the adversarial courts of the common law system? Consider how and why the courtroom language strategies in the Netherlands revealed by Komter (e.g. 1994, 1998) would be possible or not possible in an adversarial courtroom.

11. If you are in a country which does not have an adversarial approach: explore the differences between court hearings in your country, and those of the Anglo adversarial system examined in the sociolinguistics literature discussed in this chapter. In your comparison, consider the extent to which Komter's (1994, 1998) work in the Netherlands is relevant to your situation. You should also check with Vidmar (2000a) for any discussion of jury courts relevant to your country (e.g. Japan, Spain, Russia).

4
Second language speakers and interpreters

1. Introduction   64

2. Assessing and understanding the need for an interpreter   66

3. Arguments against the need for an interpreter   69

4. Understanding the role of the interpreter   70

5. Linguistic challenges in courtroom interpreting   72

    5.1. Semantic challenges   *72*

    5.2. Grammatical challenges   *72*

    5.3. Pragmatic challenges   *73*

    5.4. Cultural challenges   *76*

    5.5. Additional challenges for creole speakers   *77*

6. Second language speakers without interpreters   77

7. Deaf sign language users   78

    Assignments and further research   *81*

Second language speakers and interpreters

1. Introduction

In Chapter 3 we saw that courtroom talk is unusual in a number of ways. For example, it appears to be dyadic, and yet there are multiple addressees, most of whom are not permitted to speak. And it appears to be about hearing and assessing the stories of witnesses, and yet witnesses are so constrained in how they can tell their stories, that in effect it is largely lawyers' accounts of their stories which are presented and assessed.

While participating in courtroom hearings can be intimidating or confusing for many people without a legal background, these difficulties are compounded for people who are not fluent speakers of the dominant language. There is a growing body of sociolinguistic research on the participation of second language speakers in court, primarily in English-speaking countries. Central to this participation is the work of interpreters, who provide oral equivalents of what is said in English for the non-English or second language speaker, as well as what is said by this person for the English speakers. In keeping with widespread usage, I will use 'interpreting' to refer to such oral practices, and 'translation' to refer to the corresponding written practices. And following linguistic convention, I will use the term L2 speaker to refer to a second language speaker (such as a speaker of English as a second language, or a person who speaks a language other than English), and L1 speaker to refer to a person who speaks the dominant language (mostly here it is English) as their first language.

The rights of L2 accused persons in the legal process are specifically protected under international law in the 1966 International Covenant on Civil and Political Rights. Article 14 of this covenant (which is reiterated in Article 6 of the European Convention on Human Rights) states that:

an accused person has the right
a) to be informed promptly and in detail in a language which he understands of the nature and cause of the charge against him (emphasis added)
...
f) to have the free assistance of an interpreter if he cannot speak or understand the language used in court

Article 5 of the European Convention on Human Rights also extends this right to arrested people, before they are accused. However, this free assistance of an interpreter is often limited to accused persons in criminal matters. What happens to witnesses, jurors and people involved in civil matters?

While there is no international recognition of the rights of L2 speakers to interpreting assistance when they are witnesses or jurors, or party to a civil case, there are many jurisdictions which provide interpreters not just for defendants but for any witnesses who do not speak English. And some non-English speakers can serve on the jury in a few jurisdictions where interpreters are provided for jurors speaking specified languages, namely:

- monolingual Spanish speakers in New Mexico (US) since 2000 (Montalvo 2001);

- monolingual speakers of Indigenous languages in Northwest Territories and Nunavut (Canada) since 1989 (Vertes 2002);

- Deaf people in many states in the US: under legislation for Americans with Disability (Napier *et al.* 2007);

- in New Zealand in 2005 an interpreter was provided for a deaf juror (Napier *et al.* 2007).

In these instances we see the legal system recognising the rights of citizens who are monolingual in a language other than English. This recognition means that accused people are more likely to be tried by a jury which includes some of their social, cultural and linguistic peers.

Exercise 4.1

Prepare a submission to the Attorney-General or Minister for Justice in your state/country, arguing for the provision of interpreters for jurors. As background research for this submission, you'll need to research:

- the numbers of people who speak languages other than English in the state/country
- which languages are spoken by how many people
- the specific provisions made for interpreters in legal proceedings, e.g. which languages are catered for? who makes the decision that an interpreter is required in a particular case?
- any relevant sections of the Constitution or Bill of Rights

You will also need to research the role of the jury and consider how its function is compromised if citizens of non-English-speaking background can never serve on a jury.

Underlying the legal system in many countries is the assumption of monolingualism. This is part of a much wider assumption that societal monolingualism is the norm, and the best way for countries to work. However, a great many of the world's societies are multilingual, and for this reason the assumption that societal monolingualism is the norm is increasingly being referred to as the myth of monolingualism (see Edwards 2004). We see this myth of monolingualism in the way in which interpreting works. For example, it is typical for the official transcript in English-dominant countries to record only English utterances. Thus all other utterances have no legal status, and only the interpreter's words can be referred to in appeals. So, the interpreter's English version is the basis of any decision or appeal. And Angermeyer (2008: 385) shows how, in the US small claims courts that he studied, the monolingual bias of the court 'forces bilingual participants to act as monolinguals, thereby creating the appearance of monolingualism as the norm' (see Section 2 below).

Most of the research on courtroom language has been done in countries where courtrooms are monolingual. However, there are some jurisdictions where two languages are used, such as Malaysia (Malay and English), Hong Kong (Chinese and English) and Sri Lanka (Tamil or Sinhala and English). R. Powell (2008: 155) finds that bilingual courtrooms can be an important step in making legal processes more transparent, but they can 'obscure the need many participants have for translation'. Another issue which Powell draws attention to is that while practical acceptance of two languages 'may increase participation in judicial proceedings ... it cannot overcome the fact that individual bilingualism varies widely'. But despite this reality of different degrees of bilingualism, many monolingual people assume that bilingualism is the same as parallel monolingualisms. However, many people use their first language for certain social functions (often in the home and in religious settings) and another language in other social functions (such as basic conversations with outsiders), and they may not be equally fluent in both languages. As we will see in the next section, speaking English as a second language does not always mean that you can handle the English in a legal matter without an interpreter.

2. Assessing and understanding the need for an interpreter

We have seen that an accused person has the right to free assistance of an interpreter if they cannot speak or understand the language used in court. So, who decides if an interpreter is needed? Generally this important decision is made in court by the presiding judicial officer (i.e. the judge or magistrate), typically on the basis of this officer's impression of the L2 speaker's answers to a few basic questions, such as *How long have you been in this country?*, *Where did you learn English?* and *Where do you live now?*

But later questions in a courtroom hearing can be much more complex. Here is an example of a complex lawyer question (from Brennan 1995: 81):

And is that because of what you have told is that he threatened to, not just bash you but bash, I think your words, all of you?

Exercise 4.2

Take the question from Brennan (1995: 81) above and work with a partner on each of the following steps. For each step, record the activity for later playback and analysis.

a) Read the question aloud once at normal speaking pace, and then ask your partner to repeat it without looking at the transcription.
b) Break the question into three or four segments, and read each segment once, with your partner repeating each segment before you read the next.
c) Do a), but this time your partner interprets it into a language you both know.
d) Do b), but this time your partner interprets it into a language you both know.

Replay the recording and compare the repetitions with the original.

What inaccuracies do you observe in your partner's repetition of the question? and in the interpreted version?

This would also be an interesting question to experiment with in terms of accuracy of written transcription. You could do a) and b), but have your partner write down the question as you are reading it. No repetition allowed.

What conclusions can you draw from this exercise about understanding and interpreting (and transcribing) courtroom questions?

It is clear that the legal system needs a better test of language proficiency than is currently used to inform the decision about the need for an interpreter (a practical challenge for applied linguists). Cooke (2002) describes a pilot interview-based test, which comprises a series of questions designed to stimulate structures and types common in cross-examination (see also Law Society of the Northern Territory 2004: 8).

The difference between straightforward questions such as *When did you arrive in this country?* and complex questions, such as the cross-examination example above, is important when we think about L2 speakers in the legal process. Applied linguistic research on how languages are learned and used has found that we can talk about two different types of language proficiency. Basic Interpersonal Communication Skills (BICS) is the term used to refer to the language proficiency which people can acquire in their second language as they go about basic communication, such as shopping, telling people where they live, when they arrived in the country and so on. These are the kinds of topics typically asked about by judges when they are 'testing' a defendant to see if an interpreter is needed. But researchers have found that this basic language proficiency is not enough for educational success. Cognitive Academic Language Proficiency (CALP) is the more complex and abstract language proficiency which a learner needs to acquire in order to succeed academically in another language. To oversimplify the complex research on this topic, the evidence indicates that school-aged children generally take at least five years to add CALP to BICS (see Cummins 2000).

But what kind of language proficiency is needed to successfully get through the legal process, for example to understand that long and tortuous cross-examination question we saw above? And what about the fine differences of meaning that can be at issue in struggles between lawyer and witness over word choice (such as we saw in Section 4.3 of Chapter 3, and will see in Sections 4 and 5 of Chapter 6). Perhaps we could say that what is needed in the legal process might be called something like LIMP: Language Intricacies and Manipulation Proficiency. As yet there is little research that examines what we might call LIMP in terms of second language speakers (but see Cooke 1995a, 1996, 2002; Gibbons 2001). We're not talking here about the technical legal terms that we see in written legal documents, but about spoken language complexity, such as subtle differences in word choice, tricky manipulation of presuppositions, and asking three questions in one. A particularly common type of cross-examination question is one which asks something like *Do/Would you agree that you said ...,* referring to a witness's earlier telling of their story – for example in a police interview or during their cross-examination. You will remember questions of this type in Extract 3–ii in Section 4.1 of Chapter 3 (Turns 7, 9 and 13).

In some jurisdictions, there is a recognition of both the rights of L2 speakers to interpreting assistance, and the fact that not all questions and answers will need to be interpreted. But more typically we see what we might call the all-or-nothing view of language learning and use, that is, the belief that a person either needs an interpreter throughout or doesn't need an interpreter at all. This approach ignores the distinction between BICS and LIMP.

A striking illustration of the different kinds of language proficiency required in the legal process is found in Cooke's (1996) case study of an Australian woman, Daphne. Daphne was from a remote Aboriginal community in Northeast Arnhem Land in the Northern

Territory. Her first language was Djamparpuyngu, and she also spoke fairly fluent English for telling stories and answering straightforward questions. Daphne's story is a long one, about how she escaped her abusive spouse during one of his many violent outbursts. But things took a tragic turn, and she ended up in court facing a murder charge. In an unusual departure from typical practice, the judge allowed her to have an interpreter sitting beside her, so that she could just answer the questions without worrying about what language she spoke in. (This type of courtroom interpreting is referred to as 'stand-by interpreting', see Angermeyer 2008: 391.) Her examination-in-chief started off with fluent and articulate answers in English to questions such as *Where were you living at that time?*, *Who was there?* and *What happened then?*

But as the questions got to some of the worst abuse she had suffered, questions such as *What happened then?* and *What were you thinking?* led to her answers in Djamparpuyngu, as she struggled to explain her state of mind. Here is the English interpretation of some of her Djamparpuyngu answers to questions such as *What were you thinking?* (Cooke 1996: 286):

at the time when I was holding the knife all these thoughts were flashing through, the past treatment and I lost myself. .. My mind and head turned ... kind of like – blackout. ... My mind was blank, I was just moving my hand anyway, not conscious of exactly where I was hitting ... it was like when someone yells at you in an angry way so hard you can behave in a way where you are not conscious of actions, that's the kind of feeling

Daphne was able to give evidence about everyday happenings, and to narrate in English much of the story of the abuse she suffered, but when it came to explaining her mental state, she switched to Djamparpuyngu. The judge in her case recognised the difference between these different kinds of language use, and allowed her to speak through an interpreter when necessary. Reflecting on this story, maybe we need to add to LIMP suggested above another term LIMS: Language Intricacies and Mental States.

The use of stand-by interpreting in Daphne's case contrasts with the situation investigated by Angermeyer (2008) in his study of 40 cases in three small claims courts in New York City. Angermeyer found numerous occasions on which either interpreters or arbitrators (the judicial decision-makers in these courts) instructed litigants who had requested interpreters that they could not use any English. For example, one litigant who had requested a Russian interpreter gave several short answers in English, until the arbitrator said 'Speak in Russian sir. If you need an interpreter, then be interpreted' (p. 388). Such restriction of the language choice of bilingual litigants cannot be explained in Angermeyer's study in terms of legal strategy: the small claims courts are not bound by strict rules of evidence as in other courts, and it is also rare for litigants to have lawyers. Angermeyer argues that it is the monolingual language ideology of the legal system which explains such a restrictive approach to the realities of multilingual language practices (an issue we will take up in Section 4.4 of Chapter 11).

While debate and contest are common in a number of countries over whether or not particular individuals need interpreting assistance, a rather different situation exists in New Zealand, where approximately 14% of the population is indigenous Māori. With the 1987 declaration of Māori as an official language of New Zealand, came the right for any person (not just a defendant) to speak Māori in any legal proceedings, regardless of their proficiency in English. It is the responsibility of the officer presiding over the proceedings (such as the judge) to ensure that a competent interpreter is available (Lane *et al.* 1999). Similarly, in Wales, the Welsh Language Act of 1993 legislated the right of all Welsh speakers to use that language in any court, also regardless of their proficiency in English (Colin & Morris 1996: 76–77).

3. Arguments against the need for an interpreter

Regardless of a person's limited proficiency in the second language, there can be arguments against the need for an interpreter. One of the reasons for this is that in the adversarial system, interpreters are often viewed with suspicion and mistrust, particularly in situations where a witness speaks some English. Interpreters are often seen, not as meeting the basic human right of a defendant, but as some sort of ally or even advocate for the defendant. Thus lawyers have raised a number of objections about the request for an interpreter in a courtroom hearing. Cooke (1995a: 69) gives the example of a lawyer who spoke of a witness using 'the support of an interpreter to try and dream up some explanation'. This suggestion was rejected by the presiding judicial officer as 'utterly impertinent'. See also Angermeyer (2008: 392–393) for an example of an arbitrator in a small claims court rejecting a lawyer's attempt to discredit a litigant's request for an interpreter.

There can be many reasons for arguments against the request for an interpreter. Some of these objections might sometimes result from a lawyer's previous experience when an insufficiently trained and skilled person has worked as an interpreter. Obviously any such bad experience has to be set aside when approaching a new case with a qualified interpreter. But on some occasions, arguments against the request for an interpreter appear to relate more to the widespread xenophobia of monolingual people towards someone speaking in another language. The popular fear that *they might be talking about me but I don't know* appears to sometimes shift slightly in courtroom contexts to *the interpreter might be helping the witness but I don't know*. A third reason for arguments against the request for an interpreter may relate to the lawyer's strategies for handling the case, and may be part of this lawyer's exercise of power over the opposing side.

The following questions indicate some of the concerns that lawyers have about interpreters in court:

- *Will the interpreter modify an answer?* This question indicates lack of understanding of the work of interpreters. It may also indicate distrust, lack of respect and resentment. Interpreters swear an oath to 'interpret to the best of their ability and skill' and are bound by a code of professional ethics, which includes confidentiality, accuracy and impartiality (see AUSIT, also Berk-Seligson 2002a: Appendix 4, Appendix 5; Home Office 2007). And just as lawyers are expected to act professionally – for example not telling witnesses what to say in their evidence – interpreters also should be treated as professionals.

- *Will the interpreter help the witness?* Again, we can ask why should we expect that the interpreter would not be professional? Is the judge going to favour one party? Admittedly, there can be complications when the interpreter is from the same country or ethnic group as the person they are interpreting for. For example, the witness might expect that the interpreter will help them. This adds challenges to the work of the interpreter, but it is unfair to expect that the interpreter cannot deal with such challenges in a professional manner.

- *Will it give extra time for the witness to prepare an answer?* It may be that the witness gets part of the gist of the question, when it is first given (in English). However, this can turn out to be a disadvantage, if they didn't fully understand the question.

- *Will it be harder to gauge the credibility of the witness?* This may certainly be harder if we don't understand the witness giving their evidence themselves, because it is in a language we don't understand. But this should not be grounds for interfering with the right to an interpreter.

- *Will the interpreter provide a 'buffer' between lawyer and witness?* Certainly having an interpreter makes interaction more complex – the lawyer asks a question which the interpreter repeats in the witness's language, then the witness answers, and the interpreter repeats the answer in English. Does this process protect the witness from excesses of cross-examination? Does it soften the blow, so to speak? Perhaps it can to some extent, but it also introduces an extra complexity for the witness.

Many of these arguments against the request for an interpreter can be seen to relate to resentment about provisions for some community groups and individuals – *are they getting something I can't get?* But this resentment, while often connected to monolingual biases, can also be based to some extent on a mistaken understanding of the way in which interpreters provide language assistance.

4. Understanding the role of the interpreter

The interpreter's aim is to 'remove the language barrier and to the best of their skill and ability place the non-English speaker in a position as similar as possible to that of a speaker of English' (Hale 2004: 10). Put another way, the interpreter's job is 'to replicate the original source language message in the target language in a manner that would have the same effect on listeners'. The interpreter's job is not to help the person understand what is going on, because that is what could give the L2 speaker an advantage over many others in the legal system. A question which arises here is about whether even English speakers can understand the language used in court. In fact, studies such as Heffer (2005) suggest that criminal courts at least don't use much technical language – of the sort we see in written legal documents, for example. But the linguistic trickery which is used in court is arguably a type of linguistic practice which many people, even those who speak English as their mother tongue, can find hard to understand and deal with at times.

Another area in which there is a widespread lack of recognition about how language works is when monolingual people complain that the witness said a few words, but the interpreter said many, or vice versa. There is often confusion over what accurate interpreting involves. As Colin and Morris (1996: 99) explain in their book on legal interpreting in the UK:

... lawyers not infrequently instruct court interpreters to say exactly what the witness has said – to "translate literally". What they should mean by this is: tell me no more and no less than the speaker has said. This is a perfectly acceptable requirement. What they should *not* mean is: give me a word-for-word transposition of what the speaker has said.

In fact a literal word-for-word translation can often produce ludicrous results, as we see particularly in the case of idioms. For example, a word-for-word translation of the German sentence *Ich will nicht hinter schwedische Gardinen* would be the nonsensical *I don't want behind Swedish curtains*. An accurate interpretation would be *I don't want to go behind bars*.

A central difficulty then in the way in which second language speakers can access their basic human rights in the criminal justice system concerns misunderstandings about the role of interpreters in the legal system. Their role is often poorly understood by legal professionals, as well as second language speakers. The interpreter's job is not that of legal assistant, or advocate or support person, but of language professional. In some jurisdictions this is seen to be like a language 'machine' (or conduit), and in others as that of a communication facilitator (see Hale 2004; Laster & Taylor 1994). In discussing the predicaments faced by court interpreters, Morris (1999: 7) says that they often feel like a piece of gum stuck to a shoe: 'ignored for all practical purposes, but almost impossible to remove'.

Interpreters are clearly essential in the way in which linguistic diversity works in the legal process. It is interesting to hear how legal professionals talk about the participation of interpreters in the legal system – do they talk about 'using' interpreters or 'working with' interpreters? There are many indications that interpreters are not recognised as language professionals: they are mostly poorly remunerated, having a low hourly rate, and working mostly as casual employees with no secure employment or career structure. They are typically poorly accommodated and resourced. And their needs are often poorly understood – it is common for interpreters to be provided with no contextual information, and no time to prepare for what can be extremely complex interpreting assignments. Further, most courts do not take into account interpreters' needs for breaks. Unlike anyone else in the court, they typically have to talk all day, as they interpret whatever is spoken by any participant.

Related to the lack of recognition of courtroom interpreters as professionals, and the widespread view among lawyers and judges that the interpreter's role is like that of a language machine, is the view that having an interpreter does not, or should not, change anything in the courtroom. Several scholars have shown that this is an unrealistic view, starting with Berk-Seligson's study in the US of interpreted courtroom proceedings. Berk-Seligson shows a number of ways in which the interpreter is inevitably 'an intrusive element' (2002a: 96). These include occasions in which the interpreter has to ask for clarification, and occasions on which lawyers or judge speak directly to the interpreter. A number of studies of interpreting in various contexts (not just legal ones) show that interpreting can never be mechanical, it is an interactional activity (e.g. Wadensjö 1998). As Berk-Seligson shows, bilingual courtrooms cannot be expected to be identical to monolingual courtrooms.

5. Linguistic challenges in courtroom interpreting

5.1. Semantic challenges

As with interpreting in any other context, legal interpreting involves a number of linguistic challenges. Semantic challenges abound in situations where words or expressions in one language do not have easy equivalents in the other language. While idioms are the classic case of such a challenge, there are many others. For example, Stern (1995: 24) reports the difficulties for interpreting into Russian parts of the day in English, such as *afternoon*. The day is subdivided differently in Russian and English, and it can be difficult to find Russian equivalents for English expressions, such as *late morning, early afternoon* and *late afternoon*. And Moeketsi (1999: 161) says that Sesotho interpreters in South Africa face a challenge in interpreting some English generic verbs, such as *assault*. As the Sesotho language does not have a generic verb corresponding to English *assault*, interpreters have to choose between verbs such as *-otla* (beat), *-tlatlapa* (illtreat, abuse), *-hlekefesta* (treat roughly), *-hlasela* (attack) and *-lematsa* (hurt). Moeketsi recommends that interpreters should explain this lack of exact equivalent to the judicial officer, and ask that the original speaker rephrase the utterance. But such advice is often difficult for interpreters to follow, because of the fear that a request like this may wrongly lead legal professionals to mistrust the linguistic skills of the interpreter. It is clearly important for judges and lawyers to receive training in how to work with interpreters, and this training would explain the nature of translation and interpretation, as well as fundamental findings from sociolinguistics and applied linguistics on such topics as bilingualism and language acquisition.

5.2. Grammatical challenges

Important work on grammatical challenges comes from Lee's (2009a, 2009b, 2010) study of Korean interpreters in Australian courts. Lee shows how grammatical differences between Korean and English can make it very difficult, if not impossible, for interpreters, even those with accreditation and considerable experience, to accurately interpret within the constraints of courtroom hearings. For example, Korean does not have a single form that indicates definiteness such as the English definite article *the*. While demonstratives such as *i* ('this'), *ku* ('that/the') and *ce* ('that') may substitute for English definite determiners to some extent, there is no one-to-one lexical equivalence between Korean *ku* and English *the* (Lee 2009b: 384).

In a telling example, Lee discusses the evidence of a Korean complainant in a sexual assault case. During her cross-examination, the complainant consistently denied that there had been any discussion on the night in question between herself and the defendant about a condom (if there had been, this might have been taken to indicate consent to sexual intercourse). Later in cross-examination, the defence lawyer quoted from a transcript which was a translation of a phone call made by the complainant to the defendant several days after the alleged incident. This phone call had been organised by the police, without the defendant's knowledge. The English transcript records the translation of one of the complainant's (Korean) questions to the defendant as *Did you have the condom on?* The complainant responded that she asked this question because she was *asked to ask like that* (Lee's translation of the complainant's answer). However, Lee points out that the English transcript of the phone call records another question from the complainant to the defendant, three turns later, as *I asked you whether you had condom on, on that day?* As Lee comments, it is impossible to know what the complainant had actually said in this phone call, as she spoke in Korean, but only the English translation was available. (This reflects a common situation where the actual utterances of witnesses in court and police interviewees are not considered to be evidence, but only the official English translation of these utterances, as we saw in Section 1 above.)

However, Lee points out that given the difference in use of the definite article between Korean and English, it is quite likely that the complainant had not been asking about a particular condom, previously discussed with the defendant. In other words, it seems quite likely that in both of the Korean questions during this surreptitious phone call the complainant was talking about *a condom* and not *the condom*. While this might seem like a trivial grammatical point, it assumed great significance in the trial. During his closing argument, the defence lawyer said (2009b: 393–394):

*the condom is of significant (0.3) proportions in this case (omitted) ... she says that she never saw any condoms (1.5) she never saw any condoms when I took her to exhibit G, I do it now (omitted) ... now you must understand (2.3) that this was in the context of police seeking evidence (omitted) .... she says (0.5) °that° she didn't see any condoms there that night.(3.1) I suggest TO you (.) by the very words she used to Richard himself (.) she's telling lies and she tripped herself UP (0.3) because she's probably forgotten what she said to Richard on the phone.(0.7) (omitted).... not a condom (0.3) THE condom, the definite article. (1.7) she could only have been talking, ladies and gentlemen, of the CONDOM which she would've KNOWN about back on ** March 200* and she did in FACT see the condom packet or packets (omitted) ... but the fact of the matter is, (0.9) she was aware that there was a condom because she SAID in her (1.0) conversation with HIM (0.6.) did you have the condom on.*

This 'analysis' by the defence lawyer shows the importance which can be placed on close analysis of language use during adversarial trials. It also shows how serious can be the consequences of unrecognised grammatical differences between languages which cause difficulties in interpretation. Here, the defence lawyer was clearly implying that the complainant had lied about the issue of a condom, and that this was proven by her use of *the definite article*. In this case, the prosecutor seemed unaware of the linguistic problem, and did not take up this point. Lee observes also that neither the interpreter for the defendant nor the interpreter for the complainant 'disclosed linguistic issues or pointed out [such] potential misunderstanding' (p. 394). This analysis and other work by Lee point to the problems of restricting interpreters to the narrow conduit approach, without providing the scope for them to provide linguistic guidance on issues such as this. This issue is also addressed by Mikkelson (1998), who calls for an expanded role for court interpreters in the US, comparable to Norway, where interpreters are required to inform the court if there are any misunderstandings.

Another example of grammatical challenges for interpreters is found in Filipovic's (2007) examination of typological differences between English and Spanish in the encoding of manner and direction in verbs of motion.

5.3. Pragmatic challenges

Pragmatics is the area of language analysis which considers speakers' meanings (in contrast to semantics which considers the meanings of utterances). This can also be explained as analysis 'that takes into account commonsense (non-linguistic) understandings that may be brought to bear on the interpretation of an utterance' (Swann *et al.* 2004: 238). Pragmatics is a central concern of interpreting. As Hale (2004: 3) explains it, accuracy in interpreting requires 'a pragmatic reconstruction of the [utterance in the] source language into the target language'. Thus, it does not suffice to simply translate the propositional content of an utterance, but its pragmatic force (sometimes also referred to as its illocutionary force) must also be conveyed. In courtroom interaction, pragmatics can play a more powerful role than in other interactions, such as community meetings, or doctor–patient consultations, for example. This is because devious interpersonal strategies can be central to communication in courts. For example, in cross-examination questions, a lawyer can express sarcasm, or frustration, or disbelief, or impatience. If an interpreter does not convey the pragmatic force of the question, then the L2 witness is only hearing part of the question.

Sometimes pragmatic force is conveyed by intonation or other prosodic features, such as volume. But often, it is deceptively small and apparently non-essential seeming words in the question which convey pragmatic force. Words like *well, so, now* are discourse markers – they don't have any independent propositional meaning, they often come at the beginning of an utterance, and they are often essential in conveying pragmatic force. They are also syntactically independent from the utterance, so that if you repeat the utterance without the discourse marker it still makes sense, although it does not convey the original pragmatic force. It is this last characteristic of discourse markers that makes them of particular concern in sociolinguistic research on courtroom interpreting.

For example, Hale has found that interpreters often completely omit discourse markers when they interpret lawyers' questions, as in the following cross-examination example:

Extract 4–i Hale's (2004: 72) transcription of audiorecording
1. L: **Well**, you were yelling and screaming at this stage weren't you?
2. Int: *Usted estaba gritanda y y y ah hablando en voz alta en se momento, ¿no es cierto?*
[translates as: You were screaming and and and uh speaking in a loud voice at this moment, isn't it right?]

Although the interpreter's version of the question transmits its propositional content, the omission of the discourse marker *well* obscures the fact that the lawyer is asking this question to contradict the witness's previous answer.

Hale (2004: 71) shows that *well* is used by lawyers in cross-examination 'as a sign of contradiction, marking disagreement'. It is a fairly frequently used discourse marker in cross-examination, and can also express the lawyer's frustration or impatience. The following extract shows the original lawyer questions and interpreter's translations of the witness's answers from an example of Hale's in which there are a number of discourse markers, indicated by bold type. (As it is the questions with discourse markers we are looking at here, I have provided the Spanish interpreted version for just these questions. See Hale for the full text.)

Extract 4–ii Hale's (2004: 73–75) transcription of audiorecording
1. L: Uh do you accept that you filled out a claim, an insurance claim for the car on the twentythird of July?
2. W: Mm, that I filled it out yes, that it was on the twentythird I'm not sure.

3. L: Uhm, **well** when you filled out the insurance claim, your wife did that on your behalf, is that correct?

   Int: *Cuando usted llenó el formulario de reclamo de seguro su esposa lo hizo por usted, ¿verdad?*

[translates as: When you filled out the insurance claim form your wife did it for you, right?]

[several more questions in which the lawyer tries to pin down the date on which the witness filled out the form]

4. L: **But** you filled out the form on the twentythird?

   Int: *Pero usted llenó ese formulario el 23.*

[translates as: But you filled out that form on the twentythird.]

5. W: Haven't I told you that I'm not sure? It's been too long.

6. L: Right, uh, **well** you accept that you filled out the form on the twentythird?

   Int: *¿Acepta usted que usted llenó el formulario el 23?*

[translates as: Do you accept that you filled out the form on the twentythird?]

7. W: I don't have the ... I don't know exactly the date when it was filled out.

8. L: **Well**, where did you get the form from to fill it out?

   Int: *¿ Dónde obtuvo el formulario para llenarlo?*

[translates as: Where did you get the form from to fill it out?]

In this example, the interpreter gave no equivalent of any of these occurrences of *well*, although she did translate *but*, as *pero*. In Hale's study of 13 local court hearings in Sydney, *well* was used as a preface in 27 cross-examination questions, but it was interpreted only eight times – so for 70% of its occurrences, it was left out of the interpreted version.

Exercise 4.3

With a partner read aloud the English version in Extract 4–ii above, each taking one role (either lawyer or witness). Read it first as presented above. Then read it a second time, omitting the three occurrences of the discourse marker *well*. Discuss the differences in pragmatic force between these two English readings.

   If there are Spanish speakers in the class, you can do this exercise by reading the whole extract.

Tag questions are also important in conveying pragmatic meaning or pragmatic force, and they are a popular tool in cross-examination in English-speaking countries (as we saw in Section 4.1 in Chapter 3). There are a number of different variant and invariant tag question forms in English. English invariant tags include *right?, correct?, is that so?, isn't that so?, true?*. Variant tags in English are formed with verbal auxiliary and subject pronoun, as in the highlighted tags in the following examples:

*You were there, **weren't you?***
*He's always waiting for you, **isn't he?***
*They might identify him, **mightn't they?***
*He saw you, **didn't he?***

Tag questions can play an important role in a number of cross-examination strategies, including intimidation, confusion and attempts to lead the witness to give contradictory answers. Thus, accurate interpreting of tag questions into a second language must pay attention to the pragmatic force of the particular tag question chosen. But most languages apart from English have only invariant tags, and thus the interpreting of the wide range of English tag questions is tricky. How can the distinctions in pragmatic force found in the range of English tag questions be conveyed in a language which has only invariant tags? Does the language have the same scope for fine-tuning the impact of questions in cross-examination? Several sociolinguists have addressed this issue for Spanish, most notably Berk-Seligson (1999), Hale (2004) and Rigney (1999).

Sociolinguistic research on pragmatic aspects on courtroom interpreting have led Hale and Gibbons (1999) to observe that interpreters are more likely to achieve accuracy in interpreting utterances or parts of utterances which deal with the external reality or the propositional content of questions (e.g. the events about which the witness is being questioned), than the courtroom or pragmatic reality (e.g. the discourse markers which index the questioner's stance of sarcasm) (see also Hale 2004).

5.4. Cultural challenges

To date little research has investigated cultural challenges for interpreters. The greatest concentration of sociolinguistic research on courtroom interpreting has been with speakers of Spanish, whose cultures have considerable overlaps with Anglo culture (as well as significant differences). Cooke (1995b) discusses challenges for interpreting and translating between English and Djamparpuyngu, the language of Aboriginal people on remote Elcho Island in the far north of Australia, whose culture is vastly different from Anglo culture. Cooke explains the tension involved in providing a translation of a written legal document (the coroner's decision in a coronial inquiry into the killing of a local man by police). He explains how simply translating the decision without background information and explanation rendered it into a document that made no sense to the community. For example, the coroner discussed the killer's exercise of his legal right to remain silent and not to testify at the inquiry. The coroner's assertion that no unfavourable inference could be drawn against the killer for his refusal to give evidence made no sense to the community at Elcho Island. In their culture, failure to speak about the killing is a 'sign of shame or guilt' (p. 52). Thus, the translation of the document 'added far more information than is explicitly contained in the coroner's words', as the right to remain silent was explained. Cooke points out that, in contrast to the translation of this written document, courtroom interpreting does not provide the opportunity for such explanations. Thus we see that no matter how accurately an interpreter may render concepts and terms from a source language into a target language, if there are significant cultural differences, the interpreted version may not necessarily make sense. This can work both ways in court: for example in the interpreting of legal concepts to a witness, or in the interpreting of distinctive cultural obligations or concepts to the court (see also ARDS 2008; Edwards 2004: 63–64; Morphy 2007). Mikkelson (1998) points out that in the Northwest Territories of Canada judges and lawyers are permitted to ask interpreters for cultural explanations.

5.5. Additional challenges for creole speakers

It is likely that speakers of creole languages face particular disadvantages in court. This is because creoles often sound quite like the dominant language of the court, and yet they are separate languages. Take, for example, the creole language spoken in several regions of northern Australia, which is known as Kriol. It developed from an earlier Aboriginal Pidgin English which was a rudimentary form of communication between Aboriginal and non-Aboriginal people, and which was not spoken by anyone as a first language. When people were moved from quite wide geographical areas to live together on a mission early in the 20th century, children began speaking this language variety as their first language. So, it expanded in complexity and contexts of use. In linguistic terms the pidgin became a creole language. While much of the vocabulary of Kriol comes from its lexifier language, English, Kriol words do not necessarily have the same meaning as similar English words. Further, much of the grammar of Kriol comes from the Aboriginal languages spoken in the regions from which the families of these children had been removed.

An educational kit for teachers of Kriol in Australia (CEOKR 1994: 43–44) gives an example of possible miscommunication if English speakers do not recognise that a creole language is not English. The sentence *Mai waip bin dran la riba* (written in a phonemic spelling system), sounds quite like the English sentence *My wife been drown la river*. If you know that in Kriol *bin* is the past tense marker and *la* is the preposition meaning *at, on* or *in*, then you might think you can understand this sentence. But it does not mean *My wife drowned in the river*. The Kriol verb *dran* has come from the English verb *drown*, but it does not have quite the same meaning. As the kit for teachers explains (CEOKR 1994: 44):

Kriol *dran* denotes an event in relation to the surface of a liquid. It does not give any information about the state of the thing affected which can be human, animate or inanimate e.g. a biscuit can *dran* in tea.

So this sentence *Mai waip bin dran la riba* probably best translates into English as *My wife swam/bathed in the river*. This example provides an indication of the importance of interpreters for Kriol-speaking witnesses. The website of the Katherine Regional Language Centre in the Northern Territory[14] argues that there 'is really no excuse for not using interpreters' for Kriol speakers in legal and health contexts in the Northern Territory, where the government funds the interpreter service and the language centre provides training and support for the interpreters.

While there appears to be no published research on speakers of creole languages in court, we will see in Section 4.1 of Chapter 8 that there is some work on police interviews with speakers of Jamaican Creole.

6. Second language speakers without interpreters

We saw in Sections 2 and 3 above that L2 speakers are not always provided with interpreters. At this stage there is little sociolinguistic research which investigates the testimony of such witnesses. But Cooke (1995a, 1998, 2009) provides some valuable insights, such as the complications and misunderstandings that can arise with one word answers to Yes/No-questions.

We saw in Chapter 3 that witnesses often give very short answers, and that a large number of questions can be answered by *yes* or *no*. Given that these two answers provide the opposite answer, it would be disturbing to find out that witnesses' answers of *yes* in their L2 English are equivalent to L1 English speakers' *no*, and vice versa. But this may be exactly what is happening in answer to negative questions for speakers whose first language has the opposite pattern from English, in the interpretation of answers to such questions. A few examples from northern Australia will highlight the problem. Cooke explains that in the Yolngu languages, people 'frequently say *yes* to confirm the veracity of a negatively framed proposition in a situation where the English speaker would say *no*' (Cooke 2002: 24). Speakers of these languages who speak English as L2, often carry over this pattern of answering questions into their L2 English, as in the two examples in Extract 4–iii. I have added in square brackets the answer which would convey the same meaning in English.

Extract 4–iii Cooke's (2002: 26) transcription of audiorecording
1. L: You can't answer that?
2. W: Yeah, I can't answer that.
   [No, I can't answer that]

....

3. L: You had never seen a person speared before in your life before you saw the spear in Ian Wurrawul, had you?
4. W: Yes. I haven't seen. Sorry
   [No, I hadn't.]

The L2 English answers in Extract 4–iii are instructive, because the witness did not stop at *Yeah/Yes*, but amplified his answer in a way that made his meaning clear. But if he had given a one-word answer without this amplification, L1 English speakers may well have mistakenly taken them to mean *Yeah, I can answer that* and *Yes, I had seen a person speared before*. So you can see how tricky it can be understanding answers from L2 speakers of English who speak a Yolngu language as their first language. Japanese is another language which uses the same pattern for answering negative Yes/No-questions, so the same miscommunication can arise from L2 speakers of Japanese answering Yes/No-questions. They may be following the pattern of their L1, or they may be following the pattern of their L2.

7. Deaf sign language users

A particular group of people who do not have English as a first language are deaf sign language users, who may experience even greater disadvantage in the legal process than other second language users, for several reasons.

First, many people do not realise that deaf sign languages are full and complex languages, which are the first language of their users. Not all deaf people are proficient in English, and for those who do read and write English, it is as users of English as a second language (Brennan 1999). In the US, the lack of understanding that the deaf sign language (American Sign Language (ASL)) is a language different from (non-oral) English is something of a two-edged sword. On the one hand, deaf people can serve on the jury in the US, unlike deaf people in most other countries. But this is because this right is provided for people with disabilities, and deaf people are considered to be disabled users of non-oral English. On the other hand, this approach wrongly implies that ASL is a manual form of English. However it is not English, but a distinct language, and its users may not necessarily have good proficiency in reading and writing English. And some courts in the US have failed to understand the crucial difference between ASL, and manually transliterated forms of English, such as Signed English. Thus, in some jurisdictions in the US, interpreters have been directed to use Signed English (rather than ASL) for deaf jurors, because of the mistaken belief that this would somehow make the interpretation more accurate (Mather & Mather 2003). This approach is problematic because it requires that the deaf person is bilingual, and knows English as well as ASL.

Second, many people fail to recognise hearing impairment or deafness, and can wrongly attribute certain behaviours, including silence, to non-cooperation or resistance (McKee 2001: 132–134). And similarly, facial expressions which convey emotions in hearing people, may function quite differently as part of sign language.

Sign language interpreters face a number of additional challenges to those which confront all court interpreters. First, whereas interpreting between speakers of two different (oral) languages involves just spoken interaction, interpreting for a deaf person involves two different modalities, spoken and sign (see Brennan 1999; Turner 1995). Second, while most interpreters for witnesses in court interpret in consecutive mode, it is customary for sign language interpreters to work in simultaneous mode (Brennan 1999: 228; Napier et al. 2007: 16–17). Presumably this difference relates to the difference in modality. When a deaf witness is giving evidence, the witness is using only the visual channel, and thus the interpreter can use the oral channel, and interpret simultaneously (and vice versa for questions addressed to the witness.) But this is more cognitively demanding and tiring for the interpreter, who has no time to process a question, or an answer, before providing its interpretation. And it is arguably not equitable for the deaf person, as research has shown consecutive interpreting to be more accurate than simultaneous interpreting (Russell 2002).

Important linguistic differences between signed languages and spoken languages also present particular challenges for interpreting in the highly constrained communicative events in the legal process. Spoken language is linear, comprising one meaningful unit spoken after another. But sign languages use several different signs in combination to make meaning. Thus, as Hoopes (2003) points out, a sign language interpreter must pay attention to all of these articulators at once: (1) dominant hand, (2) non-dominant hand, (3) eye gaze, (4) eyebrow posture, (5) cheek posture, (6) mouth posture, (7) head movement and posture, (8) shoulder posture. Hoopes reports that second language learners of sign languages have been found to concentrate on manual aspects of the language, with less successful use and interpretation of the other (non-manual) signs, such as mouth posture.

Regardless of the expertise and experience of the interpreter, there are specific challenges for sign language interpreters which result from specific linguistic differences between spoken languages and sign languages (Napier et al. 2006). For example, sign languages such as Auslan (in Australia) and NZSL (in New Zealand) use fewer 'category' or 'super-ordinate' terms than English. Thus, English generic words which are frequently used in criminal trials have to be interpreted more specifically: for example the English word *assault* has no lexical equivalent in these sign languages (in the same way as there is no equivalent for *assault* in Sesotho, as we saw in Section 5.1 above). It would have to be signed as 'punch', 'stab', 'kick', 'slap', or similar. Similarly the English word *disorderly* would have to be signed more specifically as 'drunk', 'fight' or 'swear'. (See also Brennan 1999 and Reed *et al.* 2001 for parallel comparisons between English and British Sign Language.) Napier *et al.* (2006: 124) point out that 'there is often no simple solution to such linguistic differences'. But one strategy that interpreters use is that which is referred to by Brennan and Brown (1997) as 'borrowing'. They use this term to refer to the way in which sign language users use fingerspelling and/or mouthing the English word to provide an English gloss for the word they are signing. In this way, for example, as Napier *et al.* (2007: 15) explain, the English word *murder* might be interpreted with the sign for strangle, or stab, or shoot, or slit the throat, while simultaneously either mouthing the word 'murder', or fingerspelling the word.

Class discussion

Imagine a witness saying *I went into a pub, bought a pint of beer, and was short-changed by the bar-tender.* Discuss the dilemmas for sign language interpreters which are revealed in the account below from Brennan and Brown's (1997: 121–122) explanation of the difference between English and British Sign Language [BSL] in conveying this sentence.

We know that in English we could embellish this account in all sorts of ways, but a typical BSL account would include certain types of visual information automatically; it would be more unusual to exclude those rather than include them. Thus, we may well be able to glean from the BSL account what kind of doors the pub had, e.g. double swing doors, a single swing door, a door with a round knob or a door with a vertical handle; we may well be able to discern that the bar-tender was a large man with stubble and a cigarette hanging out of his mouth; we may be able to tell that the counter was curved, that the place was crowded and that the person had to elbow his way in and so on. Now it is quite possible to present all of this information in the English language. However, when we say 'I went into a pub' in English we do not typically add information which indicates how we went in, what kind of door we opened, what kind of handle it had and so on. In BSL, not only is it typical to include such information, it is often unavoidable (cited in Napier *et al.* 2007: 14).

Class debate

Debate the proposition that interpreters give speakers of English as a second language an unfair advantage in court. In preparing for this debate, you might like to make a list of all the ways in which the interpreter can be an active participant in court from Berk-Seligson's 2002a study, especially Chapter 5.

The winning side should be decided not only on the basis of their persuasive debating skills, but also on the extent to which their arguments reveal an understanding of relevant sociolinguistic issues.

Assignments and further research

If you are a fluent speaker of a language other than English, then you may find scope for researching the challenges to courtroom interpreting for speakers of this language. If your research is for a class project, essay or term paper, you might address one or two of topics 1–5. For a thesis/dissertation, you might address all five topics.

1. Start with background research on the courtroom interpreting needs for speakers of this L2, addressing such questions as:

   ▪ How many L1 speakers of this language live in the city/state/country served by the courthouse on which your research is focused?

   ▪ How many L2 speakers of this language live here?

   ▪ How many accredited interpreters of this language are available for court interpreting?

   ▪ Are there significant dialectal variations within this language which might affect court interpreting for speakers in this courthouse? If so, how are these dialectal issues addressed in the provision of interpreters?

   ▪ What are the hiring arrangements for interpreters? Consider such aspects as remuneration, reimbursement of expenses, career structure, union representation.

2. **(Lx)** Observe some courtroom hearings in which evidence is given in this language. On the basis of your observations, write a report which discusses such aspects as:

   ▪ occasions on which the interpreter is clearly an active participant, following Berk-Seligson's (1990 [2002a]: Chapter 5) discussion of this issue;

   ▪ evidence of challenges faced by the interpreter in any or all of the following areas:

     ○ understanding of the interpreter's role by lawyers, witnesses, judicial officer, others;

     ○ particular linguistic challenges, e.g.
       – semantic,
       – grammatical,
       – pragmatic;

     ○ particular cultural challenges.

3. If possible, interview court interpreters and legal professionals whom they have worked with in cases involving this language. Find out what they think about the challenges involved in ensuring that speakers of this language are equal before the law in this courthouse.

4. Interview speakers of this language who have given evidence in court through an interpreter, or have observed a relative or friend doing this. Find out what they think about the challenges involved in ensuring that speakers of their language are equal before the law in this courthouse.

5. **(Lx)** Analyse the bilingual interaction in one or more cases involving this language. Remember that this will take time to negotiate permission to purchase recordings of courtroom hearings (see Section 5 of Chapter 2), or to make your own recordings. Once you have recorded and transcribed the hearings, examine the process of interpretation, paying particular attention to such aspects as:

   - any discussion about the right to an interpreter for any of the witnesses;

   - any objections to or legal discussion of any specific aspect of the interpreter's work;

   - specific linguistic challenges and how the interpreter dealt with them, e.g.
     - interpretation of English invariant tags, see Section 5.3 above;
     - interpretation of discourse markers (see Hale 2002 or 2004: Chapter 4);
     - interpretation of lawyers' pragmatic force (see Hale 1999, 2004: Chapter 3).

6. **(Lx)** If you speak Spanish, compare the discussion of the interpretation of tag questions in cross-examination in the studies of Berk-Seligson (1999), Hale (2004) and Rigney (1999).

7. Critically discuss the issues involved in the inclusion of deaf people on juries. Pay particular attention to the research project by Napier *et al.* (2007). Explain what the study set out to investigate, why and how, and how its findings impact on this issue.

5
Vulnerable witnesses

1. Introduction	84
2. Children	84
2.1. Unclear and confusing questions	85
2.2. Do you remember questions	86
2.3. Suggestibility and credibility	87
2.4. Provisions for child witnesses	88
3. Second dialect speakers	88
4. Cultural differences impacting courtroom talk	92
4.1. Cultural presuppositions about language use in court	92
4.2. Cultural presuppositions about actions outside of court	93
4.3. Cultural presuppositions and courtroom discourse structure	95
5. Legislative protection for vulnerable witnesses	99
Assignments and further research	102

Vulnerable witnesses

1. Introduction

In the previous chapter we saw that courts in such countries as Australia, New Zealand, England and the US are not only monolingual, but typically assume that society functions 'normally' in a monolingual way. This assumption disadvantages people who are not first language speakers of English, as we saw. In this chapter we consider some other social groups whose members experience disadvantage in court, also due to enduring aspects of their social identity and distinctive aspects of their language use: children, second dialect speakers and people from different cultural backgrounds. We will see that second dialect speakers share some characteristics with second language speakers. However, interpreters are generally not provided or considered suitable for second dialect speakers, who, by definition, share a considerable amount of language use and meaning with speakers of the dominant dialect (= the language of the court).

Legal systems often make some provision for people defined as vulnerable witnesses. This term is usually applied foremost to children, and the category often also includes people with mental, learning and sometimes physical disability. We will see why second dialect speakers and those whose cultural differences impact on courtroom communication should also be included as vulnerable witnesses. This chapter is unable to consider people with disabilities, given the lack of relevant sociolinguistic research. Also, we will not consider people who are disadvantaged in court because of their *situated* identity in the legal matter in which they are participating, for example victim-witnesses. But this is an issue we will return to in Section 5 below and Section 6 of Chapter 6.

2. Children

Perhaps the greatest disadvantage in the legal process is experienced by children, particularly those who are called on to give evidence in cases in which they have been victims of abuse. Cases in which children are accused of crime generally take place in specialised children's courts, where some recognition of the special needs of children can be accommodated. But child complainants in abuse cases (sometimes called 'victim-witnesses') have to give evidence in an adult court, in any case in which the accused is an adult. In many ways it seems unfair to subject a child to such difficulty. Yet this is often the only way in which the accused can be brought to court, as the child complainant is often the only person with direct evidence supporting the allegations of the prosecution against the accused. Not only is the child's evidence (in examination-in-chief) essential to the prosecution, but also the rights of the accused to question the accuser mean that such a child must endure cross-examination.

It is not easy to carry out research on child witnesses as courtrooms are typically closed during cases of sexual abuse (as are childrens courts for all cases). However, a few linguists have succeeded in gaining necessary permissions, notably Walker (e.g. 1993) in the US and Brennan and Brennan in Australia (e.g. Brennan 1994, 1995; Brennan & Brennan 1988). These scholars have combined empirical investigation of cases in which children have given evidence with research on children and language generally to provide insights into the ways in which children are disadvantaged in court. Walker (1999) is a handbook which gives direct and practical advice to legal professionals questioning children, especially in court, supported by extensive references to the research literature. This includes psycholinguistic research on general child language acquisition, which has established a considerable knowledge base about developmental aspects of child language. Walker also draws on extensive psychological research on children, which has examined such issues as memory, culpability, understanding, and the ability to distinguish truth from fantasy.

While children have often been seen as unreliable witnesses, perhaps the most important research finding is that 'Even very young children can tell us what they know if we ask them the right questions in the right way' (Walker 1999: 2). But asking the right questions in the right way is something that is often not done, whether for reasons to do with rules of evidence, legal manipulation, ignorance or incompetence.

2.1. Unclear and confusing questions

A major problem with questions addressed to children in court is that they are often unclear or confusing, and often they use grammatical constructions that are too complex for child witnesses. Thus, one of Walker's basic guidelines is that legal professionals should reduce the processing load that children must carry, by aiming for simplicity and clarity in questions. You might think this should be self-evident to anyone interviewing children, but the real-life data in Exercise 5.1 shows that it is not necessarily so.

Exercise 5.1[xiv]

Read the following questions addressed to children in court which are all confusing in some way (from Brennan 1995 and Walker 1999). For each question, state what makes it confusing. Linguistics students should analyse this in terms of relevant aspects of linguistic structure, such as passive voice or nominalisation. Rewrite the questions to make them less confusing.

do you remember ? = Problematic; multipart

(a) So, you told us that you don't remember, do you remember saying that a moment ago? (to 10 year old)

Rephrase as tag = you don't remember, right ?

(b) How far was the trampoline from you when you were first helped on the bike by Mr Brown? (to 7 year old)

Re Phrase :

(c) Well I know, I understand what you say you have been talking to her today, but you see what I am asking you is this, that statement suggests that you said those things which you now say are wrong to the police, Did you say it to the police, or did you not? (to 9 year old)

unclear deixis

(d) Now you had a bruise, did you not, near one of your breasts, do you remember this? (to 11 year old)

statement   Tag   leading (smuggling)   embedded/multipart
Do you remember   Where was your bruise?

(e) But do you recall going to the hospital and will you tell us why you went to the hospital? (to child aged between 4 and 6 years old)

Discuss these questions: Do you think that lawyers should be asked by the judicial officer to rephrase confusing questions such as these, addressed to children? Or do you think this might be an unfair interference with cross-examination attempts to expose problems in the evidence of the witnesses involved?

Other guidelines for interviewing children in legal contexts are perhaps less self-evident than the one about aiming for simple clear questions. These guidelines reveal the importance both of ongoing research on child language, as well as training of those who work with children in the legal process. For example, Walker (1999: 55) cites research which shows that a child's ability to count cannot be taken to mean that the child understands the concept of number. Similarly, pre-adolescent children can often talk 'freely, in grammatical and appropriate ways' (p. 56) about time, without necessarily being able to give reliable specific time information. So, Walker says that just because a child freely uses expressions like *two months ago*, *three hours* or *in the spring*, this does not mean that such answers should be taken literally, without further probing.

2.2. Do you remember *questions*

Another problem in interviewing children in court relates to the specific way in which questions with the form *Do you remember/recall X?* are used in this context, as for example in questions (a), (d) and (e) in Exercise 5.1 above. This is a common element in the courtroom questioning technique referred to as 'refreshing the witness's memory' or 'reviving the witness's memory' (e.g. Mauet & McCrimmon 2001: 121). In examination-in-chief this is a common way in which lawyers focus their witnesses on the particular event or part of the event before beginning their specific questions about it. But in cross-examination these questions are frequently used as part of the strategy of discrediting the witness's memory and/or truthfulness. So, in cross-examination these *Do you remember* questions are typically used to expose inconsistencies between two different tellings of the story by the same witness – for example, contrasting what the witness told an investigator with what the witness said in examination-in-chief. A typical example might be *Do you remember telling the inspector that you saw an old man on the street corner?* This can be followed with a question seeking to contradict the witness's earlier statement, such as *Now that didn't happen did it?* (In this chapter we will not take up the complexities involved in treating inconsistencies as lies; see Section 4.3 of Chapter 11).

But these *Do you remember* questions can be particularly tricky for children, who are not always able to process the structure of the embedded proposition in a question such as *Do you remember telling the inspector that you saw an old man on the street corner?* A *yes* answer to this question would be taken to confirm that the witness remembers telling the inspector something, specifically that he saw an old man on the street corner. But a child may answer *yes* meaning to confirm that he did see an old man on the street corner, and thus such a question may not alert the child witness to the fact that the question is about the interview with the inspector.

Walker (1993: 70–71) gives an example of such a question from the cross-examination of a five-year-old girl who had purportedly witnessed a murder: *Do you remember when Don asked you 'What color was their skin, like mine or like Martha's?'*. The child answered *Like yours*, ignoring the scope of the *Do you remember* question, simply answering the last of the three embedded questions. A similar problem arose when the child was asked another *Do you remember* question (p. 71), in which the lawyer was probably reading from the transcript of an earlier interview with the child: *And Martha said 'I sure would like to get those boys. I don't like it when someone hurts my friends. You're my friend. Can you tell me who Mark is?' Do you remember that question?* Again the child ignored the metaquestion, about whether she remembered being asked the question *Can you tell me who Mark is?*, and instead answered this embedded question, saying *Mark is one of Doug's friends.*

These two examples make it clear that on each occasion the child was not answering the *Do you remember* question, but the question embedded in it. But it is more tricky when the *Do you remember* question queries a proposition which itself may be negated with *No* or confirmed with *Yes*, as in another question addressed to the same child: *Do you remember telling somebody that night that you saw somebody throw a knife at Doug?* The child's *Yeah* answer to this question may have been intended to answer that she did remember telling somebody …, or it may have been an answer parallel to the two *Do you remember* questions we have already discussed. In that case her answer may have been that she saw somebody throw a knife at Doug.

Walker's analysis of these and other *Do you remember* questions in this child's cross-examination shows that they often function as ambiguous questions, and the answers may also be similarly ambiguous. (In her 1999 book, Walker labels these *Do you remember* questions which introduce at least one more proposition – or embedded clause – as DUR/X questions.)

We have seen that these *Do you remember* questions which are used to introduce extracts from an earlier witness account play a particular strategic role in cross-examination, and are difficult for children to process. But another factor which makes them particularly tricky, is that they appear very similar to other questions which also begin with *Do you remember* but which introduce a WH-question, rather than a proposition, and thus function as WH-questions. For example *Do you remember what time you entered the house?* has the structure of a Yes/No-question, but it can function, both in the courtroom and in other contexts as a WH-question, that is with the meaning of *What time did you enter the house?* In fact questions like this – Yes/No structure with WH function – are common in a variety of contexts, with a range of auxiliary verbs, as in questions like *Can you tell us his address? Did she say what his address was?* These questions are labelled by Walker (1987) as YNW questions, to indicate their blending of Yes/No-question form with WH-question function. Danet *et al.* (1980: 225) call them requestions, indicating that they can be interpreted either as questions about ability to answer, or as requests for information. Interpreting questions of this structure literally, as questions about ability to answer, and thus answering with either *Yes* or *No*, can be a source of humour or irritation. (Question (e) in Exercise 5.1 above contains the requestion *will you tell us why you went to the hospital?*

2.3. Suggestibility and credibility

A particular concern with child witnesses relates to their suggestibility, that is their ability to be influenced by suggestion. This is an area in which there is considerable psychological research (for reviews see Ceci & Bruck 1993; Poole & Lindsay 2002). Suggestibility is also a matter for sociolinguistics, especially given the prevalent use in cross-examination of Yes/No-questions, many of which are leading questions (as we saw in Section 4 of Chapter 3). But it is not just that children – particularly young children – can be easily lead to a particular answer. A number of psychological studies have also found that their recall is more accurate in response to open-ended questions (such as *What happened then?*) than to Yes/No-questions (such as *Did he touch you then?*). In this way, the linguistic form of questions can affect not only suggestibility but also memory, both of which impact on the credibility of the child witness. Fivush *et al.* (2002: 350) summarise studies of children's credibility in this way:

Under conditions in which young children are being interviewed about highly distinctive, personally meaningful events and are asked only open-ended questions, their ability to give accurate reports even after long delays is quite impressive. But when children are interviewed in suggestive and misleading ways, especially if these suggestions are repeated across interviews, and if interviewers rely on yes-no questions, young children's memory cannot be considered at all credible. It is not so much a question of children's memory per se, as the way in which memory is elicited in the interviewing context. The question is not how credible are child witnesses, the question is how careful are forensic interviewers.

This influence of the linguistic form of questions not only on the answers children give, but also on their memory, raises serious problems for the examination of child witnesses in court. It is also relevant to any other interviewing of children in legal contexts, and we will come back to this topic in the discussion of police interviews in Section 5 of Chapter 8.

2.4. Provisions for child witnesses

Courts in a number of countries have made some provisions for the vulnerability of child witnesses, although these provisions generally do not directly address the linguistic difficulties. Thus, in some jurisdictions, child witnesses are allowed to give evidence on closed-circuit television, in order to alleviate them of the trauma of being face-to-face in court with a suspect against whom they are testifying. Another innovation provides for a videotaped interview with a child witness to take the place of their examination-in-chief. However, child witnesses (like all other witnesses) are generally required to be present in court for cross-examination. They are sometimes provided with some support by a screen between the child and the accused. Some countries, such as Canada and England, extend provisions such as these to witnesses who have difficulties in communication because of either a physical or mental disability.

Class discussion

Analysis of the linguistic (and other) difficulties faced by child witnesses leads some people to argue that children should not have to answer questions in court. What do you think? Consider the situation in which a serious crime has been committed, and the only witness is a child. How would an ideal justice system approach the child's evidence in this case? In your discussion, spend some time 'in the shoes of' an accused person: what rights would you expect in relation to questioning the child witness?

---

3. Second dialect speakers

Second dialect speakers are people who do not speak the standard dialect used in the legal process, but rather a related dialect. This is often an unstandardised dialect which is stigmatised and denigrated in the society generally. Although communication difficulties are not as extreme as with second language speakers, in some ways second dialect speakers can be at a greater disadvantage than some people who speak a second language. This is because they are often wrongly assumed to be speakers of the dominant dialect, or to be people who are too uneducated, lazy or ignorant to speak 'properly' (if you don't have a linguistics background, you might like to go back to Section 3 of Chapter 1).

This negative relationship between the use of a non-standard dialect and legal reactions to its speakers is revealed in Jacquemet's (1992, 1996) study of the large mid-1980s trial of Mafia gang members (*camorra*) from the Naples area of Italy. Defence attorneys tried to impugn the credibility of witnesses on the basis of their use of the non-standard Neapolitan dialect in their courtroom testimony, appealing to the general regulation that all courtroom participants should speak 'Standard Italian'. Jacquemet (1992: 114) argues that this was part of the legal strategy of the defence in trying to link in a negative way a witness's 'inability to perform within courtroom canons to his claim to be a reliable man, a man of truth'. So the implication was that witnesses using a non-standard dialect were 'untrustworthy individuals'. However, the use of this dialect caused no comprehension difficulties for any of the participants, many of whom were themselves from Naples, and the judge refused to disallow its use.

Despite the indications that in many countries a large number of participants in the legal process are likely to be speakers of non-standard dialects, there is remarkably little relevant linguistic research. African Americans in the US are six times more likely to be imprisoned than white Americans (Walker *et al.* 1996: 1). And African American English has been the focus of a considerable amount of linguistic and sociolinguistic research since the 1960s. Much of this research has paid attention to educational implications of dialectal difference between African American English and Standard American English. But there is almost no linguistic research which examines African American interactions in the legal process (but see Fuller 1993; Hobbs 2003a, discussed in Section 5 of Chapter 3).

Most of the research on speakers of non-standard dialects in court (and other legal contexts) has focused on Australian Aborigines, many of whom use a dialectal variety of English in their dealings with the law. Aboriginal English in Australia varies from 'light' varieties, which are closest to other varieties of Australian English, to 'heavy' varieties which are least similar to these varieties, and closer to the creole language, Kriol (mentioned in Section 5.5 of Chapter 4).[15] Dialectal differences can impact on courtroom talk at every level of language.

A powerful semantic example comes from Cooke's (1995a: 91) analysis of the cross-examination of an Aboriginal witness in a Northern Territory coronial inquiry. This witness gave evidence that on a particular night there was a *half moon* shining, and *that he knew this because he remembered looking at the moon that night*. One of the cross-examining counsel who was *confident that there was no half moon on that night* saw a chance to present the witness as unreliable, saying to him *You're sure you're not just making this up now?* In this situation, the manipulation of dialectal difference – which was possibly unwitting – was averted by the interpreter's interjection. As a result, the witness was asked to draw the moon that night, and 'it became evident that he was using the [Aboriginal English] expression 'half moon' to mean what is referred to in Standard English as a crescent moon'. On most occasions on which Aboriginal speakers of varieties of English give evidence, there is no interpreter and thus no mechanism for dialectal differences to be drawn to the attention of the court. But this was an unusual case because an interpreter was present in the court on stand-by for witnesses who did not speak enough English. His initiative and skill in drawing the attention of the court to possible dialectal difference in the meaning of the expression *half moon* was complemented by the court's openness to receiving such communication facilitation.

Koch (1985: 180) gives a good example of miscommunication involving an Aboriginal English-speaking witness in a land claim hearing in Central Australia. Giving evidence about the relationship between two people, the witness said *Charcoal Jack – properly his father*. This was understood by the court as the witness being unsure of the family relationship in question, consistent with it being recorded in the official transcription as *Charcoal Jack – probably his father*. But this was a misunderstanding, in which several features of heavy Aboriginal English were ignored, including the interchangeability of the *b* and *p* sounds, and the use of the adverb *properly* to mean 'real'. So, a subtle but important misunderstanding arose because of phonological and semantic differences, combined with a cultural difference, namely the usage of the word *father* to refer to a person's biological father as well as any of this biological father's brothers (and thus the qualification *properly* to specify a person's 'real' or biological father). The witness was not expressing lack of certainty about the relationship. On the contrary, he was being specific about what kind of father-relationship was involved. (For further discussion about misrepresentations of Aboriginal English in transcripts of land claim hearings, see Walsh 1999).

Most of the research on Aboriginal English in the legal system has focused on speakers of light varieties, which overlap to a considerable extent with other varieties of Australian English. Despite the fact that these Aboriginal English varieties do not sound very different from General Australian English, there are important pragmatic features, which are often unrecognised or misinterpreted, and which can affect speakers in their dealings with the law. This may well be a major reason why the participation of second dialect speakers in the legal system has not attracted much linguistic research – where lexical and grammatical differences between the stigmatised and the standard dialects are not great, the pragmatic and cultural differences can be overlooked.

For example, in the Anglo legal system and society generally, silence in answer to a question is generally 'interpreted to the detriment of the silent person', for example as implying that the person asked the question has something to hide (Kurzon 1995: 56). And Conversation Analysis research has found that in western Anglo societies, the 'standard maximum tolerance for silence' is about one second (Jefferson 1989). After that, someone will break the silence, which after about one second, makes people feel uncomfortable. In contrast, many speakers of Aboriginal English, as well as traditional Aboriginal languages, use silence as a positive and productive part of communication. But this use of silence is often not understood by legal professionals – of whom very few are Aboriginal – and considerable miscommunication can arise in legal interviews, whether in a lawyer's office, a police station or a courtroom. Many people who interview Aboriginal people are unaware that their answer will often begin with a silence. Not hearing an immediate reply to the question, the interviewer often moves on to another question. In effect, the interviewer has interrupted the first part of the reply, and thus prevented the Aboriginal interviewee from providing an answer (see Eades 1994, 2007a).

Another pragmatic feature found to be crucial in understanding Aboriginal participants in the legal process is 'gratuitous concurrence' – namely, freely saying *yes* in answer to a Yes/No-question (or *no* to a negative question), regardless of either the speaker's understanding of the question, or their belief about the truth or falsity of the proposition being questioned (Eades 1994; Liberman 1981). One reason that this pragmatic feature is particularly prevalent in Aboriginal societies, relates to the widespread cultural norm that harmony and agreement should be preserved at an immediate level, and differences can be worked out in due time. But the use of gratuitous concurrence in legal contexts can be problematic for Aboriginal interviewees. Once a person has agreed to a proposition in a context such as a police interview, it can have life-changing implications. This pragmatic feature has been observed in intercultural communication in Indigenous Australia for many decades. Morrow (1993, 1996) reports a similar communicative pattern among English-speaking Yup'ik Eskimos, as does Berk-Seligson (2009) for US Hispanics. It is likely that it is also found in many other intercultural communication situations around the world. Further, it is undoubtedly more prevalent in situations of power asymmetry, which characterise interactions in the legal process. In such interactions it can have disastrous consequences for the minority participant (see Gibbons 2003).

In my research on Aboriginal speakers of varieties of English in courts, I have found that some lawyers seem to have a good understanding of some Aboriginal ways of using English. For example, some lawyers use their knowledge of the positive Aboriginal use of silence to the advantage of their clients, as Extract 5–i shows. This example comes from the sentencing hearing of an Aboriginal defendant who had pleaded guilty to assault. In answering questions which could help to establish grounds for minimising the severity of his sentence, he was invited by his lawyer to show remorse for his actions to the judge.

Extract 5–i Eades' (2000: 172) transcription of official audiorecording
1. DC: And do you tell his honour that you know you shouldn't- and that you're sorry for having done that?
2. W: Uh well- yeah- I am- sorry (6.7) when we're not- oh sorry- when we're not drinkin' you know- we don't even fight or nothin'- you know- when we're drinking it's a bit of a problem- it's one of them things- drinking.

Exercise 5.2[xv]
Assign one student the role of lawyer, and one the role of witness for this exercise. These two students should <u>read aloud</u> Extract 5–i above, taking care to allow the full 6.7 second silence in the witness's turn. <u>Discuss the pragmatic force of this long silence,</u> considering the following questions:
a) how did the silence feel for the person acting as the lawyer?
b) how did the silence feel for the person acting as the witness?
c) how did the silence feel for the people listening?
c) what possible interpretations might be made of this long silence?
d) how might these interpretations be affected by knowledge about the use and interpretation of silence in Aboriginal conversations?

It seems obvious that lawyers, magistrates and judges need to be made aware of such cultural differences in communicative style. And in fact, in my experience, many legal professionals are excited to learn about this aspect of intercultural communication, as the following example (from Eades 2007b: 312) illustrates:

A 1992 hearing of the Queensland Criminal Justice Commission (CJC) was investigating an allegation of police misconduct, and I was asked to appear as an expert witness. In addition to explaining some of the subtle ways in which communication patterns differ between Aboriginal and non-Aboriginal speakers of English, I was asked to advise the Commission specifically on more effective ways of hearing the evidence of Aboriginal witnesses to this tribunal. As part of this process, I listened to an Aboriginal woman being questioned by lawyers. This woman had originally approached the Commission wanting to tell her story (related to her witnessing of police misconduct in the matter under investigation), and no disadvantage could occur to her as a result of her evidence. However, under questioning by the lawyers, she provided very little information. The lawyers asked her questions, and she appeared unable to provide answers. I was then asked to advise the Commission about communication with this witness, in her absence. I recommended that the lawyers should wait after each question, until the witness answered. I explained that this means asking a question and then *shutting up.* Given the uncomfortable feeling that this leaves with many (non-Aboriginal) people, I suggested that the interviewing lawyer could shuffle papers, or say something like *there's no need to rush.* In answer to the Commission's question *how long should we wait?,* I replied: *until after the answer.*

Following a short adjournment, the witness was asked to return to the witness stand, and this revised style of questioning took place, with remarkable results. The same witness who had earlier that day appeared shy, difficult to communicate with, and of little help to the Commission's investigation, was now an articulate witness with a clear and important story to tell the Commission. The only significant change was that the interviewing lawyers allowed time for the silence which began quite a few of her answers to their questions.

4. Cultural differences impacting courtroom talk

4.1. Cultural presuppositions about language use in court

We have seen above that understanding dialectal differences between speakers of Aboriginal English and General Australian English requires an understanding of differences in the use and interpretation of silence. I have discussed this difference above in terms of dialect, but it can also be seen in terms of cultural difference, and it is likely to be relevant to many other social groups beyond Australian Aboriginal people. Specifically, people from different cultural backgrounds may have different expectations about how silence is used and what it means, and thus they bring different cultural presuppositions to the interpretation of silence. Sociolinguistic research generally (not in legal contexts) has found distinctive uses of silence in a number of sociocultural groups, including the Amish (Enninger 1987), Japanese (Lebra 1987) and Chinese (Young 1994). So, there is a possibility of intercultural miscommunication in the legal process in countries like Australia and Canada (among others) with people from these ethnic groups. Further, a number of sociolinguists and anthropologists have pointed out that Native Americans use silence quite comfortably in their interactions (e.g. Basso 1970; Gumperz 2001; Philips 1993).

Researchers have pointed to legal implications of misinterpretation of silence in other situations of intercultural communication. For example, in the Hernandez case in the US in

1990, the US Supreme Court upheld a state court's decision, which had disallowed Spanish speakers from serving as jurors in a case in which evidence was to be given in Spanish and interpreted into English. The main reason for the decision was that two of the Latino jurors hesitated before agreeing that they would accept the interpreter's translation of the testimony (rather than relying on the original Spanish testimony). Montoya (2000) argues that a misunderstanding of the brief silence (or pause) of two jurors in this case, led to a decision which amounted to linguistic discrimination. The decision also prevented Mr Hernandez from being tried by a jury of his peers.

Given the importance placed in the legal process on the 'demeanour' of witnesses as an indication of their truthfulness and credibility, then different cultural presuppositions about communicative style in court can play a crucial role. Such non-verbal behaviour as eye contact is widely recognised in sociolinguistic and communication research to vary between different cultural groups (e.g. Bauer 1999; Eades 2008a; Palerm *et al.* 1999; Ta 1999). To what extent are such cultural differences recognised and understood by legal professionals? And to what extent are they implicated in the effective or non-effective participation of members of minority cultural groups in the legal process? These are some of the questions awaiting further sociolinguistic research.

4.2. Cultural presuppositions about actions outside of court

Cultural differences can impact courtroom talk and understanding, even when language or dialectal differences seem minimal, as the discussion of silence above has indicated. But another impact of cultural differences is in the ways in which actions outside of the court are dealt with in court. For example, there may be culturally specific assumptions presupposed in lawyer questions which are not shared with the witness. And, conversely, there may be culturally specific assumptions presupposed in witness answers which are not shared with the lawyer.

A telling example comes from Cooke's (1995a) work with Aboriginal witnesses in the coronial inquiry in a remote area of Arnhem Land in the Northern Territory, which we saw above in Section 5.4 of Chapter 4. In the following two extracts we see opposing cultural presuppositions about health and illness in the examination of an Aboriginal witness about the habits of a deceased man whose death was being investigated. This mentally ill man carrying a fishing knife had been chased by five special task force police, all armed with shotguns, who surrounded him, before one of them shot him dead. The witness was a volunteer tracker for the police, who was related to the deceased, and was a witness to the fatal attack on this man by police. Extract 5–ii comes from his questioning by the lawyer for the police association.

Extract 5–ii Cooke (1995a: 89–91) based on official court transcript
1. L: This dead man, did he used to catch fish all around the island?
2. W: Yes.
3. L: And he'd move around the island on foot?
4. W: Yes.
5. L: And he used to travel a long way by foot?
6. W: Yes, because of that sick, that's why he goes – he travels with his foot.

7. L: But he could walk a long way by foot?
8. W: Yes, because of his sickness.
9. L: Could he walk all the way to the other end of the island?
10. W: Yes.

In this exchange, we see the tracker reporting that the deceased man's habit of walking a long way was *because of his sickness* (in Turns 6 and 8). The (non-Aboriginal) lawyer appears to have interpreted this habit of walking a long way as evidence of the deceased man's health. As we see, he countered the witness's explanation with *but* at the beginning of Turn 7, and he used the ability modal *could* in Turns 7 and 9, and he emphasised the *long* distances he could walk in Turns 5, 7 and 9. The lawyer went on to separate mental health from physical health:

Extract 5–iii Cooke (1995a: 89-91) based on official court transcript
11. L: And apart from his sickness in the head was he physically fit?
12. W: Not really.
13. L: There was something wrong with him apart? – I'm not talking about the sickness in his head, I'm talking about his body.
14. W: Not really.
15. L: Was there something wrong with him?
16. W: Yes.
17. L: What was it?
18. W: Same thing, head.
19: L: Yes, but apart from that, forget that. Was anything wrong with his body apart from his head?
20. W: What do you mean, apart from his body.
          [to Int: *Bulany, nhaltjan ngayi ga wanga?* 'Bulany, [term for interpreter] how is he talking?']
21. L: Was there anything wrong with him physically?
22. Int: Do you mind if I assist?
23. L: Yes, I do mind. Did he have anything wrong with his arms?
24. W: No.
25. L: Or his legs?
26. W: No.
26. L: Or his stomach or chest?
28. W: Yes, from his head to his body.

The witness's question to the interpreter between Turns 20 and 21 is evidence of miscommunication between the lawyer and the witness. Cooke explains this miscommunication in terms of the contrast between the Anglo view which separates mental and physical health (distinguishing the *sickness in his head* from *anything wrong with his body* or *wrong with him physically*) from the Aboriginal view that sees the two as inseparable (as the witness puts it he had something wrong from *his head to his body*). Thus these two extracts reveal the cultural presupposition in the lawyer's questioning that although the deceased may have suffered with a mental illness, he had nothing *wrong with his body*, and further he *could walk long* distances. The Aboriginal witness interprets the deceased's tendency to go for long walks on his own, as a symptom of *his sickness*, which pervaded his whole being *from his head to his body*. Interestingly, the interpreter, who was sitting beside the witness in stand-by interpreting mode, was ready to provide some intercultural explanation (in Turn 22), but the lawyer prevented him from *assisting*.

> **Class discussion**
>
> Extracts 5–ii and 5–iii above come from a coronial inquiry in which there was no jury. But what happens in jury trials when there are cultural differences in presuppositions about language use in court or about actions outside of court? Can we expect jury members to know about these differences in cultural presuppositions? If not, whose responsibility is it to inform jurors? How should this be done? To what extent are members of minority cultural groups represented on juries? To what extent can bicultural jurors analyse and articulate different cultural presuppositions?

In Australia there are also extreme cases of mismatch in cultural presuppositions in land claims and native title hearings, as explored in the work of Morphy (2007) and Walsh (1995, 1999, 2008). In these cases, Aboriginal groups have to demonstrate for the court that they are entitled to claim certain areas of land under specific land claim legislation, or to have their ownership in Aboriginal customary law recognised by native title legislation. Anthropologists and linguists are closely involved as expert witnesses in these legal processes (e.g. Henderson & Nash 2002; Sutton 2003; Walsh 1995). These scholars and legal professionals involved in the process (e.g. see also Gray 2000; Neate 2003) have provided powerful examinations of the cultural and linguistic challenges involved for Aboriginal people trying to fit a round peg (their customary legal system) into a square hole (the Anglo legal system), as it were. At the basis of this mismatch are fundamental cultural and epistemological differences in understandings about the social, physical and spiritual world. For example there are different presuppositions over what land ownership means and entails, and over who has rights to talk about their knowledge of land and its usage. Walsh (1995, 2008) discusses assumptions within the Anglo legal system about the identity of 'traditional Aborigines' – a central construct in land claim and native title processes, given the legal requirements involving traditional attachment and continuing connection to areas of land. Walsh's analysis leads him to conclude that many Aboriginal people are in a *Catch-22* situation: if they are articulate and literate, they appear less traditional and may be suspected of reading information about their land, rather than knowing it as part of cultural tradition (which is oral). But if they have not read information published about their land, they can be seen as not really interested in their traditions, which could call into question their legal entitlement. However, if they are judged to be inarticulate in the legal proceedings, it is hard for their knowledge to be revealed for assessment. The perceived lack of articulacy relates to many interactional and intercultural dynamics about language in legal proceedings discussed in this book, especially in Sections 5 and 6 of Chapter 4 and Sections 3 and 4 of this chapter (see also Walsh 1994).

4.3. Cultural presuppositions and courtroom discourse structure

In the example discussed above with Extracts 5–ii and 5–iii, it is unlikely that either the Aboriginal witness or the lawyer could have perceived, analysed and articulated the different cultural presuppositions revealed by Cooke. This case took place in a remote island off the far northern tip of Arnhem Land in the Northern Territory where traditional Aboriginal ways of living remain strong, and where few non-Aboriginal people reside for more than a few years. It is to be expected that cultural differences will pervade intercultural communication, although, as we saw with the example, the extent of the differences appears to be generally unrecognised.

But in other areas, where cultural differences are not so extensive, they can still play an important role in intercultural communication in court (as in other areas of social life). For example, in my research in a courthouse in a country town in New South Wales (only six hours drive from Sydney), I found Aboriginal witnesses trying to explain aspects of their lifestyle and culture relevant to the questions they were being asked. But the strict constraints on the structure of courtroom talk, that we saw in Chapter 3, made it difficult for witnesses to succeed in their attempts to shed light on cultural issues.

For example, a witness I refer to as Mrs Walsh was giving evidence in her sentencing hearing, after pleading guilty to an assault which occurred during a factional brawl. Her lawyer (defence counsel) was asking her questions – in examination-in-chief – about her generally good character and contributions to the community over many years, relevant to his argument that a prison sentence was not called for in her case. Several of the lawyer's questions elicited information about Mrs Walsh's work in establishing a housing cooperative, a legal service and a football club for Aboriginal people. The judge then asked her how she set up a legal service, as we see in Extract 5–iv:[16]

Extract 5–iv Eades' (2000: 182–183) transcription of official audiorecording slightly edited

106. J: How did you set up a legal service?
107. W: Um- we never had any- any Aboriginal organisations in Jonestown at that time- and what I did I um- I was living in a house [where

108. J: [Sorry you lived where?
109. W: I was living in a house at Smithville, and they um- wanted to get me out of that house because of [um

110. J: [I'm not hearing you very clearly I'm afraid.
111.W: They wanted me to move out of the house that I was occupying at the time.

112. J: Ye:s=
113.W: =And they wanted to set up the alcoholic uh rehabilitation centre.

114. J: Ye:s.
115. W: It wasn't running (there) but they wanted me out of the house so that they could uh move into it- they uh turned my water off- my children was in and out of hospital with uh sores and diarrhoea and all kind of sickness=

116. J: =Ye:s.
117. W: So what I did I contacted all the um- Aboriginal organisations all over New South Wales=

118. DC: =I might be able to assist your honour- um- I have been able to cut through some of this=
                 [and (.......)
119. J: =Good [well you put it in legal terms for me ...
120. DC: [Would you like me to do that?
121. J: Yes. [(Go ahead) ...
122. DC: [(......) permit me to lead=

123. Pros: =I've indicated to my friend he can lead your honour=
124. J: =Good.
125. Pros: =It will come out more coherently perhaps.

126. J: =Well you- you listen and Mr Thomson will tell you what he thinks of the facts and you tell us whether that's right or not.
127. W: (Yes).

128. DC: Now- is it the situation that you had this trouble with your house and you contacted various organisations for Aboriginal people- particularly in Sydney?
129. W: Yes [(.........)

130. DC: [And you ended up getting in touch with the legal service that was based in Sydney?=
131. W: =Yes.

132. DC: Then after your agitation they sent up someone to organise a legal service in Jonestown?
133. W: Yes.

134. DC: And you were then on their board?
135. W: Ah well my parents got on the Board of Directors.

136. DC: They got on as directors?=
137. W: =Yes and my brother was [(..........)

138. DC: [All right And you worked for them too?
139. W: Yes I was involved in organising everything=

140. DC: =All right- I would hope that perhaps answers your honour's initial inquiry.
141. J: Yes it does thank you.
142. DC: Thank you your honour.

143. DC: Now moving to Mapletown- it's correct to say that you continued your involvement with the Aboriginal community?
144. W: Yes.

Although the judge wanted to hear how Mrs Walsh set up a legal service, he had trouble with her answer. First, he had physical problems hearing her, as we see in Turns 108 and 110. But then, his *ye:s* answers in Turns 112, 114 and 116 appear to have been taken by Mrs Walsh's lawyer to indicate that the judge was impatient with her explanation. (Note particularly that the third of the judge's *ye:s* answers – Turn 116 – is latched on the witness's answer, as indicated by the = symbols in the transcript. This latching could be perhaps taken here as impatience.) So the witness's lawyer took over at Turn 118, suggesting that he might be *able to cut through some of this*.

What then developed was the judge's open request (119) that DC put the defendant's words *in legal terms for [him]*, followed by technical discussion between DC, the prosecutor and the judge about the use of leading questions (120–124). This discussion was not explained to the defendant; she was simply told (126) to listen to her lawyer and effectively to return to one-word *Yes* or *No* answers. In place of the narrative which the defendant had attempted to provide to explain how she set up the legal service, she was given six very generalised facts as a summary (128, 130, 132, 134, 136, 138). This summary presented her lawyer's perspective on what was relevant about how she had set up a legal service. It is interesting that the lawyer's perspective on the witness's story was taken as putting her story *in legal terms* for the judge. Perhaps, following from Heffer's work discussed in Section 7 of Chapter 3, we might have expected a legal argument along paradigmatic lines. But this is not what Mrs Walsh's lawyer did. He simply provided a brief narrative account that focused on her actions and *cut through* the other details of her story.

It is also interesting that the lawyer's version of this story not only summarised Mrs Walsh's narrative, but effectively depersonalised it: her story, about how *they* (government housing authorities?) had been trying to move her out of the house to take it over as an alcohol rehabilitation centre, and how her children had been so sick that they were in and out of hospital, was summarised as *this trouble with your house* (128). In Mrs Walsh's version, arguably the trouble was not with her house, but with people: the authorities (*they*) and her sick children. But her lawyer's version of her answer to question 106 (presented in the six Yes/No-questions from Turns 128–138) had no people apart from Mrs Walsh and a representative of one of *various organisations*.

In Turn 132 the lawyer presented the fact that after Mrs Walsh's agitation, the legal service based in Sydney had sent someone up to organise a legal service in Jonestown. It appears from Mrs Walsh's earlier Turn 117 that she had been going to narrate in more detail what was involved in persuading the Sydney legal service to take this step, seemingly finding that relevant to answering the judge's question (106). Then the lawyer tried to establish Mrs Walsh's role on the board of the newly established legal service, and limited her attempts to explain the roles of close relatives. Here we see another cultural difference in that Aboriginal people in Mapletown, as throughout Australia, see family as central to all aspects of life.

In this situation the judge's broad WH-question (106) was replaced with six Yes/No-questions and the judge's metalinguistic directions that Mrs Walsh was simply to agree or disagree with the proposition for each question. Here we see how the Yes/No-questions, combined with the judge's metalinguistic directions, silenced the witness and prevented her from explaining. Further, in her answers to the lawyer's version of how she set up a legal service, Mrs Walsh was interrupted in both instances where she attempted to go beyond a simple *yes* answer (Turns 129 and 137). So, the lawyer effectively 'hijacked' Mrs Walsh's story, after the judge's difficulties with hearing the witness had been resolved, and at the point where her own elaboration and explanation was gaining momentum. The lawyer's version of the story was not only brief and rather depersonalised, but it removed the elements of frustration and struggle which began before Mrs Walsh's control of the story was hijacked (and which surfaced later to some small extent in her cross-examination, before she was told by cross-examining counsel: *all we're trying to find out is ...* and by the judge: *I don't really want you to go into- in the case- into a great history ...*).

This example of Mrs Walsh's questioning by the judge and her own lawyer about how she had set up a legal service provides an illustrative example of how cultural differences in lifestyle, expectations and explanations can be impacted by the rigid structure of courtroom talk. From the outset, there was a significant cultural difference involved about Mrs Walsh's establishment of a legal service. Legal professionals in Australia would not expect a repeat offender who has pleaded guilty to an assault charge, to reveal, in her defence as to her good character, that she had established a legal service in her community. In Aboriginal societies, however, this would not seem to be particularly contradictory, owing to the way in which controlled physical settlement of disputes can be accepted, and not used in evidence against a person's good reputation (Langton 1988; Macdonald 1988). This could probably have been explained to some extent in Mrs Walsh's evidence, had she been allowed to answer the questions addressed to her. But, as we saw in Extract 5–iv from Mrs Walsh's questioning, the preoccupation of both her own lawyer and the judge with getting answers to questions seriously compromised any chance she might have had in providing a meaningful explanation.

The cultural presuppositions underlying the discourse structure of courtroom talk have also been found to be at odds with those of English-speaking Yup'ik Eskimos. Morrow (1993: 5) points out that 'the primary flow of information in Yup'ik society is not through direct questions and answers', and she argues (1996) that the way in which Yup'ik people deal with repeated direct questions in the court leads (non-Yup'ik) attorneys to mistakenly interpret Yup'ik clients, defendants and witnesses as compliant.

5. Legislative protection for vulnerable witnesses

This chapter and the previous one have considered witnesses who are disadvantaged in court because of aspects of language use specific to their social group. A number of governments around the world have recognised the need to address this type of disadvantage to some extent, for example with interpreter services for second language speakers, and with some provisions for child witnesses to give their evidence-in-chief by video link, rather than in the witness box, facing their alleged abuser. Interpreter services fulfil a fundamental human right (to enable defendants to hear accusations and evidence against them), enshrined in international law (as we saw in Chapter 4). But other provisions for disadvantaged witnesses appear to be limited to the provision of some protection from possible extremes of cross-examination to people defined as 'vulnerable witnesses' (and thus do not begin to deal with the issues discussed in Sections 3 and 4 above). In the terms of such legal provisions, vulnerable witnesses are usually defined foremost as children, and the category often also includes people with mental, learning and sometimes physical disability (as in the UK, see Luchjenbroers & Aldridge 2008). The protection offered to vulnerable witnesses during cross-examination typically centres on the kinds of questions which are not allowed to be put to them, generically referred to as 'improper questions', for example questions which are 'indecent' or 'scandalous'.

In recent years, a number of jurisdictions have widened the type of question which can be disallowed (as we will see below), as well as the scope of the term 'vulnerable witnesses', for example including not just age and disability, but such characteristics as level of understanding and cultural background. Section 41 of the uniform Evidence Acts in Australia[17] stipulates that in disallowing certain questions, the court must take into account 'any relevant condition or characteristic of the witness'. Concerns with the treatment of complainants in sexual assault cases have highlighted the point that a witness's vulnerability may not derive from their enduring membership of a social group (such as children or intellectually disabled), but rather on occasions to their situated social identity, for example as victim-witness of a distressing attack.

The Australian Law Reform Commission (ALRC 2005) provides a thoughtful and detailed consideration of vulnerable participants in cross-examination, in the report of its extensive research on evidence legislation (carried out in conjunction with the Law Reform Commissions of the two most populous states, New South Wales and Victoria). The report draws on a range of legal, psychological, sociolinguistic and community publications, submissions and experiences, and is recommended reading for anyone interested in pursuing any of the topics introduced in this chapter. The report evaluates the advantages and disadvantages of specifying the grounds under which a witness may be defined as vulnerable. One of the disadvantages of such specification, which may become complex, is that it may result in lengthy legal contests about whether a witness fulfils the requirements specified in the relevant legislation. It has been argued that the focus should be on whether or not questions are misleading or confusing for the particular witness, regardless of whether or not the witness has a particular vulnerability (ALRC 2005: 5.99).

Another important issue is whether constraints on the cross-examination of vulnerable witnesses should be the responsibility or duty of the presiding judicial officer, or whether this person merely has the option of exercising such constraints. If the latter is the case, then such a constraint might only be considered after one of the parties has requested it. In coming to its recommendations on this matter, the ALRC took the view that the presiding judicial officer has a responsibility to exercise such constraints over cross-examination questions, regardless of whether counsel raise an objection or not. This view is encapsulated in the powerful comments of NSW Chief Justice Spigelman cited in this report (ALRC 2005: 5.79):

Judges play an important role in protecting complainants from unnecessary, inappropriate and irrelevant questioning by or on behalf of an accused. That role is perfectly consistent with the requirements of a fair trial, which requirements do not involve treating the criminal justice system as if it were a forensic game in which every accused is entitled to some kind of sporting chance.

A strong version of the law concerning vulnerable witnesses in found in S257A of the New South Wales *Criminal Procedure Act* 1986, including its 2005 amendment. (And it is this strong version which was adopted by ALRC in its recommendation.) You will see that it is focused on questions that can be disallowed in cross-examination, and thus would not be relevant to Mrs Walsh's attempts to tell her story, discussed in Section 4.3 above. While this legislation is directly relevant to many of the issues raised in this chapter, it will also be relevant to Chapter 6, and we will return to it in Section 6 of that chapter. Section 275A (titled 'Improper questions') of this legislation states that:

(1) In any criminal proceedings, the court must disallow a question put to a witness in cross-examination, or inform the witness that it need not be answered, if the court is of the opinion that the question (referred to as a "disallowable question"):
    (a) is misleading or confusing, or
    (b) is unduly annoying, harassing, intimidating, offensive, oppressive, humiliating or repetitive, or
    (c) is put to the witness in a manner or tone that is belittling, insulting or otherwise inappropriate, or
    (d) has no basis other than a sexist, racial, cultural or ethnic stereotype.

(2) Without limiting the matters that the court may take into account for the purposes of subsection (1), it is to take into account:

> (a) any relevant condition or characteristic of the witness, including age, education, ethnic and cultural background, language background and skills, level of maturity and understanding and personality, and
>
> (b) any mental, intellectual or physical disability to which the witness is or appears to be subject.

(3) A question is not a disallowable question merely because:

> (a) the question challenges the truthfulness of the witness or the consistency or accuracy of any statements made by the witness, or
>
> (b) the question requires the witness to discuss a subject that could be considered to be distasteful or private.

(4) A party to criminal proceedings may object to a question put to a witness on the ground that it is a disallowable question.

(5) However, the duty imposed on the court by this section applies whether or not an objection is raised to a particular question.

(6) A failure by the court to disallow a question under this section, or to inform the witness that it need not be answered, does not affect the admissibility in evidence of any answer given by the witness in response to the question.

Exercise 5.3

Examine the NSW rule on improper questions in cross-examination given above, in the light of the discussion throughout this chapter, and answer the following questions about provisions in this state for the cross-examination of vulnerable witnesses:

1. Who is protected by this legislation? How inclusive is it of the disadvantaged groups and vulnerable witnesses mentioned throughout the chapter? Do you think it is sufficiently inclusive? too broad? Why(not)?

2. Who is the person responsible for ensuring that certain witnesses are protected from improper questions? What do you think is the actual process by which this takes place?

3. What criteria are used in the definition of improper questions: linguistic? legal? situated/contextual? other? What advantages and disadvantages do you see in the way in which improper questions are defined?

4. Imagine that you are an advocate for one of the following groups of people: children, sexual assault victims, intellectually disabled people, second language speakers, second dialect speakers. Would you be satisfied with this legislation? If not, why not? What changes would you want, and why?

5. Imagine that you are a defence advocate (and thus you often represent the interests of accused people). Would you be satisfied with this legislation? If not, why not? What changes would you want, and why?

Assignments and further research

1. Investigate the participation of children in courts in your country or state? How does the law define a child? Are there different age limits in different states? How does the relevant legislation (e.g. the *Evidence Act*) deal with the evidence of children? What is the role of childrens court? What can you find out about ways of using language in childrens court? Are there special provisions for child witnesses in other courts? You might want to read the Australian Law Reform Commission's report on children in the legal process (ALRC (1997) http://www.austlii.edu.au/au/other/alrc/publications/reports/84), and the UK Home Office's report on interviewing 'vulnerable and intimidated witnesses, including children'. (Home Office 2000 http://www.homeoffice.gov.uk/documents/ach-bect-evidence/).

2. Some jurisdictions have legislated special provisions to protect child witnesses, for example the state of Queensland, in its 2003 amendments to the *Evidence Act*. Examine Sections 9E and 21 of this Act (available online at http://www.austlii.edu.au/au/legis/qld/consol_act/ea197780/. Discuss the ways in which the rules of evidence for Queensland courts attempt to address the needs of child witnesses. Do you think these provisions are adequate? If not, what needs remain unaddressed? (In considering these questions you might like to consult Eades 2008a, especially Section 3 of Chapter 11.) Compare this Act with similar rules of evidence in a different jurisdiction (that is the Evidence Act or its equivalent in a different state or country).

3. **(Lx)** There is a wealth of psychological research on child witnesses. Students with a background in both psychology and linguistics could examine some of this psychological literature and identify unanswered questions to which sociolinguistic analysis could make a contribution. A few good starting places are in Walker's (1999) references and Ceci and Bruck (1995).

4. **(Lx)** Investigate the use of African American English in court. This exercise is designed as a class project, but could be adapted for individual students, and it could be used in this way as a scoping study prior to thesis/dissertation work in this area.

   - Read about linguistic and sociolinguistic features of AAE (or AAVE) (two good references to start with are Green 2002 and Mufwene *et al.* 1998).

   - Prepare a checklist of features of AAE: phonological, lexical, grammatical, semantic, discourse structure, pragmatic. Different features should then be allocated to different students.

   - Spend a day or half-day observing court proceedings in a courthouse where you will hear AAE speakers. Make notes about any features you observe, focusing specifically on the features allocated to you, and who is using AAE in what contexts. Also make notes about any instances of the following:
     ○ possible miscommunication due to dialectal difference;
     ○ possible negative attitudes to a speaker related to dialectal difference;
     ○ evidence of bidialectalism of a speaker;
     ○ code-switching: note any possible factors involved.

- Discuss your court observations, paying attention to:
    - connections to linguistic and sociolinguistic research on AAE;
    - connections to linguistic and sociolinguistic research on courtroom talk;
    - possible further research topics.

5. **(Lx)** Topic 4 above could be adapted for any non-standard or stigmatised dialect, or for any pidgin or creole language.

6. **(Lx)** If you have a background in psychology and linguistics, you could investigate language use in court by people with intellectual or mental disability. A literature-based study could examine the literature on language use in court (as introduced in Chapter 3, and also drawing on relevant material in the other chapters in this Part). Then discuss the relevance of these findings to people with a specified intellectual or mental disability.

6

Courtroom talk and societal power relations

1. Introduction   106

2. Courtroom power revisited   106

3. Courtroom talk and the liberty of the individual   108

4. Courtroom talk and patriarchal power   112

5. Courtroom talk and neocolonial power   115

6. The power of courtroom talk   122

   Assignments and further research   127

Courtroom talk and societal power relations

1. Introduction

In the last chapter we examined vulnerable witnesses in court, focusing on those who are vulnerable because of enduring aspects of their social identity and distinctive aspects of their language use. But at the end of the chapter, we saw that legislative protection of vulnerable witnesses is not always restricted to members of particular social groups. Indeed, in the particular Australian legislation we considered in Section 5, the court has to take into account 'any relevant condition or characteristic of the witness'. Sometimes the most relevant characteristic of the witness may be their situated identity in the courtroom hearing, for example as victim-witness in an abuse or assault case.

This chapter includes a consideration of people who may be thought of as vulnerable witnesses from a different perspective, namely in terms of societal power relationships. We saw in Chapter 3 that courtroom talk has been examined for three decades in terms of situated power relationships within the courtroom. In this chapter, we turn to the ways in which power relationships and struggles at a societal level come into the courtroom. We will see that sociolinguistic analysis of courtroom talk is shedding light on mechanisms involved in the reproduction of societal power relationships.

2. Courtroom power revisited

In Chapter 3 we have seen plenty of evidence of the asymmetrical power imbalance in the courtroom. Not only do lawyers have the power to control witnesses' stories, but lawyers and judges have enormous power to control witnesses in other ways – whether they stand or sit, when they can talk, what they can talk about and when they have to remain silent.

However, despite the power imbalance, witnesses can exercise some power. In a 1980s study in magistrates courts in England, Harris (1989) found that some defendants resisted the power of the court to some extent, by interrupting their questioner, or by asking 'counter-questions', as we see in Extract 6–i below. This amusing extract took place (at a time when colour television was relatively new) in an Arrears and Maintenance Court in an English County Magistrates Court. This is a court at the lowest level, where defendants try to justify why their payment of fines or maintenance is in arrears. Defendants argue their case directly with the magistrate, with no legal representation, and in this way talk in this court is not as constrained as in many of the (higher level) courts, which have been the focus of most of the sociolinguistic research. You will see that the magistrate's questions in this extract were functioning as rebukes as much as they were functioning as requests for information:

Extract 6–i Harris' (1989: 144–145) transcription of audiorecording; slightly edited

1. M: Do you think that it is a reasonable thing that a wife and your child shall be without your support whilst you enjoy the additional pleasure of colour – in television in your home – does that seem a reasonable thing to do?

2. D: Depends on which way you look at it don't it?

3. M: Well looking at it from any <u>reasonable</u> point of view – is it <u>reasonable</u> for anyone to have the pleasure and the uh- luxury of a colour television set when a wife and a child could be going without food? Whichever way you look at it is that <u>reasonable</u>?

4. D: Well I don't know because if I didn't have a colour telly I'd just spend my time – in the pubs then wouldn't I?

Exercise 6.1[xvi]

Extract 6–i above from a hearing in this Arrears and Maintenance Court differs from a trial in a number of ways. <u>Make a list</u> of the differences, and <u>discuss</u> the ways in which these differences appear to impact on ways of talking in the hearing.

More subtle witness resistance is found in Drew's studies of complainants in rape cases, as we saw in Section 4.3 of Chapter 3 in the negotiation of word choice and meaning (an example was seen in Extract 3–v). Other examples of witness resistance in cross-examination are found in the work of Cotterill (2003), Drew (1992), Eades (2008a), Ehrlich (2001) and Matoesian (1993, 2001, 2008). The witnesses in Harris's study had no particular training or experience to equip them in the power struggle in court with magistrates, and in terms of the Duke study of witnesses' answers, discussed in Section 4.1 of Chapter 3, they would be seen as powerless witnesses. You might like to consider how the witnesses in the Cotterill, Drew, Eades, Ehrlich and Matoesian studies would be considered in terms of the Duke study of powerful versus powerless witnesses.

Ehrlich and Sidnell (2006) have analysed the testimony of a witness who would certainly rate as powerful in this dichotomy: he is privileged socially, and has had plenty of experience in language manipulation. This witness's experience was at a high level of politics: he was the then premier of one of Canada's provinces. In his answers to cross-examination questions during an inquiry into deaths resulting from water contamination, this experienced politician skilfully resisted and challenged damaging presuppositions. His ability to analyse the questions while answering them revealed that he was much more of a match for the lawyers than most witnesses. For example, in answer to one question, he replied: *Well you assumed that ... and I think that's not an assumption you ought to make* (p. 664). The answers of this witness show that questions are not inherently more powerful than answers, although this appears to have been assumed in many of the sociolinguistic studies of courtroom language.

These quite different examples of witness resistance to lawyer power serve to illustrate the point that the power imbalance in the courtroom is not static and it is not absolute. Indeed, like any power relationship it is something that is worked for and negotiated. Many aspects of courtroom hearings are weighted against the witness: such as the intimidatory physical setting, formalised rituals and various constraints on the witness's participation. But witnesses can and do exercise some power in some ways.

[handwritten margin note: Vuln. Wit. tend to not challenge]

The studies of power in courtroom talk which we examined in Chapter 3 can be described as studies of situational power within the courtroom. Some of the recent work on courtroom talk goes beyond situated power imbalances in the courtroom, and connects with sociolegal work which examines the impact on society of what happens in the legal process. Conley and

O'Barr (2005) call on both sociolinguists and sociolegal scholars to move beyond the shortcomings of their fields in isolation, and bring together insights and analyses from both fields. They argue that the interdisciplinary field of law and society (or sociolegal studies) has documented 'the law's failure to deliver on its biggest promises, especially the equal treatment of all citizens', without explaining how this failure occurs (p. 13). On the other hand, sociolinguistics has documented 'a great deal about how social differences are encoded within language', but has generally failed to ask 'whether language variation is truly consequential in social life' (p. 12). But, they argue, bringing sociolinguistics and sociolegal scholarship together can uncover 'how the power of law actually operates in everyday legal settings' (p. 14).

In this chapter, we consider the role of courtroom talk in wider societal power relations and struggles, drawing in particular on the work on variations in the ways in which judges take guilty pleas, as well as rape trials, and a case against police officers charged with abduction of three Australian Aboriginal boys. These studies provide an understanding of the relationship between social structures, such as the legal system, patriarchy and neocolonialism on the one hand, and the agency of individuals on the other hand – what people actually say and do in particular situations, for example in courtroom hearings. We will see that the power of law is not fixed and it is not restricted to the legal process. But rather, an examination of courtroom talk and its social consequences sheds light on the actual mechanisms by which societal power relations are perpetuated. This approach to the study of courtroom talk is part of the widespread 'critical turn' in the social sciences, introduced in Section 5 of Chapter 1. Several theoretical traditions that focus on situated language use are currently experiencing this critical turn, including interactional sociolinguistics, discourse analysis, linguistic anthropology and applied linguistics.[18]

The 'critical turn' provides us with more refined concepts than have typically been used in the sociolinguistic work on situated language and power in courtroom talk. Many critical theorists have taken up Gramsci's (1971) point about two different kinds of power. While Gramsci has been criticised for being overly deterministic, his basic point about two different kinds of power is still quite helpful: coercion (or 'direct domination') is exercised by legislative or executive powers, or expressed through police intervention, while hegemony involves the dominant group securing the consent of the society. Van Dijk (1993: 254) succinctly expresses this distinction, when he says that 'a powerful group may limit the freedom of action of others [coercion], but also influence their minds [hegemony]'. And as 'managing the minds of others is essentially a function of text and talk', the analysis of language use is central to the analysis of power. For example we will see in the study of rape trials how courtroom talk has the power to define the ways in which women are expected to control unwanted sexual advances. Thus, sociolinguistic attention to the ways in which power is exercised through talk involves more than the immediate interaction in the courtroom. It must be seen as part of the wider societal exercise of power.

3. Courtroom talk and the liberty of the individual

One of the sociolinguistic studies which illustrates this approach is Philips' (1998) analysis of one of the shortest events that takes place in courts, namely the spoken guilty plea. If a person pleads not guilty, then a trial is held to determine their guilt or innocence. But if a person pleads guilty, the next stage in the legal process is the sentencing. In lower courts, the sentencing generally takes place immediately after the guilty plea, or the court's finding that a defendant is guilty. In higher courts, the guilty plea is often a separate hearing, and sentencing takes place on a later occasion. There are variations in the way in which the guilty plea is made or presented to the court. In some courts, a court official reads the charge, the defendant pleads guilty, and the judge ascertains that this guilty plea conforms to legal requirements. In other courts, a defendant's lawyer presents a written guilty plea signed by the defendant (which can sometimes be a 'change of plea' from an original not guilty plea). Again, the judge ascertains that this guilty plea conforms to legal requirements. These legal requirements are that the guilty plea is made with the defendant's understanding of the nature of the charge, as well as the nature and range of possible sentences, and the rights which the defendant forgoes by pleading guilty, as well as the fact that the defendant has the right to plead not guilty. You might think that the guilty plea would be so short and procedural as to be too boring for a researcher. There are no tricky lawyer questions, no witnesses and no jury. It is, in effect, a discussion in court between a defendant and a judge on a fairly restricted topic.

But Philips' (1998) study of guilty pleas in US criminal courts is a powerful example of how careful and rigorous sociolinguistic analysis can show us the workings of power in the legal system. Her study took place in the Superior Court in Tucson, Arizona, and at the descriptive level it begins with an investigation of the structure of the plea event. Philips refers to this event as 'the spoken guilty plea', but note that the act of pleading guilty is carried out by the presentation to the court of the signed guilty plea document, which is then the basis of the judge's questioning. Based on her analysis of 44 audiorecorded pleas taken by nine different judges, Philips was able to analyse the topics which defendants are asked about by judges. Figure 6.1 presents a summary of this structure, with topics which do not always occur indicated by square brackets:

---

1. Opening
          Call of the case
          Self-Identification by Lawyers
          [repair slot][19]
11. Substance of procedure
          [Social background questions]
          Nature of charge
          Plea agreement comprehension questions
          Conditions of plea agreement
          Sentencing possibilities
          Constitutional rights
          Coercion questions
          Factual basis
          [repair slot]
          Findings
111. Closing
          Sentencing arrangements
          Probation investigation arrangements

Figure 6.1 Structure of the spoken guilty plea (Philips 1998: 29–30)

Having established what happens in this event, Philips then examined in more detail the systematic variation in the way in which different judges in her study took the plea. Which questions were left out by which judges in which cases? Which judges varied the order of questions? Which judges tailored their questioning to individual defendants, and which followed the same questions in the same order with all defendants before them?

Philips' examination of this systematic variation was accompanied by research on the social context of judicial work, particularly in the light of ongoing debate in the US about the appointment of judges. In some US jurisdictions judges are appointed and in others they are elected. In Arizona at the time of Philips' study, judges were appointed by the state governor, in a complex system that involved nominations from a commission comprising attorneys and non-attorneys, chosen in a variety of ways. Being appointed rather than elected, the judges in Philips' study saw themselves as non-political. But Philips came to a different conclusion at the end of her study.

Her investigation involved detailed ethnographic interviews with the nine judges whose guilty plea events she was studying. This interview part of the study focused on judges' beliefs about society, social problems and the role of the courts, and it found, unsurprisingly, that not all judges have the same beliefs. When Philips examined the judges' linguistic behaviour in asking questions of defendants in the guilty plea event, she found some interesting patterns in relation to the judges' beliefs about society. To summarise and slightly oversimplify Philips' study, she found that the judges took one of two rather different views about the relationship between the state and the individual. These fundamentally different political philosophies or ideologies can be seen as either conservative or liberal. The judges with a liberal ideological stance held the view that people are not all equally capable of protecting their own liberty, and that the state should take on the role of protector of human liberties, particularly for powerless people. On the other hand, the judges with a conservative ideological stance believed that all individuals are equally capable of taking care of themselves and don't need the state to help. These judges expressed the view that the state should interfere in lives of individuals as little as possible.

Philips found an interesting relationship between these two different ideological stances, and the ways in which the judges conducted the guilty plea hearings. The ideologically conservative judges followed the minimal requirements of case law, involving the defendant as little as possible. These judges were most concerned with making a good record, that could not be overturned by an appellate court. Philips calls these judges 'record-oriented judges', and she says that they 'aspire to a fixed script' in taking the guilty plea. On the other hand, the judges who were more ideologically liberal were more likely to vary the order of topics they asked the defendant about, as well as the formulation of questions. This was consistent with their concern to determine in each instance that the defendant was pleading knowingly and voluntarily. Philips calls these judges 'procedure-oriented judges', and she says that they tailor the procedure to each defendant, and see their 'scripts' for taking the guilty plea as inherently variable.

Exercise 6.2[xvii]

'Coercion questions' refers to the questions which the judge asks the defendant to ascertain whether they have been coerced to plead guilty. Read the two extracts below from two different guilty plea hearings, and decide which of these judges exemplifies the record-oriented judges and which exemplifies the procedure-oriented judges in Philips' study. Give reasons for your answer. Which approach do you prefer? Why? What are the advantages and disadvantages of each approach?

Extract 6–ii Philips' (1998: 153) transcription of audiorecording
Judge X Coercion Questions

1. Judge:	Did anybody else- did anybody make any other promises than just that to you?
2. Defendant:	No, [sir.
3. Judge:	[in exchange for your plea. Did anybody use any force against you, or make any threats against you?
4. Defendant:	No, [sir.
5. Judge:	[to get you to change your plea? I have to be satisfied that this is something you're doing voluntarily. Uh is it?
6. Defendant:	Yes, sir?
7. Judge:	Have you discussed it fully and carefully with Mr Martin?
8. Defendant:	Yes, sir.
9. Judge:	D'you think he's giving you good advice?
10. Defendant:	Yes, sir.
11. Judge:	You're satisfied with his representation?
12. Defendant:	Yes, sir.

Extract 6–iii Philips' (1998: 172) transcription of audiorecording
Judge Y Coercion Questions

1. Judge:	Have any promises been made to you to uh cause you to enter pleas of guilty at this time other than the promises contained in the written plea agreement?
2. Defendant:	No.
3. Judge:	Has any one used any force or any threats to cause you to enter [pleas of guilty at this time.
4. Defendant:	[No.

Philips' conclusion is that the procedural diversity which she observed in the spoken interaction in guilty plea hearings is tied up with the ideological diversity found among members of the judiciary. It is a myth to view trial court judges as non-ideological: even in the apparently simple courtroom event of taking the plea, judges are practising not only law and courtroom control, but also politics, related to the role of the state in the lives of individuals. Philips' examination of actions (what judges say in court) in relation to ideological stances (judges' views on equality and the role of the state) exemplifies Conley and O'Barr's (2005) position that combining sociolinguistic and sociolegal analysis can show how the power of law actually operates. And we can see the wider social consequences of courtroom talk: when a defendant goes to court to plead guilty, this person may face a record-oriented judge who processes their plea with a focus on the legal record of this event, and with little or no concern for this person's circumstances or real understanding of the consequences for their rights and freedom. Or by chance, this person may face instead a procedure-oriented judge who takes great pains to try to ensure that the defendant is pleading guilty knowingly, willingly, and not as a result of any coercion or promise. In this case, there may be quite different consequences for the defendant's rights and freedom.

4. Courtroom talk and patriarchal power

While Philips' work on the guilty plea examines the ways in which judges' talk is involved in the treatment of defendants pleading guilty, the work of Matoesian and Ehrlich is about the ways in which courtroom talk in the cross-examination of complainants in rape cases reproduces patriarchal domination and redefines (or represents) rape, particularly in acquaintance/date rape cases.

Regulations generally referred to as rape shield laws are supposed to 'shield' complainants from questions about their sexual history. Matoesian (1993, 1995, 2001) addresses the question of why the introduction of rape shield laws does not seem to have achieved the goal of making it easier for complainants in rape cases to give evidence.[20] This sociolegal question, which is seemingly about structural issues in rape trials, is answered by Matoesian's detailed microanalysis of courtroom interaction in such trials. He argues that the cross-examinations of complainants in rape cases involves transforming the victim's experience of violence into one of consensual sex. But more than this, Matoesian shows how 'rape as an enforcement of the social order is reproduced in trial talk' (1993: 71). At the centre is patriarchal domination, 'a system organised around the subordination and sexual control of women' (p. 219). When a woman who has been raped goes to court (as a prosecution witness in the case against the alleged rapist), it is common for defence lawyers to ask questions in such a way as to blame the complainant, and to allocate responsibility to her for what happened. Matoesian uses Conversation Analysis to analyse these linguistic strategies, which include puzzle/solution pairs (similar to Drew's contrast device, discussed in Section 4.4 of Chapter 3). In Extract 6–iv we see an example which combines three other linguistic mechanisms – namely, repetition, lawyer silence and emphatic delivery – to convey a particular stance of the lawyer. The question is about the complainant's evidence about how much she had to drink at the bar at which she met the defendant, before accepting a ride home from him:

Extract 6–iv Slightly simplified version of Matoesian's (1993: 145) transcription of audiorecording
1. DC: Is it your testimony:::? (1.0) under swor:::n SWORN oath (0.8) that in four hours at the
          Grainary [bar] you had only two drinks?
2. W: (1.2) Yes.
3. DC: (45.0) Linda ...

> **Exercise 6.3**
>
> Read Extract 6–iv aloud, preferably with a partner. Pay careful attention to the detailed transcription provided by Matoesian (see Section 8 of Chapter 1 for transcription conventions). Discuss the impact of the lawyer's two turns in this extract. How do you think this extract might have contributed to a strategy of blaming the complainant for what happened to her? If you were on the jury in this case, how might you discuss with other jurors the lawyer's stance conveyed by the use of repetition, lawyer silence and emphatic delivery in this extract?

Ehrlich's examination of language use in rape cases sheds valuable light on how courtroom talk defines consent, in its construction of rape incidents as consensual sex. One of Ehrlich's concerns is with the 'substantive ideological work' done by questions in the cross-examination of complainants. Much is written about the meaning and scope of the term 'ideology', which is an important concept in critical studies, and which we will come back to in Section 4 of Chapter 11. One useful explanation comes from Fairclough (1989: 2), who defines ideologies as 'common-sense' assumptions which 'are a means of legitimizing existing social relations and differences of power, simply through the recurrence of ordinary, familiar ways of behaving which take these relations and power differences for granted'. In the rape cases analysed by Ehrlich, it is taken as common sense that women can resist unwanted sexual aggression with aggressive and direct physical resistance, an ideological position that ignores the role of the victim's fear. When witnesses said that they were too afraid, they were questioned in ways similar to the witness in Extract 6–v:

Extract 6–v Ehrlich (2001: 74); official court transcript
1. L: You had what I would call a subjective fear of this man. In other words, you were genuinely scared of him, right?
2. W: Yes.
3. L: But he didn't do anything overt to cause you to be fearful? By overt, he didn't do anything outward to make you afraid, never threatened you?
4. W: He never uttered any threats.
5. L: No. Never punched you or mistreated you physically in any way?
6. W: No.

In this extract, the lawyer began by acknowledging the complainant's *subjective fear* and that she had been *genuinely scared* of the defendant. But the following questions reshaped or reformulated the concept of fear, so that the jury would be led to think *why was she afraid of someone who didn't do anything overt, like punching or making overt threats to her? Why couldn't she resist someone who wasn't even violent?* Notice that the witness made one attempt to qualify this view when she said that *he never uttered any threats* in Turn 4. She was leaving the opportunity for an alternative view in which a person may feel threatened even if no *overt threat* has been made. What aspects of the situation do you think might cause her to feel threatened? If this discussion was taking place in an informal context or argument, perhaps the complainant could have explained why she felt threatened. But remember that the witness can only answer the question which has just been asked, and she has no opportunity to argue against the lawyer's reformulation of the grounds for her fear. You might like to go back to the hierarchy of question types discussed in Section 4.1 of Chapter 3. What kind of questions was the lawyer using in this extract?[xviii]

Another way in which defence lawyers change the claim of forced sex to one of consensual sex, is by rephrasing the complainant's account of what happened. This often involves tricky linguistic mechanisms for shifting blame or for removing responsibility or agency for particular actions. For example, Ehrlich (2001) analyses the linguistic means used to attribute non-agency to a defendant. Using the term 'grammar of non-agency' to refer to this, Ehrlich shows that it includes the use of unaccusative constructions (where an action is presented as simply happening), and the nominalisation of actions (using an abstract noun instead of a verb). These two grammatical strategies are powerful in removing agency, as we see in one of the cross-examination questions that the complainant was asked by the defence lawyer: *Well, your shirt came off first as a result of fondling of the breasts, right?* (Ehrlich 2001: 53). In this question, no one is responsible for either of the actions referred to: it was the agentless *fondling* (a nominalisation) which was responsible for the complainant's shirt coming off (in an unaccusative construction). Such a question could be asked differently in order to attribute agency to the defendant, for example *Well, when he was fondling your breasts, he took off your shirt, right?*

Exercise 6.4[xix]

Examine the following examples (Ehrlich 2001: 53) of questions addressed to complainants in rape trials, and discuss the linguistic means used to attribute non-agency to the defendant. Rephrase these examples in order to attribute agency to the defendant. Then see if you can rephrase them to attribute agency to the complainant. (Linguistics students should discuss these examples and possible alternatives in terms of syntactic choices.)

(a) Was there any exchange around this point where your pants are removed where you are asking him or he is telling you 'do you like me?'

(b) And were your arms still in the same position above your head and crossed over and being held by one hand?

Ehrlich's work on rape trials shows how the cross-examining lawyers' questions presuppose and assert common-sense assumptions about the choices and options that women have when confronted with sexual aggression. We saw in Extract 6–v above the assumption that the complainant had no grounds to fear the defendant. Ehrlich also shows how this assumption is found in judges' decisions which construct consent as the absence of resistance. She points out (2001: 24) that legislation defines consent as 'the voluntary agreement of the complainant to engage in the sexual activity in question'. But the patriarchal reasoning implied in cross-examination questioning and behind judicial decisions is one of 'implied consent': if the complainant did not actively and physically engage in resistance, then her (in)actions are taken as consent. Such questions are the mechanisms through which patriarchal ideologies are used in the courtroom to define or 'represent' rape and to reproduce power relations which legitimise violence against women.

People usually get frustrated or angry with lawyers when they hear about rape trials, whether it is from media reports, experiences of participants in the proceedings or research. Maybe it would be better to get rid of lawyers from this process? In Chapter 10 we will see that this is increasingly happening in small civil cases (in small claims courts) and in areas of family law, such as custody disputes. Laypeople have the chance to tell their story without it being controlled and transformed by questions from lawyers on both sides. You might like to discuss this issue in relation to rape trials, not ignoring the rights of the accused to question their accuser and to be treated as innocent until proven guilty. Ehrlich (2007) raises an important issue about the role of lawyers, pointing out (p. 136) the 'danger in unduly privileging narratives or accounts of experience that are *unmediated* by lawyers' advice and questioning strategies as "natural" or "true"' (emphasis in original). This danger is illustrated with an incest case in which a woman gave evidence about her father's repeated sexual abuse since she was eight years old. This complainant several times used the verb phrase *had sex*, in such expressions as *my dad was having sex with me*. As Ehrlich points out, this verb phrase could give the connotation of consensual sex, which is not legally possible with a child or young teenager. So, although this complainant was alleging sexual abuse in this case, some of the ways she reported this in her evidence involved her apparent adoption of 'culturally hegemonic meanings' and ways of talking about non-stranger rape (pp. 136–137). What would happen to the evidence of complainants like this woman if their evidence was not mediated by their lawyers' advice and questioning strategies?

5. Courtroom talk and neocolonial power

While the work of Ehrlich and Matoesian has shown the role of courtroom talk in the workings of patriarchal power, my work with Australian Aboriginal witnesses has examined the role of courtroom talk in the workings of neocolonial power. Neocolonial power can be defined as the power which a former colonial ruler exercises over its former colonial subjects. In Australia, excessive police intervention in the lives of Aboriginal people was a central part of colonial rule, and it remains central in contemporary neocolonial control. Criminologists have documented the excessive rate at which Aboriginal people are arrested and imprisoned. They have also pointed out that police discretionary decisions in minor matters – such as the use of so-called 'offensive' language or noise in the streets – result in a greater proportion of Aboriginal people being arrested and charged for matters for which non-Aboriginal people are simply cautioned, or even ignored. Sociolegal scholars use the term 'criminalisation' to refer to such ways in which police intervention in the lives of Aboriginal people has the effect of making many of them 'illegal' because of their Aboriginality.

In my recent book (Eades 2008a), I present a detailed analysis of a mid-1990s Brisbane case – known as the Pinkenba case – which provided clear evidence of the role of courtroom talk in legitimising excessive police intervention in the lives of Aboriginal people. In Conley and O'Barr's (2005) terms, this analysis of courtroom talk shows the actual mechanisms through which the legal system fails to deliver justice.

The Pinkenba case involved three Aboriginal part-time street kids (aged 12, 13 and 14) who were walking around a shopping mall near the downtown area of Brisbane late one night. They were approached by six armed police officers, told to get into three police vehicles and then driven 14 kilometres out of town to a dark and swampy industrial wasteland, where they were threatened, before the police drove off, abandoning the boys. This was not the first time that police had done this to Aboriginal people, but for the first time, the families of the boys made an official complaint.[21] As a result, the police officers were charged with 'unlawful deprivation of liberty' – in ordinary English this was an alleged abduction.

The Aboriginal community was outraged that police had removed the boys like this, never charging them with an offence, and ignoring legislated guidelines about how to deal with young troublemakers (if indeed they had been making trouble that night). The incident also had occurred just six months after an 18-year-old Aboriginal young man in the same city had died while in a police van, where he had been detained for disturbing the peace. In fact, by the time the Pinkenba case got to court, it was invested with enormous political and social significance in the 200-year-old struggle between police officers and the Aboriginal community, about the police removals of Aboriginal people.

This case resembled a rape trial in some ways. Both rape and abduction are actions which would be legal if the complainant had agreed to the action, either engaging in sex or going for a ride. But without the complainant's consent, the action is illegal. And typically in both rape and abduction cases, the only witness is the complainant, so the cross-examination is typically focused on showing that the complainant either consented or did not object.

But in the Pinkenba case, this was only part of the cross-examination strategy. In fact, more than half of the cross-examination of the three boys was not about what happened the night the police took them for a ride. Instead, it was devoted to presenting the boys as lying criminals who could not be trusted to tell the truth, and who were so experienced in talking to police, that they must have known they did not have to go with these police officers in the cars. There were also many questions which asserted, implied or presupposed that the boys were a threat to public safety on the streets. (No doubt was ever raised that the police officers did take the boys out to Pinkenba that night and leave them there.)

In this construction of the boys as lying criminals who are a threat to public safety, the defence lawyers used a number of linguistic mechanisms. One of them relates to the choice of words, discussed in Section 4.3 of Chapter 3. There we saw that lawyers carefully choose labels for key events, people and situations, which promote their theory of the case. And in Section 4 above, we saw that this involves not just lexical items but grammatical choice as well (as in the grammar of non-agency). The way that lawyers take a witness's story and re-present it in different ways is an example of recontextualisation: taking a story from one context – such as its original telling in examination-in-chief – and retelling it in a new context – such as cross-examination. Recontextualisation is a common discursive activity, which can be carried out by the original teller or a different person. It plays a central role in the legal process, and we will come back to it in Section 7 of Chapter 7, Section 5 of Chapter 9 and Section 4.3 of Chapter 11.

During cross-examination recontextualisation of a witness's story, lawyer and witness can struggle over the choice of words to describe events, people or situations. For example, the boys all said in their examination-in-chief that they were *walking around* the Valley (Fortitude Valley near the Brisbane city centre), before the police officers approached them and told them to get in the police cars. *Walking around* is a commonly used general Australian English, as well as Aboriginal English, description for a frequent and widespread youth activity in many cities throughout the world. This activity is not illegal. In cross-examination, the first of the two defence counsel (DC1) did not accept 13-year-old David's term *walking around* from his evidence-in-chief, and instead substituted his own term *wander around*. David did not directly dispute this term, although he did not use it, as we see in Extract 6–vi:

Extract 6–vi Eades' (2008a: 130) transcription of official audiorecording

1. DC1:   You **wandered** around the streets of Brisbane- we know that you were in the mall up in the heart of the town we know you walked down towards North Quay- we can see you on-tapes- we know you were in the Valley.

2. David: (2.7) Mm.

3. DC1:   And you were just **wandering around** (2.0) [weren't you?
4. David: [Yes.

5. DC1:   For [what?
6. David: [Yes.

7. DC1:   For what?
8. David: (2.3) Looking.

9. DC1:   Looking (1.5) At what?
10. David: (2.3) We was just **walking around** for nothing.

Despite David persisting with his expression *walking around* to describe what the boys were doing that night, DC1 persisted with his alternative *wandering around* in later questions. This might seem to be a subtle difference, but it is not a trivial one: while *walk around* does not imply a destination, it does imply a purpose (e.g. *walking around window-shopping* or *walking around and looking at the people*). *Wander around* on the other hand seems to connote neither destination nor purpose, and it collocates easily with the adverb *aimlessly*.[22]

David's answer in Turn 8 to the *for what?* question is interesting: *looking* or 'observing the comings and goings of others around them' (Eades 1988: 104) is indeed an important Aboriginal social activity. As *walking around looking* is not an activity commonly practised by middle-class adults, it is possible that DC1 did not understand David's answers. And as DC1 persisted with his term *wandering around* in later questions, the 13-year-old Aboriginal witness was not able to counter the linguistic skills with which the defence counsel recontextualised his story of what he had been doing that night in the Valley. The difference between these two verbs may seem like a minor matter in terms of the witness's allegation of being unlawfully deprived of his liberty. But it played an important role in the construction of him and his two mates as a threat to public safety, particularly in combination with evidence about their criminal records – in effect, it was a linguistic tool used to construct these boys as vagrants.

A similar, but more powerful, change of wording of the witness's story by the lawyer took place with the oldest witness, who was 15 years old at the time of the hearing. He also told the court that what he and his two mates were doing that night in the Valley was *walking around*. This was substituted by DC1, not with *wandering around*, as we saw with the youngest witness, but with *prowling around*, as we see in Extract 6–vii:

Extract 6–vii Eades' (2008a: 133) transcription of official audiorecording

1. DC1:   (3.2) And just **prowling around** <u>looking</u> for <u>mischief</u> weren't you?
2. Barry: (3.2) No- just **walking around**.

Central to the meaning of *prowl* is that the agent is in search of something that is not legitimately theirs: *prey* or *plunder*, as the *Macquarie Dictionary* expresses it. Thus, this word *prowl* was a clever tool in the implication that the boys had been intending to engage in criminal activity, and thus were 'fair game' for law enforcement activity. Although no evidence was produced to indicate that the boys were engaged in criminal activity that night, their story about what they were doing was taken over by the lawyers in cross-examination, using such linguistic strategies as we have seen in these two extracts.

Although Barry was able to counter the accusation that he and his mates were *prowling around looking for mischief* (in the form of criminal activity), DC1 exercised his greater control over Barry's story to use this loaded verb *prowl* in the presupposition of a later question, asking of Barry's previous activities (for which he had already been dealt with by the courts): *What sort of things did you steal- when you were wan- prowling around the streets?* DC1 started to say the word *wandering* and changed it to *prowling*, suggesting the deliberateness of this lexical substitution strategy here.[23]

Although this is just one small example (with two parts), it indicates the ways in which lawyers' power to re-present witnesses' stories can invoke and perpetuate cultural stereotypes. In the Australian media, Aboriginal people are constantly linked with crime (e.g. Jakubowicz *et al.* 1994: 38–39). Using a number of linguistic strategies, the two defence counsel in this case succeeded in connecting to and contributing to this widespread view of Aboriginal people as a criminal threat to public safety. In addition to the lexical substitution we have seen here, another important strategy was to present as assertions, presuppositions and questions for confirmation details of the boys' criminal records, with 'questions' such as:

- *What are you going to do when you grow up – go on to bigger and better criminal activity?*

- *Have you taken <u>lots</u> of things away from shops?*

- *Sixteenth of february nineteen ninety three you appeared in court for breaking and entering the council chambers- that right?*

It might be hard to imagine why a complainant giving prosecution evidence about his alleged abduction has to answer questions about his criminal record, especially when he had already been to childrens court to face the law. But the rules of evidence allow questions which are related to the witness's credit, credibility and trustworthiness, and thus a complainant's criminal record is generally considered fair game in cross-examination.

In my (2008a) analysis of this case, I show that there was more going on in the Pinkenba case than simply the reliance on and reproduction of negative stereotypes about Aboriginal people. This case played a central role in the power struggle between the police and the Aboriginal community over the rights of police officers to remove Aboriginal people from public places. And it was a very unbalanced struggle – three young teenage Aboriginal part-time street kids being questioned by the two most highly paid barristers in the state. But as Matoesian has pointed out 'power is always bi-directional, even in the most systematically asymmetrical relationships' (1993: 208).

The boys did attempt some resistance in their answers, as seen in the following example of 13-year-old Albert, almost at the end of his two hour cross-examination. Albert had made little overt resistance to this point, although it is quite possible that some of his *I dunno* answers were more about non-cooperation than a report on his knowledge. But in Extract 6–viii, we see that he was fed up with the lawyers' questions and was attempting to answer back.

Extract 6–viii Eades' (2008a: 232) transcription of official audiorecording

1. DC2:   How many?
2. Albert: (1.9) <u>Told</u> you there were six of them.

3. DC2:   (1.0) A all six standing around were they?
4. Albert: Yes.

5. DC2:   Or were some in the police cars already?
6. Albert: Nuh (0.6) (I'm) not [silly.

7. DC2:   [Eh?- Pardon?
8. Albert: (1.0) They was all standing around.

9. DC2:   All standing around? (2.2) tell us exactly where then please °(Albert)°?- at the cars- were
            they?- a couple at each car or what?
10. Albert: <u>AROUND</u> us.

11. DC2:   Around where around you?
12. Albert: Oh °where do you think°?

13. DC2:   Mm? (2.8) the only thing that was said was this one thing was it? (1.5) (by) one police
            officer- hop in the car (0.8) mm? (1.5) that's the only thing you can remember being said
            (1.2) right? (1.8) is that right Albert? (2.7) Albert?
14. Albert: °Nuh you tell lies°.

Much of Albert's cross-examination had been about his criminal record, and had included repeated allegations that he tells lies. Now, at the end of his questioning, the second defence counsel was trying to present Albert as having an unreliable memory about the occasion on which the police had approached him and his friends before they took them for the ride. But DC2 went too far for Albert. His answers in Turns 2, 6 and 12 reveal defiance and impatience with the questioner, something which had only been glimpsed on a few earlier occasions. But it is Albert's answer in Turn 14 which was most defiant, accusing DC2 °you tell lies°. While there is no indication of which of DC2's propositions Albert saw as lies, this bold and substantive accusation may well have related to DC2's earlier distortion of what had happened when the police told the boys to get in the car. However, Albert's °you tell lies° was uttered very quietly, and it is not clear if DC2 heard it. He did not respond to it.

These examples of resistance are not as subtle and delicate as the negotiation engaged in by adult witnesses examined in work by Cotterill, Drew, Ehrlich and Matoesian (referred to in Section 2 above). Indeed, in the Pinkenba case the boys' overt resistance is more like typical teenage 'answering back' to parents or teachers when being questioned or rebuked in a disciplinary context (and in this way these answers have some similarity to the resistant answers we saw from the English Arrears and Maintenance Court in Section 2 above). Thus, while such answers as *You don't have to know my things what I do*, and *What's the matter with that?* are clear examples of witnesses refusing to accept lawyers' control, the defiant stance of the boys actually served to support the defence counsels' aim of presenting these witnesses as delinquents, who were a threat to safety on the streets (and thus somehow legitimately removed by the police and abandoned out of town). Thus, rather than gaining the boys some control, these answers of overt resistance paradoxically supported the defence strategy, as we see in the following example from the cross-examination of 15-year-old Barry. This extract occurred after Barry had been questioned by the first defence counsel about whether he had *ever gone for a ride in a stolen car*. Barry answered *I don't remember*, and DC1 pressured him on this point with further questions as *Oh you'd remember Mr Coley if you'd ever been in a car that had been borrowed without the consent of the owner you'd remember that (1.0) wouldn't you?*. Barry was becoming increasingly irritated and finally shouted *I DON'T KNOW I SAID I DON'T REMEMBER*. DC1 seized the opportunity to present Barry as a defiant person who could not be pushed around, with the following questions:

Extract 6–ix Eades' (2008a: 251-252) transcription of official audiorecording

1. DC1:   I notice Mr Coley that you're not a person to be er- uh- overborne- are you? (2.6) are you?
2. Barry: I don't know what it means.

3. DC1:   What it means is that you've been quite prepared to snap back at me haven't you? (1.4)
          haven't you? (4.5) you accept that don't you Mr Coley?
4. Barry: (1.1) ˚Yeh˚.

5. DC1:   (1.8) Don't you?
6. Barry: Yeh.

7. DC1:   (4.1) You're not the sort of person who can be forced into things are you? (5.5) are you?
8. Barry: (4.9) Nuh.

You will notice that Barry appeared reluctant to agree to this characterisation, saying *I don't know what it means* in Turn 2, answering very quietly in Turn 4, and waiting for a considerable time before answering in Turn 8. But DC1 cleverly used Barry's resistance in answering questions as support for the portrayal of him as someone who would not go in a police car if he did not want to. His use of the term of address *Mr Coley* also highlighted DC1's construction of him as an adult.

Exercise 6.5ˣˣ

Read the extract below from the Pinkenba case, discussed above. Consider the ways in which the defence lawyer was using a similar strategy to that in the rape trial discussed in Extract 6–v above. Do you agree with the lawyer's definition of *force* here? Why(not)?

Extract 6–x Eades' (2008a: 140–141) transcription of official audiorecording

1. DC2:   You got in the car without being forced David- didn't you?
2. David: (1.5) No.

3. DC2:   You told us- you've told us a ((laughs)) number of times today you did.
4. David: (1.3) **They forced me.**

5. DC2:   Eh?
6. David: **They forced us.**

7. DC2:   Tell us- tell us how David come on?
8. David: **They told us to jump in the car.**

9: DC2:   They told you to jump in the car?=
10. David: =Yeh.

11. DC2:   That's all that was said?
12. David: (1.0)Yeh.

13. DC2:   Nothing else was said to you apart from- jump in the car (2.2) that right?
14. David: (1.2) Yeh.

15. DC2:   And you did get in the car?
16. David: Yeh.

17. DC2:   You weren't pushed in the car- or held in the car?
18. David: No.

19. DC2:   You never asked to get out of the car?
20. David: (1.4) No.

21. DC2:   (4.6) And- all that happened because- you didn't think you were in any trouble- did you?
22. David: (1.8) No.

23. DC2:   CORRECT?
24. David: (1.9) °Yeh°.

25. DC2:   And that's why you had no trouble going out there getting in the car and travelling with
            the police. You didn't think you were in any trouble- did you?
26. David: We weren't.

[5 turns omitted here involved DC2's difficulty in hearing the answer]

27. DC: You weren't- that's right- that's right- what you're saying is I think- that if you'd just been
            walking along the street- you wouldn't have jumped in the car yourselves- **you got in the
            car because the police said to.**
28. David: Yeh.

29. DC2:   Ok- that's what you mean isn't it?
30. David: Yeh.

31. DC2:   **When you say forced- all you mean is- the police said so?**
32. David: Yeh.

33. DC2:   Mm?
34. David: Yeh.

Exercise 6. 6[xxi]

Read the extract below from the Pinkenba case, discussed above. Discuss the ways in which language is used in the presentation of Barry as a vagrant.

Extract 6–xi Eades' (2008a: 262) transcription of official audiorecording

1. DC2:   What were you doing [walking around the mall late at night]?
2. Barry: (4.8) I dunno just walk (1.8) walk around.

3. DC2:   (What were you doing David?) I'm sorry Barry what were you doing?
4. Barry: (1.5) Just walking.

5. DC2:   Looking for some money Barry?
6. Barry: Nuh (1.8) no-one was around anyway.

7. DC2:   (1.8) (aha) Looking for someone who might have been around in that lonely place?
8. Barry: Nuh.

9. DC2:   (2.1) It's not a bad place to- steal some money is it from someone?
10. Barry: Nuh.=

11. DC2:   =Deserted sort of area?
12. Barry: Nuh.

13. DC2:   Is that why you went to the top of the mall?
14. Barry: Nuh.

---

6. The power of courtroom talk

In this chapter we have seen that sociolinguistic considerations of language and power in the courtroom cannot be restricted to the examination of lawyers dominating and controlling witnesses. Most of the early sociolinguistic studies of courtroom talk conceptualised power as unidirectional control over witnesses by lawyers, as members of a dominant group (and this approach is consistent with Van Dijk's position quoted in Section 2 above). But scholars influenced by Foucault and post-structuralism see power not in terms of a static attribute or a monolithic oppressive power structure, but rather in terms of relationships. These relationships of power are dynamic and complex, and as we have seen in this chapter, they are not completely one-way. Despite all the controls on witnesses in court, we have seen examples of witnesses exercising their agency through acts of resistance. In this way witnesses challenge the situational power relationship between lawyers and witnesses, as well as societal power relationships, for example between police officers and Aboriginal young people.

The critical sociolinguistic work examined in this chapter provides examples of research which responds to Conley and O'Barr's (2005) call for sociolinguistic studies that examine the actual mechanisms through which the legal system fails to deliver justice. In this specific analysis of power relations in court and beyond court, this work resonates with Blommaert's call for sociolinguistic work which analyses 'power effects, or the outcome of power, of what power does to people, groups and societies, and of how this impact comes about' (Blommaert 2005: 1–2, emphases in original).

And we have seen that the examination of power relations in court should not be restricted to interaction between lawyers and witnesses in the highly charged event of cross-examination. Philips' study of a seemingly routine and non-contested courtroom event – the guilty plea – explodes the myth of judges as non-ideological. We saw that fundamental beliefs about the liberty and equality of individuals have an impact on how judges talk to defendants pleading guilty. Judges are generally seen to be outside politics, and the guilty plea is generally considered to be a non-political event. But judges who believe that the state should actively help powerless people to protect their human liberties have been found to work hard to ensure that defendants pleading guilty know what this means, and that they have not been coerced into pleading guilty, but are doing so of their own free will. In contrast, judges who believe that all individuals are equally capable of protecting their own human liberties are likely to use a formulaic approach to questioning defendants pleading guilty. The contrast between these two approaches of judges questioning defendants pleading guilty highlights the social consequences of courtroom talk.

Other social consequences of courtroom talk have been demonstrated in sociolinguistic studies of rape cases and Aboriginal complaints about police abuse, in which we have seen the perpetuation of patriarchal and neocolonial power, respectively. These studies have highlighted the extremes to which cross-examination can go in the unbalanced power relationship between lawyer and witness. These cases have shown us that through their questioning lawyers can reproduce in court the domination that was experienced by victims in the original event. And to the extent that judicial officers allow lawyers to treat witnesses in this way, they too are agents of this courtroom reproduction of the domination over the victim-witnesses.

We have seen that there is more going on in these cases than a situated power struggle between two sides in an adversarial contest. In the rape cases studied, defence lawyers define consent and naturalise the patriarchal view of women as teasers who lead men along and who should expect that such actions as flirting in bars will end with sexual intercourse. In this way a woman's experience of violation is transformed into one of consensual sex.

But in an adversarial contest, can't the prosecution define the victims' experiences in a different way, for example in a feminist way? While this seems logically possible, it does not appear to have been studied. However, Ehrlich (2002) has examined a civil case, in which a woman who sued a doctor for sexual assault and breach of trust was represented by a feminist lawyer. In this case, the lawyer asked questions of the complainant in such a way as to challenge dominant understandings of sexual assault. For example, after the complainant provided detail of an abusive pelvic examination, the lawyer asked *Did anyone else force you to engage in non-consensual sex during your teenage years?* (p. 205). In this question, the feminist lawyer rephrased the complainant's description of a pelvic examination as *non-consensual sex*, a term usually restricted in criminal trials to sexual intercourse. But the lawyer's rephrasing, or recontextualisation, was not always allowed by the judge, as we see in the following extract from this case. Here the complainant was answering questions about an earlier experience of non-consensual sex, which had occurred when she was a teenager.

Extract 6–xii Ehrlich (2002: 206); official transcript

1. W: When I was on a holiday in the Bahamas, I was – I had met a tennis coach there and he also had sex with me without my permission.

2. L: Can you expand on the circumstances that gave rise to this event?

3. W: Well, he offered me something to drink in his car. ... [several lines omitted detailing the tennis coach luring her to his hotel room] ... and then the next thing I know he was telling me to get into the bed and we were having sex.

[several turns omitted]

4. L: What was your reaction to the **sexual activity that was forced on you?**

5. W: Just- I didn't just-

6. J: She **didn't say he forced it on her**, Ms V., she said without her permission. If you're going to lead her you'd better get it correct.

7. L: Was there **any physical force applied** by the tennis coach in prevailing upon you to have the sex?

8. W: No. I was just scared and just did what he wanted me to do.

You can see that there was a contest here between the judge and the lawyer over the use of the term _force._ The lawyer referred to the complainant's _sex without my permission_ (Turn 1) as _sexual activity that was forced on you_ (Turn 4). But the judge did not allow this meaning of the word _force_, resulting in the lawyer asking about _physical force_ (Turn 7). Interestingly, this resulted in the complainant explaining a situation which is typical of many women's experiences of sexual violation: _I was just scared and just did what he wanted me to do_ (Turn 8). As Ehrlich (2002: 207) explains, questions such as Turn 4 in this extract presuppose 'the abusive, violent and forced nature of non-consensual sex ... [and] these presuppositions (which have a taken-for-granted quality) create a discursive space in which the fear and trauma that accompanies sexual violation and objectification make sense'. Interestingly, the lawyer's feminist response (in Turn 7) to the judge's intervention provided a mirror-image to the defence lawyer's strategy in Extract 6–x in Exercise 6.5 above. In that extract, we saw DC2 contesting David's use of the expression _they forced me_ to refer to police actions which did not involve any physical violence or threat. In Extract 6–xii on the other hand, the feminist lawyer used the term _forced_ to refer to _sex without [her client's] permission_, and distinguished that from sex in which _physical force [was] applied_ in response to the judge's criticism. This lawyer, like the teenage Aboriginal boy, was presumably taking a contextual view of the way in which a person can be _forced_ to do something against their will – taking into account such issues as imbalance between the participants in terms of their physical strength and control of the immediate situation, as well as the victim's fear and trauma. So, this civil case examined by Ehrlich (2002) shows the way in which a complainant's lawyer may reformulate a witness's story in such a way as to highlight her claims. It is not known whether there are also prosecutors in criminal rape trials who take an anti-patriarchal approach to questioning complainants in examination-in-chief. There are some structural parallels between the role of prosecutors in such cases and the role of the complainant's lawyer in civil cases such as Ehrlich has analysed. However, there are also important differences: in the criminal cases the prosecutor (or district attorney) is a government employee acting for the state, while in civil cases the lawyer is employed by the complainant to act as her advocate.

We have seen that in criminal trials the redefinition or reformulation of the complainant's account does not have to be restricted to the complainant's experiences during the event which is the subject of the case, such as the rape or abduction incident. As we saw in the Pinkenba case, defence counsel may ask more questions about the witness's background, character and earlier troubles with the law, than about the incident which is the subject of the case. This approach is allowed under rules of evidence, as it is considered to be relevant to the witness's honesty and credibility (also referred to as 'credit'). Thus, this provision enabled defence lawyers in that case to construct the identities of the complainants not as the victims of abuse, but as criminals who are a danger to society. In this way, the Aboriginal boys in the Pinkenba case were once again punished, humiliated and controlled in court. In my (2008a) analysis of this case, I concluded that the boys were taken for a ride literally by the police, and metaphorically by the justice system.

At this point, let us go back to the discussion of vulnerable witnesses in Chapter 5, and particularly to legislative developments, such as the New South Wales (NSW) law on improper questions (introduced in Section 5 of Chapter 5). Aboriginal child witnesses would be considered vulnerable witnesses in many jurisdictions because of both age and cultural background. Complainants in rape cases are also clearly vulnerable in this situation, and could also be provided some protection from improper questions under the NSW legislation (under the provision in subsection 2(a): 'any relevant condition or characteristic of the witness'). However, even in this comprehensive provision, the constraints on asking improper questions remain at the discretion of the court, that is the presiding judge or magistrate (see subsection 1 in Section 275a: '... if the court is of the opinion'). Thus, the ways in which witnesses can be harassed and humiliated, and the ways in which their stories can be changed, ultimately depend on the discretion of the individual judge or magistrate. And this discretion may well depend to some extent on the forcefulness of arguments made by lawyers on either side. Further, legislation in many jurisdictions is not as comprehensive and inclusive as in NSW, and their rules do not consider aspects of situated identity in assessing the relevance of provisions for vulnerable witnesses.

I conclude this chapter, and this Part on courtroom talk with a major issue about language and power. Many people question the injustices in the justice system, and even feel that the adversary system is 'out of control' (as reported by Conley and O'Barr 2005: 138). There are multiple reasons for this – for example, success in court often seems to be related to how much you can afford to pay a lawyer, as much as it does to justice. But not all of the reasons are financial: there are social, and political reasons, as we have seen. And there are many linguistic reasons for the feeling that the adversary system is out of control. In this Part of the book, we have seen a range of linguistic mechanisms which are allowed in the frequently unbalanced contest between lawyer and witness (Eades 2008a examines this issue in some depth). Sociolinguistic research shows that the basic human right of all people to be equal before the law appears to be currently unattainable for many people. What changes are required to address this fundamental injustice?

Exercise 6.7[xxii]

List some of the specific linguistic mechanisms allowed during cross-examination which support the feeling that the adversary system is out of control, drawing on examples in this chapter, and where relevant from earlier chapters. Then discuss to what extent the NSW legislation on improper questions in cross-examination (presented in Section 5 of Chapter 5) might be useful in addressing the most unjust excesses of cross-examination. Can you suggest other law reform measures to address the extremes of cross-examination?

Assignments and further research

1. Review Philips (1998) and examine the relevance of this study for your state/country. For example, how are judges selected there? On the basis of your observation of guilty pleas, is there variation in the ways in which judges interact with defendants during this event? Design a research study which could address questions about ideology in the languages of judges in your state/country.

2. **(Lx)** Read Matoesian (1993, 2001) and Ehrlich (2001) focusing on the linguistic means by which the patriarchal domination of women is reproduced in rape trials. Make a list of these linguistic means and give an example of each. Then, critically discuss Conley and O'Barr's (2005: 31–38) contention that the use of linguistic mechanisms which revictimise women in rape trials is not any different from 'the ordinary mechanics of cross-examination'.

3. **(Lx)** At the end of my analysis of courtroom talk and neocolonial control in Australia (Eades 2008a), I raise the question of the relevance of the Australian experience to that of other colonised people in former British colonies, such as Aboriginal people in Canada, Native Americans in the US and Māori people in New Zealand. Using the questions on p. 337 of that book as a point of departure, design a research project which would investigate this question in relation to one of these indigenous groups.

Part 3
Police interviews

7
Police interviews

1. Introduction		132
2. Communicating the suspect's rights		132
	2.1. Police caution/Miranda rights	132
	2.2. Rewriting the rights: a linguistic approach	134
	2.3. A sociolinguistic approach	135
	2.4. Do you understand that?	137
	2.5. Scripted cautions: for and against	141
	2.6. 'Perilously easy to waive ... nearly impossible to invoke'	142
3. Putting the Miranda rights in context		143
4. Truth or proof?		145
5. Cognitive interviewing and conversation management		147
6. Suspect resistance		149
7. From interview to written report		153
	7.1. Fabricated confessions and policespeak	153
	7.2. The blurring of source distinctions	156
	Assignments and further research	158

Police interviews

1. Introduction

Interviewing is a vital part of the work of police officers, and involves two types of interview: with suspects and with victims or witnesses. Most (socio)linguistic attention has focused on interviews with suspects in police custody, which are referred to in the US as 'interrogations'. In many other jurisdictions this term is no longer used because of its negative connotations and because it 'doesn't take account of the possibility of a willing subject' (Schollum 2005: 3). Instead the term 'investigative interviewing' is used to refer to any interview with victims, witnesses or suspects. There is little sociolinguistic research on interviews with victims and witnesses – apart from those involving child victim-witnesses in abuse cases. Thus, any students interested in pursuing either witness or victim interviews as an area of research, whether with children or adults, should start with the literature on police interviews with children discussed in Section 5 of Chapter 8.

For interviews with detained suspects, there has been linguistic interest since the late 1970s in the comprehensibility of rights texts, such as the Miranda warning in the US and equivalent police cautions in the UK and Australia.[24] These terms 'Miranda warning' and 'police caution' refer to the advice police are required to give suspects at the beginning of the interview about their rights, such as the right to a lawyer, and the right to silence. Following our examination in Section 2 of the rights delivery section of police interviews, we turn to approaches to questioning in police interviews. Section 3 shows how research in the US finds that police use interview strategies which enable them to 'get around' the rights of suspects. Section 4, looking at research in England and Wales and Australia, suggests that suspect interviews can be focused more on proof of guilt than simply obtaining 'the truth' about an event. And Section 5 introduces the two most influential approaches to the training of investigative interviewers: cognitive interviewing and conversation management. We then move in Section 6 to examine how suspects resist coercive police questioning. In Section 7, we look at how stories told to police by witnesses to events being investigated are transformed into written reports for the legal process. This connects to some of the work we saw in Section 4.3 in Chapter 3, and Sections 4 and 5 in Chapter 6 on recontextualisation of stories, and it will be taken up in Section 5 of Chapter 9, where we examine the language of lawyer interviews, and again in Section 4.3 of Chapter 11.

2. Communicating the suspect's rights

2.1. Police caution/Miranda rights

When a suspect in a criminal case is arrested by police, the suspect is then described as being under arrest, or detained, or being held in custody. It is often said that the main function of an interview with a detainee (or an interrogation) is to elicit the information required in order to make a charge (e.g. Auburn et al. 1995; Heydon 2005: 208; Shuy 1997: 178). A seminal review of literature and issues involved in the psychology of confessions in the US (Kassin & Gudjonsson 2004: 41) goes further, saying that the police interview of a detained suspect 'is a guilt-presumptive process, a theory-driven social interaction led by an authority figure who holds a strong a priori belief about the target and who measures success by the ability to extract an admission from that target'. However, current policing in some jurisdictions appears to take a different approach, as we see for example in an Australian manual of investigative interviewing (Ord *et al.* 2004) which says that the 'purpose of an interview with a suspect is no different to that with a witness: to ascertain the truth of the matter under investigation' (p. 73). These two different perspectives on the aim of police interviews with suspects are indicative of the wider debate on this point, characterised by Schollum (2005: 39) as aiming to induce a confession versus aiming to reach the truth. It seems that recent developments in police interviewing in England and Australia are directing police towards the 'reach the truth' approach, while in the US, the goal remains to induce a confession. Leo's (2008) detailed study of interrogations (= police interviews of detained suspects) in the US has revealed (p. 6) that 'their goal is to elicit incriminating statements from suspects in order to build the strongest possible case against them and thereby assist the prosecution in securing conviction and incarceration'.

People who are detained by the police have no right to leave, and police must advise them of their rights while in custody. It is this communication of rights which has received most linguistic attention in research on interviews with detained persons. While these rights appear to be well known from television police dramas, research has focused on the extent to which they are comprehensible. Do you know what these rights are? Can you recite any version of them?

In the US these rights are referred to as 'the Miranda rights' (also 'the Miranda warning'), after the name of the 1966 case which established that suspects being held in police custody should be advised of their rights before being interviewed (or interrogated) by police. The wording of the rights can vary slightly, but they are based on the judgment in the *Miranda* case which established them. (You will find one version on the next page, but don't turn the page before you have attempted to remember them yourself!)

In the US, police often carry a printed card which lists the Miranda rights (Leo 2008: 123). Rock (2007: 146) reports that there are also scripted cautions (= advice for detained persons about their rights) in Northern Ireland and Australia. In other countries the police caution is not necessarily scripted, meaning that police have some flexibility in how they advise detainees of their rights. Rock (p. 138) reports that for England and Wales there is an official wording, but police are at liberty to deviate from it, or to explain it in their own words, and Berk-Seligson (2009: 40) says the same liberty is permitted in the US. The same is also true for some jurisdictions in Australia, including New South Wales (NSW). What is the situation where you live?

Currently, rights for detained people in England and Wales are more complex than in other countries such as the US and Australia. This is because of changes in 1994 to the right to remain silent in police interviews. Detainees now receive this advice:

If you are asked questions about a suspected offence, you do not have to say anything. But it may harm your defence if you do not mention something which you later rely on in court. Anything you do say may be given in evidence [i.e. later, in court]. (Rock 2007: 272)

This explanation of the right to silence and its possible negative consequences, referred to in England and Wales as 'the caution', is typically delivered orally at the point of arrest (Rock 2007: 147). Rock (pp. 139–142) explains the legal background and consequences of this far-reaching modification of the right to silence. (And note that it is parallel to the situation, also in England and Wales, in which unfavourable inferences may also be drawn from a defendant's failure to answer a question or questions in court, see Note 5 in Chapter 2.)

Probably the earliest linguistic work on how police communicate suspects' rights to them was done by Brière (1978), in connection with an expert witness opinion he was asked to provide for court. In this case, the question was whether the suspect – who was from Thailand and had 'limited English speaking ability' – would have been able to understand his Miranda rights. As part of his work on this case, Brière investigated the linguistic difficulty of a typical formulation of the Miranda rights at that time. His method involved the use of several then-current psycholinguistic measures of readability and comprehensibility, which were based on measuring such features as the relative frequency of familiar to unfamiliar words, and the average sentence length in number of words. Based on these standardised tests, Brière concludes that the typical wording of the US Miranda Rights requires the equivalent reading skills of an 8th grade high school student for 50% comprehension, and of an 11th grade student for 100% comprehension. However, when adjustments are made for the oral nature of the delivery of the rights, the level of education required for 100% comprehension is raised to 13th grade.

Below is a typical version of currently used Miranda rights in the US (from Leo 2008: 123). It is a little simpler than the version which Brière (1978: 235) examined, and also than the version quoted by Berk-Seligson (2009: 40).

- You have the right to remain silent.
- Anything you say can be used against you in a court of law.
- You have the right to an attorney.
- If you cannot afford one, one will be appointed to you free of charge.

Leo also explains that there are additional statements in the Miranda rights advice in some jurisdictions. He gives this example (2008: 123): 'If you agree to answer questions, you may stop at any time and request a lawyer, and no further questions will be asked of you'. Were you successful in your earlier recall of the US Miranda rights? Can you see how the US right to silence differs from that in England and Wales (also given above).[xxiii]

2.2. Rewriting the rights: a linguistic approach

In Australia, the wording of the NSW police caution, particularly as it impacts on second language speakers of English, has been investigated by Gibbons (1990, 2001). Gibbons (2001) points out that there are actually several cautions, referring to the right to silence, the fact that the interview will be electronically recorded, and the question(s) which check that the interviewee has not received 'any threat, promise or inducement' (p. 456) to give specific answers, as well as a 'resumption' question used when an interview is about to recommence after an interruption. (While detainees also have the right to have another person present during questioning, who may be a lawyer, the communication of this right does not appear to be part of the official caution in NSW (NSW Police Service 1998.)

Exercise 7.1[xxiv]

Read the extract below from the version of the police caution being used in NSW in the 1990s (from Gibbons 2001: 451). Discuss with a classmate this part of the caution, which deals with the right to silence. Linguistics students should analyse the linguistic structures which could make this caution difficult to understand. Rewrite the caution in simpler language.

I am going to ask you certain questions which will be recorded on a video-tape recorder. You are not obliged to answer or do anything unless you wish to do so, but whatever you say or do will be recorded and may later be used in evidence. Do you understand that?

In discussing your work on this exercise with your teacher, you will have dealt with some grammatical features widely recognised by the 'plain language/plain English movement' as contributing to difficulties of understanding (see e.g. Charrow & Charrow 1979; Gibbons 2001: 448–450, 2003: 166–200; Tiersma 1999: 211–230).

Exercise 7.2[xxv]

Compare your revised version of this NSW right to silence caution with that recommended by Gibbons, and that finally adopted in the police Code of Practice for that state (as made available in the Teachers' notes). Discuss how you would approach the delivery of this part of the caution if you were a NSW police officer – as in England and Wales, you would not be obliged to use the exact wording of the scripted caution (NSW Police Service 1998: 52).

Gibbons explains (2001: 448) that there is a problem with using scripted (or prepared) cautions, such as the one prepared for NSW, in that they are designed for two quite different audiences. The primary audience is the suspect: if the caution is not intelligible to suspects, then it will have failed its primary purpose. But the caution must also be 'legally watertight', being acceptable in court as having provided the necessary information and rights to the suspect. Thus, this second audience comprises lawyers and judge, and possibly also a later appeal court. You will see that this is a similar problem to one of the problems of communication in court, discussed in Section 7 of Chapter 3 and also Section 2 of Chapter 2. Exercises 7.1 and 7.2 have looked at only a part of the NSW police caution and Gibbons' work on it. You are encouraged to read more about work on revising other sections of this police caution in Gibbons (2001, 2003: 196–198).

2.3. A sociolinguistic approach

We have seen that Brière uses a psycholinguistic approach, assessing the language of the Miranda rights in terms of measures of readability and comprehensibility, and Gibbons uses a linguistic approach to deconstruct the grammatical complexity of the right to silence part of the police caution in NSW. In a large study in England and Wales, Rock (2007) takes a sociolinguistic approach to the question of the comprehensibility of 'rights texts' – both spoken and written – used in police interviews. Central to this approach is an interactional perspective on understanding. Thus, Rock problematises 'restrictive notions of comprehension and comprehensibility' (p. 12), in which the text is examined without its users and contexts of use. Instead, the sociolinguistic approach focuses on meaning-making, both by police officers who deliver the rights, and by detainees who receive them. Thus, Rock is interested in more than the linguistic analysis of the form of rights texts (i.e. the wording of these texts), and she investigates the ways in which rights texts are presented and explained, and how detainees respond. Her multifaceted study includes analysis of seven different versions of the written rights text, interviews with 52 detainees about their reading and understandings of this written document, and examination of the delivery of 151 oral cautions in four major police forces in England and Wales, as well as interviews with 48 police officers.

In England and Wales the written rights text – a *Notice to Detained Persons* brochure – must be given to detainees before they are interviewed, and the rights which it must advise about are (Rock 2007: 36):

• the right to consult [police] *Codes of Practice*
• the right to have someone informed of their arrest
• the rights (sic) to consult privately with a solicitor
• the right to a copy of the *Custody record*
• the right to silence [discussed in Section 2.1 above]

The *Notice to Detained Persons* brochure goes further than the oral rights texts in other countries by also advising detainees of their entitlements while in custody, in addition to their rights, as listed above. These entitlements, which specify how the detainee should be cared for while in custody, include the provision of clean bedding and three meals a day with drinks, and details about provision of medical attention if required. Rock shows how the original version of the written rights and entitlement text (which she refers to as the 'parent text') was rewritten by a sergeant in the late 1990s. Rock discusses this revision, and the five different rewritings of it which she requested from writers working for a private communications (document design) company. Her detailed analysis highlights some of the complexities involved in simplifying written texts. But going beyond grammatical, lexical, typographic and organisational detail, Rock examines the diversity of ways in which the detainees respond to the text, showing that 'it is a great challenge to institutional texts' to respond to a variety of different purposes to which they are put by their intended audience (2007: 108). So, apart from those detainees who cannot read, and others who choose not to read the Notice, some simply skim the document to assess its relevance ('reading-to-assess'), some use it as a reference, for example while answering questions in the interview about whether or not to call a lawyer ('reading-to-do'), and others read it in their cells or even take it to read before detention ('reading-to-learn') (p. 108).

Rock's examination of the oral delivery of the caution points out that this oral caution is basically 'a written formulation which is spoken in use' (p. 143). In this way it is similar to other legal texts, such as pattern jury instructions, discussed in Section 6 of Chapter 3 above. One of the most interesting findings of this part of Rock's research is that there is much more than explanation going on in the seemingly highly regulated conversations surrounding detainees' rights in police interviews. She shows how both police officers and detainees can also be variously engaged in reassuring, persuading, making suggestions, empathising, learning, presenting identity and showing affiliation. We can see from this study that the communication of rights in police interviews involves much more than the form of words used.

2.4. Do you understand that?

Rock's work on the interactional nature of understanding resonates with Heffer's (e.g. 2005) work on communication with the jury, discussed in Sections 6 and 7 of Chapter 3 above. The sociolinguistic approach taken in these rather different studies of language in the legal process reminds us that 'understanding is something which one does rather than something which one has' (Rock 2007: 22). In this section we will look at the thorny issue of how police officers ascertain whether a suspect has understood the explanation or statement of their rights.

In NSW (Gibbons 2001) and the US (Shuy 1997), police are obliged to check the suspect's comprehension of the rights after they have been delivered orally, while in England and Wales it is optional (Rock 2007: 205). It is common for police officers to do this by asking a question like *Do you understand that?* after they have delivered the caution/Miranda rights. It seems that an affirmative answer to this question is taken as meaning that the suspect understands their rights. But Shuy (1997: 182–183) reports that in some of the cases he has worked on, suspects say *yes* to this question, when there is evidence that in fact they have little understanding. Sometimes the particular answers provide reason to doubt that a suspect has understood the rights, as in the example in Exercise 7.3.

Exercise 7.3
Read the extract below from an audiorecorded police interview with a murder suspect in a country town in NSW (check the transcription conventions Section 8, Chapter 1).

Extract 7–i Eades' unpublished transcription of official audiorecording

1. PO: OK- as I've already explained to you, Detective Bentham and I are making inquiries in relation to the death of Jonathan Fletcher- Jonathan died earlier this evening at the Mansfield Hospital as a result of a stab wound that he received to the stomach area- I'm going to ask you further questions about this matter- you do not have to say or do anything- but anything you say or do may be used in evidence- do you understand that?=

2. Sus: °°Yes I do°°.

3. PO: I'll just ask you again just to keep your voice up if you don't mind=

4. Sus. = °Yes I do°.

5. PO: My questions and the answers given by you will be recorded on the machine as this interview takes place- do you understand that?

6. Sus. = °Yes I do°.

7. PO: OK- the interview will be recorded simultaneously on three audiotapes- now we're having some problems with the videotape and the machine will not accept the videotape at this point in time- so we're just going to have to continue with the interview just on three audiotapes- all right?

8. Sus: °OK°.

> Discuss the suspect's answers, in particular any evidence which might suggest that he has not understood the questions he is answering. (The data for this extract and its continuation in Extract 7–ii below come from my work on this case in preparing an expert witness report for the defence.)

You will have noticed in this example that the suspect gave three identical answers in a row, in a barely audible voice, in Turns 2, 4 and 6. Interestingly, this rather formal and formulaic answer – *Yes I do* – was latched directly onto the question in Turns 4 and 6, indicating that the suspect had taken no time to think about the answer. None of these features of the answers can necessarily be taken to indicate either understanding or lack of understanding. However, the second *Yes I do* answer in this extract (in Turn 4) is a strange answer to the request given in Turn 3. In fact, the propositional content of this answer appears to suggest an unwillingness to cooperate with the request to speak with an audible volume (i.e. *Yes, I do mind*). However, the cooperative tone of voice and the subsequently slightly more audible volume in the answers, would suggest that the intention in this answer was to cooperate with the request. It is interesting that this answer is the formulaic *Yes I do* which was also given in the immediately preceding and following answers. This instance of apparent disjunction between the question in Turn 3 and the answer in Turn 4, might suggest that the suspect was not listening very closely to the questions, and/or not completely understanding them. This raises the definite possibility that the answers to these questions may not be agreement with the proposition in the question, but may in fact be answers of gratuitous concurrence. You may want to go back to Section 3 of Chapter 5 to refresh your memory about gratuitous concurrence. And, in answer to your question about the suspect's ethnicity in this example: yes, he is Aboriginal. (Although gratuitous concurrence is not restricted to Aboriginal people, it is widely used by them.)

We can see that asking *do you understand that?* after giving information or an explanation is not a good way of actually ascertaining whether a suspect has understood. Yet, this is exactly the approach recommended in a number of police forces, as we saw above. But there can be a number of reasons why an interviewee might answer *yes* to such a question when they don't understand, or are not sure if they understand, that is, why they might answer with gratuitous concurrence. Rock's (2007: 207–210) study sheds valuable light on this point. In the 151 police interviews she observed, 119 interviewees responded audibly to the comprehension checking question. Of these, 116 (= 97%) positively evaluated their comprehension, and not a single interviewee 'admitted complete incomprehension' (p. 207). Rock asked 85 of these detainees immediately after the interview to explain the caution in their own words. Only one interviewee explained all three parts of the caution, while more than half of them explained it incompletely and more than a quarter explained it incorrectly. Rock (pp. 207–209) discusses a number of reasons why detainees might claim to understand the caution and yet be unable to demonstrate this understanding. These reasons include conversational preference for agreeing to such a question, as well as psychological issues of acquiescence, and institutional pressures on detainees to say that they understand. And in Section 3 of Chapter 5, we saw some cultural reasons which are relevant to Australian Aboriginal people answering such a question with *yes* even when they don't understand it. But, as Shuy (1997: 184) points out, 'a self-reported measure of a person's ability to understand falls far short of adequacy in diagnosing that person's comprehension'.

What alternative approach could be recommended to police officers? The NSW Police Service (1998: 49) Code of Practice suggests a strategy of inviting the suspect to repeat the caution in their own words (see also Gibbons (2001: 445–447):

Before questioning suspects be satisfied they understand the caution and implications of the actions following it. Where you feel they do not understand the caution, ask clarifying questions and record the answers in full: e.g. *What do you understand by what I have just said?*

You can see that this strategy is recommended for situations where the interviewing officer feels that the interviewee does not understand the caution. Thus, there may well be situations where a suspect's *yes* answer to the *do you understand?* question is accepted without this further comprehension checking question, even though the suspect has not actually understood the rights. Now, let us return to the interview with the NSW murder suspect which started in Extract 7–i above. After the four questions we saw in that extract, there were six questions relating to the suspect understanding the protocol about the audiotaping of the interview, and confirming that he agreed to being electronically interviewed. Then the interview continued with the questions and answers given in Extract 7–ii.

Exercise 7.4[xxvi]

Read below the continuation of the police interview which began in Extract 7–i above.

(a) Discuss the first four questions in this extract (Turns 1, 3, 5, 7) and their answers in the light of Philips' (1998) work on 'coercion questions' asked in guilty plea hearings, discussed in Section 3 of Chapter 6 above.

(b) Discuss the police officer's checking of the suspect's understanding of his rights (which had been read to him before the tape recording started). How effective do you think the comprehension checking was? What evidence supports your assessment? How might this have been done differently?

(c) Discuss any other evidence which might suggest that the police officer was attempting to communicate clearly with the suspect.

(d) Discuss any questions which might have been asked in a different way in order to facilitate clearer understanding.

Extract 7–ii Eades' unpublished transcription of official audiorecording

1. PO: Has any person made any threat, promise or offered you anything to take part in this interview tonight?
2. Sus: (0.7) No.

3. PO: OK- no- nobody has threatened you at all?
4. Sus: No.

5. PO: OK- and nobody has promised you anything to take part in the interview?
6. Sus: No.

---

7. PO: And we haven't offered you any money or gifts or any advantage like that at all?

8. Sus: [no audible reply]

[biographical questions omitted here, dealing with full name, date of birth, address, employment, etc]

9. PO: OK- now do you agree that just a short time ago in the company of Wally Peters you were- Sergeant Allen read you your rights- as a person in custody?

10. Sus: °Yeah°.

11. PO: And that was this form here- this Caution and Summary of Part 10A on the Crimes Act?

12. Sus: °Yeah°.

13. PO: OK- and you signed that?

14. Sus: °Yes- I did- yeah°.

15. PO: OK- Now did you understand that=

16. Sus: =Yes.

17. PO: **What do you understand by- by your rights?**

18. Sus: Oh (0.8) my rights?

19. PO: Do you understand that this- while you're in police custody that police have certain – they have a duty of care to do certain things for you?

20. Sus: Yeah.

21. PO: OK- are you also aware that you're entitled to a support person?=

22. Sus: =Yes.

23. PO: And Wally's that support person- is that right?

24. Sus: Yes.

25. PO: And you're happy to have Wally as your support person?=

26. Sus: =Yes.

27. PO: OK- and do you also agree that you're entitled to some legal advice?

28. Sus: Yes, I am.

29. PO: And did you- now I understand that you waived your right- that you didn't want that legal advice or you=

30. Sus: °No I didn't (want)°.

31. PO: Now did you speak to someone earlier this afternoon about it?

32. Sus: No I never.

33. PO: You didn't speak to anyone? OK- but I think they were- they were contacted- I believe Kay Best from Aboriginal Legal Service was contacted.

34. Sus: I didn't know that.

35. PO: OK- and she was advised of the situation- now I understand that you don't wish to have a legal advisor here?

36. Sus: No.

37. PO: You don't wish to speak to anyone in relation to that?

38. Sus: No.

Why did the police officer in this interview provide no meaningful opportunity for the suspect to explain his rights in his own words, after having invited him to do just that (in Turn 17)? Why did he respond to the suspect's apparent lack of certainty in Turn 18 with a monologue in Turn 19, one that involved specialised legal register in the expression *a duty of care to do certain things for you*? Rock's analysis of police interviews, and her interviews with detainees and interviewing police officers found evidence that both parties tend to see a comprehension checking question – such as *what do you understand by your rights?* – as a face threatening act which amounts to a challenge to the detainee. Thus some detainees in Rock's study replied to comprehension checking questions from a police officer with defensive-sounding answers such as *I do know me rights* and *well I understand it anyhow* (2007: 210). Rock (pp. 212–214) also details 10 different strategies used by some police officers in attempts to present the comprehension checking question in a non-challenging way. Thus, one approach taken by officers is to present this as something that will be mutually beneficial for both officer and detainee, by saying something like *so that I'm satisfied you understand what it means*. Another police officer strategy is to present the request as a procedural one, by asking suspects to explain what they understand by their rights *for the benefit of the tape*.

> **Exercise 7.5**[xxvii]
> Role play the interaction between interviewing police officer and suspect in the act of delivering the caution and checking the suspect's comprehension of it. (Choose one of the three versions provided in this chapter, or research a version used in your local police station.) The student acting as police officer should endeavour to assist the suspect in understanding their rights, and should take as much care as possible in ascertaining whether the suspect understands the rights. The student acting as the suspect can think creatively about what kinds of confusion might arise in understanding what the police officer is communicating. Discuss the implications of this interaction for the work of police officers in rights delivery and comprehension checking.

2.5. Scripted cautions: for and against

We have seen that Gibbons (2001) worked with the NSW police force on revising the scripted caution in use in that state. Other linguists have discussed the advantages of a standardised scripted caution (Cotterill 2000: 21; Russell 2000: 45). And Solan and Tiersma (2005: 88–89) have suggested a preferred version for a scripted Miranda rights caution in the US. But Rock's detailed (2007) study of how cautions are delivered in practice, and of how suspects respond to the delivery has led her to problematise the use of scripted cautions. She points out (p. 162) that the use of a standardised scripted caution assumes that there is 'one optimal formulation for delivering any given proposition(s) to all people, across settings and situations'. Allowing officers to reformulate the caution in their own words recognises the problem with this assumption. However, this alternative approach leaves the onus of clear communication on individual police officers, who have to work out how to tailor the rights for each suspect, often after only brief contact with them.

Rock reports on the practical work which she did in conjunction with a police sergeant whose task was to produce a revised version of the *Notice to Detained Persons* brochure for national distribution throughout England and Wales. As Gibbons (2001) found in his work in helping to rewrite the police caution in NSW, not all of Rock's suggestions were taken up. Further, the final version distributed to police stations in England and Wales involved alterations made without consultation with either the sergeant or Rock, which resulted in making the document unnecessarily more complex than it need be, and included some problematic sentences such as 'The police will help you get in contact with a solicitor for you' (2007: 259).

Class debate[xxviii]

Debate the proposition that the Miranda rights/police caution should be delivered in a standardised, scripted wording. In preparation for this debate you should read Rock (2007: Chapter 8), also Cotterill (2000), Gibbons (2001), Russell (2000) and Solan and Tiersma (2005: 87–93). You should also go back to the discussion in Section 3 of Chapter 6 above about Philips' (1998) work on judges taking the guilty plea.

2.6. 'Perilously easy to waive ... nearly impossible to invoke'

Above we have seen psycholinguistic (Brière 1978), linguistic (Gibbons 2001) and sociolinguistic (Rock 2007) approaches to the ways in which police officers communicate rights texts. In the US, linguist-lawyer Ainsworth (1993, 2008) combines a legal approach with a sociolinguistic one in examining appeal cases which have dealt with how suspects can take up their Miranda rights. So, these are cases in which defendants have appealed to a higher court on the grounds that police had ignored their attempts to invoke their Miranda rights – for example to have a lawyer present – during the interview (interrogation) in which a confession was elicited. Examining a large number of appeals relating to the issue of whether particular suspects had waived their Miranda rights, Ainsworth (1993) shows how the legal doctrine which underpins the exercise of these rights privileges a direct, assertive speaking style, e.g. saying to the police officer *I want to have a lawyer here*. But taking up Lakoff's (1975) and subsequent sociolinguistic work on the tendencies of women to communicate in a less assertive, indirect style, Ainsworth argues that women are disadvantaged by this difference in communicative style. A statement like *I think I need a lawyer*, which contains a hedge (*I think*), can be ignored, because it is seen as not clear and unambiguous. While Ainsworth refers to the less assertive, indirect style as the 'female register', she believes that it is also used by members of certain ethnic communities and people who are 'socio-economically powerless' (1993: 286), consistent with the findings of the Duke courtroom research, discussed in Section 4.2 of Chapter 3. This important pragmatic issue raised by Ainsworth is yet to be researched for other social and cultural groups (but see the discussion of a related issue for Canadian Aborigines in Section 4.2 of Chapter 8).

In a new analysis of more recent cases, Ainsworth (2008) examines the linguistic ideologies[25] which underlie the legal insistence in the US on suspects' use of bald and completely unmodified imperatives such as *Give me a lawyer* or *I want a lawyer* in order to exercise this constitutional right. Ainsworth finds, for example, that language is seen to be 'essentially a transparent and objective medium of communication', and that the dominant view is that it is 'entirely fair to require speakers to conform to objective norms of communication, as those norms are imagined by the courts' (2008: 16–17). Based on this view of how language works, the legal rules governing the Miranda rights are 'applied acontextually, without regard for either conversational implicature[26] or for the ways in which power asymmetry may affect register selection[27]' (p. 16).

Exercise 7.6[xxiv]

The utterances listed below are all questions or statements made by detained suspects during police interviews (reported and discussed in Ainsworth 2008). In each case, the suspect was denied the right which they appeared to be invoking – that is, to have a lawyer brought into the interview. Also in each case, an appeal court determined that a valid invocation of the right had not been made.

For each utterance below, debate the proposition that it is an invocation of the right to a lawyer. Linguistics students should pay particular attention to the pragmatic meaning of the utterances.

1. Could I get a lawyer?
2. It seems like what I need is a lawyer ... I do want a lawyer.
3. I think I would like to talk to a lawyer.
4. If I'm going to jail on anything, I want to have my attorney present before I start talking to you about whatever it is you guys are talking about.
5. I'll be honest with you. I'm scared to say anything without talking to a lawyer.

Ainsworth's discussion of these and other examples comes to a rather depressing conclusion. She says (2008: 19) that 'citizens still have the constitutional rights outlined in *Miranda*, but as a practical matter, these rights are perilously easy to waive and nearly impossible to invoke'. Arguably, this situation which makes it almost impossible for defendants to invoke their Miranda rights suggests that the 'guilt-presumptive' nature of police interviews with suspects in the US – pointed out by Kassin and Gudjonsson (2004) (see Section 2.1 above) – extends beyond the courtroom to judicial stages of the criminal justice system.

3. Putting the Miranda rights in context

While Ainsworth has concluded that the Miranda rights are effectively unavailable to many suspects, Leo's (2008) comprehensive study of police interrogation in the US leads him to go further, saying that Miranda is 'largely irrelevant to modern American police interrogations' (p. 37). Arguably, his work would suggest that there is not much point in linguists continuing to pay attention to the wording of the Miranda rights. To understand how police have 'minimized the impact of Miranda by successfully adapting to it' (p. 124), see Leo (2008, especially 124–132 , also 1996a, 1996c).

Over many years, Leo has studied more than 2000 interrogations: through direct observation of hundreds of police interrogations, as well as analysis of electronic recordings of other interviews and transcriptions of others. He has also interviewed police interrogators, criminal justice officials and criminal suspects, studied police training manuals, and attended numerous police interrogation training courses and seminars. His findings present an alarming picture of police interrogations in the US, and are playing an important role in the movement to uncover police-induced false confessions and related wrongful convictions (see http://www.innocenceproject.org/).

While Leo's criminology research does not examine the details of talk, it provides important understandings about the strategies – verbal and non-verbal – used by US police to achieve their aims in this interview process, which is clearly guilt-presumptive. His work is essential reading for anyone who wants to do (socio)linguistic work on police interviews with suspects in the US. For these reasons, I will briefly summarise some of the most important findings of Leo's work (e.g. 2008, also 1996a, 1996b, 1996c).

First, according to Leo (e.g. 2008: 16), the legal process is supposed to separate four functions: investigative, prosecutorial, adjudicative and penal. But in the US, police are 'committed to the goal of incriminating the accused in order to assist the state in its prosecution' (p. 20). In this way they overstep their investigative function, taking on the prosecutorial function and they conduct interviews in an adversarial style (which should be reserved for courtroom hearings).

Second, interrogation methods are designed for guilty suspects, so police only interrogate people that they have decided are guilty. This decision is based on police officers' analysis of a suspect's verbal and non-verbal behaviour, using a variety of diagnostic tools. These tools purport to use such features as micro-tremors in the suspect's body, or the suspect's use of pronouns, to reveal deception. Leo's review finds that these tools are all fundamentally flawed: 'until a unique human lie response is discovered and can be measured there will be no reliable lie detector machine or technology' (p. 104).

Third, police interrogation is 'strategically manipulative and deceptive' (p. 5) and 'firmly rooted in fraud' (p. 25). Unlike the situation in other countries, police in the US are allowed to lie to suspects about matters such as the seriousness of the crime, as well as other evidence in the case. Leo found that police often tell suspects lies about fingerprint, or DNA, or polygraph or accomplice evidence. These lies purport to show that a suspect was at the scene of the crime, or involved in the crime, or committed the crime. At the same time, police often present themselves as wanting to help suspects, and they suggest that by cooperating and providing a full confession, suspects can receive a lighter sentence. In this way police take on the adjudicative and penal functions of the criminal justice process, over which in fact they are supposed to have no control.

Leo's research (e.g. 1996c, 2008) found that these 'sophisticated interrogation strategies' developed by police in response to the Miranda requirements 'are grounded in manipulation, deception and persuasion' (Leo 1996c: 284). These strategies are summarised (Leo 2008: 134, emphases in original) in this way:

Police interrogators use *negative incentives* to break down suspects' resistance, reverse his denials; lower his self-confidence; and induce feelings of resignation, distress, despair, fear and powerlessness (see Leo 1996a). Once a suspect is broken down, police use *positive incentives* to motivate him to see the act of complying and admitting to some version of the offence as his best available exit strategy and option, given his limited range of choices and their likely outcomes (Leo 1996a). Together, the use of negative and positive incentives are meant to make the suspect view the interrogation as a negotiation in which he has little meaningful choice but through which he can put an end to this distressing process and gain a better outcome before it is too late.

Leo analyses these negative and positive incentives in terms of their structure and psychology. But given that these strategies are carried out through talk, then they would warrant sociolinguistic attention. For example, how do police reverse suspects' denials and lower their self-confidence?

At the time of revising this book manuscript for publication, Berk-Seligson's (2009) analysis of coerced confessions in four cases involving Spanish speakers with varying degrees of English proficiency had just appeared. This important book contains the first detailed sociolinguistic examination of how US police succeed in coercing confessions in interviews with suspects. Given the focal importance in Berk-Seligson's study of the issues involving incipient bilingualism, we will discuss this study in Section 2 of Chapter 8. In showing 'ample evidence of coercion' by police (p. 214) in each of the four cases, Berk-Seligson gives linguistic substance to Leo's ethnographic analysis of police strategies of manipulation and deception, which he finds central to the widespread occurrence of false confessions and wrongful convictions. Some of the linguistic mechanisms which Berk-Seligson finds in coerced confessions are (pp. 110–111):

- extensive use of controlling or coercive questions;

- infrequent use of questions that invite narration, such as open-ended questions;

- interruptions;

- questions that involve multiple propositions;

- 'the repeated, frequent use of a monotonic declarative intonation pattern' suggesting the answer rather than asking a question;

- 'the creation of a veiled threatening tone through repeated admonitions to the suspect that he "answer carefully" because he was "under oath"'.

4. Truth or proof?

There seems to be a significant difference in police interviews with suspects in the US on the one hand, and countries such as England, Wales and Australia on the other. We have seen that suspect interviews (= interrogations) in the US are guilt-presumptive (Kassin & Gudjonsson 2004: 41), 'grounded in manipulation, deception and persuasion' (Leo 1996c: 284) and 'clearly based on interrogation and obtaining a confession' (Schollum 2005: 80). In England and Wales, on the other hand, suspect interviews have been seen as based on 'interviewing and obtaining the facts' (Schollum 2005: 80). (As we saw in Section 2.1 above, Schollum (2005: 39) characterises the two approaches as aiming to induce a confession versus aiming to reach the truth.) However, it must be pointed out that Leo's extensive study of what actually happens in police interviews in the US has no comparable counterpart in any other country. Thus, we cannot be sure about the extent to which police interview practice, as distinct from policy, is really distinctive in the US. But it does seem likely that mandatory electronic recording of suspect interviews in countries like Australia, England and Wales might have some influence on the ways in which police interview suspects, and on the development of what Milne and Bull (1999: 157) refer to as 'the investigative interviewing ethos'.[28]

However, there are some studies in England and Wales, and Australia which suggest that police are doing more than obtaining facts. As Baldwin (1993: 350–351) explains it, a key element in police interviews with suspects is 'concerned with future rather than past events'. The future events are the possible trial and any following legal proceedings. Thus, a 'main purpose of [police interviews with suspects] is … to seek to limit, close down, or pre-empt future options available to the suspect'. Baldwin's conclusion of his study of 400 videorecorded and 200 audiorecorded interviews in England and Wales is that police are aiming to construct proof rather than establish truth. Baldwin's (1993) investigation of police interviewing techniques found that most interviews involved 'relatively simple and straightforward interchanges with reasonably compliant suspects' (p. 331). Almost two-thirds of the interviews took less than half an hour, and a third of all suspects admitted culpability at the beginning of the interview (and many of the suspects had seemingly also done this before the interview). In many of the interviews police officers had a presumption of guilt in their questions, including some in which 'admissions were obtained only in response to a series of leading questions' (p. 341).

The interviews examined by Baldwin were carried out in 1989–90, only about five years after significant changes to policing in England and Wales with the introduction of the 1984 Police and Criminal Evidence Act.[29] Further, these interviews were done before the national introduction of police interview training began in 1992, drawing on cognitive interviewing and conversation management approaches (to be introduced below). Now that training has been well established for close to two decades, it would be important to investigate police interviews with suspects to see if Baldwin's conclusion in his study of interviews done 20 years ago still applies to suspect interviews today: a good thesis/dissertation topic! In Section 7 of Chapter 8, we will see how one thesis (Jones 2008a) uses sociolinguistic microanalysis to investigate police interviews with ten Afro-Caribbean and ten White British suspects. A major finding of Jones' study is that there was a 'marked contrast' between the two groups of interviews. In the Afro-Caribbean interviews 'the police followed a preferred version of events in which the suspects were guilty'. But in the White British suspect interviews 'responses which did not point to guilt were not rejected' (p. 224).

While Baldwin's approach does not involve analysis of the details of talk, Heydon's (2004, 2005) analysis of 13 Australian police interviews with suspects uses sociolinguistic microanalysis to examine how police officers structure and manage the interviews. Police conduct the interviews to fulfil institutional requirements (such as delivering the caution) as well as eliciting a confession. Using Goffman's (1974) work on participation frameworks and participant roles, Heydon shows the difference in the way that talk is ordered in the opening and closing sections on the one hand and the information gathering section on the other. In the opening and closing sections, the interviewing police officer is the animator of the talk – that is the person who produces the actual utterances – while the police institution is assigned two roles: of author, having produced the cautions delivered by the officer, for example; and principal, being ultimately responsible for what the police officer says in these official sections of the interview. But during information gathering, interviewing officers work to produce a participation framework in which the suspect fulfils all three roles. In Heydon's study, suspects only cooperated with this framework if the police version of events was congruent with their own.

5. Cognitive interviewing and conversation management

Before we move from looking at what police do in suspect interviews to how suspects can resist, this section will outline the most influential approach to suspect interviewing, known as 'cognitive interviewing', and then briefly introduce the approach known as 'conversational management'. Although the work on these approaches has not been done by sociolinguists, it is important for a textbook on sociolinguistics and law to introduce these approaches. Any training or technique for interviewing is essentially about how to ask questions and respond to interviewees' answers. Although cognitive interviewing and conversation management have been developed primarily from psychological, communication and training research, future sociolinguistic research can contribute to understandings of how these approaches work in practice.

Cognitive interviewing is central to policing in England and Wales, and in many other jurisdictions. Originating from US psychological experimental research (e.g. Geiselman *et al.* 1984), the cognitive interview is based on four principles which enhance memory-retrieval for eyewitness reports. These four principles ('general memory retrieval techniques' p. 76) are summarised in Schollum's (2005: 58) easily accessible review for the New Zealand Police Commissioner of investigative interviewing literature. (For a fuller discussion see Milne and Bull 1999.)

Report everything (RE): The witness is asked to report everything remembered about the incident and all surrounding circumstances (no matter how fragmentary and regardless of apparent importance
Reverse order (RO): The witness is asked to recall the events in a variety of chronological sequences (e.g. beginning to end, reverse order, forwards or backwards from particular points)
Change perspective (CP): The witness is asked to consider the event from a different perspective (e.g. from the point of view of someone else present at the scene)
Context reinstatement (CR): The witness is asked to focus his or her mind on the context surrounding the incident (e.g. features of the physical environment, his or her thoughts and feelings at the time, and so on)

Fisher and Geiselman (1992) incorporate these principles of memory enhancement in their cognitive interview format, which has five ordered sections: Introduction, Open-ended Narration, Probing Memory Codes, Review and Closing the Interview (p. 145). Although it was developed by psychologists as a result of research on memory, cognitive interviewing should be of considerable interest to sociolinguistic studies of police interviews, given that it provides guidelines for the discourse structure of investigative interviewing and the linguistic form of interviewers' turns.

Key features of the Introduction section are the need to control any eyewitness anxiety and to develop rapport, as well as to explain the aims of the interview. In the Open-ended Narration phase, the interviewer focuses on eliciting free narratives within the 'report everything principle'. Linguistic features of this section include the use of open-ended questions (to be discussed below), as well as not interrupting the interviewee and allowing for their pauses. Following the witness's open-ended narrative, the interview moves to a more focused phase (Probing Memory Codes), taking up on images of people, objects and actions mentioned by the witness and asking probing questions. These questions, both open-ended and closed questions, aim to 'encourage the witness to develop the image in [their] mind as sharply as possible, and ... describe it in detail' (Fisher & Geiselman 1992: 153). In this section the interviewer also provides opportunities for the interviewee to reverse the order of their account, and to change perspective, consistent with the principles introduced above. In the Review phase, the interviewer repeats the relevant information provided by the interviewee, and provides an opportunity for any further memories to be volunteered. At this stage, the interviewer can also probe for more information. The final section – Closing the Interview – has three specific goals, namely '(a) collecting background information, (b) extending the functional life of the interview, and (c) creating a positive, lasting impression' (p. 156).

As its use in real-life situations has increased (after its initial basis in experimental work), the cognitive interview approach has been widely promoted as a framework for structuring investigative interviews.[30] Since its original development for police interviewing of eyewitnesses, cognitive interviewing is now recognised in many jurisdictions as the preferred approach to investigative interviewing of any cooperative interviewee, and thus is also often seen as applicable for many suspect interviews. As Powell et al. (2005: 12) point out, there is considerable overlap between various police interview protocols, most of which are influenced to a greater or lesser degree by the principles of cognitive interviewing. These various protocols generally 'acknowledge that the most useful information obtained in any forensic interview is that which is given in a free narrative response' (p. 18). Thus, consistent with the Open-ended narration phase in cognitive interviewing, the recommended procedure is to start with invitations for the interviewee to tell their story in their own words with a prompt such as *Tell me everything you can remember about [the day or the event in question].* Such an invitation or directive is often referred to in the interviewing literature as an 'open-ended question' (although linguists typically restrict the label 'question' to utterances with a question form, for example including rising intonation).[31] Powell et al. (2005: 19) give a definition of open-ended questions that reflects the use of this term in the interviewing literature, namely: questions 'that require multiple-word responses and allow interviewees the flexibility to choose which aspects of the event they will describe'. Other similar 'open-ended questions' can then be used to encourage the interviewee to expand on their narrative, such as *What else can you remember about [one particular part of the day or event]?* Milne and Bull (1999: 22) point out that an important benefit of using open-ended questions is that they give the interviewee control of the flow of information, and they minimise the risk of interviewers imposing their own version of events on the interviewee. Open-ended questions elicit free narratives, which have been found in psychological research to result in the most accurate information, but not necessarily the most detail. Thus, interviewers are generally encouraged to follow up the free narratives elicited by open-ended questions with more focused questions, which fill in more detail, such as *What time did you leave the club? Who did you leave with?* (Ord et al. 2004: 90).

In Section 5 of Chapter 8, we will see the influence of cognitive interviewing in a number of protocols for investigative interviewing with children. There is scope for sociolinguistic research to complement existing psychological research on memory by examining the interactional dimensions of remembering, and implications for ways of talking in interviews. This could follow on from work in discursive psychology which examines remembering as a social activity rather than memory as a personal mental capacity, such as Edwards and Potter (1992) and Middleton and Edwards (1990). Such an approach is consistent with sociolinguistic work on the interactional processes involved in storytelling (e.g. Norrick 1998, 2005; Schiffrin 2006), which we will glimpse in relation to the production of written summaries of police interviews (in Section 7.2 below), written affidavits based on lawyer interviews (in Section 5 of Chapter 9), as well as the assumptions about storytelling and retelling (in Section 4.3 of Chapter 11).

While the cognitive interview and related approaches have been developed for interviewing cooperative interviewees (whether witnesses or suspects), some police interview guidelines have developed alternative and/or additional strategies for interviewing uncooperative interviewees (also whether witnesses or suspects). These approaches seem to differ from cognitive interviewing approaches by the addition of 'challenges', in Ord et al.'s (2004: 81) terms, which serve to enable police officers to 'confront ... lies and inconsistencies'. Ord et al. recommend that once an objective has been selected for challenging, the interviewer should start using open questions to seek an account of the issue being challenged. Once the interviewee has provided an explanation, the interviewer should probe the explanation with WH-questions (such as *who, where, when, why, how*), and then 'summarise, checking for accuracy and correct interpretation' (p. 95).

A comprehensive approach to interviewing non-cooperative or resistant witnesses or suspects is the approach developed by Shepherd (e.g. 2007), known as 'conversation management'. Based on the view that interviewee non-cooperation is often a result of the way the police officer conducts the interview, the conversation management approach aims to 'assist the interviewer to understand the witness's motivational blocks to volunteer information and to parry the witness's conversation diverting tactics by redirecting the conversation to the task at hand' (Powell et al. 2005: 12). Milne and Bull (1999: Chapter 4) provide a good summary of the details of conversation management, which are too complex to deal with here. They include five pre-interview steps, four interview phases, two post-interview steps, six micro-skills and four macro-skills. Some of the micro-skills are cognitive, involving observation and memory, for example. Others are linguistic, such as 'appropriate questioning which allows the elicitation and subsequent probing of the initial and subsequent interviewee accounts' (Milne & Bull 1999: 63). The macro-skills are primarily cognitive and analytical, such as 'the ability to detect changes in emotional state, motivation, attitude and disposition'. To date, there does not appear to have been any sociolinguistic analysis of how conversation management works in practice. A good thesis/dissertation topic perhaps?

6. Suspect resistance

We now turn from a focus on what police do in suspect interviews to what suspects do. It is not easy for researchers to access data from the information gathering section of police interviews, owing to its confidential nature and its role in not-yet-completed legal proceedings. Occasionally, official transcripts of police interviews are made publicly available, as was the case in 2004 with two of the many police interviews from a high profile English murder case, that of Dr Harold Shipman, who in 2000 was found guilty of the murder of 15 of his patients. Two different sociolinguistic studies have been carried out on these interviews (Haworth 2006; Newbury & Johnson 2006), and at the time of writing this book, the transcripts and tapes of these two interviews are still available online.[32] These two sociolinguistic analyses were both published in late 2006, and seemingly the authors of each of these studies were unaware of the complementary study. Neither of these studies focuses on the police officers' approaches to questioning.

Interestingly, both studies highlight the ways in which the suspect, Shipman, resisted the power of the police interviewer over him (although the scholars had not chosen to examine the same interview). As Heydon (2005) found with her Australian police interviews, Shipman was in his interviews 'broadly cooperative, but at times resistant' (Newbury & Johnson 2006: 215). These studies take up a theme we looked at in relation to courtroom talk in Section 2 of Chapter 6. While the interviewer in legal contexts – both courtroom cross-examination and police interviews – has a great deal of situational and institutional power over the witness, this power is not static. Indeed, the suspect in these two police interviews exercised considerable situational power in the interview, and as Haworth (2006: 746) points out, the interviewing police officer had to 'continually assert his power in order to maintain it'.

For example, in the interview examined by Haworth, the police officer opened the questioning by saying *there's one or two points we'd like to pick up on from*, but he was overlapped by the suspect saying *can I clarify something first?* (p. 745). This led to the suspect introducing the first topic of the interview, rather than the police officer, who would typically be the participant to control the topical agenda of the interview. Another way that this suspect exercised power over the police officer was by asking him questions, such as *may I ask whether the house was searched?* (p. 751). Haworth notes that this is the same strategy reported by Harris (1989) in her study of defendants asking 'counter-questions' of magistrates in an English County Magistrates Court (discussed in Section 2 of Chapter 6 above).

These two studies of the Shipman police interviews remind us that power is not some static thing held by interviewing officers because they are members of the police force. Rather, power is a dynamic relationship, which interviewer and interviewee work for. As with lawyers in court, officers in police interviews have many advantages in this power relationship: due to their institutional role, their general control over the topics of the interview, their ability to ask coercive questions, and their legal power to detain suspects against their will. Legally, suspects have the power to withhold answers, although as we have seen above, this power may be compromised by a number of strategies used by the police. What other power do suspects have in police interviews? Their legal power also includes the right to have a lawyer present, who may intervene in police questioning (for some examples, see Newbury & Johnson 2006: 236, Turns 95, 101, 103, 105). The situated interactional power of suspects also includes the power to negotiate control over the talk to some extent, by changing topic and asking questions, as we have seen.

Further examples of the situated interactional power exercised by Shipman are found in
Newbury and Johnson's (2006) examination of the second of the two publicly available police
interviews in this case. In their discussion of Shipman's resistance, they show how he 'actively
resist[ed] powerful moves by the police questioner ... through contest, correction, avoidance
and refusal' (p. 214). In using these strategies he appeared to be cooperating in the interview,
but he was adopting 'strategies of resistance ... that are acceptable within the rules and roles
constituted by the institutional interviewing situation' (p. 214).

Exercise 7.7[xxx]

Read the following interactions taken from the Shipman police interview analysed by
Newbury and Johnson (2006). Discuss for each of the examples which strategy of
resistance to police power is being used: contest, correction, avoidance or refusal. Also
discuss Newbury and Johnson's claim that Shipman was appearing to be cooperative
while he was using strategies of resistance.

(a) **Extract 7–iii official police transcript**
1. P: ... You told her you can remember she refused the treatment and that's what's put on these
          false records isn't it?
2. Sus: You see you're stating the obvious, that doesn't need an answer.

(b) **Extract 7–iv official police transcript**
1. P: You attended the house at 3 o'clock and that's when you murdered this lady and so much
          was your rush to get back, you went back to the surgery and immediately started altering this
          lady's medical records. We can prove that only minutes after 3 o'clock on that date you were
          fabricating that false medical history for this woman. You tell me why you needed to do that?
2. Sus: There's no answer.

(c) **Extract 7–v official police transcript**
1. P: I'd like to put it to you doctor, that you were the person who administered that lady with the
          drug, aren't you?
2. Sus: No.

(d) **Extract 7–vi official police transcript**
1. P: From the progression you've noted on your records this was not something that would have
          been expected.
2. Sus: This was a progressive angina. And people do die of coronaries with no preceding history of
          angina.

In using these strategies of resistance, the suspect Shipman worked to exert his own power
in the police interview. You might see some similarity here with the answers in courtroom
cross-examination of a provincial premier in Canada, whose resistance has been analysed by
Ehrlich and Sidnell (2006), and discussed in Section 2 of Chapter 6 above. Ehrlich and
Sidnell show how this witness challenged the presuppositions in questions put to him in
cross-examination. In making these challenges to presuppositions, he used strategies such as
Newbury and Johnson's avoidance (e.g. Ehrlich and Sidnell 2006: 664, Extract 8b) and
correction (e.g. Ehrlich and Sidnell 2006: 672, Extract 12a, starting at Line 23), in addition to
directly addressing presuppositions, with such comments as *you assumed ... and I think that's
not an assumption you ought to make* (p. 666). Both the premier in this courtroom hearing and

Dr Shipman were interviewees who had considerable institutional status and social privilege. Perhaps it is not surprising therefore, that these interviewees had some success in their situational power struggles with their interviewers, the lawyers and the police officer. In fact, Haworth (2006) shows how Shipman overtly appealed to his institutional status in answering accusatory questions in the police interview. The police officer pointed to a problem with Shipman's records on the victim's medical file, saying that *it doesn't actually say you'd taken a blood sample from her.* His reply was ... *it's not the custom of most general practitioners to write 'I have taken a blood sample which would consist of this this and this'.*.... Haworth points out that with this reply Shipman used 'his professional status as a shield, shifting the focus of blame onto the institution to which he belongs, instead of on himself as an individual member' (p. 747). Shipman also attempted to undermine the institutional status of the interviewing police officer. Towards the end of the interview, the police officer made a direct accusation of murder, saying *I suggest to you that you have injected Mrs Grundy with a fatal overdose of morphine and brought about her death.* Shipman's answer started with a bald denial, and then his indirect explanation of how the victim died of a drug overdose was delivered in the form of a criticism of the police officer's professional credibility: *No- and you tell me that people in Hyde don't have access to drugs- I think you should talk to your drug squad.*[33]

We have seen that language use in the information gathering phase of police interviews can be a ripe area for investigating power struggles and their discursive enactment. But Haworth (2006: 756) reminds us that there are other important issues which researchers may miss if we focus only on the immediate context of the police interview. Despite Shipman's skilful use of resistance in his answers to questions in the police interview, many of these answers became problematic to his defence during the trial, because of eyewitness evidence presented by police. For example, to counter Shipman's explanations that the victim Mrs Grundy was a drug user and his assertion that he did not keep dangerous drugs, police presented evidence of an eyewitness who had seen him remove drugs after the death of a patient, and they had also found one of the drugs in question at his home.

The interviewee studied by Haworth, and Newbury and Johnson was clearly someone with pertinent educational and social experiences which might help to equip him with linguistic resources to resist coercion in an interview. But the same cannot be said of the 18-year-old undocumented Mexican man arrested for murder and attempted rape in San Francisco, whose resistance to police coercion is investigated by Berk-Seligson (2007, 2009: 71–100). The strategies he used included responding to questions in brief, non-elaborated answers, as well as vague, unspecific expressions, and repeating the same answer, whether or not it answered the question being asked. Although this man was found guilty at trial of both first-degree murder and attempted rape, the first of these convictions was overturned on appeal 'on the basis of the use of coercive interrogation tactics by the police in extracting a confession from him' (2007: 18). Interestingly, the conviction of attempted rape was not overturned – apparently because of the convincing physical evidence – and Berk-Seligson found that in his police interview he 'never relented on' denying this accusation (p. 39). The issues in the case are complex, and they include the use of one of the interviewing police officers as interpreter (as discussed in Berk-Seligson 2002b, 2009: 38–70, see Section 2.1 in Chapter 8 below). Berk-Seligson provides a thought-provoking discussion of this case and the reasons for this suspect's unwavering resistance on the attempted rape accusation – although on the murder accusation he finally 'implicated himself sufficiently to be considered to have confessed' (2007: 19). (See Assignment topic 8 at the end of this chapter.)

7. From interview to written report

7.1. Fabricated confessions and policespeak

We have seen research on police questioning and on how witnesses resist police coercion. Another concern of sociolinguists has been with the transformation of what witnesses and suspects say in police interviews into official records of the interview or summary statements.

Some of the earliest forensic linguistic work was focused on cases in which suspects alleged that confessions attributed to them in their police interview had been fabricated. In Australia, this practice was so widely suspected and discussed before mandatory recording of confessions, that for several decades it has been referred to in Australian English with a single lexical item *to verbal*, meaning to fabricate a confession. The corresponding noun *a verbal* refers to a fabricated confession.

Can fabricated confessions be detected through linguistic analysis? The short answer to this question is 'sometimes'. For example, in a Queensland case in which I gave expert evidence in the mid-1980s, an Aboriginal English-speaking appellant alleged that he had been verballed in the police interview, which provided an apparent confession to a gruesome murder. My analysis showed how the allegedly verbatim answers attributed to this man in the typed police record of interview used English differently from typical Queensland Aboriginal English usage at the time, as well as from this man's speech patterns in other interviews (Eades 1993, 1995a, 1997, 2007b). Other Australian linguists have given similar evidence in verballing cases involving speakers of English as a second language, in which the allegedly verbatim confession revealed a proficiency in English which was significantly higher than that of the suspect (e.g. Gibbons 1995; Jensen 1995).

In England, the best-known linguistic work on fabricated confessions has not been in cases with second language or second dialect speakers. Without such clear clues of dialectal difference or unbelievable levels of language proficiency ascribed to second language speakers, how can linguists contribute to questions of authorship? Coulthard (e.g. 1994a, 1994b, 2004) has used corpus analysis in some striking and controversial cases, including those of the Bridgewater Four and Birmingham Six. For example, in his work for the review of the 1950s Bentley case (Coulthard 1994a, 2000; see also Coulthard & Johnson 2007: 173–180), Coulthard was struck by the use of the temporal adverb *then* in the allegedly dictated confession of 582 words (at the time of the Bentley case, confessions were produced as monologue narratives, rather than answers to interview questions). Figure 7.1 summarises Coulthard's comparison of the use of temporal *then* in Bentley's alleged confession, with its use in a small corpus of three ordinary witness statements, and a small corpus of three statements from police officers. What was more striking about the frequency of temporal *then* in the Bentley 'confession' is its occurrence after the subject (linguistically referred to as 'postpositioning'), as in *I then caught a bus to Croydon*. You can see that its use in the Bentley confession was strikingly similar to its use in the statements by police officers, compared to its absence from the ordinary witness statements. And yet even more striking is the comparison between the use of postpositioned temporal *then* in the expression *I then* in the Bentley 'confession' with its quite rare occurrence in the large Cobuild Corpus of Spoken English, a subset of the corpus known as the Bank of English. (You can see that when Coulthard did this analysis the Cobuild Corpus of Spoken English comprised 1.5 million words.)

Corpus	Derek Bentley 'confession'	Ordinary witness oral statements	Police officer written statements	COBUILD Corpus of Spoken English
Total words	582	930	2270	1.5 million
Temporal *then*	once every 58 words	once in 930 words	once every 78 words	[Not given]
I then	once every 194 words	nil	once every 119 words	once every 165,000 words

Figure 7.1 Temporal *then* in the Bentley case (based on Coulthard 1994a)

Linguists who investigate allegedly fabricated confessions have examined a number of linguistic features in questioned documents and compared them to other features of spoken and written texts. As with the example from the Bentley case, a number of cases in which linguists have given expert evidence relating to fabricated confessions have revolved around linguistic features which are clear linguistic hallmarks of either written texts or 'policespeak' (rather than stories or answers from suspects as they purport to be).

'Policespeak' is the term first used by Fox (1993) to refer to the linguistic features which characterise police statements, which we could also call police register. Fox examined a corpus of 'less than twenty police statements', and found a number of features which were quite unusual, when compared to the Bank of English corpus, which at the time of her research contained 150 million spoken and written words.[34] Although Fox's policespeak data for this project comprised written police statements, several of the features have also been found in spoken police talk (see Coulthard and Johnson 2007: 76–77; Gibbons 2003: 85–87; Hall 2008). The following list presents some features of policespeak (we have already seen an example of feature (i) in the discusssion above:[35]

(i) Expressions of time and frequency (such as *then, at first, continually*) are often found immediately following the subject, compared to more typical usage where these expressions either precede the subject or follow the verb.

(ii) The passive voice is used frequently.

(iii) Vocabulary is often much more formal than in conversational usage (such as saying that police *retain* possession of property, rather than *keep* it, and that jewellery is *recovered* rather than *found* or *got back*). Sometimes this formal vocabulary may be used for specific legal reasons.

(iv) A focus on precision often results in over-elaboration (Gibbons 2003: 85) or 'unnatural overspecificity' (Fox 1993: 188), such as referring to a man as *a male person*.

(v) A focus on legal accuracy may result in using generic reference rather than a common specific word (for example using the term *residential address* rather than *house*, in order to include possible reference to a house, or apartment).

Features (i), (iii) and (iv) are found in a typical popular, but accurate, representation of policespeak: *The male person then proceeded in a northerly direction.* Do you remember seeing an example of policespeak in an earlier chapter?

Exercise 7.8[xxxi]

Examine the statement (repeated from Exercise 1.1 in Chapter 1) made by a police officer to an eighteen-year-old suspect in a recorded interview in the police station:

As I already informed you Jane, I'm making inquiries in relation to an amount of green vegetable matter which was located in the glove box of a motor vehicle today searched by myself and Detective Sergeant John Miller.

What features of policespeak can you find in this statement?

Since the introduction of mandatory electronic recording of police interviews with suspects in cases involving serious crimes,[36] there is much less linguistic expert evidence required in cases of verballing. However, the linguistic analysis of texts in order to resolve disputes over authorship has expanded into other forensic fields (such as the analysis of written threats, where the identity of the author is unknown, and suicide notes, where the author's identity might be contested). Authorship analysis has also been developed for the detection of plagiarism (see Woolls & Coulthard 1998; Woolls 2003). The forensic linguistic field of authorship analysis is beyond the scope of this textbook, but if you are interested in pursuing it, you could start with Chaski (2001), Grant (2007, 2008) and Howald (2008), in addition to the references cited in this section.

Interestingly, there appears to be little attention in the US to the linguistic analysis of fabricated confessions. Shuy (1998: 94–104, 154–173) discusses two apparent cases, and Stygall (2008) analyses the alleged confessions of four women to child sex abuse. Stygall's narrative analysis found 'unusual differences' (p. 221) between the 'confessions' attributed to these women and their narratives in other contexts. She also found (p. 225) that the confessions were 'too much alike'. And Berk-Seligson (2009: 171–200) analyses a confession statement attributed to a Spanish speaker, pointing to a number of linguistic features which support the accused's appeal lawyers' claim that the statement was 'inauthentic' (p. 179).

Perhaps it is not so surprising that there has been little other analysis of fabricated confessions in the US, when we consider Leo's (e.g. 2008) findings about police interviews with suspects, discussed in Section 3 above. The highly coercive, deceptive and manipulative nature of police interrogations in that country may mean that it is often 'unnecessary' for police to fabricate confessions. Leo provides case examples of police officers apparently instructing suspects under great pressure about what information to give in answer to their questions. It appears that the tactics which are allowed in US police interrogations are often sufficient to induce suspects to produce a false confession in their own words. This is a subtle difference from the situation in Australia and the UK, where – before mandatory tape recording of suspect interviews – police were able to attribute their own words to suspects in so-called 'confessions'. While linguistic analysis has been used to examine questions of allegedly fabricated confessions, as we have seen, it is not able to address the question of whether or not a suspect's confession was his or her own idea.

7.2. The blurring of source distinctions

Even when police interviews are electronically recorded, there can be concerns about the ways in which police produce summaries of these interviews. These concerns do not necessarily relate to allegations of police malpractice, but rather to the ways in which interactionally produced texts are presented in a summary monologic form. This work connects to work on other ways in which the recontextualisation of a person's story at various stages in the legal process can result in some significant transformations – for example, in cross-examination in court as we saw in Sections 4 and 5 of Chapter 6, and in the production of affidavits following lawyer interviews as we will see in Section 5 of Chapter 9. (Another example from a police interview will be discussed in Section 4.2 of Chapter 8.)

Rock (2001) examines the process by which a witness's account of an event to an interviewing police officer is worked into a witness statement, over its four tellings in the police interview. In her analysis of this one particular story in her database of more than 20 statements, the interviewing officers' questions worked over time to co-construct with the witness an account of what had happened. Rock compares the production of the witness statement with the way in which the 'sea mills rocks into stones and stones into sand' (p. 45). Her analysis of this question–answer work in producing the witness's story, leads her to conclude that 'a tremendous amount of interactional currency is spent in the production of a witness statement' (p. 69). For example, the final written witness statement included the sentence 'At about 6pm or earlier we left Jerry's house' (p. 56). Rock shows the process by which the police officer worked with the witness to co-produce this statement over several different occasions during the interview, first asking the witness *at what time did you leave?* The witness's answer was *we left about- we was there for about- say about three hours I think I'm not sure- bout three hours two hours*. The police officer then suggested *til about six o'clock do you think?* Although the witness replied *yeah around six o'clock yeah*, later in the interview he did not accept the police officer saying *so you all left about 6 o'clock*. He said *I'm not sure if it was about six it's probably earlier about more earlier than that ... I'm not sure of the time*. Still later in the interview the police officer suggested *you left there- about six o'clock or earlier*, to which the witness replied *yeh*. It is this formulation made by the officer and agreed to by the witness – *about six o'clock or earlier* – which appeared in the summary witness statement. Rock argues (2001: 58) that 'in view of the way [this] was discovered, we might want to question its usefulness as evidence and a potential investigative foothold'.

Rock's analysis resonates with two European studies which also highlight the process by which stories are generated in police interviews. These studies, by Jönsson and Linell (1991) in Sweden and by Komter (2002, 2006b) in the Netherlands, examine police interviews with suspects, which in these countries are presented in court in a written summary monologic form. Thus they function rather differently from police interviews with suspects in countries such as England and Wales, the US and Australia today, where the full transcript of the interaction – comprising questions and their answers – can be, and often is, used during court proceedings. Despite this difference in how the summary functions in the legal system, the sociolinguistic research on the production of these summaries is directly relevant to the concerns raised in Rock's work on witness statements, and to broader concerns about the production of summary statements in the legal process (to be taken up again in Section 5 of Chapter 9, and in Section 4.3 of Chapter 11).

Jönsson and Linell's (1991) study examines 30 police interrogations in Sweden, focusing on what they call the 'story generation processes', by which written police reports result from 'dialogic interviews'. Their study compares the two versions of the suspects' stories, finding differences in several respects: compared to the suspects' oral accounts, the written monological versions had a more clearly elaborated narrative structure and a legally relevant perspective, as well as more precision, coherence and a clear chronology, and an objectively identified sequence of events. While many of these differences are seen by the authors to typify differences between orality and literacy, they also conclude that 'written products look the way they do because they are not genuine first generation messages' (p. 438), but have been extensively reworked, as with the statement in Rock's (2001) study.

Jönsson and Linell's analysis makes an important point about what they term 'the blurring of source distinctions' (1991: 434). They explain that 'one cannot know from reading the reports under what conditions a given piece of information has been introduced'. For example, has it been introduced 'more or less spontaneously by the suspect in a narrative turn', or is it introduced in the proposition of the interviewer's question and only then 'confirmed (or sometimes, modified or denied) by the suspect'? Thus, in Rock's example discussed above, the final witness statement 'At about 6pm or earlier we left Jerry's house' blurs the source distinction about the timing of this event. The statement gives no indication that the time of 6pm was introduced by the police officer (on two different occasions in the interview), before being agreed to by the witness in the phrase *about six o'clock or earlier*. (Evidence of the blurring of source distinctions can also be found in Komter 2002, and in Shuy's work on undercover FBI recordings, e.g. 2005).

In her study of 20 police interrogations in the Netherlands, Komter (2006b) also investigates the interactional construction of written police reports. Her detailed analysis of one police interview of a suspect shows how the interviewing officer produced a typed monologue text, which showed no hint of its interactional production, but which was then treated in court as if it actually represented the talk in the interrogation room (see also Komter 2002).

These studies all highlight that the police statement is produced interactionally, although it is presented as the product of a single person, namely the witness or suspect interviewed. In Section 4.2 of Chapter 8 we will see another problem which can arise from police written summaries of police interviews, namely an inaccurate summary which misrepresents what the interviewee was saying.

Exercise 7.9

Read the police interview with Shipman given as an appendix in Newbury and Johnson (2006: 232–238). Working with a partner, write a one-page summary of the information elicited in the interview. Compare your summary with others in the class in the light of issues raised in Section 5.2 above.

(Note that if police officers were preparing such a summary, they would be working with a significant constraint: namely their aim is to produce a summary of the information elicited from the interview in a way that maximises its relevance to the law relating to the likely charges to be laid. This constraint is not practical to impose on this exercise, without students and teachers having a thorough knowledge of the relevant laws.)

Assignments and further research

1. Critically examine published data from the information gathering section of police interviews with suspects (in Auburn *et al.* 1995; Berk-Seligson 2007, 2009; Heydon 2005; Jönsson & Linell 1991; Komter 2002, 2006b) in the light of the findings on witness resistance to coercive questioning in Haworth (2006) and Newbury and Johnson (2006). Make sure that you consider such similarities and differences as the nature of the crime being investigated, and the institutional and societal power of the witness.

2. **(Lx)** Analyse the two publicly available Shipman police interviews in terms of the frameworks presented in the published sociolinguistic studies, by examining the interview about the death of Mrs Mellor in the light of Haworth (2006), and the interview about the death of Mrs Grundy in the light of Newbury and Johnson (2006). You will find the tapes and official transcripts online at http://news.bbc.co.uk/2/hi/in_depth/uk/2000/the_shipman_murders/the_shipman_files/613627.stm

3. Analyse the two publicly available Shipman police interviews in terms of the principles and methods of cognitive interviewing. See Section 5 above for some useful references.

4. Critically compare and contrast cognitive interviewing and conversation management interviewing approaches to police interviews with suspects with the approach promoted in the most widely used police interrogation manual in the US (Inbau *et al.* 2001).

5. **(Lx)** [for students who have done sociolinguistic study of language and gender] Critically consider the research on gendered policing, paying particular attention to the work of McElhinny (e.g. 1995, 2003) and Ostermann (e.g. 2003a, 2003b). Assess the contributions made by this research to the study of language and gender.

6. Examine published police interview data in the light of literature on the linguistic features of policespeak (Coulthard & Johnson 2007: 76–77; Fox 1993; Gibbons 2003: 85–87; Hall 2008). Can you draw any tentative conclusions about differences in police use of English depending on the particular event, for example comparing the delivery of rights texts to the information gathering section of an interview? Can you propose any future research project which could shed more light on this issue? (See Assignment topic 1 above for sources of published police interview data.)

7. Ainsworth's analysis of appellate decisions in the US has led to her conclusion that the Miranda rights are 'perilously easy to waive and nearly impossible to invoke', as we saw in Section 2.6 above. To what extent is this finding relevant to the invocation of parallel rights in your country? An investigation of this question would require an examination of relevant appellate decisions in your country, as well as an investigation of rights delivery sections of police interviews with suspects in the light of Ainsworth's (2008) approach, and the work of Rock (2007) on the communication of rights (see also Solan & Tiersma 2005: 54–62).

8. Berk-Seligson (2007: 36) concludes that 'even when subjected to what appellate courts deem to be "coercive" interrogation techniques', suspects 'have within their power a

certain degree of ability to resist such coercive questioning tactics' (see also Berk-Seligson 2009: 71–100). Critically discuss this conclusion in the light of:

- data from police interviews with suspects in publications such as those listed in Assignment topic 1 above;

- Leo's analysis (e.g. 1996a, 1996b, 1996c, 2008) of police interviews with suspects in the US.

This might be good preparation for a thesis/dissertation which examines a corpus of police interviews with suspects collected for the purpose. Such a study should consider the contextual components which are likely to mitigate against resistance, as well as those which facilitate resistance.

9. **(Lx)** [suitable for a thesis/dissertation] Examine the impact of electronic recording of suspect interviews in the US on the deceptive and manipulative strategies which have been found by Leo (e.g. 2008) to characterise interviews with suspects. This would require detailed examination of a corpus of electronically recorded suspect interviews. In addition to examining these interviews, you could also consider the extent to which the interview techniques recommended in the Inbau *et al.* (2001) police training manual are followed in these interviews.

8

Police interviews with members of minority groups[37]

1. Introduction   162

2. Second language speakers   162

    2.1. Interpreters in police interviews   162

    2.2. Linguistic challenges in interpreting suspects' rights   165

    2.3. Second language speakers without interpreters   167

3. Deaf sign language users   170

4. Speakers of creole languages and second dialects   172

    4.1. Creole speakers   172

    4.2. Second dialect speakers   172

5. Children   176

6. Intellectually disabled people   180

7. The politics of police questioning   180

    Assignments and further research   184

Police interviews with members of minority groups[37]

1. Introduction

In this chapter we continue our examination of police interviews, taking up some of the issues from Chapter 7, and looking specifically at members of minority groups – as suspects, witnesses or victims in police interviews. A basic human right is that of equality before the law. Sociolinguistic research discussed in this chapter will reveal that this right can be a complex ideal, which many people cannot access.

2. Second language speakers

2.1 Interpreters in police interviews

We saw in Section 2.1 of Chapter 7 that the earliest linguistic work on the communication of suspects' rights by police was undertaken by Brière (1978) in relation to the comprehensibility of the Miranda rights for a suspect with limited English proficiency. This is an issue investigated by linguists in a number of countries in specific cases involving speakers of English as a second language (e.g. Berk-Seligson 2009; Cooke 1996; Gibbons 1990; Roy 1990; see also Eades 1997: 19). The comprehensibility of suspects' rights in police interviews has been addressed in some jurisdictions with the provision of written translations of the caution. For example, in England and Wales translations of the *Notice to Detained Persons* are now available in more than 40 languages (Rock 2007: 39, 145), and by 2002 the police caution had been translated into 15 Aboriginal languages in the Northern Territory of Australia (Cooke 2002: 32).[38]

But shouldn't second language speakers, and people who do not speak English at all be provided with interpreters in police interviews? In many jurisdictions, there appears to be no overtly expressed or legislated right to an interpreter in a police interview (in contrast to the situation for accused people in court, which we saw in Section 1 of Chapter 4). The decision to call an interpreter usually rests with the police officers involved or their superior officers. In some ways, the situation is parallel with that in court, where the decision about the need for an interpreter is typically made by a judge with no training in assessing language proficiency (see Section 2 of Chapter 4).[39] In the Australian state of New South Wales (NSW), police officers are directed to interview through an interpreter if the person (suspect or witness) being interviewed:

- is unable to communicate in English

- has a limited understanding of English

- is more comfortable communicating in their own language

- is deaf, hearing impaired or speaking impaired

- is a child and the appropriate adult or support person requires one wants one (sic) (NSW Police Service 1998: 51)

While police officers are not trained in assessing language proficiency, in NSW they are advised that 'just because someone can speak English to do everyday tasks does not mean they can cope with the added stress of a police interview. If in doubt, get an interpreter.' (NSW Police Service 1998: 51).

But it seems that it is not just the interviewee's English proficiency which is taken into consideration when police decide whether or not to call an interpreter. Gibbons (2003: 234–237) found that police in NSW have been reluctant to call an interpreter for a number of reasons:

- There are often practical difficulties in calling an interpreter at night, but police are reluctant to delay the interview till morning.

- Police officers have to use the local police budget to pay interpreters.

- Police feel that using an interpreter may make it harder for them to assess the suspect's non-verbal communication and demeanour, factors often used by police officers to assess a suspect's guilt.[40]

- Police do not want the suspect to have extra thinking time before answering a question.

- Some police officers perceive interpreters as advocates for the suspect.

Class discussion

Critically discuss the reasons given to Gibbons by police officers in explanation of their frequent reluctance to call an interpreter to interviews with suspects who speak English as a second language. What arguments can be given to counter these reasons? What changes might be made to counter this reluctance?

In preparing for this discussion, you should go back to Section 3 of Chapter 4, where some similar issues were dealt with in relation to the use of interpreters in court.

In contrast to most jurisdictions, in the Northern Territory of Australia, where a considerable proportion of the population speaks an Aboriginal language, the right to request an interpreter is one of the suspect's four rights communicated in the caution phase at the beginning of the interview. The others are the right to let others know of your detention, the right to nominate a prisoner's friend who can assist you during the interview, and the right to silence (Cooke 2002: 31). Despite the right to request an interpreter, and despite the high proportion of Aboriginal people in the Northern Territory who do not speak much English, or any English, Cooke found that some police only involve an interpreter for the caution phase of the interview, and then carry out the rest of the interview in English (p. 1). He also found (Cooke 2004: 5, 49–51) that police in remote northern areas of Western Australia are often reluctant to call an interpreter.

Cooke further found that in the Northern Territory and Western Australia the prisoner's friend has often been called on to also act as an interpreter (e.g. Cooke 2004: 46–48). But the role of the prisoner's friend is quite different from that of interpreter. The main function of the prisoner's friend is 'to advise the suspect, and to assist him during the interview process to choose freely whether to speak or to remain silent' (Mildren 1999: 142). Justice Mildren of the Northern Territory Supreme Court explains the problem with having a prisoner's friend also doing the interpreting in a police interview: 'the role of the prisoner's friend is in conflict with that of the interpreter. The latter must be impartial, but the former is required to be partisan' (p. 141). Further, as Mildren explains, people chosen by suspects to sit with them during the police interview are rarely trained as interpreters.

The use of untrained people – who may or may not be friends of the suspect – as interpreters in police interviews, is not limited to Australia. Berk-Seligson (2000, 2009: 13–37) found a troubling situation when she searched appellate decisions in three populous US states for cases in which police had made use of unqualified interpreters during investigative interviews. Reviewing all such appeals between 1965 and 1999 in California, Florida and New York, she found 49 cases which dealt with the use of unqualified interpreters. Instead, the following types of people acted as interpreters: police officers, police informants, relatives of the person being interviewed (including children), crime scene witnesses, a fellow prison inmate and even a suspect's confederate. Berk-Seligson discusses obvious compromises for the justice system in terms of conflict of interest and quality of interpreting.

Berk-Seligson's (2009) investigation of the use of police officers as 'interpreters' is disturbing reading. There are two major problems: the inadequate language proficiency of some of the officers who are acting as interpreters, and the conflict of interest involved whenever a police officer acts as an interpreter. Looking first at the interpreting police officers' language proficiency, Berk-Seligson found that police departments are increasingly encouraging officers to take brief 'survival Spanish' courses, which might be equivalent to about one year's high school study (p. 142) or between 16 and 24 hours of instruction over two or three days (p. 143). Berk-Seligson's detailed analysis of two cases involving police officer 'interpreters' with this kind of training leads to her strong criticism of the 'implicit assumption by police departments that a limited level of proficiency in a second language is sufficient for carrying out a custodial interrogation'. The limited level of proficiency of such police 'interpreters' clearly compromises the rights of second language-speaking suspects to equal treatment before the law.

These problems are compounded by issues surrounding the conflict of interest. Berk-Seligson found that US police officer interpreters are not necessarily expected to follow the code of ethics that typify the work of professional interpreters – such as impartiality (see Section 3 of Chapter 4 above). An appeal in the Californian Supreme Court in 1992 (*People v Márquez* 1992) shows the way that the court viewed the role of police officers acting as interpreters for suspects. In this case the Spanish-speaking defendant Márquez had argued that statements he made to police should not have been used in his trial, because the interpretation was provided by the police officer (Detective Parrott) who was 'also an investigating officer and an interested party' (Berk-Seligson 2009: 26). The appeal court rejected this argument, saying that the defendant's 'characterization of Detective Parrott as an interested party and improper interpreter is premised on authorities and standards relating to court interpreters at trial. Detective Parrott was not acting as a court interpreter; she functioned as a facilitator for the police investigation'. On the face of it, perhaps it might seem reasonable to some (as it did to the appeal court) that the role of an interpreter in a police investigative interview is significantly different from that of an interpreter in a trial. What do you think?

For Berk-Seligson, the issue is clear: suspects in police interviews who require an interpreter should be provided with a non-partisan qualified interpreter. Berk-Seligson's detailed microanalysis of three cases in which a police officer has acted as an interpreter lead her to conclude that 'police should not serve as interpreters' (2009: 217) because of the conflict involved in simultaneously acting in two different roles. For example, in her (2002b, 2009: 38–70) analysis of one such interview, the police officer blurred what should have been two distinct roles – namely, investigator and interpreter. Furthermore, he used coercion to elicit a confession, thus violating the suspect's rights. (In Section 6 of Chapter 7 above, we saw that Berk-Seligson (2007, 2009: 71–100) also investigates suspect resistance in this case.) Even fluently bilingual police officers can 'subvert the intent of the law' when combining these two roles (p. 212), as Berk-Seligson highlights with her analysis of one such case (2009: 171–200). Her study sheds important light on US police interviews with second language speakers and provides micro-linguistic detail of some of the ways in which miscarriages of justice occur. Her conclusion is that the potential for miscarriage of justice 'rises substantially when the suspects being investigated are not fully proficient in English, and rises even higher when the police officials who themselves are not fluent in the language of the detainee conduct interrogations in that language' (p. 211).

2.2. Linguistic challenges in interpreting suspects' rights

But even when suspects are provided with non-partisan, qualified interpreters, there can be considerable challenges in interpreting the suspect's rights, which have been highlighted in two studies (Nakane 2007; Russell 2000).

Russell (2000) examines the difficulties experienced by interpreters in 20 police interviews with French speakers in England. Her focus is on the right to silence caution and its explanation. One of the main problems is that interpreters often try to match the small segment of the original English with a word-for-word translation (something that would presumably be even more problematic with languages that are not related to English). Extract 8–i illustrates one of the problems Russell found in the interpretation of the police officers' explanations of the caution:

Extract 8–i Russell's (2000: 38) transcription of audiorecording
1. PO: Should this matter go to court
2. Int: Donc si cette affaire va au tribunal
(trans: so if this matter 'goes' to court)

Do you speak French? If so, then you would have seen that this is a rather strange translation. Russell says that a translation based on meaning rather than form would use the verb phrase *passe en justice* rather than *va*. French speakers might like to read Russell (2000) to find other examples where interpreters seem to follow each English word in their translation, resulting in rather strange-sounding French.

One of the problems for the interpreters in Russell's study relates to the way that the police officer breaks up the caution and its explanation into small segments for consecutive interpretation. While segmentation is inevitable, it can be a source of considerable linguistic difficulty in any consecutive interpreting (see Angermeyer 2008: 397–398). This difficulty is examined in Nakane's (2007) analysis of six interpreted police interviews in Australia with Japanese suspects. She found that the caution was interpreted more accurately when it was broken by the police officer into small segments for interpreting, than when the interpreting break was after a long segment. But in addition to the length of turns, the accuracy of the interpretation seemed to be affected by both turn construction and turn boundary (i.e. where the police officer stopped to allow for consecutive interpreting). For example, in one of the interviews (Nakane 2007: 101–102), the police officer delivered the right to silence in two parts, as we will see in Extract 8–ii. Nakane points out that the police officer may have broken this caution in this way in order to be helpful. But look at how the interpreter provided the Japanese version to the suspect:

Extract 8–ii Nakane (2007: 101); lawyer's transcription
1. PO: I must caution you do not have to say or do anything
2. Int: Anoo moshi iitaku nai kotoba ga areba desu ne,
3. Sus: Hai.
4. Int: iwanakutemo kekkoo desu.
5. PO: Unless you wish to do so and anything you do say or do may later be given in evidence.
6. Int: Sorede, ittan oshaberini natta kotoba wa, atoni natte desu ne,
7. Sus: Hai.
8. Int: shooko to natte nokori masu node,
9. Sus: Hai.
10. Int: sono ten ni chuui shite kotaete kudasai.
11. Sus: Hai.

translation (by Nakane)
1. PO: I must caution you do not have to say or do anything
2. Int: U:m if you have words that you don't want to say,
3. Sus: Yes.
4. Int: You don't need to say them.
5. PO: Unless you wish to do so and anything you do say or do may later be given in evidence.
6. Int: And the words you speak, later,
7. Sus: Yes.
8. Int: will remain as evidence, so,
9. Sus: Yes.
10. Int: Please answer with caution to that point.
11. Sus: Yes.

Exercise 8.1[xxii]
Discuss the interpreter's version of the police caution in Extract 8–ii.
(a) Has anything been omitted?
(b) Has anything been changed?
(c) If you were the police officer, where would you have made the turn boundary (i.e. how would you have broken up this caution), and why?
(d) If you speak Japanese, explain how you would interpret this caution, discussing differences between your version and that provided in this extract.

Class discussion

Nakane (2007), Russell (2000) and Berk-Seligson (2009) conclude that a standard scripted version of the caution needs to be prepared in languages other than English. Do you agree or disagree? Why (not)? Discuss this view in the light of the discussion in Section 2.5 of Chapter 7, being careful to think about similarities and differences between interviews with native speakers of English and those with people who speak little or no English. Do you have any other recommendations for improving the interpretation of the caution and its explanation in police interviews?

2.3. Second language speakers without interpreters

We saw in Section 2.1 above that second language speakers of English do not always have access to interpreters. Apart from the work of linguists reporting on a few individual cases in which they have given expert evidence, there appears to be little research which examines second language speakers in police interviews. But these individual cases reveal some important issues. Cooke (1996, 2002) provides evidence of a problem for second language speakers in understanding the right to silence from two different cases with Aboriginal speakers of English as a second language in northern Australia.

Exercise 8.2[xxiii]

Read the following extract from the caution section of a police interview with an Aboriginal suspect who spoke English as a second language. Discuss the questions which follow the extract.

Extract 8–iii Cooke's (1996: 280) transcription of audiorecording
1. PO: Ummm- and if you don't want to answer any of my questions you just have to say 'I don't want to answer that question' and then you don't have to answer it- OK?
2. Sus: Yes.
3. PO: Ummm- now what did I mean by that- y'know- if I ask you a question it's gonna be on there [i.e. the videotape]- and if you answer you answer it'll be on there but if you don't wanna answer you just say you don't wanna answer- what does all that mean?
4. Sus: If I'm not sc- scare I'll do my best=
5. PO: =Right=
6. Sus: =to answer every questions.
7. PO: All right- OK- now an' if you don't want to answer any more questions.
8. Sus: I'll try answer it- answer it back.
9. PO: But if you don't want to answer it- what do you say?
10. Sus: No.

Discussion questions
(a) Do you think that the suspect understood the right to silence? Discuss any evidence from the transcript which supports your view.
(b) If you were the police officer interviewing this suspect, what would you do differently in either the delivery of the right to silence caution, or the comprehension check, or both?
(c) Discuss this extract in the light of Section 2.4 of Chapter 7.

Your discussion of Extract 8–iii no doubt centred on problems which arise from police officers not really listening to suspects' answers when they ask comprehension checking questions. This extract also reveals a problem that many second language speakers have with the English modal expression *don't have to* which is often found in explanations of the police caution (as in Turn 1 of Extract 8–iii above). Cooke's (2002: 9–10) work on another case sheds some light on the nature of this problem for Yolngu Matha speakers of English as a second language (which includes the suspect in Extract 8–iii above, and the witness in Extract 8–iv below). In this second case, the witness, referred to here as James, was giving evidence in court about his double role as prisoner's friend and interpreter in the police interview of his older brother (Harry). You will recall from Section 2.1 above that while it is a practice of police officers to sometimes ask prisoner's friends to provide interpreting for the suspect, this puts the person in a situation of conflict of interest. The audiorecorded police interview provided evidence of this conflict in this case, particularly as it showed how James assisted police in explaining the caution (in his role as interpreter), and then went on to tell his brother that it would be good for him to talk to the police (in his role as prisoner's friend). As this advice was given in the Yolngu Matha language, police were not aware of it. The defendant's lawyer argued in court that the police interview, which contained a confession, should not be admissible, because Harry had not been supplied with an independent interpreter, and also because the role of prisoner's friend had not been adequately explained to either of the two brothers involved. Extract 8–iv below is taken from the cross-examination of James about the evidence he had given in examination-in-chief. There he had talked about his reluctance to be involved in the police interview of his older brother (apparently because of cultural norms about talking to an older brother about matters involved in the sexual assault about which he was being investigated). (Note that it is possible that James's use of the preposition *about* in Turns 6, 10 and 18 would be equivalent to *to* in Standard English.)

Extract 8–iv Cooke's (2002: 9–10) transcription of audiorecording
1. DC: James- you said you weren't feeling comfortable being there- remember you said that? is that right?
2. W: Yes.

3. DC: Is it the fact that you weren't comfortable- because Harry is your older brother?
4. W: Yes.

5. DC: Why would that make you uncomfortable?
6. W: I- I- I **don't have to** talk about my brother- older brother.

7. DC: You **don't have to?**
8. W: Yeah.

9. DC: I'm not sure I understand.
10. W: I'm an Dhudi-nha in Yolngu system- we **don't have to** talk about older brother- 'cause he's our old- older brother.

11. DC: Well that means **you don't have to- can you if you want to?**
12. W: No.

13. DC: Why do you say that?
14. W   Skinship system-[41] have to to respect older brother.

[some questions and answers omitted]

15. DC: You said that you were uncomfortable because you are his younger brother- is that right?
16. W: Yes.

17. DC: Perhaps you could just explain to his honour why that makes you feel uncomfortable?
18. W: Well- look- he's my brother and he's my- my- a leader in a more or less way- that's back home-
and like- we respect our older brother- we **don't have to** talk about- I mean= all that bad things
about our brother- like my brother or we **don't have to** swear our brother- like older brother.

Did you find this witness's evidence confusing? What if you learn that it is common for
Aboriginal speakers of interlanguage varieties of English to use *don't have to* to mean *must
not*? Then you can see that what this witness is saying would translate into Standard English
as *I mustn't talk about my brother* (in Turns 6, 10 and 18). Or, as indicated above, it might be *I
mustn't talk to my brother*. Cooke explains that the misinterpretation of the expression *don't
have to* is frequently found with Aboriginal people from non-English-speaking background
across the Northern Territory, including speakers of Kriol. And now you can see the particular
relevance of this Extract 8–iv to the discussion in this section of second language speakers
being interviewed by police without interpreters. The expression *you don't have to* is central to
the right to silence caution, as in the police officer's explanation in Turn 1 of Extract 8–iii
above: *if you don't want to answer any of my questions you just have to say 'I don't want to answer
that question' and then you don't have to answer it.*

But this non-modal auxiliary expression *you don't have to* can cause confusion for second
language speakers of English. This expression is the negative form of the expression *you have
to*, which could also be expressed as *you are obliged to* or *you must*. But there can be two
different negative forms of *you are obliged to*, either *you are not obliged to* (= *you don't have to*),
or *you are obliged not to* (= *you must not*). In Extract 8–iv above, the witness James uses *I (we)
don't have to* where he means *I (we) must not* (see especially Turns 10–14). In Extract 8–iii, the
suspect seems to understand the expression *you don't have to answer my questions* to mean *if
I'm not scared, I'll do my best to answer [the questions]*. This interpretation does not seem to
relate to either the *you are not obliged to* (= *you don't have to*), or the *you are obliged not to* (= *you
must not*) interpretation. It seems quite possible that in the asymmetrical institutional power
situation in which she found herself, the words *you don't have to answer my questions* did not
make sense to her in either interpretation (obligation or permission). Thus, it seems that she
simply presented her attempt to cooperate with the interview.

However, when police officers say to second language speakers *you don't have to answer my
questions*, this may sometimes confusingly be interpreted by some as *you must not answer my
questions* (consistent with James's use of *I don't have to talk about my brother* to mean *I mustn't
talk about my brother*).[42] Let us now look at how Cooke (1998: 343) removed this potential
problem in his plain English version of the caution which was used as the basis for translation
into Aboriginal languages in the Northern Territory (i.e. the 'front-translation version'):

... the police will ask you if you want to tell them about that trouble or if you want to sit silently without
talking.
    You must decide for yourself if you want to tell police about that trouble or not. The police want to
ask you questions about that trouble. The law says you can tell the police about that trouble if you want
to, or, if you don't want to talk about the trouble the law says you can sit silently and not talk to the
police. This is a decision that you make for yourself.

You can see that this plain English version of the right to silence caution completely avoids the *you don't have to* structure found to be problematic for Aboriginal speakers of English as a second language. In doing so, it uses many more words than the standard versions of this caution. This is consistent with a basic principle of plain English: explaining something clearly in ordinary language often results in a longer explanation than the original (see Tiersma 2006: 19).

A similar problem with the expression *you do not have to* was found for French interpreters in Russell's study. For example, one interpreter started interpreting the *you do not have to* ... part of the right to silence caution with word-for-word form-based interpreting. You can see in Extract 8–v below that the interpreter had two false starts, the first of which *vous ne devez* is the French equivalent of *you mustn't*. The final and accurate version settled on by the interpreter is one based on meaning rather than form:[43]

Extract 8–v Russell's (2000: 37) transcription of audiorecording
1. PO: And the caution is that you do not have to say anything (1.5)
2. Int: .hhh la caution qui dit que vous ne devez- vous n'avez- vous n- n'êtes pas obligé de dire quoique
            ce soit
(trans: .hhh the guarantee that says that you must not- you have not- you do not have to say anything)

Cooke's examples in this section have highlighted grammatical and semantic problems which can arise when second language speakers are not provided interpreters in police interviews. Berk-Seligson (2009: 101–141) analyses a case with a Spanish speaker of English as a second language which highlights pragmatic problems. In this case, the suspect appears to acquiesce readily to controlling questions in the police interview in a way that Berk-Seligson finds to be consistent with the gratuitous concurrence found to typify Australian Aboriginal participation in formal interviews (discussed in Section 3 of Chapter 5 above). Berk-Seligson's analysis of this police interview also highlights a range of linguistic mechanisms used coercively with this second language speaker (as mentioned in Section 3 of Chapter 7 above).

3. Deaf sign language users

In Section 7 of Chapter 4 we saw that deaf sign language users face many challenges and disadvantages in the legal system. To date, there has been little research focused specifically on police interviews.

> **Exercise 8.3**
> Reread Section 7 of Chapter 4. Make a list of particular challenges and disadvantages faced by deaf users of sign languages throughout the legal system. Discuss these issues in terms of what you have learnt specifically about language use in police interviews.

As with speakers of second languages, sign language users often face difficulties in having access to competent interpreters. In some US jurisdictions, police officers are trained to work as interpreters, as we saw in Section 2.1 above. The principle of giving police officers some lessons in a second language and then having them work as interpreters in police interviews has been examined by Hoopes (2003) in relation to police officer interpreters for deaf sign language users in one large US city. In this city deaf suspects are interviewed by police officers who have a little training in American Sign Language (ASL). On the one hand, the police officers' attempts to use ASL in giving the Miranda rights (= police caution), and in carrying out the interrogation, indicate a positive development in recognising communication needs of deaf people. But on the other hand, the results – in cases where the training is not adequate, and the police officer is not a fluent sign language user – can be disastrous for deaf suspects, in terms of lack of understanding of their rights, as well as the charges against them, and particular questions during the interrogation. Following Berk-Seligson (2002), discussed in Section 2.1 above, there are also questions of conflict of interest in having police officers acting as interpreters.

Hoopes (2003) has raised other concerns about the level of training of ASL interpreters used in police interviews. He carried out an experimental study in which nine ASL interpreters at varying levels of competency – who were not native signers – interpreted the Miranda rights, which were judged by 10 native signers of the language for comprehensibility. He found that the signed interpretations of the three beginning interpreters were incomprehensible, while those of the three intermediate interpreters were 'uniformly found to be confusing' (p. 44). It was only the signed interpretations of the [three] advanced interpreters that were found to be 'fairly clear or clear' (p. 45). Interestingly, only the advanced interpreters successfully used the syntactic non-manual signs that are essential to sign languages, for example conveying negation and conditional construction with movement of various parts of the body. (Remember from Section 7 of Chapter 4 that hand movements are only one component of the body movements used in sign languages.)

Hoopes' study focuses on the need for skilled sign language interpreters, especially in the context of police forces believing that a little ASL training is sufficient to equip a police officer to deliver the Miranda rights and to carry out an investigative interview. Castelle (2003) raises another important issue about police interviews with deaf people, namely about the interpretation and misinterpretation of facial expressions. He points out that facial expressions which convey emotions in hearing people, may function quite differently as part of sign language. For example, while raised eyebrows in hearing people typically convey surprise, and at times, disbelief, they function grammatically in ASL. Thus, in ASL a Yes/No-question is formed by raising the eyebrows throughout the signing of the proposition being questioned. On the other hand, a WH-question is formed by lowering the eyebrows throughout the signing of the proposition being questioned (Hoopes 2003: 31). But police officers are often trained to study facial expressions and other non-verbal behaviour of suspects generally, without an understanding of relevant differences between spoken and sign languages. Castelle (2003: 172) points out that 'the "bible" of police interrogations' in the US, Inbau et al. (2001), contains an extensive discussion of the evaluation of such non-verbal behaviour. But this manual of police interrogation 'does not contain a single reference to the interrogation of deaf people, let alone a discussion of the special communication issues involved'.

4. Speakers of creole languages and second dialects

We saw in Section 5.5 of Chapter 4 and Section 3 of Chapter 5 that speakers of creole languages and non-standard dialects face subtle but significant challenges in the courtroom. The same linguistic and social issues affect their participation in police interviews. There is very little published research on this topic, so it would be an excellent area for thesis/dissertation research.

4.1. Creole speakers

Brown-Blake and Chambers (2007) examine miscommunication in UK police interviews with speakers of Jamaican Creole by police and customs officers, as well as official transcriptions of these interviews. Jamaican Creole (also known as Jamaican language) is the first language of most people in Jamaica and many Jamaicans in the UK. As with many other English-lexified creole languages, there is a widespread misconception that people speaking Jamaican Creole are speaking some kind of English. In one case (pp. 276–277), a witness to a shooting incident told investigating police *Wen mi ier di bap bap, mi drap a groun and den mi staat ron*. The English translation of this Jamaican Creole sentence is 'When I heard the bap bap [the shots], I fell to the ground and then I started to run'. But the person transcribing the police interview was apparently unfamiliar with differences between Jamaican Creole and English, and thus, this utterance appears in the official transcript as 'When I heard the shot (bap, bap) I drop the gun and then I run'. The Jamaican Creole clause *mi drap a groun* ('I fell to the ground') sounded to the transcriber like *I drop the gun*. You can imagine how significant this mistake could be for implicating the interviewee in a shooting incident! This example is probably the tip of the iceberg of miscommunication with speakers of creole in police interviews. As Brown-Blake and Chambers point out, despite some lexical similarities between Jamaican Creole and English, it is important that speakers of the creole language are provided with interpreters, and that interpreters (or translators) are also involved in the production of official transcripts. This study also reveals problems for suspects in understanding the police caution, as might be expected for speakers of creole languages who are not provided with interpreters.

Another important example, this time for speakers of the creole languages in Australia (Kriol and Torres Strait Creole), is that the word *kill* in these two languages means 'hurt or maim' rather than 'cause to die'. So, if a person assaults someone and, speaking Kriol or Torres Strait Creole, threatens to *kill* them, this should not lead to charges relating to (attempted) murder (see Cooke 2002: 4; Trezise 1996).

4.2. Second dialect speakers

To date, there has been almost no research investigating second dialect speakers in police interviews (but see Section 7.1 of Chapter 7 for linguistic expert evidence in specific cases involving fabricated confessions). However, Fadden (2007) compares the police interviews of three Canadian Aboriginal English-speaking suspects with three non-Aboriginal suspects. She finds that, in contrast to the non-Aboriginal suspects, the Aboriginal suspects said very little, and that when they did directly address the investigating officer, they were generally non-confrontational and used hedges. This study connects with Ainsworth's (1993: 286) concerns about suspects from 'certain ethnic groups' being disadvantaged by using a 'less assertive, indirect style' in invoking their rights in police interviews (as discussed in Section 2.6 of Chapter 7). This is clearly an issue for further investigation.

My work for the defence in the case of an Aboriginal English speaker in coastal New South Wales provides a telling example of the way in which subtle dialectal difference can lead to misrepresentation when a police interview is summarised in a written report.[44] In this case, the accused man (whom I will refer to as 'Jack') was charged with murder after he stabbed his drunk and out-of-control brother ('Mick'). In his police interview, Jack freely confessed to stabbing Mick. In a number of answers, Jack gave specific details of Mick's violence when he was drunk, which he referred to several times as *the way he carries on when he's drunk*. For example, Jack told the police that Mick had got very drunk on the day in question, and that while they were at their aunty's house, Mick *started carrying on- pushing [a woman] around*. When the police ask him *What sort of- where- do you know why he was pushing [this woman] around?* he replied *No- he just carries on- he just carries on like that*. The police officer then asked about this *carrying on*, saying *All right and what- what sort of things was he saying?* Jack answered *What sort of things was he saying? No- he was just pushing her around.* You can see that Jack made it clear that this *carrying on* didn't involve *saying* anything, it was about actions.

Exercise 8.4

Discuss the following questions:

(a) What does it mean in your dialect of English to say that someone was *carrying on when he was drunk*?

(b) Which of the following actions can it refer to: swearing? shouting? arguing? throwing glasses? punching someone? pushing someone against the wall?

(c) After probing your native speaker intuitions, find out what a dictionary of your dialect of English gives as the meaning(s) for *carry on*.

The *Macquarie Dictionary* of Australian English defines *carry on* as 'c. to behave in an excited or foolish manner' and 'd. to exhibit signs of being in a temper'.[45] It is not specific about whether it is only verbal activity that is involved, or whether it can also refer to physical actions. In my usage of this expression, I would generally expect it to refer to verbal behaviour. If physical behaviour was involved I would add something specific to this effect. For example, if someone told me *spectators at the soccer match were carrying on*, I would interpret this to refer to such actions as shouting, arguing, or screaming, but not fighting. But there is a subtle difference between General Australian English here and Aboriginal English – where *carry on* is often used to describe physical behaviour. And the Aboriginal English meaning of Jack's expression *carry on* is clear from his police interview. In answer to various questions about Mick's behaviour on the day in question and on previous occasions when he had also been drunk, Jack used *carry on* to refer to violent behaviour. For example, Jack told the police about an incident which had occurred some 10 months before the police interview, when Mick had stabbed Jack in the eye. When the interviewing officer asked Jack what Mick used to stab him with, Jack replied *A knife- that resulted from- it's come from nothing- he was intoxicated again- that's the way he carries on when he comes home drunk.* And in answer to a general question about what Mick does when he is drunk, Jack said *he carries on silly in the house- smashin' up things.*

In addition to the verb *carry on* having different meanings in Aboriginal English and General Australian English, the adjective *silly* is also not the same in both dialects. In General Australian English it means 'lacking good sense, foolish, stupid', or 'absurd or ridiculous' (*Macquarie Dictionary*). In Aboriginal English it can have the same meaning as in General Australian English. But it can also mean 'insane, out of one's mind', or 'wild or violent as a result of being drunk' (Arthur 1996). Thus Jack's description of his brother that *'he carries on silly in the house'* does not refer to something like singing the national anthem in a falsetto voice (as it might in General Australian English), but to *smashing up things.*

It transpires that it is not just *things* that were *smashed up* when Mick was *carrying on silly.* Mick had on other occasions injured a number of relatives: he had threatened a female relative with a knife, struck the same woman in the breast, knocked another female relative unconscious by hitting her on the head with a fence paling, assaulted a 13-year-old nephew, struck the same nephew in the head and arm with a hockey stick, and broken Jack's spine with a golf club, in addition to threatening him on another occasions with a knife and wounding his eye (as we saw above).

In his answers in the police interview Jack said that Mick had been *pushing* a woman *around* earlier that day at their aunty's house. Then when Mick came home he *started picking on [their] sister, hassling* her, as well as *picking up the mattress* she was lying on, and she had *sang out* [= called out] to Jack for help. Jack was well aware of the injuries that their sister could receive from Mick's *carrying on silly.* But Jack's numerous indications of Mick's violence when drunk, as well as his rough physical treatment of the other woman at his aunty's house that day, and then their sister that night, did not make it into the written police report, which emerged from this interview and was contained in the Fact Sheet.

This three-page Fact Sheet – which was the basis of the murder charge – contains one page of biographical information about the accused, as well as the names of the arresting and interviewing police officers. The remaining two pages comprises a 661-word report with the arguably erroneous title 'Full Facts'. This is a summary of what is alleged by the police to have happened in the incident in question – that is, a summary recontextualisation of Jack's story. About half of this Full Facts report (FF) purports to comprise a summary of what Jack told the police during the interview, taking the form of 10 clauses beginning with 'The accused stated ... ' or 'He stated ... '. The choice of this verb belies the fact that Jack's 'statements' were in fact answers to questions, and thus produced interactionally (consistent with the studies by Jönsson & Linell 1991, Rock 2001 and Komter 2006b referred to in Section 7.2 of Chapter 7).

Most relevant to this discussion is the FF report of Jack's 'statement' to the police concerning Mick's actions on the day in question. Despite the fact that several of Jack's answers in the police interview had implicated both rough physical treatment on the part of his brother and the expectation of physical violence (as we have seen in the examples above), FF gives no indication of either. There are only six actions attributed by Jack in the FF to his brother. These are in bold in the following quotations from FF:

Extract 8–vi Quotations from written Full Facts summary

He stated that ... his brother Mick **arived (sic) home**, where he **started to pick on their sister**, Emily

He stated that he'd had enough of his brother's **antics** ...

Mick **dared** Jack to carry out his threat ...

Mick then **fell** to the floor, where he **blacked out** ...

The two statements which are relevant here are in the first two sentences, in which Mick's provocative actions are given as *started to pick on their sister*, and *antics*. Neither of these terms conveys physical actions in General Australian English, despite Jack's clear indication in a number of answers (some of which we have seen) that Mick had begun to use physical violence with their sister, and that use of physical violence was typical of his behaviour when he was drunk.

So, there is a striking change to the way in which Jack's answers in the police interview were reported in the FF: the Aboriginal English expression *carry on silly* which refers to physical violence when drunk, was 'translated' as *antics*. And the only verb attributed to Jack in reporting his brother's actions that night was *started to pick on*. This police summary obscured the reason for Jack making the attack on his brother, explaining it in terms of impatience with antics, rather than an attempt to stop a dangerously violent person. This case reveals how dialectal differences in word meaning can make a crucial difference in understanding: following receipt of my linguistic report, the prosecutor dropped the murder charge, substituting it with a charge of manslaughter to which the accused pleaded guilty.

This case provides a troubling insight into the potential consequences of subtle dialectal differences. The accused in the case spoke a very light (or acrolectal) variety of Aboriginal English. If you look at the example answers given above, there are no distinctive grammatical features. Further, Jack's accent, while recognisably Aboriginal, would have been unlikely to cause comprehension difficulties. There was no evidence in the interview that the police officers had problems with understanding Jack, apart from their misconception that *carrying on* referred to *things he was saying*. It is common for related varieties of English to be very similar, and yet to have some lexical items which do not have the same meaning. For example, *I'm pissed again* has quite a different meaning in Australian English and American English.

Class discussion[xxxiv]

Discuss the case summarised above, paying attention to the following questions:
(a) Should the police officers in this case have known what Jack meant by *carrying on* and *carrying on silly*?
(b) Does it matter that they didn't? Why(not)?
(c) What implications can you draw from this case for the police interviewing of suspects who speak a related dialect? Would you recommend any policy changes? Discuss any suggested changes.

---

5. Children

In Section 2 of Chapter 5, we read about concerns with how children are questioned in adult courts. But before children get to court to give evidence, generally they must be interviewed by one or more police officers.[46] Police interviews with child victims of alleged abuse have been the focus of a considerable amount of psychological research, and an understanding of this work is essential to any sociolinguistic consideration of children in police interviews. The research has led to the development of guidelines and protocols for interviewing children. I will briefly report below on summaries of some of this research and guidelines. If you are going to investigate interviews with children in any depth, you should go to the works cited in this section to find references to specific studies (see Wakefield 2006 for an overview).

The main questions of sociolinguistic interest dealt with by the psychological research concern children's memory and the most effective ways of eliciting accurate information about children's experiences. One of the leading researchers in this area provides a summary of the findings (M. Powell 2008: 189), saying that 'decades of controlled research in both field and laboratory settings has resulted in clear international consensus regarding the most effective way of eliciting reliable and clear statements from children'. What do you think this involves? If you have experience in talking to children, you might like to reflect on how you find out important information from them. The consensus on interviewing children shares with many approaches to investigative interviewing of adults the aim of obtaining 'a comprehensive narrative account of the alleged offence, with as little specific prompting as possible from the interviewer' (p. 189, see also Powell *et al.* 2005). The importance of avoiding prompting is especially important with child witnesses, as children have been found to be particularly susceptible to coercion (Ceci & Bruck 1995).

Several different protocols have been developed for investigative interviewing of children, of which some of the best known are:

- *Memorandum of Good Practice on Video Recorded Interviews for Child Witnesses in Criminal Proceedings* introduced by the Home Office in England and Wales in 1992 (see Aldridge & Wood 1998);

- the revisions to these guidelines in 2000 in *Achieving Best Evidence in Criminal Proceedings: Guidance for Vulnerable or Intimidated Witnesses, Including Children* used throughout the UK: http://www.homeoffice.gov.uk/documents/ach-bect-evidence/ (see Aldridge 2007);

- the Stepwise approach introduced in Canada in 1996 (Yuille *et al.* 1993);

- the National Institute of Child Health and Human Development structured interview protocol (see Sternberg *et al.* 2002, used mostly in the US, Israel and Europe, according to Powell 2005: 193).[47]

If your country is not represented in this list, you might like to find out if there are official guidelines for police interviews with children, and how they are similar to or different from guidelines in other countries.

Exercise 8.5

Investigate one of the protocols given above for investigative interviewing of children. List the ways in which it is similar to and different from the general cognitive interviewing approach to police interviewing, as introduced in Section 5 of Chapter 7.

Wilson and Powell (2001: 44–45) point out that the various protocols for investigative interviewing with children comprise 'the same essential stages and elements', namely:

- greeting and establishing rapport with the child;

- introducing the topic of concern;

- eliciting a free narrative account from the child;

- specific questioning;

- closure.

From a sociolinguistic perspective it is the third and fourth items on this list that are of greatest interest, namely eliciting a free narrative account from the child, and specific questioning. In order to elicit a free narrative account, and to avoid the possibility of 'contaminating' a child's story of their experience, interviewers are advised to use open-ended questions as much as possible. Indeed, Powell (2005: 138) finds that the open-ended question 'has become the "gold standard" for investigative interviewers'. You might want to go back to Section 5 of Chapter 7 to refresh your memory about the meaning of the term 'open-ended questions'. M. Powell (2008: 191, emphasis in original) reports that research in the last few years shows that although 'children's *initial* response to free recall or open-ended prompts may be brief and lacking in detail, gentle persistence with open-ended questions (particularly those that use children's utterances as cues for further information) can often result in extensive or contextually elaborate accounts', even with children as young as four years old. In their practical guide for counsellors, police, lawyers and social workers, Wilson and Powell (2001: 54–55) illustrate this point with the following example:

Extract 8–vii Wilson and Powell (2001: 54–55); transcription details not provided
1. Iv: What happened when you went into his bedroom?
2. Ch: He hurt me, he hurt me bad, I told him to stop but he didn't.

Wilson and Powell say that following up this interaction with closed questions such as *who hurt you?* and *how did he hurt you?* are likely to elicit less information than using 'open-ended questions' such as *Tell me what happened,* and echoing parts of the child's answers (a well-recognised strategy from ethnographic and counselling interviews).

While most of the literature on investigative interviewing of children either reports psychological experimental studies or recommends practical strategies, there is a little sociolinguistic research, which enriches these other works with microanalysis of actual police interviews with children. Aldridge and Wood (1998) present a sociolinguistic study of 100 transcripts of videorecorded police interviews of children in abuse cases in North Wales. It provides a wealth of interview extracts which illustrate how police officers following the *Memorandum* (referred to above) actually talk to children in the different phases of the interview. And in examining how children answer questions in these interviews, Aldridge and Wood's book reveals linguistic details of miscommunications, as well as difficulties involved in understanding children's stories and in asking them questions.

For example, from this large corpus Aldridge and Wood (1998: 149) are able to detail specific types of words which interviewers may not realise are difficult for children under about eight years old. These include:

- legal terms, such as *arrest* and *witness*;

- terms for genitalia;

- pronouns, such as *it* and *that* (a demonstrative used as a pronoun);

- prepositions, such as *in* and *on*, and temporal words, such as *before* and *after*.

An example of a five-year-old child misunderstanding the interviewer's use of *that* is seen in Extract 8–viii:

Extract 8–viii Aldridge and Wood's (1998: 177) transcription of videorecording
1. Ch: My Mum doesn't let me have felt pens.
2. Iv: No?
3. Ch: Yeah, don't tell my Mum.
4. Iv: So, if we don't tell Mum that you've got a felt pen in your room, what sort of thing is **that**?
5. Ch: A black pen.

In this example, the interviewer wanted the child to recognise the characteristics of *a secret*, which was the intended answer to the question in Turn 4. But the answer in Turn 5 shows that the child was unable to recognise the intended referent of the demonstrative *that* (used as a pronoun).

Aldridge and Wood (1998: 130–132) also explain that children acquire proficiency in *what, where* and *who* questions before *when, how* and *why* questions, which they may not fully acquire until at least eight years of age. They found that young children gave either meaningful answers to the *what, where* and *who* questions, or else answered with either silence or *I don't know* or *I can't remember*. But with the *when, how* and *why* questions, they found a lot of answers which indicated that the child being questioned answered as if it was a different question, as we see in the examples from young children of different ages in Extract 8–ix:

Extract 8–ix Aldridge and Wood's (1998: 130–133) transcription of videorecording
How-questions answered as if they are *when*-questions:
(a) 1. Iv: **How** did he do it?
2. Ch: Years ago (5 year-old).

(b) 3. Iv: Can you tell me **how** he did that?
4: Ch: When I had my jeans on (5 year-old).

Why-question answered as if it was a *where*-question:
(c) 5. Iv: **Why** does grandad smack you?
6. Ch: Here [pointing] (3 year-old).

You might like to compare these examples of questions asked of children in police interviews, with the examples in Section 2 of Chapter 5 of questions asked of children in courtroom hearings. The courtroom questions are more complex and tricky than the police interview questions cited. Aldridge and Wood's work on the difficulties and miscommunications which can arise from these relatively simple questions highlights just how problematic the cross-examination of children in court can be, where much more complex questions can be commonplace. The contrast between questions asked of children in police interviews with those asked in cross-examination has been addressed by Aldridge (2007). Unsurprisingly, given the adversarial nature of cross-examination and the rights of defendants to question complainants, she finds (p. 79) that while 'the children's experiences in the police interview are generally positive, this certainly is not the case in the courtroom'.

Sociolinguistic research by Aldridge and Wood on children in police interviews reinforces work by Walker (e.g. 1999) on questioning children, which we discussed in relation to children in court in Section 2 of Chapter 5. Both Aldridge and Wood (1998) and Walker (1999) should be essential reading for any research on children in police interviews.

Exercise 8.6[xxxv]

Discuss the questioning of child victims of alleged abuse in the two main legal contexts: police interviews and courtroom cross-examination. (Note that in some jurisdictions, children in such cases do not have to answer questions in examination-in-chief, as their electronically recorded police interview is played in court as examination-in-chief, see Powell *et al.* 2005: 11; Aldridge 2007: 65).
Examine the different types of questions asked in police interviews, for example in Aldridge (2007), Aldridge and Wood (1998) and Johnson (2002).
Compare and contrast these question types with those asked of children in court, for example in Brennan (1994, 1995) and Walker (1993, 1999).
From your understanding of courtroom questioning obtained from your work in Part 2 of this textbook, discuss the possibility of changes to cross-examination to take account of research on questioning children.
If possible, research any special provisions for child witnesses in court, in the light of the research on interviewing children discussed in this chapter. To what extent does it address linguistic issues (rather than other issues such as children's fear of intimidation by defendants). Here you might want to go back to Section 5 of Chapter 5, and see also Assignment topic 2 in Chapter 5.

The research on children in police interviews has, like that of children in court, been focused on child victims of alleged abuse. Presumably the findings of this research and the issues that it raises are also relevant to police interviews of child suspects. However, that does not appear to have been subject to sociolinguistic research, although there has been both legal and psychological attention to the issue of children's and adolescents' comprehension of their rights in police interviews (see Solan & Tiersma 2005: 80–81).

6. Intellectually disabled people

Research in the US (Drizin & Leo 2004) has found that people with intellectual disability are over-represented in the statistics of people who have been found to have made false confessions. Part of the explanation for this may be found in psychological research which shows that people with intellectual disability have a tendency to say *yes* to a range of questions, even absurd ones (Kassin & Gudjonsson 2004: 53). This clearly can have disastrous consequences for a person's ability to invoke the right to silence and other rights. Further, Solan and Tiersma (2005: 78) cite evidence which indicates that intellectually disabled people are not likely to understand their rights in police interviews. Clare (2004) reports on work to revise the *Notice to Detained Persons* in England to make the sections on the 'special provision' of an 'appropriate adult' more comprehensible. And Shuy (1998: 154–173) discusses a 1995 US case in which he provided an expert report in the defence of an intellectually disabled teenager who (unsuccessfully) contested his murder charge, on the grounds that his signature to a murder confession was not made freely.

Most of the work on intellectually disabled people in relation to police interviews has been done by scholars in psychology. For example, Fisher *et al.* (2002: 270–271) report on three studies with 'intellectually impaired or learning disabled children and adults'. These studies found that the use of cognitive interviewing had similar results as for 'unimpaired adults and children' in terms of the improvement of correct recall and levels of accuracy. Milne and Bull (1999: Chapter 7) summarise a number of psychological studies of intellectually/learning/developmentally disabled people in police interviews.

There appears to be little linguistic work examining intellectually disabled people in police interviews, with the exception of that done by two Australian researchers in the mid-1990s, Brennan and Brennan (1994). The aim of this work was to address communication issues affecting the ways in which police officers respond to people with intellectual disability. Brennan and Brennan's work draws on the Australian Law Reform Commission's consultations with intellectually disabled people, as well as their own interviews with police officers. The latter revealed a number of misconceptions about intellectual disability, and it resulted in the production of training materials for police officers. This material provides a framework for assessing communicative effectiveness, which includes such linguistic issues as helping police officers to understand the complexity of certain question types. This pioneering work highlights the need for sociolinguistic analysis of interactions between intellectually disabled people and legal professionals (not limited to police contexts, but also investigating other legal contexts, such as lawyer–client and courtroom interactions).

7. The politics of police questioning

Police officers have considerable situational power over interviewees. This is especially true with suspects, whom they are legally authorised to detain, and if necessary to keep in custody, and in some jurisdictions even in handcuffs and shackles. In addition to this obvious physical power, police officers have linguistic power: to direct a witness's story, to choose what aspects to focus on in a summary of their story, and to ask questions of suspects in a coercive way. In Section 6 of Chapter 7, we saw that this power relationship in police interviews is not all one-sided. Police officers work to produce their version of events in an interview, and we have seen some ways in which interviewees struggle against this control. In this chapter, we have seen some ways in which police officers have particular additional power over interviewees who are members of minority groups: to interview second language speakers without interpreters, and to misrepresent the account of a speaker of a creole language or a second dialect, for example.

But how does this power within the police interview connect to broader societal power struggles, or to power behind the interview, in Fairclough's (1989) terms? In Chapter 6, we looked at some sociolinguistic studies of courtroom talk that ask a parallel question. To date, the sociolinguistic study of police interviews has hardly considered this question, but a thought-provoking beginning has been made by Jones (2008a) in relation to police interviews of Afro-Caribbean suspects in England and Wales (see also Jones 2008b). The Afro-Caribbean suspects in Jones's study, unlike those in Brown-Blake and Chambers (2007) discussed in Section 4.1 above, do not appear to be speaking Jamaican Creole in their police interviews. It is not miscommunication which Jones examines, but the linguistic mechanism of coercion, and its apparently different use with the Afro-Caribbean suspects than with the White British suspects in her study.

There were 10 Afro-Caribbean suspects and 10 White British suspects in this study, and they are all British residents, and they appear to have all spoken the same mainstream variety of British English as each other and as the police officers interviewing them. Jones's interest is in the linguistic strategies used by police officers to steer a suspect to produce a story which points to their guilt. Such an outcome would count as success in a suspect interview, in which an important aim is to elicit information which can result in a charge being laid.

Jones's analysis found several ways in which police officers treated the Afro-Caribbean suspects differently from the White British suspects. For example, 'the Afro-Caribbean suspects had their answers rejected through repetition of questions', whereas 'the White British suspects did not' (2008a: 238). While there were some instances of the police interviewers repeating questions to the White British suspects, they did not repeat the same question three or four times, as happened with the Afro-Caribbean suspects. Another important difference involved questions starting with the discourse marker *so*, known as *so*-prefaced questions. Following Gibbons (2003) and Newbury and Johnson (2006), Jones distinguishes between *so*-prefaced questions which are information seeking from those which are confirmation seeking. Information seeking *so*-prefaced questions can be:

- open questions, such as *So if I take you back to that day, can you tell me ...*, or

- WH-questions, such as *So who was there then?*, or

- Yes/No-questions, such as *So was she already there when you arrived?*

While these questions all function to seek information from the interviewee, *so*-prefaced confirmation seeking questions present a proposition for the interviewee to confirm or deny, taking the form of a statement, such as *So she was already there when you arrived?* In Jones's study, police asked the White British suspects more information seeking questions than they asked the Afro-Caribbean suspects, thus appearing to invite the White British suspects' versions of their story more than they did with the Afro-Caribbean suspects. On the other hand, Afro-Caribbean suspects were asked more confirmation seeking *so*-prefaced questions. Given that such questions usually present the interviewer's version of the story for the interviewee to confirm or deny, they provide less scope for the suspect to present their own version.

Using analytical categories from Conversation Analysis, Jones distinguishes within *so*-prefaced confirmation seeking questions between gists and upshots. Gists are 'essentially a summary of the prior talk' (Jones 2008a: 61), and thus they do not challenge the interviewee's version. For example, a suspect provided information about when his brother had arrived at his house with a stolen video recorder. This was followed by the police officer asking the *so*-prefaced gist question which summarised these previous answers: *So he turned up at your address at two o'clock on either thursday or friday?* But upshots 'draw out a relevant implication which [the interviewee] is expected to ratify' (p. 65). For example, a suspect was answering questions about how he knew that a particular firearm was a replica gun. His answer *Because I know what a replica looks like*, was followed by the police officer asking a *so*-prefaced upshot question *So you know about guns?* As Jones explains (p. 186), this upshot question 'transforms the agenda from how [the suspect] knew the gun was a replica to the [arguably more damaging allegation] that he knows about guns'. Jones found that upshots constrained suspects 'to take up and defend a new agenda, which is not necessarily in tune with what they originally meant' (p. 164). In this way, upshots enabled the police officers to override the suspects' stories with their own, something that they did more with the Afro-Caribbean suspects than the White British suspects.

Jones is careful to avoid attributing intentions to the police officers in the study, who may not realise that they were treating the Afro-Caribbean suspects differently from the White British suspects. However, she points out that the racial inequality uncovered in her small study is arguably related to the larger social issue of institutional racism in England and Wales, which has been of concern for several decades to sociolegal researchers and has been exposed in government inquiries. And we know that the police officers were conscious of the skin colour of the Afro-Caribbean suspects, because it was common for them to refer to this identifying feature before any other in talking to these suspects. For example, one police officer said to a Jamaican suspect: *you are black ... [and] the description we have is that a tall large built Jamaican male was involved in the sale of a handgun* (2008a: 201). For the White British suspects, however, skin colour was not mentioned in the interviews, rather such physical features as hair colour and build. The highlighting of the racial identity of the Afro-Caribbean suspects in these interviews needs to be seen in the wider context of the treatment of Afro-Caribbeans (also referred to as 'blacks') in the criminal justice system in England and Wales for many years (as discussed in Jones 2008a: 9–21, 198–225). Government statistics for the year 2005–2006 show that Afro-Caribbean people are seven times more likely to be stopped and searched by police than white people, and 3.5 times more likely to be arrested (p. 19).

Some important questions emerge about the connection between Jones's microanalysis of police interviews and the complex and controversial relationship between police and Afro-Caribbean people. Do the police officers in this study interview the Afro-Caribbean suspects in a more coercive way than the White British suspects because they believe them to be more likely to be guilty of an offence? Is the interaction revealed in this small study typical of the ways in which British police conduct interviews with suspects? Are there parallels with interviews in other countries with suspects from minority groups which are widely stereotyped in terms of law and order problems? (see for example Eades 2008a, especially 60–63, 336). These are just a few of the kinds of questions which should be addressed in future sociolinguistic research on the politics of communication in police interviews.

Assignments and further research

Any empirical study of police interviews with members of minority groups will require the collection of a corpus of police interviews, as there is so little published data. Thus these questions would be suitable for a thesis/dissertation, and not practical for an essay or term paper.

1. **(Lx)** Examine the use of scripted translations of the police caution in communicating the rights to suspects who speak English as a second language, or suspects who do not speak English. Start your background reading with Berk-Seligson (2009), Nakane (2007), Rock (2007) and Russell (2000).

2. **(Lx)** Examine interpreted police interviews in a language you know well, paying particular attention to linguistic challenges such as turn construction (Nakane 2007; Russell 2000). Also investigate any particular linguistic features of the second language involved which may create challenges for the interpreter (see for example Filipovic 2007; Lee 2009a, 2009b).

3. **(Lx)** Examine the pragmatics of coercion and resistance in interpreted police interviews. To what extent is the sociolinguistic research on courtroom interpreting (introduced in Section 5 of Chapter 4) relevant to police interview interpreting?

4. **(Lx)** If it is possible to collect data from police interviews with suspects who are adolescents or children: examine the pragmatics of coercion and resistance in these interviews. What similarities and differences are there with language use in police interviews with adult suspects (as reported in sociolinguistic studies).

Part 4
Other legal contexts

9
Lawyer–client interactions

1. Introduction   188

2. Legal rules, emotions and personalities   189

3. Linguistic features associated with power, control and gender   191

4. The interweaving of text and talk   194

5. From interview to affidavit   196

6. Learning to bracket emotion, morality and social context   201

   Assignments and further research   204

Lawyer–client interactions

1. Introduction

Many people think it's hard to talk to a lawyer about their legal problems. What is behind this view? How do lawyers talk to their clients, and how do clients talk to their lawyers? In this chapter we will look at research, done mainly by sociolinguists, which addresses this question. Conley and O'Barr's (1990: 176) overview of the job of lawyers gives a good indication of what is involved in lawyer–client interactions: 'Most lawyers spend most of their time trying to understand problems stated in lay terms and transform them to meet the requirements of legal discourse' (see also Cunningham 1992; Maley *et al.* 1995). While this transformation is central, lawyers are also often involved in explaining the law to clients, for example when telling them about possible courses of action within the law and the consequences of these actions. So, a major part of the work that lawyers do for their clients involves a kind of two-way interpreting combined with puzzle-solving: interpreting what clients are telling them about an aspect of their life, working out how it fits into a particular legislative framework and interpreting the relevant law to their clients. Another major part of lawyers' work involves the generation of legal talk and text as part of the transformation of their clients' problems, for example with questions for courtroom hearings, letters to spouses' lawyers in divorce cases, or affidavits for court in protective order applications.

One of the recurring themes in the study of language use in legal contexts concerns the ways in which written law is explained, negotiated, argued and deliberated over in interactions between legal professionals on the one hand, and those who come into contact with them, on the other. Thus, in Sections 6 and 7 of Chapter 3, we saw some of the problems involved when judges explain written law in their oral instructions to the jury. In Section 2 of Chapter 7 and Section 2.2 of Chapter 8 we addressed some of the complex linguistic and sociolinguistic issues in the oral and written delivery to suspects of their rights in police interviews. But it is not only a matter of presenting written laws in oral form to people without legal training. In Section 4 of Chapter 1 we saw that spoken interaction in the courtroom is transformed into written transcript which becomes the official version of the event, and which can be used in any appeals in the future. This process can affect the way that lawyers ask questions in court, as the addressee is not only the witness, and the jury, but also the written record. We also saw in Section 7 of Chapter 7 and Section 4.2 of Chapter 8, how police officers can transform an interviewee's responses to questions into a written summary text that obscures the interactional production of the story it contains (a topic we will come back to in Section 4.3 of Chapter 11).

So, it is clear that one of the major activities involved in the legal process is negotiating between (written) text and talk, and between talk and text. This interdependence between text and talk pervades interactions between lawyers and their clients. Writing specifically about the criminal justice process, Komter (2006a: 196) says that it 'can be seen as a chain of events where encounters of spoken interaction are "wedged in" and informed by written documents and where the written documents are treated as the official basis for decision making on the assumption that they "represent" the spoken interaction'. Legal officers in police interviews and in courtroom hearings engage in talk that will always have some kind of written manifestation, representation or summary. And at times their talk originates with written text, such as when judges explain the law to jurors, or lawyers cross-examine witnesses about the transcript of a police interview. But for lawyers, the written text is at times the immediate outcome or product that they are required to produce from the spoken interaction. This happens, for example, when lawyers prepare affidavits based on what their clients tell them, as we will see in Section 5 below. And at other times, the written texts are the documents which the lawyers need to verify, amend or expand on from talk with their client, as we will see in Section 4 below. Thus, it appears that the text-to-talk-to-text nature of lawyer–client interaction is even more central than in the other two main legal contexts, the courtroom hearing and the police interview.

Unlike these two major legal contexts which have already been considered in this book, most lawyer–client interviews are private interactions, from which there is no official record.[48] This, combined with the confidential nature of the talk, mean that it is not easy for researchers to gain access to data. In this chapter, we will see that sociolinguistic and related research has begun to address the issues introduced in this section namely:

- how lawyers and their clients talk to each other;

- the relationship between text and talk in lawyer–client interactions;

- how lawyers transform their clients stories for the legal process.

This research takes us to several different countries (including Australia, Israel, the UK, and the US) and several legal contexts (involving divorce, domestic violence and criminal cases). This chapter concludes with looking at how law students learn to talk like lawyers.

2. Legal rules, emotions and personalities

Sarat and Felstiner (1995) use an ethnographic approach to study the exercise of power and the construction of meaning in 40 mid-1980s divorce cases in two US cities. Their study centres on 115 lawyer–client meetings (often called 'conferences') and 130 researcher interviews with lawyers and clients, all of which were audiorecorded over a period of nearly three years. The study pays particular attention to how lawyers and their clients talk to each other about the case and the law, as well as how they negotiate legal outcomes concerning the divorce.

One of Sarat and Felstiner's major findings about lawyer–client interaction is that lawyers work to keep legal and rational matters separate from social and emotional matters. This 'ideological separation of the legal from the social' (Sarat & Felstiner 1995: 95) is not limited to divorce cases, but it is central to the functioning of the legal process. It is an issue which we will also see in Section 5 below when we look at how lawyers and paralegals respond to the stories of their clients in domestic violence cases. And it is also important in the training of law students, as we will see in Section 6. Further, it is an important issue in the ways in which laypeople deal with the legal process in cases which do not involve lawyers, as we will see in Section 2 of Chapter 10. As one lawyer explained the legal side of divorce to her client and the client's spouse: '[In] most divorces nowadays, although there are a lot of emotions involved, and allegations of "he said" and "she did" and things like that, it really comes down to an accounting problem' (p. 65). The 'accounting problem' is about how to resolve disputes over financial matters and such custody issues as hours/days/weeks of non-custodial parenting, within the framework of the relevant law.

From the beginning of their first meeting with clients, the lawyers in Sarat and Felstiner's study explained divorce procedures according to the relevant statutes – interpreting written legal texts for their clients. Their focus was on 'accounting problems' such as property division and child support. Clients, on the other hand, talked about such things as what 'he said' and 'she did', focusing on what had gone wrong in the marriage, and why their spouse was at fault. Lawyers avoided talking about fault and blame, which have no place in no-fault divorce law, and they often remained silent when clients attacked their spouse or talked about their marriage. Lawyers did engage with their clients' talk about their spouse when it related to discussing strategies for legal negotiations with the spouse. Maley *et al.* (1995) found a similar pattern of lawyers shifting from impersonal legal talk to align with their client's evaluation of their spouse. Thus, for example, one New South Wales (Australia) lawyer in a divorce property settlement case was persuading her client to apply to move the case from the state of Western Australia, where the client's spouse had applied to begin the proceedings, to NSW. This is how the lawyer put it (p. 48):

I don't know what the judges in the family law court in Western Australia do, but I do know what they do in New [South Wales], and I know one judge in particular would have the cane toad on toast ... OK ... so that's another reason why ... [it's] better for us to bring it across here.

Maley *et al.* point out that the cane toad is a ubiquitous and despised pest, which is very ugly and puffed up in appearance. (It is also poisonous.) Thus without discussing the client's experiences during her marriage, the lawyer aligned to her client's criticism of her husband by referring to him as a *cane toad*. Further, she presented an image of a judge destroying his power, with the colloquialism of *having him on toast*.[49] As with Sarat and Felstiner's study, the authors of this Australian study found that this evaluative shifting occurred in talk about legal strategy. Maley *et al.* suggest that the shifting happens in a strategic way, that is in order to make the lawyer's suggestion more persuasive.

The Australian lawyer's suggestion of a judge having her client's husband 'on toast' is also a good example of Sarat and Felstiner's (1995) finding about how lawyers talk to their clients about judges. Although they started off talking to their clients about the legal system in terms of rules, this seemed to change if a case progressed in such a way that a court hearing was to take place rather than a negotiated (out of court) settlement. (Court adjudication was an option which lawyers encouraged their clients to avoid – because of costs, delays and problems with court hearings – contrary to popular views of 'the lawyer as "shark", eagerly stirring up trouble, fanning the flames of contention' p. 111–112.) Instead of talking about court hearings in terms of legal rules, lawyers projected their insider knowledge, giving their opinions about personalities and reputations of judges. For example, one of the lawyers prepared his client for a courtroom hearing with detailed comments on how he should sit, without having his arms over the back of the chair, with his hands in front of him, without crossing his legs, and making sure to look alert. The lawyer explained that this was important because judges *are people, and we might as well play the odds rather than have some surprises develop just because the judge doesn't like the way you are sitting* (p. 100). At times lawyers even told clients about their own personal connections within the legal system, such as one lawyer who emphasised his close connections with the local district attorney. With this focus on 'judicial powers, personalities, predispositions, and idiosyncrasies', lawyers sent a message to their clients 'that it is the judge, not the law, that really counts' (Sarat & Felstiner 1990: 140). This seems to reveal something of a paradox: lawyers did not want to engage with the personal issues that their clients tried to tell them about relating to their experiences during the marriage, yet personal characteristics of judges were important in the way lawyers talked to their clients about an adjudicated resolution of their problems. On the other hand, we saw that lawyers were interested in personal characteristics of their clients' spouse as well as their clients' experiences during their marriage, to the extent that they related to the strategy to be taken in the case. Thus, it seems that the lawyers did talk to clients about personal and social matters, to the extent that the lawyers believed them to be relevant to the legal strategy to be pursued in their client's interest. Sarat and Felstiner (1990, 1995) discuss these dimensions of the paradox in terms of two fundamental approaches to the law: known as realism and formalism. In the formalism approach, law is seen as a system of rules which govern procedures and outcomes – the lawyers typically began their dealings with their clients according to a formalist approach. But after this beginning, lawyers focused more on the personalities involved in both negotiated settlement and adjudication. Putting people rather than rules at the centre of the legal process in this way is consistent with the legal approach known as realism.

Investigating talk between lawyers and their clients in these 40 divorce cases enabled Sarat and Felstiner to address the issue of the power relationships involved, an issue we will come back to in Sections 3 and 5 below. The way in which lawyers structured conversations with their clients, for example by ignoring some, but not all, of their clients' talk about their spouse, is one way in which lawyers were able to exercise power over their clients. This is part of their professional power, as insiders in the legal system who can understand it and find their way around and through it. On the other hand, being employed as advocates for their clients means that lawyers are also under obligations to their clients, who in this way are able to exercise some power over their lawyers. In their examination of one case over more than six months, Sarat and Felstiner (1995) show that it was 'often difficult to say who, if anyone, was directing the case'. They suggest that at different times in her meetings with the lawyer, the client may have been using silence, repetition and circularity as a way of exercising her power. Thus, Sarat and Felstiner's (p. 142) conclusion about power relations in their study is that 'lawyer–client relations are sites of conflict and negotiation in which the conditions of power change from moment to moment'. This attention to the microdynamics of power relations challenges traditional views of dominant lawyers and passive clients. However, this ethnographic study does not involve close sociolinguistic analysis of the talk and the researchers' transcripts did not record sufficient detail for this to be done. The remainder of the studies which we will examine in the chapter use sociolinguistic microanalysis in their investigation of lawyer–client interaction.

3. Linguistic features associated with power, control and gender

At the time that Sarat and Felstiner (1990, 1995) were investigating lawyers talking to clients in the US using an ethnographic approach, Bogoch (1994, 1997) was approaching the same topic in Israel by focusing on particular linguistic features of the talk. Like Sarat and Felstiner, Bogoch is also interested in power relations between lawyers and clients, a theme which she investigates in terms of studies about the changing nature of professional–client relationships (1994), and studies of language and gender (1997). However, unlike Sarat and Felstiner, Bogoch has not considered the microdynamics of power relations, but has focused on what she terms 'indications' of lawyers' power, control and domination of their clients. Both of Bogoch's studies examine audiorecordings of 19 lawyer–client interviews in a legal aid office. The cases involved divorce, maintenance and custody law, as well as labour law. Each interview was the initial meeting between the lawyer and that client.

The first of these studies (Bogoch 1994) examines the extent to which lawyers use an authoritarian approach versus a participatory one, consistent with studies of other institutional settings, such as doctor–patient interaction, where the traditional authoritarian model has been giving way to a participatory egalitarian one. An important contextual factor in the study is the Israeli 'ideological commitment to egalitarian, solidary and informal relationships even between strangers' (p. 65). Thus, the interviews were examined for linguistic indications of power, distance and solidarity. If you were to select a number of linguistic features to examine power, distance and solidarity in lawyer interviews in your country, what would they be? For Bogoch's study, they were conversational openings, professional register, topic control, the expression of emotion and forms of address.

Bogoch reports that the most surprising finding was that none of the lawyers opened the conversation with their client with a greeting. They got straight into the business of the interview, for example with a request for confirmation of a detail about the case, or checking the client's name. What is the significance of this finding? Bogoch (1994: 70) argues that it shows that the lawyers did not perceive any need for 'the social rituals of everyday encounters' which have been found for example in the US 'to disguise professional power'. The lawyers in this Israeli study made it clear from the beginning that they were in charge.

We would expect that lawyers, like doctors with their patients, need to use professional register in some of their talk to their clients. Bogoch looks at how the lawyers used technical legal terms and how they explained them. For example, one uneducated woman of lower socioeconomic status interrupted her lawyer's use of legal register during an explanation, saying *I didn't understand. What does that mean? What is apotropus?*[50] As Bogoch points out, this active questioning by the client might suggest evidence of a participatory relationship between her and her lawyer. But the lawyer's reply was in a formal register, using semantic and syntactic legal features which are unlikely to have answered his client's question, when he replied *Apotropus. That is the appointment of a certain person party for another party when he is incapable when the said party is incapable of functioning.* Such formal and obscure 'explanations' of legal terminology also present the lawyer as an authority who is in control of the interaction. This control of lawyers over the interaction is also found in their determination of the topics to be discussed, their topic changes, and their introduction of apparently unrelated topics.

While Bogoch did not expect to find lawyers expressing emotions to their client, she found that lawyers tended to ignore their clients' expression of emotion, for example by changing topic. A particularly poignant example comes (1994: 77) from an interview with a woman who said to her lawyer *I'm also sick and tired of this life. I already wanted to commit suicide several times from all these troubles.* As she continued, saying *I want*, the lawyer started speaking, saying *All right. What is the phone number of the outpatient clinic?* (It is not clear whether the phone number of the outpatient clinic was related to the client's reports of previous suicidal feelings.) You can see that Bogoch's finding about lawyers not wanting to deal with their clients' expression of emotion is consistent with Sarat and Felstiner's (1995) finding about the divorce lawyers in their study who only wanted to respond to their clients' talk about emotional issues if it was directly relevant to the legal strategy to be pursued.

Bogoch's examination of the fifth feature – forms of address – is not as straightforward as with the other features. Her main finding is that lawyers and clients rarely addressed each other by name, and she suggests that this might be consistent with the neutral and bureaucratic nature of the interaction. A possible class exercise might involve summarising and critiquing her findings on forms of address. It is important to remember that the choice of address terms (such as Title + last name; or first name only) and related interpretations and expectations are not necessarily shared between and across languages.

On the basis of her findings about how these lawyers talked to their clients, Bogoch concluded that these interviews were conducted in an authoritarian approach, which was characterised by professional dominance, neutrality and distance. Bogoch does not consider the ways in which clients exercise power over their lawyers, an issue which is a part of Sarat and Felstiner's (1995) treatment of power in lawyer–client interactions. In the mid-1990s most sociolinguistic studies of language in the legal process which addressed power relations tended to take a rather one-sided and static view of power, as we discussed in Section 2 of Chapter 6. This is also true of Bogoch and Danet's (1984) analysis of one lawyer–client meeting, also in Israel, which examines how the lawyer controlled the talk. One particularly interesting characteristic of this interaction is that the lawyer established 'a dialogue that is very much like cross-examination' (p. 249), with such linguistic features as interruptions, abrupt topic switching, reformulations, repeating questions without waiting for a reply and 'unfounded presuppositions'.

Exercise 9.1[xxxvi]
Discuss your observations and intuitions about how lawyers, doctors and other professionals in your country use language to create and/or maintain a position of power over clients/patients they are interviewing. Which of the linguistic features in Bogoch's study do you think would be relevant? Why? Are there other features which you think would be relevant to a study such as Bogoch's in your country? Which ones, and why? How might such a study take into account a more dynamic and reciprocal view of power relationships, such as discussed throughout Chapter 6 above, and used in Sarat and Felstiner (1995)?

Using the same interview data collected for her first (1994) study, Bogoch (1997) looked for evidence of gendered patterning in language use. This topic connects to studies in other contexts (see for example Holmes & Meyerhoff 2003), which have found that women and men use language differently, and it will be of particular interest to sociolinguistics students who have studied language and gender.

Bogoch was interested in a question about lawyers that was similar to that investigated by the Duke study about witnesses (discussed in Section 4.2 of Chapter 3 above). That is, she investigated whether talk between lawyers and their clients shows gendered patterns of language use, or whether the speaker's role in the interaction is more significant – being a lawyer or being a client. We saw that the Duke study had examined features from Lakoff's (1975) characterisation of the features of 'women's language', such as the use of hedges and intensifiers. More than a decade after the Duke study, Bogoch took as her point of departure two different sociolinguistic approaches at the time into language and gender. Thus, she examined both the dominance and the difference paradigms in the way in which language and gender was being studied, comparing the use of certain features of language for each of the following four groups: male lawyer, female lawyer, male client, female client. The dominance paradigm holds that women and men use language differently because of men's dominance over women. To explore this paradigm, Bogoch examined such features as the amount of talk, and the control of topics. The difference paradigm holds that women and men use language differently because they belong to different sub-cultures. To explore this paradigm, Bogoch examined such features as the expression of emotion and the use of affiliative requests. Her main finding (1997: 704) is that 'female lawyers were more similar in their linguistic behaviour to male lawyers than to clients of either sex'. Thus, like the Duke study of witnesses' talk, Bogoch found that the speaker's role in the legal context was more important than their gender in relation to language use. And, consistent with her (1994) study discussed above, she found that the women lawyers 'retained their stance of professional neutrality and domination' (1997: 705). But while the clients were subordinate in terms of the features of language use examined within the dominance paradigm, women clients were most deferent with male lawyers, and 'the subordinate status of clients was mitigated when the client was male and the professional was male' (p. 704). These findings suggest that while gender was not relevant to the talk of the lawyers, it did affect the ways in which clients interacted.

4. The interweaving of text and talk

We have seen that Sarat and Felstiner's work on lawyer–client interactions uses ethnography but not sociolinguistic discourse analysis, while Bogoch's work uses sociolinguistic discourse analysis but not ethnography. By the mid-2000s, it had become more usual for studies of language in the legal process to combine both approaches, consistent with developments within the broader field of sociolinguistics. Two case studies in England combine ethnography with sociolinguistic discourse analysis to examine interactions between a lawyer and his client, in custody in a police station (Halldorsdottir 2006), and throughout the day in which a lawyer met his client, prepared his defence and represented him in court (Scheffer 2006). Both cases provide a microanalysis which highlights the pervasive and central role of written texts throughout the conversations between the lawyer and his client.

Halldorsdottir's (2006) study examines interaction between a lawyer and his client who was in custody in a police station in England. (The client's mother also participated in the interview.) The common practice in such lawyer–client interviews is for the lawyer to explain the evidence the police have against the client, as well as the law relating to the allegation, and then to ask the client to tell their story about the event. In the case Halldorsdottir examined, the first two of these activities involved the lawyer going from text to talk: first from his written notes of the police officer's oral summary of the evidence against his client (a text which had originated in talk), and then in his explanation of the law on shoplifting. The next two activities also involved an orientation to text, although it was less direct. The client and his mother took up the legal difference between theft and burglary in terms of the client's action, and then the lawyer's questioning about the client's criminal history provided information relevant to police guidelines on diversionary cautions (see Note 24 in Chapter 7). The lawyer then moved on to explaining the features of the case that could support an argument for diversionary cautioning (rather than the criminal charge of burglary). The discussion of relevant police guidelines (in a Home Office circular) continued with talk between the lawyer, his client and the client's mother about the reasonableness of the proposed request for cautioning, and the unreasonableness of the investigating officer's stated intention to lay a burglary charge. The extracts from this lawyer–client interview presented by Halldorsdottir clearly show the lawyer's work in the two-way process of 'interpretation' – both interpreting relevant parts of the law and of police guidelines to his client, and interpreting the client's actions in terms of the law. In this two-way process, texts and documents are central – whether it is the law, police guidelines or the formulation of the allegation. While these texts can be 'invoked in talk' (2006: 270), new texts can be constructed on the basis of the interview, such as the lawyer's record of the client's case.

While the suspect in Halldorsdottir's case was interviewed by his lawyer at the police station, Scheffer (2006) examines an interview between a lawyer and defendant in the courthouse cell on the morning of his court hearing. Scheffer's interest is in what he calls the 'microformation' of a criminal defence, taking us through the way that one barrister[51] in England prepared the defence of a client accused of a serious assault offence ('wounding with intent'). While trial manuals for lawyers outline steps in preparing a defence, Scheffer's examination is much more detailed and includes all of the lawyer's written activity – such as writings, jottings and text markings – as well as his discussions with his client: hence his term 'the microformation' of the defence.

The case was not a jury trial but a Crown Court hearing, and the barrister had no prior information about the case before the day of the hearing. On the morning on which he had to defend the client in court, the barrister received a file containing documentation he would need (this file is known as a 'brief', even though it is often far from brief!).[52] In addition to the formal documents such as the indictment, and the record of the police interview (together with the audiotape), the brief contained witness statements, and exhibits, such as photographs of the injuries sustained by the victim. The file had been prepared by the instructing solicitor for the case, the barrister had had no opportunity to consult with this person, and he had not met with his client before the day of the hearing. Further, there was no written statement from the client, and there were no accurate instructions[53] prepared by the solicitor, only a few scribbled notes.

Scheffer's ethnographic study involved him shadowing the barrister all day, and later analysing the barrister's notes on documents in the brief, as well as the notes the barrister produced himself. After his initial reading and marking of the documents in the brief – for example with underlining and jotted notes – the barrister rushed to the cells to interview his client. Doubtless the very limited time for preparing the defence was an important factor in the way in which the barrister took instructions from his client. We saw in Chapters 7 and 8 that there is a considerable literature about the best ways of eliciting a person's story in investigative interviews. But for lawyers there is frequently no time or justification for a carefully prepared or structured interview. Rather than asking his client *what happened?* or inviting him in any other way to tell his story, the barrister led the client through the police interview transcript, asking him to either confirm or correct it. This process therefore privileges the police interview, which might seem to be a strange situation. After all, the defence lawyer's job is to present a story from the perspective of the accused person rather than from that of the prosecution. On the other hand, this approach is not only expedient under the serious time restrictions, but it also clarifies for the defence how his client responds to the police version of events, and to the way he had earlier answered police questions.

In Section 7.2 of Chapter 7 and Section 4.2 of Chapter 8, we saw how written summary statements by police transform a conversation between suspect and police officer(s) into a single-authored narrative. Scheffer found the same process in the way that the barrister produced in his notes a monologue version of his client's story from the police interview. He did this by underlining parts of his client's answers in the police interview, omitting the questions, as well as any repetition. This version – which became the client's instructions – shares with the written police summaries we saw in Chapter 7 the characteristics of a dialogue which has become a monologue. Thus there was now only one author – the client – and the original source distinctions – who introduced what point, in what way – had become blurred.

Scheffer then traces the trajectory of the barrister's work on the case that day: including the preparation of an abbreviated list of modules that encapsulated elements of the prosecution case, the drafting of a rough map of the location of the event, the cross-examination of prosecution witnesses questioning them about their statements as prepared by the police, and the examination-in-chief of defence witnesses. In the examination-in-chief of the defendant, we see the interdependence of text and talk. The barrister drew on his list of prepared modules to formulate questions, which themselves provided the framework for the defendant to tell his story. The barrister's closing argument was based on several written sources, including notes taken while interviewing his client, marks made on the brief, notes jotted down while cross-examining, and lists of points made in preparation for the closing argument.

The conclusion Scheffer draws from his detailed investigation is that text and talk are not discrete modes in the barrister's work on this case. Rather than seeing the lawyer operating either orally or with written text, or even 'jumping from one ... to the other' (2006: 337), he says that the microformation of the defence 'operates in between, invents intermediaries [such as notes, marks such as underlinings, lists, a map], and bridges gaps' between text and talk.

5. From interview to affidavit

The two case studies by Halldorsdottir and Scheffer show the interdependence of text and talk in lawyer–client interaction at the time of arrest and on the day of a courtroom hearing. The lawyer's immediate task is to advocate for the client in relation to the client's actions which have led to arrest, and in the context of the relevant law. The most detailed sociolinguistic study of interaction between lawyers and their clients is found in the work of Trinch (e.g. 2003), who carried out an extensive study of interviews by lawyers and paralegals with Latina survivors of domestic abuse in the US. The focus of these interviews was the lawyers and paralegals obtaining the stories of abuse in order to prepare a written affidavit for the court in support of the client's application for a protective order (= restraining order). Given the similarities between the ways in which lawyers and paralegals interacted with their clients and prepared their affidavits, I will use the generic term 'lawyers' to refer to 'lawyers and paralegals' in this study, in order to avoid unnecessary clumsiness (but see also Trinch's 2001 discussion of similarities and differences).

Over a period of 13 months in two different cities, Trinch observed and recorded 163 protective order interviews, and she also did ethnographic research in nine agencies that support battered women. Her main reason for choosing to focus on Latinas was because of their demographic importance, combined with the fact that 'U.S. institutions across the country are grappling with issues of representation for minority groups' (2003: 9). Trinch makes it clear that this study is not meant to suggest that Latina women suffer more or different domestic violence than other women, or that their experiences in the legal system are different. One of the cities in Trinch's study – where Latinos make up more than 40% of the population – presents a good example of societal bilingualism, with the Latino community being largely bilingual in Spanish and English. Latina women are often interviewed by people who share their ethnolinguistic background, and many of the interviews were conducted entirely in Spanish. But the other city is quite different: there are varying degrees of bilingualism among both service providers and victims, and the interviews were either carried out in English, or in Spanish with the assistance of an interpreter. Interestingly, Trinch found relatively little code-switching in the interviews, with participants generally preferring to use either Spanish or English. (But see Trinch 2001 for discussion of the non-Latino lawyers with limited Spanish proficiency using some Spanish as a way of 'claiming common ground' with their interviewees.)

Focusing on the interaction between lawyers and their clients in these protective order interviews, Trinch found that the lawyers were actually simultaneously engaged in two jobs. Thus, they had two roles and identities, which at times conflicted, namely as advocates and as gatekeepers (see Trinch 2001, 2007). We customarily understand lawyers to be advocates for their clients, but in this situation they also had to assess the women's stories in order to ascertain whether they were eligible to apply for a protective order from the court. It might also be argued that lawyers in other cases also have some gatekeeping role. For example, was the lawyer in Halldorsdottir's study, discussed above, playing a gatekeeping role in determining the possibility of arguing for diversionary cautioning for his client, rather than a burglary charge?

Trinch's major focus is on the women's stories, told to the lawyers in the interviews, and then transformed into written summaries by the lawyers for the affidavit. You can see that this is a situation where original talk must become recontextualised as written text in order for it to play a role in the legal process. Through careful discourse analysis of the interactions between the women and their lawyers, Trinch reveals the dynamic process through which the women's stories were told. We see how the lawyer–client interactions were constrained by the lawyers' gatekeeping concerns, as well as by their attention to the required legal outcome. At the same time, we see how the stories that the women told in these interviews were shaped by the interaction, in a similar way that the stories which witnesses tell to police are shaped by the interaction between police officers and witnesses (as we saw in Section 7.2 of Chapter 7).

The interviews were structured in a way that paralleled the Domestic Violence Questionnaire form which the women were required to fill out in the waiting room before the interview. During the interviews, lawyers were writing notes or typing them into a computer, as well as asking questions. The first part of the interview is described by Trinch (2003: 98) as the 'institutional data-gathering period'. Actual stories about experiences of abuse were typically ignored if they were told in this initial part of the interview. (They were also ignored during the closing part of the interview, when the lawyer would tell the interviewee about the future steps to be taken in their case.) For example, if the victims began a self-initiated narrative at the beginning of the interview most of the lawyers either ignored it or interrupted with questions from the interview form. However, on about one-quarter of these occasions the interviewer actually acknowledged the story in some way. Extract 9–i below shows how the interviewer did minimally acknowledge the unsolicited account of abuse, but then moved the interviewee away from narrating something which was not considered relevant to that part of the interview. This silencing of parts of their clients' stories is similar to both what Sarat and Felstiner (1995) found with lawyers talking to clients in divorce cases (discussed in Section 2 above), and what Bogoch (1994) found with the Israeli lawyers (discussed in Section 3 above).

Extract 9–i Trinch's (2003: 138–139) transcription of audiorecording
1. PL: O.K. Ha have the children witnessed the abuse?
2. C: Yes- well- two weeks ago when he did what he did to me- and I got cut- my little girls- well he threw me down- and I guess I kind of like blacked out – my little girls got off the van to come and get him off of me and he pushed them all- and was- the girls told me that he had told them a lot of bad things and he had pushed them [all off- you know
3. PL: [O.K.- [for
4. C: [And that's what they were afraid of- because he had never [done
5. PL: [that before
6. C: [something to them like that
7. PL: [Eh- for statistical purposes- what is your monthly income?

You can see that the interviewee responded to a simple Yes/No-question (in Turn 1) about whether the children had witnessed her abuse by telling the story of a violent episode which had occurred two weeks previously. In Turn 3, the interviewer responded with the non-committal acceptance token *OK*, and then seemed to start saying something new (*for*). When the interviewee overlapped with a comment in Turn 4 on the violent episode (in narrative analysis terms, a coda), the interviewer overlapped to finish off that coda (in Turn 5). Then without pausing at all, and without even letting the interviewee finish that utterance in Turn 6, the interviewer changed topic and tone, asking in Turn 7 for the interviewee's monthly income.

The fact that interviewers ignored part of the women's stories while they were trying to elicit short answers for institutional data-gathering, may be explainable in terms of the lawyers' attention to the immediate task of completing the required data. But even in the main part of the interview, when they were eliciting the women's stories, lawyers often ignored parts of these stories. For example, the women's stories tended to represent domestic abuse 'as a relationship and not as just an incident of violence' (Trinch 2003: 160). But in the affidavits the lawyers had to report specific incidents of violence. Further, consistent with the women's stories representing domestic abuse in terms of relationships, some of them told of times when they had tried to stand up to their abuser. But in order to present the women as 'victims' rather than 'survivors' or even perhaps 'counter-agents', the written affidavits removed any evidence of women taking actions against their abuser. In this way, significant aspects of the women's identity and actions were removed or altered.

Exercise 9.2[xxxvii]

Extract 9–ii below is part of a woman's story told to a paralegal about an incident when her abuser attacked her and attempted to rape her. Read this extract and discuss these questions:
(a) In what ways does the client present herself as an active participant in the incident she is reporting?
(b) What part of the client's story is ignored by the interviewer and why?
(c) Do you think that the interviewer's use of the word *struggling* in Turn 13 is suitable? Why(not)? What alternative word(s) might be possible and why do you think she chose *struggling*?

Extract 9–ii Trinch's (2003: 204–205) transcription of audiorecording

1. PL: OK, um- did he do- did he do anything else- um (1.0) to you when he was there? You say- you wrote on here that he slapped you- is this when he slapped you?

2. C: Right.

3. PL: OK.
4. C: Um- and the whole time- I was- you know- crying and crying and I guess I was- I was dehydrated and he wouldn't let me up – and he finally pulled back and let me sit down for a little while- but he wouldn't let me get up- no- no- I couldn't get any water- I couldn't go to the restroom- I couldn't move- I just had to sit there.

5. PL: Do you know about how long this took?
6. C: Probably about three hours.

7. PL: Three hours?
8. C: Mhmh.

9. PL: So he was successful?
10. C: No.

11. PL: No?
12. C: Mumum ((meaning *no*))

13. PL: **So were the two of you struggling?**
14. C: **Yeah- yeah I did- you know it's like ( ) two or three times- I hit him- I bit him- anything to try and get him away from me.**

15. PL: **Was he successful in removing your clothes?**
16. C: **Mhmh.**

Exercise 9.3[xxxviii]

Extract 9–iii below is the paralegal's summary in the written affidavit of the incident which was partly reported in Extract 9–ii above. The bolded part is the summary of the part of the client's story from Turns 13–16 in Extract 9–ii above. Read this extract and discuss these questions:

(a) How has the client's agency in this episode been muted?

(b) Why do you think the paralegal has done this?

(c) Does it matter? Why(not)?

Extract 9–iii Trinch (2003: 205); written affidavit

On about [date], at [time], Hector went to my house without my permission while I was out. He went into my house and waited for me. He was drunk. Hector questioned me and then pushed me against the bathroom wall. He grabbed my arms and I sustained bruises. He ran after me in the house. Hector knocked me to the floor in the kids' room. He then got on top of me and told me he was gonna have me whether I liked it or not. Hector slapped me and tried to rape me. **I struggled with him. Hector removed my clothes, but I did everything I could to keep him from raping me.** This went on for about three hours.[54] Hector finally left. While he was gone, I called the police.

Trinch's study shows in considerable detail the ways in which lawyers can shape their client's stories, through the questions they ask and the responses they make or don't make to the women's answers. As Trinch (2001: 497) puts it, we see that the lawyers in these interviews were 'editors of a report, rather than listeners to a story'. And in their recontextualisation of the stories in written summaries, lawyers transform these stories, largely it seems to make them 'fit' the expectations in the legal system about survivors of domestic violence. But does it matter that lawyers transform their clients' stories like this? Is it necessary in order for them to be effective advocates? How and why do these narrative transformations matter? Trinch provides a number of answers to these questions, some of which you will have discussed in your work on Exercise 9.3. The lawyers were writing affidavits that would represent the women in terms of the legal system's – and the wider society's – expectations of experiences of domestic violence which should entitle women to protective orders. This includes the reporting of a few specific incidents of violence, and seems to exclude evidence of the women as agents standing up to their abusers. This approach of the lawyers at these two stages of the protective order interviews and affidavits for the court might seem to make sense, and to 'work'. It's not known whether this kind of transformation is necessary for the protective order application to work. Trinch (2006: 588) reports that almost all of the women who filed applications were granted temporary protective orders on the basis of these affidavits. They then had a court hearing for the decision about a full protective order.

But what happens if a woman ends up in court giving evidence in a related case in which her abuser is charged with assault? In Chapters 3 and 6, we saw that a common cross-examination strategy is for lawyers to take answers to earlier questions (such as in a police interview), and try to elicit some inconsistency between those answers and answers in court. So, a lawyer could use the words from a woman's protective order affidavit, and find inconsistencies between that account and the woman's own account in court. Or a woman could bring up in court some part of the incident which she had talked about in the protective order interview, but which had been omitted from the affidavit. Such a discrepancy would not be well received by judges and lawyers (and presumably also jurors). You can see how a discrepancy like this could be used as evidence that the woman is unable to tell a consistent story, and is therefore an unreliable witness (and see also Note 54).

Another problem can arise in relation to the woman's role in actively resisting her abuser or fighting back. Trinch (2003: 204) found that many women do not 'explicitly couch their own acts of physical violence in terms of self-defense'. So the interviewers may downplay or omit the report of these acts in the affidavits, as we have seen. But when sexual violence cases get to the adversarial courtroom, victims actually need to show that they actively resisted their attacker, otherwise they are considered to have consented to the actions. So, as Trinch (2003: 205) explains, 'while some level of resistance is required before a person can be considered a victim ..., too much resistance might make the person's victim-status questionable'.

Trinch (2003: 277) argues that the transformation of the stories can be seen in two different ways:

On the one hand, this can be interpreted as 'giving voice' to victims of domestic violence to ensure that they are heard. On the other hand, it can be seen as mutating or erasing the victims' voices, leaving a historical record in the form of a court document that does more to reflect what the law considers to be important in these cases than it does to represent what the women's experiences are and what they consider to be of relevance.

For this reason, Trinch argues that the women's powerlessness is reproduced by the ways in which their stories are distorted. In this way, a temporary and individual solution can be found to the widespread societal problem of violence against women. Trinch's work exemplifies how contemporary sociolinguistic studies of language in the legal process can combine fine-grained microanalysis of what people say with much larger societal issues about language and power (as we also saw in the studies discussed in Chapter 6).

Class discussion

Discuss Trinch's argument that the alterations that lawyers make to the stories of their clients in her study 'diminish women's power to represent abuse, and the transformations their narratives undergo constrain the potential their stories might have at affecting systemic change' (2003: 3).

---

6. Learning to bracket emotion, morality and social context

A continuing theme of the studies of lawyer–client interactions – which we have seen in several studies discussed in this chapter – can be summed up by Sarat and Felstiner's (1995: 24) point that 'lawyers construct a picture of a world in which reason is separated from emotion and law is separated from society'. This separation is also central to an important study of the socialisation of law students, that is how law students are taught, both explicitly and implicitly, to participate effectively within the culture of the law. Mertz (2007) shows that while students are explicitly taught to 'think like a lawyer', this 'is in large part a function of learning to read, talk and write like a lawyer [which all] involves a distinctive approach to written texts and textual interpretation' (p. 42).

Combining linguistic anthropology and discourse analysis, Mertz studied a semester of the first year Contracts class in eight US law schools. Rather than using lectures or other pedagogical approaches such as problem-based learning, law school teaching typically relies on the Socratic method. While there are variations in the way this approach is used, it centres on the teacher (referred to in the US as 'professor') quizzing individual students about cases assigned for pre-class reading, while the rest of the class listens and waits till they are targeted for quizzing. Key to this teaching style is 'combative dialogue and textual exegesis' (p. 4), which is also important in the practice of the law. So, part of the socialisation of law students to act for clients in an adversarial system takes place through the ways they have to learn to interact in the law school classroom. But Mertz is interested in more than the interactional features of this approach. She shows how, using variations of this approach, teachers socialise students into the culture of the law – the ways of understanding, thinking about and acting in various domains of the legal process.

At the base of the questions addressed in law school classrooms is the exercise of understanding written legal authorities (in the form of case judgments and or statutes), and applying relevant parts of these to the case in hand. This application involves sifting through stories and accounts of events and situations to distil relevant 'facts', and using legal reasoning to apply written legal authorities. As we saw in Section 4 of Chapter 2, facts in law have to be proved by evidence within the legal process, and it is this legal proof that establishes facts, not any information which was not accepted into evidence, or any later additional information. So, for example, as Mertz (2007: 67) explains, if a case 'has already gone to trial, and a jury has accepted one party's version of the facts, then that is the version [that has to be accepted] in reviewing the case at an appellate level'. An important part of the process of sifting through stories and accounts to distil the facts is the removal of as much personal and contextual detail as possible, in order to see how the events and situations fit the relevant law and legal authorities. Here we see another dimension of the interweaving of text (in the form of laws and case judgments) with talk (legal reasoning in teacher–student exchanges). Mertz shows that although it is 'apparently neutral in form, in fact the filtering structure of legal language taught to students is not neutral' (p. 5). In learning to see the people who are involved in legal matters in terms of the ways in which they argue and strategise, law students learn that the law erases or ignores emotion, morality and social context. Mertz points out a parallel with the way in which medical training 'requires a hardening and distancing of students' sensibilities from empathetic reactions to death and human bodies'. Similarly, 'legal training demands a bracketing of emotion and morality (as it is commonly understood) in dealing with human conflict and the people who appear in legal conflict stories' (p. 121). For example, one student was struggling with this requirement of bracketing morality in relation to contract law, and he presented this struggle with a statement about emotion:

Transcript 9–iv Mertz's (2007: 122) transcription of audiorecording
Student: ... Does anyone else feel angry? ((laughter)) I mean, I'm just furious, I mean I'm the only one in the room?
Prof: I missed something, I missed something, I don't- why are you angry (xx) you're angry at me?
Student: ((laughter)) I'm angry at the whole class ... all we can do is try and think of ways to work out of [the contract we just made]? Is that what we're trying to do as lawyers?

It is interesting to see that it did not occur to the teacher that the student might be angry with the legal system, or the course, or legal training. Instead, he assumed that the student must be angry with him, and he seemed unable to think of any reason for such anger. The student's reply that he was *angry at the whole class* is ambiguous in US English: it could refer to the group of people (students and teacher), or it could refer to the course. The teacher turned the discussion to the topic of lawyer ethics, and a practising lawyer who was sitting in the classroom commented that he 'generally just goes along with the system (with the implication being that this is in fact realistically how the system runs)'. The teacher closed the discussion by explaining that what he does is to separate his personal opinion from his professional response.

Mertz argues that getting rid of social context and individual personal differences has a 'double edge'. On the one hand, the law seems to be treating all people as equals, but on the other hand 'it obscures very real social differences that are pertinent to making just decisions'. The appearance of neutrality that is created in this way 'hides the fact that U.S. law continues to enact social inequities and injustice' (2007: 5). In Section 3 of Chapter 6 above, we saw this double-edged dimension in Philips' (1998) work on the way in which judges take guilty pleas.

Class discussion[xxxix]

We began this chapter with the observation that many people think it's hard to talk to lawyers about their legal problems. Discuss this observation in the light of the sociolinguistic and related research presented in this chapter. What factors might be relevant to perceived difficulties in communication?

Assignments and further research

1. Compare and contrast the interactions between interviewers and female domestic violence victims/survivors reported and analysed in the work of Trinch (e.g. 2001, 2003, 2005, 2006, 2007) and Ostermann (e.g. 2003a, 2003b). Make sure you take account of the similarities and differences between the roles and expectations of the workers in both studies. Note that in both studies some of the interviewers were volunteer support workers. In Trinch's US study the other interviewers were paralegals employed by the office of District Attorney, while in Ostermann's study in Brazil they were female police officers. However, these police officers were playing a special role, focused on helping to '(re) empower [female victims of gendered violence] by offering emotional and legal support' (2003a: 354).

2. **(Lx)** Examine Trinch's work (especially 2003, 2005) on narrative analysis in the light of a different institutional context in which interviewers provide written summary reports of clients' stories. This would involve collecting a corpus of interviews and summary reports, for example from police interviews with eyewitnesses, social work interviews with clients, or immigration department interviews with asylum seekers (see Sections 4.3 and 4.4 in Chapter 11 below).

3. **(Lx)** [For students who have studied language and gender]. Examine Bogoch's (1997) study of gendered lawyering in interviews with their clients, in the light of current sociolinguistic approaches to language and gender.

4. What issues face second language speakers and/or deaf sign language users in interviews with their lawyers? This question could be addressed as a term paper or essay, by examining issues raised in relevant literature for other legal contexts (see Chapter 4 and Sections 2, 3 and 4 of Chapter 8). This question could also be addressed through an empirical study for a thesis/dissertation.

5. What issues face second dialect speakers or people from a different cultural background in interviews with their lawyers? This question could be addressed as a term paper or essay, by examining issues raised in relevant literature for other legal contexts (see Sections 3 and 4 of Chapter 5 and Section 4 of Chapter 8). This question could also be addressed through an empirical study for a thesis/dissertation. (It appears that the only publications to directly address this issue are Eades 1996a, 2003.)

6. Sarat and Felstiner (1995: 96) say that lawyers talk to their clients in much the same way as they talk to each other. Investigate this claim, using Sarat and Felstiner's book for evidence of how lawyers talk to clients, and collecting your own evidence of how lawyers talk to each other. Given that it is not easy to gain research access to law practices, this topic would be most suitable as a starting point for thesis/dissertation research.

7. Discuss the suggestion that lawyer–client interactions can be thought of as intercultural interactions, to some extent. You might want to consider the ways in which this is similar to and different from other professional–client interactions, such as with doctors, immigration officials or accountants.

10

Informal and alternative legal processes

1. Introduction   **206**

2. Informal courts   **207**

     2.1. Telling your story in informal courts   *207*

     2.2. Talking about social problems in informal legal processes   *209*

     2.3. Small claims courts and arbitration   *212*

3. The microdynamics of mediation talk   **213**

     3.1. Disputing in a different way   *213*

     3.2. Mediator impartiality   *216*

     3.3. An inherent paradox of power?   *219*

4. Alternative criminal justice practices   **220**

     4.1. Restorative justice practices   *220*

     4.2. Therapeutic courts   *224*

     4.3. Indigenous sentencing courts   *225*

     Assignments and further research   *229*

Informal and alternative legal processes

1. Introduction

In Chapter 9 we saw that a pervasive element of lawyer–client interactions is 'the separation of the social and legal worlds' (Sarat & Felstiner 1995: 6). So what happens when people interact with the legal process without a lawyer? This is the legal context – or more specifically, the range of legal contexts – to be considered in this chapter. Primarily in the areas of family law and civil law, there has been a growth in the last two decades or so of ways of dealing with some legal matters without the expense and complication of being represented by a lawyer, and without the formality of a traditional court, with all of its restrictions on how people can tell their story and argue their case. You will see that there is a range of legal processes involved. And within each process, there is a wide variety in the details, which we cannot hope to completely deal with in this book. Thus, for example, there are many different approaches to small claims courts, or to mediation. Where possible, you should research your local area to find out what processes are available and how they work.

This chapter starts by looking at informal courts in Section 2, drawing particularly on the ethnographic work of Conley and O'Barr (1990) and Merry (1990), as well as a small Conversation Analysis study by Atkinson (1992). Informal courts are typically used for the adjudication of civil disputes or lesser criminal charges by judges, and in this way share some features with formal courts. Conley and O'Barr (1990: 24) explain that the most important ways in which informal courts differ from formal courts are that litigants are offered 'simplified procedures, reduced costs and delay, limitations on the right of appeal, and, above all, the chance to appear in court without a lawyer'.

In Section 3 we move away from courts to mediation, which falls within the range of processes referred to as alternative dispute resolution or ADR. This acronym is also at times taken to stand for appropriate or assisted or additional or affirmative dispute resolution (Sourdin 2008: 3). ADR is a cover term for processes in which an impartial person (a facilitator) helps disputing people (parties) to resolve their dispute.[55] It contrasts with adjudication, where a judicial officer makes a binding decision about a dispute or a criminal charge. There are three main approaches to ADR, and the most significant differences between them concern the role of the facilitator, and the extent to which the outcome of ADR is an enforceable decision. Most of the sociolinguistic work has focused on mediation, in which the disputing parties – with the help of a mediator – identify the disputed issues, develop options, consider alternatives and endeavour to reach an agreement. The mediator does not make any decisions about the content of the dispute or the outcome of its resolution, but may advise on or determine the process of mediation. And depending on the nature of the mediation, the mediator may or may not provide advice on facts or possible outcomes (Sourdin 2008: 4). Some mediation is compulsory, for example when it is ordered by a court, or is a prerequisite for a court action. Other mediation is voluntary, while on other occasions it may be part of an existing contractual agreement. Conciliation is similar to mediation in some ways. As with mediation, the disputing parties – with the help of a facilitator (a conciliator) – identify the disputed issues, develop options, consider alternatives and endeavour to reach an agreement. Unlike mediation, a conciliator provides advice on the matters in dispute and/or options for resolution. But conciliators do not make determinations. Arbitration differs from mediation and conciliation in that the decision is not made by the parties, but it is binding on them. In arbitration – which is important in labour law – the disputing parties have to present their arguments and evidence to an arbitrator who makes a determination which is enforceable. Thus, arbitration is the closest ADR approach to adjudication, although the presentation of arguments and evidence is not bound by the same rules of evidence.

The last section of this chapter deals with alternative criminal justice practices, many of which take place in alternative courts, such as drug courts and indigenous courts. These alternatives share some features with restorative justice practices, some of which also take place in alternative courts. There is almost no sociolinguistic research yet in these alternative courts and related restorative justice practices, but sociological and sociolegal research can open the door to future sociolinguistic study.

2. Informal courts

2.1. Telling your story in informal courts

Two large US ethnographic studies undertaken in the 1980s studied the discourse of informal courts. Conley and O'Barr (1990) examined 466 cases in small claims courts in six US cities in three different geographic regions. More than 150 of the hearings in these cases were audiorecorded and transcribed, and the researchers also interviewed 101 plaintiffs at the time they filed their cases, 29 litigants several weeks after trial, and all 14 judges involved in the six courts (all of these interviews were also audiorecorded). This study takes an ethnography of discourse approach, 'examining what litigants actually say in and out of court' (p. 35).[56] Conley and O'Barr provide explanation and exemplification – both methodologically and theoretically – of the ethnography of legal discourse. And in a particularly useful appendix (pp. 181–185), they discuss the limits of quantification in such a study. This book is a must-read for any students interested in sociolinguistic research methods.

You will remember from Section 4.2 of Chapter 3 that Conley and O'Barr were the two scholars leading the Duke study into how witnesses talk in (formal) court hearings. In this later study in informal courts they are also interested in how witnesses talk in court. But, consistent with developments in sociolinguistics over this time, their focus in the later study is not limited to the linguistic choices in answers, for example, whether or not hedging is used, as with powerless witness talk in the Duke study. Rather the analysis is at the level of discourse, and their unit of analysis is the litigant's encounter with the legal system (p. 29). The researchers' interest was in how laypeople analyse their legal problems and present their case when their courtroom participation is not organised and constrained by lawyers. An important part of every hearing is when the plaintiff tells their story, in response to an invitation from the judge such as *please tell your story* (p. 43) or *how did it happen?* (p. 61). Litigants in small claims courts are not bound by rules of evidence, and there are usually no lawyers to filter, shape or control the story. Conley and O'Barr found two different approaches used by litigants to tell their story: some presented their case – for example in a dispute between neighbours over who is liable for damage caused by a fallen tree – in terms of people and their relationships, histories and their general social conduct. This approach, which Conley and O'Barr term the 'relational' approach, is exemplified in Extract 10–i.

Exercise 10.1[xl]

Read the extract from the plaintiff Rawls in the case in Extract 10–i below. Rawls had sued her next-door neighbour Bennett for removing a hedge on her side of the property boundary and for allowing his bushes to grow into her property. She also charged him with general harassment over an extended period. See Conley and O'Barr (1990: 63–65) for a longer extract from which Extract 10-i has been taken.

Make a list of the points in Rawl's presentation of her side of the story and the evidence she gave to support her complaint.

Extract 10–i Conley and O'Barr's (1990: 62–63) transcription of audiorecording

And so then three years went by and they let the trees grow up like you see the picture there. ... And they're so big and then when he told me to stop taking them out because he was gonna take out that hedge, uh, the stumps, why uh, in the meantime I called a man and I had them, because I'm getting crippled up and I can't bend down sir, and here I was still taking out those trees and he wasn't coming to help me like he said he was. ... and so then I just had a, the Milehigh, uh Tree Service come uh, uh and um, a, and Mr., I had his name here – Mr. uh Cook come and he come in the house and sat down with me and he looked at that and he said well he surely should help in the shrubbery in the back because there's shrubbery in the back that was over on my line that I've got to take out and I've got pictures of that too sir. And he said he didn't know what the man or what the man was because the the tree was dead why didn't he take it out? Well all he wants to do is harass me so he leaves it there so I have to keep taking the stuff out and bending over and using my trashcan, you know. This is something else. I only got one can. Why don't he pick up his own trash?

Not all litigants in small claims courts talk about their case like Rawls did. In contrast, some take an approach which Conley and O'Barr term the 'rule-oriented' approach. This involves telling their story in court in terms of rules, duties and obligations, an approach which is generally more consonant with the logic of the legal process, and the legal concern with relevance. Extract 10–ii in Exercise 10.2 below exemplifies the rule-oriented approach.

Exercise 10.2[xli]

Read the extract from the defendant Hogan in the case in Extract 10–ii below. Hogan was representing her company in a case in which it was being sued by a former sales representative, Dan Webb, for refusing to pay him a bonus commission on the sale of an expensive scientific instrument.

Make a list of the points in Hogan's presentation of her side of the story and the evidence she gave to support her complaint.

Discuss the differences between Rawls (in Extract 10–i above) and Hogan in the way they each presented their story to the court.

Extract 10–ii Conley and O'Barr's (1990: 62–65) transcription of audiorecording

... Um, then it is my responsibility, as well as the district manager, to assist the sales reps in focusing on these sanctioned programs. Uh, in order to keep track of what we have sanctioned, we have a calculation sheet that specifically shows the sales representative what we are sanctioning. This is one

---

> for the first half. I have highlighted that that particular promotion for spectrometers was on the first half, from March until August of 1984, giving the particular payouts, and as you'll see there is a $200 payout there for 1001 Spectrometer. ... [talking about Mr Harper] Um, in early, either late October, early November, I asked him, he told me at that point about um, what was going on with Mr Webb, and I asked him at that time, I said, "Would you please call Mr Webb and tell him that you have prematurely put a promotion out that's not sanctioned and that you will honor your $200 and that Instrument Supply will not." ... Um, it is my job to encourage the sales representatives to close sales. At that time I was not aware of the fact that Dan did not know it was not 400 but only 200 through Diller and Macy. Upon his resignation, um, when he came into the office the end of December, he did at that time state the $400 and I did at that time tell him that it was $200 from Diller and Macy and not a matching $200 from Instrument Supply.

Conley and O'Barr also investigated the approach of judges in these small claims courts. Interestingly, not all of the judges used a rule-oriented approach, and the greatest satisfaction appeared to be experienced by litigants whose approach most resembled that of the judge hearing their case. While identifying these two approaches, Conley and O'Barr found that they represent points at the extremes of a continuum of approaches.

The contrast between a relational approach and a rule-oriented approach in small claims courts bears some similarity to the contrast drawn by Heffer (2005) between narrative and paradigmatic modes of reasoning, which we saw in Section 7 of Chapter 3. Some people approach the law by telling stories about relationships between people, while others focus on applying legal rules to particular situations. This is also reminiscent of Sarat and Felstiner's (1995) findings about two different approaches in lawyer–client interactions, and Mertz's (2007) findings about the training of law students: lawyers aim to separate their clients' social world from the legal world (as we saw in Sections 2 and 6 of Chapter 9). Conley and O'Barr (2005) are interested in how their rules versus relationships contrast articulates with their earlier contrast between powerful and powerless witnesses in court (which we discussed in Section 4.2 of Chapter 3). In their (1990) book, they suggest that 'factors such as gender, class and race' (p. 79) as well as social roles may impact on the distribution of both contrasts. In their (2005) book they contextualise both of these earlier studies (about powerful–powerless witness speech, and rules versus relationships in approaches in small claims cases) within the bigger picture of sociolegal studies which argues that there are many ways in which the law is unarguably patriarchal. Thus, for example, they argue that the ability to use rule-oriented accounts is an acquired skill, in which the acquisition depends on exposure to the culture of business and law. As it is largely men who have had access to these roles, and it is predominantly rule-oriented accounts which are preferred in litigation, then it follows, indirectly, that 'relational litigants – which often means women – have a harder time gaining access to justice than do their rule-oriented counterparts' (p. 73). This discussion could provide thought-provoking stimulus for future research.

2.2. Talking about social problems in informal legal processes

At the same time as Conley and O'Barr's (1990) investigation, Merry (1990) was researching cases in three lower courts in two towns in the Boston metropolitan area of the US. This study is also based on extensive data collection, which included observations of 118 mediation sessions and 30 related courtroom hearings, interviews with 124 people who had been through mediation, and extensive observations and 93 ethnographic interviews in three of the neighbourhoods involved, as well as a quantitative analysis of 868 cases in the courts studied. These courts were the small claims court (civil law), the lower criminal court and the juvenile court (both criminal law). Merry uses the term 'court' to refer to the courthouse and all of the programmes which took place in it. Most of these were informal processes – such as mediation, interviews with court officers, and pre-trial conferences – which might not necessarily be seen as 'court' in non-US contexts. In Merry's study people were almost always unrepresented, that is they went through most of the process without the assistance of a lawyer. It was only if a case went to trial that lawyers were sometimes involved. This work has considerable contextual, theoretical and methodological similarities with Conley and O'Barr's (1990) study. However, Merry's book is not an an ethnography of discourse, where talk is the object of study (see Conley & O'Barr 1990: xi), but a general ethnography, where talk provides access to people's legal consciousness. Thus for example, unlike Conley and O'Barr's (1990) study, it has almost no analysis of transcripts of interaction.

Merry's interest was in the kinds of disputes that people took to court – that is, to the informal legal process in the courthouse – and what the disputants expected from the legal process (compare Conley and O'Barr's main focus on how people told their story in court). This was early days in organised mediation, and in this study mediation programmes were run in all three kinds of lower courts and they played an important role in diverting people from adjudicated courtroom hearings. Many students might be surprised to know that citizens in the US can lay criminal charges against someone (compare Australia and the UK where only police can lay criminal charges). In the US, police charges can also result in the prosecutor taking a case to a criminal court. But as citizens can initiate a complaint against a person with the court clerk, interpersonal problems can often result in people going to the court to solve these problems. Examples of these interpersonal problems are an argument which resulted in someone hitting another person (criminal), a parent complaining about an out-of-control child or school official complaining about a truant (juvenile), and landlord–tenant disputes (small claims). In Merry's mid-1980s study, all such complaints resulted in a preliminary hearing in front of a clerk-magistrate for which the defendant was summonsed to appear. The parties were often ordered to mediation before or after this hearing. If there was sufficient evidence for a criminal charge, the case was turned over to a prosecutor who then took the case to a criminal court. Although the plaintiff had laid the charge, it was prosecuted in court by a prosecutor. A similar, but not identical, procedure was used for small claims court and for personal complaints (as opposed to charges initiated by a prosecutor) in juvenile court: claims were first assessed by a court officer, and mediation was often ordered by the court. In all three contexts, there were a series of stages, during each of which participants were encouraged to work out the problems without having to go to adjudication, that is to a decision by a judge. If disputes could not be settled without a trial, then lawyers typically become involved, although the plaintiff in a criminal trial was represented only by the prosecutor.

When people came to court to file a complaint, they were bringing problems, which were almost always 'emotionally intense struggles rather than rational differences of interest'

(1990: 97). Merry shows how these emotionally intense struggles were transformed into cases at all stages of the informal court process. She found there were three different discourses, or 'modes of talking about problems' (p. 111), namely law, morality and therapy. Disputing parties, mediators and judges used one or more of these discourses at different times, often switching from one to the other within the same setting. In mediation and pre-trial processes, it was the discourse of everyday morality which was most used. That is, problems and possible solutions were discussed in terms of moral obligations within interpersonal relationships, whether in families, neighbourhoods or business relationships such as between landlord and tenant. This discourse is consistent with Conley and O'Barr's relational approach. But in Merry's study, the legal discourse – consistent with Conley and O'Barr's rule-oriented approach – was also used, particularly in cases involving neighbourhood disputes, and more often by men than women. Therapeutic discourse, which comes from the helping professions, occurred most in boyfriend/girlfriend problems and in family problems. In this mode of discourse people talked about either themselves or someone else needing help. We should not be surprised that Conley and O'Barr did not find an approach consistent with therapeutic discourse, as Merry found this kind of discourse most in the family and relationship problems, which were not dealt with in the small claims courts cases in Conley and O'Barr's study.

While plaintiffs often first arrived at the court wanting legal action on their problem, court clerks and mediators generally attempted to 'delegalise' their discourse. But they also provided information on how the problem needed to be presented legally: with specific details of specific instances, rather than complaints about a general pattern of events. You can see that this is parallel to the way in which the lawyers and paralegals in Trinch's (2003) study had to extract information from women's stories for their protective order application affidavits (Section 5 of Chapter 9 above).

We can see how these discourses work in an example (Merry 1990: 121–127), which began with a young woman, Bridget, going to court to seek protection from a younger man, Billy, who was her next door neighbour and her ex-boyfriend. Bridget's initial request to the court was in legal discourse, charging him with harassment. In the initial mediation, the discussion shifted to moral discourse. Bridget's problem was presented as *he won't leave me alone. He is calling me at work, bothering me all the time. ... He is very jealous of my male friends and gets very upset if ever I talk to them.* The mediators, in moral discourse mode, asked Billy if he could treat her as a total stranger. His reply is interesting: *It would be hard, but I could do it. And I have to, because if I don't she will take me to court. But I could take her to court too. I could charge her with statutory rape* (p. 124). Here, Billy was switching to legal discourse, with his threat to take legal action in relation to sexual activity between him and Bridget when he was younger than the legal age of consent. The mediators never took up this legal discourse, encouraging Billy instead to think in terms of relationships, and trying – unsuccessfully – to encourage him to make a request or demand in response to Bridget's relationship-based demand (that Billy stay away from her). In her private discussion with the mediators, Bridget used moral and therapeutic discourse rather than legal discourse. She talked again about his unreasonable pursuit of her, and also her feeling that he needed counselling, because of his dysfunctional family life. This initial round of mediation concluded with an agreement made in both moral and legal terms: Bridget agreed to drop her charges of harassment against Billy, providing that he stopped trying to see her or to talk to her. But this agreement failed, and six months later Bridget returned to the court assertively demanding protection from the court in legal discourse, charging him with assault and battery. She told the clerk about violence she suffered from Billy, and although she maintained her legal discourse, the clerk tried to delegalise it. In a strong moralising discourse, he advised her to stay away from a certain bar, and instead to take beer home, saying *it is better for your kids anyway* (p. 126). However, the clerk did also advise Bridget on how she could make this complaint a legal one, focusing on dates of specific events, getting medical evidence, and not delaying in coming to court after a specific incident of harassment or violence. The clerk concluded in legal discourse with his promise that 'if there is any more trouble, just come in and I will issue a complaint' (p. 126). You can see that Bridget was like the women in Trinch's (2003) study who began the process of seeking a protective order in the legal mode, but then told their story to their lawyers in moral discourse. But their lawyers wanted specific events with legally relevant information such as dates, in the same way as the clerk in Bridget's case did. Merry's account of this story ends six months later with the report that Bridget had not returned to the court.

Merry found that people brought their problems to court with a consciousness of legal entitlement, but their experiences changed this consciousness, so that many people came to think of the courts as 'ineffective, unwilling to help in … personal crises, and indifferent to the ordinary person's problem' (1990: 170). Interestingly, Merry doesn't agree with the widely held view that people go to these informal courts because community breakdown is making the US increasingly litigious. She points out that the evidence actually contradicts this view. And she argues that it's not that community is breaking down, but that Americans are increasingly asserting their independence from community control as individualism and egalitarianism grow. Consistent with people moving out of neighbourhoods to the suburbs and choosing privacy and separation from their neighbours, they are also choosing 'dependence on the law rather than the intimacy of community' (p. 174). People are invited to bring their personal problems to court, but once they do, the court seems to do everything it can to avoid treating the problems as legal problems. Instead, these problems are subject to 'continuing supervision and management as moral or therapeutic problems' (p. 180). So this study of informal courts in the US shows that there is a 'paradox of legal entitlement'. In taking their problems out of the social arena into the legal arena, 'freedom from the control of the community comes at the price of domination by the state, in the form of courts' (p. 181).

2.3. Small claims courts and arbitration

Two sociolinguists have examined the microanalysis of interaction in small claims courts which involve arbitration: Atkinson (1992) in London, and Angermeyer (2008, 2009) in New York. Both studies involved litigants without lawyers arguing small civil claims in front of an arbitrator. Atkinson found that while the parties in the London court did not have lawyers, in practice the talk was organised by the arbitrator asking questions of both plaintiff and defendant. This might seem to be similar in some ways to how talk is organised in formal courtroom hearings (with lawyers asking questions, and witnesses, including plaintiffs and defendants providing answers). But Atkinson found some striking differences between the talk in this small claims court and that in formal courts. One of these differences relates to what happened when a party gave an off-topic answer, or tried to elaborate on an answer when a Yes/No-question had been asked. In cross-examination in formal courts, this is usually met with an interruption or rebuke by either the lawyer or the judge. But in the small claims court, the arbitrators responded to such answers by 'marking receipt', saying something like *yes* or *okay*. Atkinson sees this kind of response as the arbitrator avoiding disaffiliation. He also found in what arbitrators did not say that they avoided affiliation as well. For example, arbitrators in this study never responded to the talk of plaintiffs or defendants with responses used in everyday conversations with affiliative implications, such as *oh*. Atkinson argues that these conversational strategies of avoiding both disaffiliation and affiliation enable arbitrators to display impartiality (termed 'neutrality' in this study, see discussion of these terms in Section 3.2 below). This in turn reconciles their two potentially conflicting roles: they have to question both parties to the dispute, and then pass judgment. It would be interesting to extend the approach taken in this study to other settings which resemble the structure of this arbitrated small claims court, for example some tribunals, or courtroom hearings in inquisitorial legal systems.

Angermeyer's (2008, 2009) research on 40 recorded proceedings in three small claims courts in New York City takes a different approach from any of the other studies discussed in this chapter. His focus is on the ways in which the courts' approach to multilingualism and language choice reproduces the widespread ideology of monolingualism. We will take up this point in Section 4.4 of Chapter 11 (see also Section 2 of Chapter 4). The fact that the small claims courts are much less formal than other courts and that lawyers are rarely used, did not result in the relaxation of the all-or-nothing approach that typifies the use of interpreters in higher courts. If speakers of languages other than English requested an interpreter, then these litigants were not allowed to code-switch into English at all.

3. The microdynamics of mediation talk

In Merry's (1990) study mediation was part of the court process, usually taking place in the same building before or after court hearings, and often ordered by the court. Since the early 1980s when her study was carried out, mediation has grown and diversified, and often takes place away from courts, physically and legally, and often as an alternative to court. Sociolinguistic analysis of mediation has primarily been done by scholars using Conversation Analysis (CA), which provides a rich analytical framework for detailed investigation of talk-in-interaction.

3.1. Disputing in a different way

The aim of mediation is for disputing parties to come to an agreement with the help of a mediator. Unlike disputes that end in court, mediation involves disputing parties moving away from adversarial combat to cooperation and compromise (Garcia 2000: 315). One of the earliest sociolinguistic studies of mediation was Garcia's (1991) investigation of how talk between disputants in mediation resembles and differs from everyday arguing. Her study examined nine mediation sessions which were alternatives to hearings in a US small claims court in 1987.

Exercise 10.3[xlii]

Discuss these questions:

(a) From your general knowledge or experience, what are some of the conversational characteristics of talk between disputing parties in mediation sessions?

(b) Examine the three extracts from mediation sessions below in terms of your answer to question (a).

Extract 10–iii slightly edited version of Garcia's (1991: 824) transcription of videorecording

1. Father: ... the CHILDren coming home and him ta:king them into the BA::throom (0.4) and looking into their EYE:S because their pupils might be di:lated cause they've had too many- too much sugar from milkshakes that they drink in at my HOUSE!

(0.2)

2. Stepfather: °That's [not true at all°

3. Father: [And MY KI:DS (0.2) my kids have cry- cried over [that.

4. Mediator: [Excuse me for interrupt for just a minute I forgot to- mention one of the GROU:ND ru:les- and that i:s when- you're ((talking to father)) telling your story (0.7) you ((talking to stepfather)) say nothing.

Extract 10–iv slightly edited version of Garcia's (1991: 824) transcription of videorecording

1. Mediator: Okay Dan? If you'd like to go ahead then and- tell us your side of the story?

(0.6)

2. Dan: Okay- U:::h (0.5) I think it was approximately u:h °think it was in eighty six° (1.9) the date was u::h- Fl::ve uh seven eighty °seven I believe an I-° took the motor ho::me to u:h Mark's Auto (1.0) hh chuh! for a see- replace fan belts repla:ce upper radiator hose- inspect the air conditioning unit.

Extract 10-v slightly edited version of Garcia's (1991: 831) transcription of videorecording

Stepfather: I'm not sure how to put it I FEE:L that I BEEN:: physically and emotionally assaulted! (1.0) A::ND- I'd like to change tha:t to a more se:nsitive (0.9) °u::hm° (1.5) more sensitive communica:tion.

Garcia's study provides an exemplary application of CA to show how the interactional organisation of mediation differs from ordinary conversation (some of which you have seen in Exercise 10.3). Central to this difference is the participation framework: in contrast to an ordinary argument between two people, a mediated argument involves a third person, whose job includes remaining impartial or neutral (a point to be taken up below). Typically disputants in mediation address their talk to the mediator rather than to each other. Another characteristic feature which Garcia (1991: 832) found in talk between disputing parties in mediation is the mitigation of accusations by downgrading. Consider for example, the ex-husband who said to his ex-wife about their daughter: *I'm not saying this to hurt you uh uh I think you shou- m maybe make an e:ffort to even ca:ll her once a week! to find out- how she's doing or- or- you know make a special night a week- for her!* While the ex-husband presented a suggestion for how his ex-wife should improve her communication with their eldest daughter, who was living with him, it contained an indirect accusation which was never stated (e.g. *you neglect your daughter*).

Garcia suggests that one of the reasons that mediation works is because arguments are not allowed. But Greatbatch and Dingwall (1997) found that some mediation does involve arguments. They have found this was one of the ways that the more than 100 divorce mediation sessions in nine agencies in their UK study differed from the nine mediation sessions in Garcia's US study. Like Garcia, Greatbatch and Dingwall use Conversation Analysis for their microanalysis of how people talk in mediation. But in the sessions they studied, they found (1997) that there were no formal restrictions on opportunities to speak, and that while disputants did often address their talk to the mediator, it was also common for disputants to speak directly to each other. Further, they found that the sessions often included arguments. Perhaps it is not surprising to find differences in the structure of talk in different mediation programmes, given that there is so much diversity in approaches to mediation, and to the ways in which disputing parties come to mediation in different places. In Garcia's study, the disputants' participation in the mediation of their small claims disputes was voluntary, but the mediators had the power to arbitrate a decision if a mediated agreement could not be reached (1991: 819). In contrast, the mediators in Greatbatch and Dingwall's study of divorce mediation sessions had no power to arbitrate, and they did not even write reports for court.

While Garcia and Greatbatch and Dingwall have considered ways in which disputes in mediation are similar to or different from everyday arguments, Kandel (1994) has considered one of the ways in which disputant talk in mediation is different from witness evidence in court. In her analysis of three child custody mediation sessions in the US, Kandel is interested in how disputants used quoted speech – whether accurately or inaccurately – to 'create a dramatic, emotional involvement between speaker and hearer and to shift blame and responsibility from the speaker to the person "quoted"' (p. 881). Quoting what someone else has said is generally not allowed in courtroom hearings, because of hearsay rules (see Section 4.1 in Chapter 3). But mediation is not governed by rules of evidence, and Kandel argues that the effect of quoting someone else's words is empowering in mediation. For example, in one of the sessions a mother made the point that her child's father had a drinking problem, not with an accusation, but by reporting what her daughter said and did: *My daughter picked up a bottle and said 'my daddy smells like this'* (p. 907). In Kandel's words, the mother's 'single line of talk not only involves the hearer in a dramatic scene worthy of daytime television but also communicates a critical point of custody law' (that is, concerns over a parent's substance abuse can result in the most restrictive type of non-custodial parent's visitation rights). Following Tannen (1989), Kandel refers to the use of quoted speech as 'constructed dialogue', recognising that it can be used in a very wide range of contexts for verbatim reports, inaccurate recalls and intentional misrepresentation. Kandel found that parents' use of constructed dialogue had a persuasive effect on mediators, and she suggests that the disputant with the most effective use of constructed dialogue therefore has a persuasive advantage in mediation. She suggests (1994: 50) that mediators 'should learn to listen for and hear constructed dialogue and similar devices as rhetorical strategies of the speakers, rather than listening through them, as though they were hearing the actual speech of the people whose speech is "reported"'.

3.2. Mediator impartiality

We saw in Section 1 above that the role of the mediator is typically to help disputing parties to identify disputed issues, develop options, consider alternatives and endeavour to reach an agreement. It is clearly important for mediators to remain personally detached from the dispute and the issues, and to not favour either party. Remaining fair to both sides in a dispute is mainly about the way in which mediators talk, respond to talk and direct talk (for example with questions, directives about not interrupting etc.). Sociolinguistic research has begun investigation into how mediators work to remain fair to both parties and to not be seen as biased. In the sociolinguistic literature, this is generally referred to as 'neutrality'. However, mediation experts prefer to use this term 'neutrality' to refer to the mediator's background and relationship to the disputing parties (Sourdin 2008: 141). So, a neutral mediator is one who has not had previous contact with the parties and who has no personal interest in the outcome. A good explanation of the difference between neutrality and impartiality is provided by the Australian standards for the training and accreditation of alternative dispute resolution practitioners (NADRAC 2001: 112–113), which will be referred to from here as the Australian ADR standards:

> While neutrality is a question of interest, impartiality is more a matter of behaviour. It relates to the retention of the confidence of the parties based on their perception that they are treated fairly by the ADR practitioner throughout the process.

The distinction becomes particularly important in some contexts where it is impossible to find a neutral mediator. For example, in a small rural community how do you find someone who has not had previous contact with the parties? And in some Australian Aboriginal communities there can be an added consideration: regardless of the availability of a neutral person, it is culturally appropriate for mediation to be conducted by a respected elder who knows the participants. As NADRAC (1997: 161) points out, neutrality may sometimes be waived in some ways, but it is 'essential for the dispute resolver to demonstrate and maintain his or her impartiality at all times'.

Impartiality is a 'micro-level accomplishment' (following Heisterkamp 2006: 2062), a 'practice *in discourse*' (Cobb & Rifkin 1991: 62, emphasis in original). What features of talk can provide evidence of impartiality on the one hand, or lack of impartiality (often referred to as bias), on the other? The most important contribution to this issue is found in the work of Garcia (e.g. 2000), Greatbatch and Dingwall (e.g. 1989, 1999), Heisterkamp (2006) and Jacobs (2002), most of whom research within a Conversation Analysis framework. (However, as explained above, the researchers use the terms 'neutrality' or 'neutralism' to refer to the mediator's impartial way of conducting the mediation.) Greatbatch and Dingwall (1999: 273) point out that their study of neutralism does not involve judgements about the mediators' inherent bias or lack of bias, but rather they investigate particular patterns in the mediators' ways of facilitation which may seem to be impartial. This focus on mediators' 'neutralistic stance' (1999: 273), like Garcia's (2000: 323) 'posture of neutrality', connects to concerns within the profession about 'avoiding any appearance of partiality or bias through word or conduct' (NADRAC 2001: 108).

The Australian ADR standards (NADRAC 2001: 113) highlight the need for mediators (as well as conciliators and arbitrators) to be balanced and equal in their treatment of each party. The ways that mediators communicate with the disputing parties are important in the guidelines about how practitioners can demonstrate their impartiality:[57]

• generally treat the parties equally (e.g. spending approximately the same time hearing each party's statement or approximately the same time in separate sessions) ...
• give advice and allow representation, support or assistance equally to parties
• ensure they do not communicate noticeably different degrees of warmth, friendliness or acceptance when dealing with individual parties

Such general guidelines and standards about treating parties equally can provide a good starting place for sociolinguistic investigation of mediator impartiality. Note, that in sharp contrast to courtroom talk, mediation has no predetermined turn-taking conventions, and there are no rules of evidence prescribing who can talk about what topics, who can ask questions, who can control the talk, and what topics cannot be discussed.

In their (1989) examination of a divorce mediation session in the UK, Greatbatch and Dingwall look at what they term 'selective facilitation'. Their microanalysis of several parts of the talk in this session shows the mediator facilitating discussion about property settlement. This analysis reveals that the mediator picked up on the wife's desired outcome and actively promoted discussion of that, while inhibiting consideration of the husband's desired outcome. The aspects of talk which lead the authors to this analysis are discoursal: comments, suggestions and complaints made by the wife were taken up by the mediator much more than those made by the husband. It's not that the mediator overtly evaluated either the wife's or the husband's desired outcome. The selective facilitation happened through the ways that the mediator provided opportunities for each of the disputants to talk. As with all Conversation Analysis studies 'the devil is in the detail': it is impossible to present more than the brief outline above of the researchers' approach and findings in this study. In the Class discussion below, you are encouraged to carefully read and react to this study.

Class discussion[xliii]

Carefully read Greatbatch and Dingwall's (1989) case study, which is in a journal easily accessible online. Also read the Australian ADR standards document (NADRAC 2001), which is also easily accessible online (or a comparable document in your own country, if available). Discuss your reaction to the mediator's use of selective facilitation in this session? To what extent do you agree or disagree with Greatbatch and Dingwall's conclusions (pp. 636–639).

Although mediator impartiality is seen as central to the philosophy and practice of mediation, Greatbatch and Dingwall's fine-grained analysis questions what they see as 'a false opposition between neutrality and bias' (1989: 639). Like so many ways of conceptualising human interactive behaviour, close analysis reveals a more complex situation, and one in which mediators' talk is influenced by what disputants say, in an interactive reciprocal way (see also Garcia 2000; Greatbatch & Dingwall 1994). In their (1999) study drawing on 10 of their recorded mediation sessions, Greatbatch and Dingwall show that impartiality (which they refer to as neutralism) is 'not an individual trait' (p. 274), it is collaboratively achieved.

This study found that with one exception the disputing parties contributed to maintaining an impartial stance.

Several other studies have also looked at how mediators do the difficult job of maintaining their impartial stance while facilitating disputing parties to come to an agreement. In Jacobs' (2002: 1403) terms, what mediators are doing is 'managing disagreement while managing not to disagree'. At its most basic, this involves getting the parties to state their position, to listen to the other parties' position, to discuss possible ways of solving the dispute, and to agree on a compromise solution. We saw above that the first two of these tasks can be handled by the mediator's overt control of turn-taking. The third of these tasks – discussing possible ways of solving the dispute – often revolves around the mediator eliciting or suggesting options and encouraging parties to consider them. Garcia (1997, 2000) found three main strategies used by mediators to do this, which, following Maynard (1984), she terms solicits, proposals and position reports.

Mediator solicits can be quite general as in *who would like to start with some ideas?* (Garcia 2000: 331). While specific solicits also aim to encourage the disputants to provide a solution, they can indirectly suggest a direction for arriving at the solution. Thus in a dispute between the owner of a repair shop and the owner of a videocamera which had been serviced there, the mediator asked *what would it cost for Pete to purchase the camera?*, indirectly suggesting a way to resolve the dispute – by the shop owner buying the camera from the dissatisfied customer. You will see that both of these examples of solicits take the linguistic form of questions. In his analysis of mediator strategies, Jacobs (2002) found that mediators often used questions as a way of doing indirect advocacy. As he points out (p. 1410), mediator questions 'play a central role in the decision-making process', while enabling the mediator to avoid personally committing to any particular suggestion. (See pp. 1411–1414 for an extract from a child custody and visitation mediation session in which a mediator steers a disputant past her attempted closure of the search for a solution, using a series of 'indirect advocacy' questions, which are also examples of general and specific solicits.)

When disputants follow up a mediator solicit with a suggestion for a solution, Garcia refers to this suggestion as a position report, which she defines (1997: 225) as a suggestion that the speaker is personally committed to. Position reports contrast with mediator proposals, which are also suggestions for a possible solution, but suggestions that the speaker is not personally committed to. Mediators aim to elicit position reports from disputants rather than presenting their own proposals, and Garcia (2000) found that not all of the mediation sessions in her study contained proposals.

You can see that the generation of solutions to disputes in mediation is a collaborative effort. Mediators solicit position reports and at times contribute their own proposals for consideration by both parties. Garcia's Conversation Analysis shows the importance of the sequential organisation of talk in mediation sessions. When a disputant makes a suggestion (or position report) in response to the mediator's solicit, it is the second pair part to the mediator's request, and is not structured as a conversational initiative by the disputant. Further, being an answer to the mediator's question, it is not addressed to the other disputant. You are encouraged to read the other CA studies referred to in this section to gain a fuller appreciation of the conversational strategies found in mediation sessions.

Exercise 10.4[xliv]

Role play a mediation session on an issue in either a child custody or salesperson–customer dispute. Here is a suggested scenario, but you may wish to develop an alternative one.

A divorcing couple discuss their argument about child custody and a mediator tries to help them reach an agreement. The mother wants the two children (aged 4 and 10) to live with her, and visit their father on alternate weekends. She also wants an assurance that his new partner won't be in the house at that time, because she feels the partner is very immature and self-centred, and would prevent the children's father from properly taking care of them. The father feels that the mother is overprotective with the children and that they should spend more time with him and his new partner. His view that the mother is not a very good parent is part of his argument for the children to spend every second week with him.

Prepare for this role play by rereading Sections 1 and 3.2 of this chapter, and by reading the Australian ADR standards (NADRAC 2001: 100–114) or something comparable in your country. You will need three people for the role play, and other students can observe and take notes for later discussion. The mediator should use a number of questions as solicits for a solution, and the disputants should try to avoid providing suggested solutions or position reports (for the purposes of the role play). Make an electronic recording of the role play. After the role play, briefly discuss these questions:
(a) What discourse strategies did the disputants use to resist the mediator's invitations for them to provide solutions?
(b) How successful were these strategies?
(c) How did the mediator display impartiality?
(d) How did these displays of impartiality relate to those discussed in this section?
(e) Were there any instances which seemed to reveal lack of impartiality by the mediator?
After initial discussion of these questions, replay the recording of the role play, to see what further detail you can add to your analysis of the participants' strategies.

3.3. An inherent paradox of power?

We saw above that Greatbatch and Dingwall (1989) observed a mediation session in which the mediator's selective facilitation gave indirect support to the wife's proposed solution to the dispute, while clearly disfavouring the husband's. Interestingly, the researchers express the view that the outcome that the mediator was effectively promoting in that session – that is, what the wife wanted – 'was probably more just than the one that might have otherwise been reached' (p. 617). This comment raises the issue of the relationship between the mediator's impartiality and power relations between disputants. Although alternative dispute resolution is often seen as a more accessible and inherently preferable way of solving disputes than court litigation, several sociolegal scholars have raised questions about whether it can in fact be a less fair way. Abel (1981: 257) puts it this way: 'compromise produces unbiased results only when opponents are equal; compromise between unequals inevitably reproduces inequality'. Kandel (1994) provides a helpful summary of the debate between opponents and proponents of mediation (see also Sourdin 2008: 63–67 for discussion of power and inequality issues in mediation; also Cobb & Rifkin 1991 and Dingwall 1988). The fundamental question is whether resolving a dispute through compromise rather than adjudication enables the more powerful disputant to succeed. Does the need to compromise bring with it the danger of some disputants relinquishing rights which a court might instead protect? These issues have been particularly addressed in relation to the pervasive working of patriarchy in divorce and custody disputes (e.g. Conley & O'Barr 2005). To what extent is the privileging of a rational rather than emotional approach (which we discussed in Chapter 9) carried from the formal legal sphere into mediation sessions? Grillo (1991: 1576) has raised concerns about 'societal prohibitions against female anger' affecting the ways in which women can participate in mediation. And Merry (1990: 149) argues that although talk in mediation sessions is frequently highly emotional, 'the person who plays the trump card of rationality wins the day'.

In Section 2.2 above, we saw Merry's paradox of legal entitlement: in taking their disputes to the informal court process (including mediation), disputants avoid community control, but are subject to new control by the state, through the courts. Kandel (1994: 886) finds another paradox in divorce mediation, that she calls an 'inherent paradox of power': 'freeing the participants from the domination of courtroom constraints [mediation] risks the possibility that the stronger parent may dominate the weaker'. Maybe disputants are more equally matched in a dispute when each is represented by a lawyer in court?

Class debate[xiv]

Debate the proposition that mediation provides greater opportunity for individuals' rights to be overborne in settling disputes than does adjudicated litigation. Make sure that your discussion of this topic draws on sociolinguistic research about how talk works in mediation and in court.

---

4. Alternative criminal justice practices

Mediation is used most in family law and civil disputes. In this section we turn to criminal law where there have been some radical initiatives in the last two to three decades, resulting in some departures from traditional ways of dealing with offenders in the courts, and from punishments involving prison sentences. In the common law countries, these initiatives began in several different jurisdictions in Canada, the US and New Zealand, and spread quickly to other countries including Australia and the UK. These initiatives are often collectively referred to with the term 'restorative justice'. However, I will follow the work of Marchetti and Daly (2007) in separating the practices which follow the principles of restorative justice (in Section 4.1) from two other types of alternative criminal justice practices which differ from restorative justice in significant ways, namely therapeutic courts (in Section 4.2) and indigenous courts (in Section 4.3).

4.1. Restorative justice practices

It is not easy to provide a short definition of restorative justice as the term has developed to describe a variety of practices which have developed in different jurisdictions. These practices have all developed as alternatives to the conventional processing of criminal offenders through courts and prisons, a process which is often ineffective in preventing reoffending, and which largely ignores the needs of victims (see Johnstone & Van Ness 2007). Restorative justice focuses on restoring social balance and redressing the effects of harmful actions, and is often contrasted with retributive justice, which centres on punishment (but see Roche 2007 for questions about this dichotomy). Regional reviews in Johnstone and Van Ness (2007) indicate that there are diverse restorative justice practices in all continents and in countries with every kind of formal legal system. Further, Braithwaite (2002: 5) believes that restorative justice has been 'the dominant model of criminal justice throughout most of history for perhaps all the world's people'. At the heart of restorative justice is the belief that when a crime is committed, it has an impact on the victim(s) and the community, and that to restore balance to the community and repair harm to the victim requires an approach which brings victim, offender and community together. Many scholars have pointed out that restorative justice approaches apply some civil law practices to criminal law. Johnstone (2003a: 8–14) provides an overview of some of these applications, which include:

- The criminal act is seen primarily as a harmful act perpetrated by one person (the offender) on another person (the victim) – whereas in criminal law the criminal act is seen primarily as a breach of the law.

- The state initiates the action against the offender on behalf of the victim and the community – whereas in criminal law it is the state taking action against the offender.

- The outcome is often centred around the offender repairing the harm caused and restoring the balance disturbed by their offence – whereas in criminal law the outcome is typically centred around the punishment deserved by the offender.

- Moral education, healing and restoration are seen as the goals – whereas in criminal law, the main goals are punitive.

Two other characteristics of restorative justice distinguish it from both typical criminal law and typical civil law. First, restorative justice involves informal processes, and no restrictions on talk such as courtroom rules of evidence (although as we saw in Section 2 above, informal courts also share this characteristic). And second, restorative justice involves consensual decision-making about penalties. Restorative justice is probably used most as an alternative to court with youth justice conferencing and family group conferencing, and as an addition to court with victim–offender mediation.

Some of the most influential empirical research and theorising about restorative justice is found in the work of Braithwaite (e.g. 1989, 2002) who introduced the concept of reintegrative shaming, which refers to 'disapproval of the [criminal] act within a continuum of respect for the offender and terminated by rituals of forgiveness' (Braithwaite 2002: 74). He argues that loving families use reintegrative shaming as a form of punishment for particular actions while maintaining mutual respect between people. Further, he argues that societies that use reintegrative shaming of members who have done wrong have a lower crime rate than those who use disintegrative shaming or stigmatisation. The difference between these two approaches to shaming an offender lies in the emphasis on the shamefulness of the action, rather than the person, and the question of whether or not the offender is brought back into the community group. Thus a significant difference between restorative justice and the traditional criminal justice system is that the first involves reintegrative shaming, while the latter involves disintegrative shaming, which is at its most disintegrative in cases where the offender is imprisoned. Braithwaite (1989: 68) argues that reintegrative shaming is 'superior to stigmatization because it minimizes risks of pushing those shamed into criminal subcultures, and because social disapproval is more effective when embedded in relationships overwhelmingly characterized by social approval'.

With such a different approach to the criminal justice process, we would expect interaction in such restorative justice processes as youth justice conferencing to be quite different to the criminal court hearings studied by sociolinguists.[58] What are these differences? Are there also similarities? How do people use language in these alternative legal contexts? These are some of the main questions which can be addressed by sociolinguistic research.

At the time of writing this textbook, sociolinguistic work on restorative justice is beginning with Martin and his colleagues' project on youth justice conferencing in New South Wales, Australia. Beginning in this state in the late 1990s, youth justice conferencing is an alternative to court sentencing for youth offenders (i.e. under 18 years old) who have admitted their guilt and who agree to participate in the conference (Cunneen 2008: 201). The conference typically involves the offender – with support person(s), such as family members, the victim – also with support person(s), a police officer, and a convenor, and in relevant cases, an ethnic or Indigenous community liaison officer. The offender also may take a lawyer. Successful conferences result in an agreed upon outcome plan, specifying what the offender must do to repair the harm caused by their offence (often referred to as 'reparation'). The offender does not receive a criminal record unless they do not fulfil the requirements of their outcome plan. This can result in the offender being sent to court.

Martin *et al.* (2009: 43) provide the following 'provisional characterisation' of the elements that comprise what they refer to as the 'macro-genre' of youth justice conferencing (parentheses indicate optional elements):

gathering
legal framing
commissioned recount of the offence
exploring consequences for various parties
(apologies and acknowledgments)
tabling possible remedies
(break and private negotiations)
brokering a collective agreement
ratification of outcome plan
(apologies and acknowledgments)
formal closing
(shared refreshments)
dispersal

Of particular interest for this short introduction to issues of sociolinguistic interest in restorative justice practices is the work of Martin and his colleagues on how language is used to negotiate shaming. Their microanalysis of the details of talk in youth justice conferencing uses the systemic functional linguistics (SFL) framework (see Zappavigna *et al.* 2008). For example, the researchers have used SFL to analyse the structure and function of interactions in one sample conference of a young person alleged to have stolen a phone. Like the other conferences studied by the researchers, this conference (Martin *et al.* 2009: 58) had the features of 'pedagogic [discourse] with regulation projecting integration'. That is, the talk in the conference was teaching the young person (for example community norms about theft), by regulating his talk and working to reintegrate him into his family and community. Students familiar with SFL will want to read this work in detail, while it is only possible to provide a brief summary of some of the findings here. Conversational exchanges in the conference were regulative in organising what the young person was required to say, for example when the convenor said *so what I need you to do is admit you're guilty* and the young person replied *OK*. And the conversational exchanges were integrative when they worked to 're-align the young person with the values of his or her family, ethnic group and community and diminish the relatively malign influence of peers' (p. 56). This (re)integrative discourse within the conference enacts the intended wider social reintegration of the young person to which the conference aims to provide a significant contribution. An example of integrative discourse is in Extract 10–vi below, in which the convenor is shaming the young offender in terms of how his father must have felt when the police contacted them. (Con stands for convenor, and YP for young person.)

Extract 10-vi Martin *et al.*'s (2009: 63) transcription of videorecording
1. Con: And who did they ring when they brought you to the police station?
2. YP: My dad.
3. Con: OK. And what did your dad say? Was he angry, happy?
4. YP: ((nods)) Angry.
5. Con: Angry. ((laughs)) Yeah. OK.

One of the issues examined by Martin and his colleagues is how the young offenders gave evaluations of the events in question and situations related to the events. In the conferences studied to date, the offenders took little initiative in any of the talk. When invited to tell what had happened, the young people did give a short narrative, analysed by Martin *et al.* (forthcoming) in terms of the structure of commissioned recounts. But apart from this short recount, there appears to be a striking similarity between courtroom talk and the question–answer discourse pattern in which most of the talk in the conferences was organised, structured and controlled by the convenor (and at times the ethnic liaison officer). In answer to the convenor or liaison officer questions, the young offenders often gave minimal answers, such as in Extract 10–vi above. The researchers also found that the young offenders rarely used 'the evaluative language of affect, appreciation and evaluation', and when they did, it was through the co-construction and guidance of other participants (forthcoming). This is illustrated in Extract 10–vi above: it was the convenor who provided the evaluative language – here about the reaction of the young person's father to his son being taken to the police station.

An important part of restorative justice is the offender's apology to the victim. This central speech act is of obvious sociolinguistic interest. Do you remember Extract 5–i in Section 3 of Chapter 5? You might like to go back to that example of an appellant expressing remorse to the judge in court for his attack on his wife. We saw in that apology that the offender not only said *I am sorry*, but gave an explanation of the problems which led to this action. Martin *et al.* are examining how young offenders apologise in youth justice conferences. Referring to Hayes' (2006) concerns about problems with the ideal of apology and forgiveness in youth justice conferences, Martin *et al.* (forthcoming) say:

> To these misgivings we can now add our observations concerning power relations inherent in the genre, and the regulatory role taken up by convenors, police and liaison officers, which seem to leave little room for the young person to do other than respond compliantly to evaluations introduced by others. What kind of 'sincere' sounding apology is possible when the young person is so heavily scaffolded?

What does it mean to scaffold a young person in their act of apologising? 'Scaffolding' is a term from education research which is used in the literature on second language learning to refer to the practice of a fluent speaker guiding the learner's response, for example using questions or modelling an utterance as a framework for the learner. In the language learning research, scaffolding is seen as a constructive element in helping the learner to gain fluency or communicative competence. In Extract 10–vi above, we saw the convenor scaffolding the young person's talk about his father's emotions. However, Martin *et al.* also found examples where an apology 'drifted' into a mitigating account (following Hayes 2006), as we see in Extract 10–vii. You can see that the young person accepted that he has no right to hurt people, but then provided a mitigation of the wrong (ELO is the ethnic liaison officer, and YP is the young person):

Extract 10–vii Martin *et al.*'s (forthcoming) transcription of videorecording
ELO: What gives you the right to go and hurt other people?
YP: No right, but he hurt my mate.

If you are interested in research in restorative justice processes, I recommend you start with Braithwaite (1989, 2002), and both the *Handbook of Restorative Justice* (Johnstone & Van Ness 2007) and *A Restorative Justice Reader* (Johnstone 2003b). An understanding of the current sociolegal concerns relating to restorative justice will provide a starting point for framing sociolinguistic research questions.

4.2. Therapeutic courts

The second type of alternative criminal justice practice comprises therapeutic courts – also known as problem-oriented courts – which began with drug courts in the US in the late 1980s. The main therapeutic courts today are drug (and alcohol) courts, family violence courts and mental health courts.[59] They all operate as courts, typically within lower court buildings. But both sentencing and offender fulfilment of sentencing requirements involve community and government representatives from such sectors as health and housing, in addition to judicial and police officers.

A brief outline of the drug court in Queensland, Australia (based on MCQ 2008: 95–97) will provide a glimpse into how therapeutic courts work and how they differ from the restorative justice courts discussed above.[60] Established in Queensland in 2000, drug courts are an attempt to break the drugs–crime–imprisonment cycle for heavy drug users through individually tailored court-ordered drug rehabilitation programmes. The five specific goals of the drug courts are (MCQ 2008: 95):

• to reduce the illicit drug-dependence of offenders
• to reduce the criminal activity associated with illicit drug use
• to reduce the health risks associated with illicit drug use by offenders
• to promote the rehabilitation of drug offenders and their reintegration into the community
• to reduce the pressure on court and prison systems

The court-ordered programme is an alternative to imprisonment: in effect, it is the sentence. It involves three phases – detoxification, stabilisation and reintegration – and takes about 12 to 18 months to complete. It may involve rehabilitation in a residential programme, and training for job-readiness. The main focus in therapeutic courts is on 'change in justice practices for a more humane and holistic response to individual offenders' aiming to encourage them to use available treatment programmes (Marchetti & Daly 2007: 438). I have been unable to find any research about language use in therapeutic courts: a possible area for thesis/dissertation research perhaps?

4.3. Indigenous sentencing courts

Among the earliest alternatives to criminal justice practices in common law countries have been those developed for Native American communities in the US, First Nations/Aboriginal people in Canada and Māori people in New Zealand. It is often claimed that these indigenous courts are based on traditional indigenous justice systems. However, Cunneen (2007: 128) believes that this claim is an oversimplification, and it can be trivialising (2008: 298) to dichotomise pre-modern indigenous restorative justice and modern state-centred systems of justice.

It is impossible to provide even an introduction to all of the indigenous courts currently operating in common law countries. I will restrict this overview to Australia, where Indigenous sentencing courts operate in all states and territories.[61] This overview is based to a considerable extent on Marchetti and Daly (2007), as well as my informal conversations with magistrates and Aboriginal justice officers involved in several states. Indigenous courts in Australia range from more formalised to less formalised; some are held in the local courthouse, while in NSW they are held in venues away from the courthouse. The main features shared by all of these courts are that the offender must be Indigenous, must have pleaded guilty, and must have agreed to have the matter heard in the Indigenous sentencing court. Further, the charge must be one that is normally heard in the lower court (called magistrates court in some states, and local court in others). In all of the Indigenous courts, the magistrate has the final power in the sentencing decision. But the sentencing hearing is convened by the magistrate with a small number of Indigenous elders and/or (other) 'respected persons', who play an active role in the proceedings. This active role includes talking to the offender, and offering support and encouragement, as well as rebuke and reintegrative shaming. It also includes deliberating with the magistrate on the sentence, and often coming to a joint decision about it with the magistrate. Like the restorative justice practices discussed in Section 4.1 above, such as youth justice conferencing, Indigenous sentencing courts focus on the offender's situation, the harmful effects of the offence, the impact on the victim, and the need for balance to be restored in the community following the offender's harmful action. But a major difference is that the active involvement in the Indigenous courts of the respected people, including elders, from the local Indigenous community enables the hearings to be more culturally appropriate than conventional courtroom hearings, both in the ways in which they are conducted and in the sentence eventually handed down to the offender.

Marchetti and Daly (2007: 428) argue that this active role of Aboriginal community members is central to the 'distinct theoretical and jurisprudential basis' which separates Indigenous courts from restorative justice and therapeutic jurisprudence. There are certainly similarities between the Indigenous courts on the one hand and restorative justice and therapeutic jurisprudence on the other: for example, all three alternatives differ from traditional criminal justice in placing the needs of the offender as one of the priorities in the process. Also, all three processes involve the participation of people who are not normally involved in criminal court hearings, such as family members of the offender, victims and victim support people. But the Indigenous courts are unique in their 'power-sharing arrangements' (Potas et al. 2003: 4). As Cunneen (2008: 300) sees it, in opening up the justice system to greater Indigenous control, these courts provide 'an opportunity to reconfigure the justice system with different values, different processes and different sets of accountability'. In this way, Indigenous courts in Australia 'are more explicitly concerned with a political agenda for social change in race relations' (Marchetti & Daly 2007: 443).

These Indigenous courts are new and are still pilot projects in some jurisdictions, but they should be important settings for sociolinguistic research in the future. In the state of NSW, the Indigenous court is known as circle sentencing. Non-Aboriginal participants in circle sentencing (including police prosecutors, defence lawyers and magistrates) have reported on the benefits of having 'everyday language replac[ing] complicated legal terms, facilitating communication within the circle and making it more comfortable for participants to voice their opinions' (Schwartz 2004: 4). Aboriginal participants have commented favourably on the fact that they can use 'Aboriginal English, rather than the language used in other courts' (Potas et al. 2003: 20), and that 'you can use your own language and [the other circle members] know what you mean or understand, and most importantly you are respected for who you are at the same level' (p. 43). But even a cursory glance at these new practices from a sociolinguistic perspective (including my discussions with magistrates and others involved, and my reading of a complete transcript of one circle, see Exercise 10.5 below) also indicates that there are important differences in discourse structure between circle sentencing and traditional courts. These differences are likely to be of far greater consequence than the avoidance of 'complicated legal terms', which in my observations in courts do not actually occur very frequently at all in talk addressed to witnesses, but much more frequently in talk between legal professionals.

From my understanding of circle sentencing, there are important ways in which its discourse structure differs from that of traditional courts. Most importantly, there is no rigid control of discourse structure. While the magistrate convenes the circle, and acts as the facilitator, the aim is to encourage participants to talk, not to control their contributions. Thus the talk is free-flowing, and typically participants often take long turns (and this may also be quite different from youth justice conferencing; see Section 4.1 above). Repetition is not a problem, and relevance is not an issue – there is a widespread recognition that the issues facing the circle are complex, and interrelated, and that many factors need to be considered. In the Indigenous court in the state of Victoria – the Koori Court – the first sitting magistrate and the first Aboriginal Justice Officer who organised the Koori Court wrote about their experiences (Auty & Briggs 2004). Here is their reflection on the way that talk is working in this court (p. 33):

What is impressive about the court at this early stage is that many Aboriginal people have found their voice in it. We wait and take time, we invite rather than compel engagement, we back-track and re-enter dialogue from other places. We are listening to what we are told.

You can see that this refers to a very different approach to talk than that found in conventional courtrooms. A glimpse at part of a transcript from the website of the national television broadcaster (in Extract 10–viii below) provides some indication of the ways in which interaction in New South Wales circle sentencing differs from regular magistrates courts.

Exercise 10.5[xlvi]
Read the extract from the circle sentencing hearing of an Aboriginal man who has pleaded guilty to charges of assault on the mother of his children and to multiple breaches of apprehended violence orders (= protective orders). Discuss the ways in which the talk in this extract contrasts with talk in conventional courtroom hearings. (MaEl stands for male elder, D for defendant, Oolong is an Aboriginal residential alcohol rehabilitation centre and AA is Alcoholics Anonymous, a self-help organisation for people with alcohol problems.)

Extract 10–viii ABC TV's *Four Corners* edited transcript accessed online October 2005[62]
1. MaEl: Richard, would you openly admit that you've got a problem, you do have a problem with drugs and alcohol together?
2. D: Yeah I I admit that. I honestly admit it because um through um Oolong you you've got to go um they're compulsory, you've got to go to AA meetings and you know in AA meetings and you've got a chance to
3. MaEl: That's only the start of the journey.
4. D: I know that, I know that.
5. MaEl: You've got a long way to go.
6. D: And as soon as I walked out them walls up there it's it's been hard you know, like it's it's really hard at the moment cause that place is sort of like a safe house. Whatever you did um you had the support and that. Now at the moment I'm not saying I've got no support now but everything's back on my shoulders and, as I say I don't want that anymore in my life, you know.
7. MaEl: Do you want to disgrace all the time? Do you want to go through this again somewhere else?
8. D: I don't.
9. MaEl: And you won't get the chance we're going to, we're trying to give you here.
10. D: I'm sick of hurting everyone I love, you know like, and that's it, you know.

It is important to point out that Indigenous courts in Australia are sentencing hearings for defendants who have already pleaded guilty, or been found guilty. So they replace hearings in which there is often a reduced role for cross-examination. Thus, no matter how successful and popular such sentencing courts become, it is hard to see how they can replace trials, where cross-examination is an essential ingredient to the presumption of innocence until proven guilty, which is the cornerstone of the legal system.

But in bringing law together with people's lives, relationships and emotions, Indigenous sentencing courts, like the other alternative approaches to criminal justice discussed in this chapter, have begun a revolution in the legal process. Central to this revolution is the way that language is used. Thus these alternative legal processes are excellent contexts for future sociolinguistic research.

Assignments and further research

1. Merry (1990: 111) found that the three discourses of law, morality and therapy 'constituted the dominant frames of meaning in (lower) court and mediation' in her study. How relevant are these three discourses in other informal and alternative legal processes? You could answer this question through an examination of published studies of one or more of the processes dealt with in this chapter. Or you could use this question as a way of analysing your own empirical study of one of these processes.

2. Compare and contrast Merry's (1990) and Conley and O'Barr's (1990) studies of informal US courts. In Section 2 above, I have outlined some similarities and differences between these two contemporaneous ethnographies in similar legal contexts. In undertaking a more thorough investigation of these two studies pay attention to data collection, theoretical framework, methods of analysis, findings and implications. What questions emerge from these two studies which might be addressed in future research? (I have not found any published discussion by either Merry or Conley and O'Barr about the similarities and differences between the findings of their two studies.)

3. Is mediation a 'good thing'? Critically evaluate research on what mediation is intended to do, how it actually works, and claims about its effectiveness and shortcomings. Section 3 of this chapter will provide some useful starting references and see also Conley and O'Barr (2005: Chapter 3).

4. **(Lx)** Greatbatch and Dingwall conclude their (1997) study of argumentative talk in divorce mediation sessions with three big questions about interactional organisation. These three questions (p. 165) could form a good starting point for thesis/dissertation research on language use in mediation:

   First, does the use of turn-taking procedures that preclude direct exchanges between disputants enhance the likelihood of reaching agreements? Second, to what extent are such procedures consistent with the notions of empowerment, facilitation, and neutrality that underlie the rhetoric surrounding the use of mediation? And third, in what ways do different turn-taking procedures contribute to the objective of improving the disputants' ability to resolve future conflicts through direct negotiation?

5. **(Lx)** Examine the discursive management of mediator impartiality in intercultural mediation and/or mediation which includes an interpreter for a second language speaker. To what extent does such mediation reveal a similar use of conversational strategies as those used in the mediation sessions studied by Garcia (e.g. 1991, 1997, 2000), Greatbatch & Dingwall (e.g. 1989, 1997, 1998, 1999), Heisterkamp (2006) and Jacobs (2002).

6. Investigate the variation in mediator approach between mediators oriented towards a therapeutic approach and those oriented towards a bargaining approach (Silbey & Merry 1986, see also Candlin & Maley 1997; Maley 1995; Tracy & Spradlin 1994). How does this variation relate to other variations in courtroom talk and informal legal processes discussed in this book? For an essay or term paper, this investigation could be based on the literature

which analyses this variation, combined with an application of the sociolinguistic analysis presented in this literature to other empirical studies of mediation referred to in this chapter. For thesis/dissertation research, this topic might be a good starting point for a new empirical study.

7. Conley and O'Barr (1990: 178) set out a number of questions for further research, which thesis/dissertation students are encouraged to consider. To what extent have these questions between addressed in the two decades since they were proposed? In particular, you might to like to think about the ways in which Heffer's work (e.g. 2005, 2006, 2007, 2008) on jury instructions, and Philips' work (e.g. 1998) on judges taking the guilty plea connect to Conley and O'Barr's question (3) about the significance of the rules–relationships continuum at other points in the legal process.

8. If you are a thesis/dissertation student, you could consider empirical research in an alternative legal process. I recommend that you begin by investigating what alternative legal processes are used in your region. The next step would be preliminary reading on the relevant sociolegal issues, starting with references given in this chapter. After that, you should start negotiating research access (which may be quite tricky). My suggestion is that you start with a broad sociolinguistic question, such as how language is used in this alternative legal process, and how this language use compares to language use in another legal process (e.g. courtroom hearings). As you collect data and begin sociolinguistic description, a more focused research question should emerge, informed by relevant sociolegal research.

Part 5
Conclusion

Part 5
Conclusion

11

What (else) can sociolinguistics do?

1. Introduction   234

2. Expert evidence   234

3. Legal education   239

4. Investigating inequality   240

    4.1. Language ideologies and inequality   241

    4.2. Language and understanding   243

    4.3. Storytelling and retelling   247

    4.4. Linguistic and cultural difference   251

5. Conclusion   256

    Assignments and further research   257

What (else) can sociolinguistics do?

1. Introduction

In the first 10 chapters we have seen a wide diversity of ways in which sociolinguistics can show how language works – and doesn't work – in the legal process. For example, in Chapters 3–6 we've seen how the extremes of questioning in cross-examination can impact on the stories of witnesses, and we've seen some of the particular effects in interviews with children, second language speakers and witnesses from different social backgrounds. Taking a different approach to interviewing, and not being restricted by courtroom rules of evidence are some of the factors that are involved in rather different ways of investigative interviewing of children, for example by police officers. Also important in this context are the results of sociolinguistic and psycholinguistic research on child language use and development, as we saw in Chapter 8.

The rest of this book deals with a practical question: What else can sociolinguistics do? The answer to this question will start by looking at ways in which sociolinguistics responds to the law, as expert evidence (in Section 2) and in legal education (in Section 3). Then in Section 4, we consider how sociolinguistics is applied to the law, particularly how it contributes to the understanding of issues of fairness and equality in the legal system (following Conley and O'Barr's (2005: 178)) distinction between sociolinguistics applied to the law or responding to the law). There are no exercises provided in this synthesis of what sociolinguistics can do in studying language use in the legal process. Teachers could assign class work by having students research and report on some of the different studies introduced here, using the references cited in this chapter.

2. Expert evidence

Sociolinguistic analysis can be presented as expert evidence in court on any topic to which it is relevant. In this section I will introduce some of the main questions on which sociolinguists give evidence. Our concern in this book is sociolinguistics, rather than linguistics in its entirety, but most of the issues about expert evidence apply equally to sociolinguistics and to linguistics. The presentation of expert linguistic evidence in court is often referred to as forensic linguistics. This is the narrow use of the term, which more broadly refers to linguistic study of language in the legal system.

The process of presenting sociolinguistic evidence in court is initiated by a lawyer who decides, during the preparation of a case, that an expert witness may be able to help in relation to one or more issues to do with language use. Scholars who agree to give expert evidence are in a difficult position. In most common law situations they are contracted by one side in the adversarial contest, but their role is to give an expert opinion as a scholar, not as an advocate. While the lawyer's prime responsibility is to advocate their client's interests, the expert witness is not an advocate, but an impartial expert. Probably the most frustrating part of being an expert witness is remaining true to scholarly ideals – such as being cautious, weighing the evidence and considering all possible explanations for a finding – in the face of adversarial cross-examination from lawyers who typically try to lead the expert witness into aggressive defence of categorical positions. As Ainsworth (forthcoming) explains:

The role of the lawyer – to unswervingly serve the best interests of the client – is quite different from the role of the expert witness – to unswervingly serve the interests of accurate fact-finding through articulation of the science of linguistics as applied to the issues in the case.

Expert witnesses are usually cross-examined in the same way as regular, or fact, witnesses, apart from one important difference: courtroom rules of evidence allow expert witnesses to give opinions – but only those which are held on the basis of their expertise – while fact witnesses are not allowed to give opinions. But expert witnesses can be subject to the full range of linguistic mechanisms which serve in the adversarial contest (some of which we saw in Chapter 3 and Chapter 6). I am not the only sociolinguist who has left the witness stand after cross-examination with the feeling that I must be guilty (of something)!

But, a recent Australian innovation removes expert witnesses to a considerable extent from the adversarial competition. Justice Gray of the Federal Court of Australia explains (Gray 2010) that in this court experts who will be called as witnesses by opposing sides in a case are typically ordered by the court to confer with each other before the trial in order to produce a jointly authored document for the court. This document specifies the matters on which the two experts agree, as well as those on which they do not agree, with the reasons for the disagreement. Then, during the trial, expert witnesses are not called to give their evidence during the course of each party's case for examination-in-chief and cross-examination. Rather, they are both called at the end of all the other evidence. After being sworn or affirmed, the two experts then have to directly debate between themselves the matters on which they disagree. It is only after they have finished this professional scholarly debate on the issue that lawyers are allowed to ask questions, and the judge can too. This breakthrough – called 'hot-tubbing' – should go a long way in ensuring that scholars remain impartial experts and resist the temptation to see themselves as part of the legal team on one side.[63]

The earliest sociolinguistic expert evidence appears to have been in relation to fabricated confessions, which we discussed in Section 7.1 of Chapter 7. There we saw that sociolinguists have examined typed confessions alleged to be verbatim reports of what a suspect had told police. Sociolinguistic analysis can sometimes address the question of whether the speech attributed to an individual appears to be an accurate representation of the person's speech patterns. In recent years, the original work on fabricated confessions has developed to other forensic questions related to attributing authorship – including whether a suspect is likely to be the author of incriminating written or spoken texts, such as a suicide letter or a bomb threat. If you are interested in pursuing authorship analysis, you should start by reading Chaski (2001), Coulthard (e.g. 1994a, 1994b, 2004), Coulthard and Johnson (2007), Grant (2007, 2008) and Howald (2008).

Sociolinguistic and linguistic anthropological evidence is an important part of the legal processing of Indigenous claims to land in Australia (see Section 4.2 of Chapter 5). This evidence is primarily concerned with the ways in which language knowledge and usage of claimants relates to their claims about ownership and connection to land.

In the US, Shuy (1993, 1998, 2006) has written three popular books about his considerable experience in providing sociolinguistic expert evidence. In these books, he details some of the cases, and discusses some of the issues involved in providing expert evidence. Much of Shuy's expert evidence focuses on language crimes, that is crimes committed through language, which include bribery, threatening and perjury (see also Solan & Tiersma 2005). Many of these cases involve the analysis of undercover recordings of conversations made by officers of the Federal Bureau of Investigation. These analyses address the question of whether the suspect being secretly recorded in conversations with undercover agents is initiating or at least cooperating with the planning of illegal activity. Shuy (1990) explains how he uses topic analysis, not to determine what speakers meant during a conversation, but rather to examine the structure of the conversations which 'leaves clues' (p. 87) about their intentions. Topic analysis involves 'tracing the various topics raised ..., noting the specific responses of the individuals to those topics and whether the topics were recycled or reintroduced several times by the same person' (p. 86). Response analysis examines the range of ways in which speakers respond to the topics raised by their interlocutor. For example, speakers may use minimal responses (or 'feedback markers') such as *uh-huh* or *OK*, without signalling agreement. And some topics raised by the agent may be responded to by the suspect changing the topic, or deferring the topic, or even by silence. Shuy shows that in one such undercover recording a man suspected of soliciting the murder of his wife was consistently cooperative about small talk topics, but never cooperative about substantive topics (what the goal of the conversation was about). He was occasionally cooperative about corollary topics (defined as 'ways of achieving or arriving at the substantive topics' (p. 87)). Shuy (1998) has also written about expert sociolinguistic evidence he has given concerning the coerciveness of questioning in police interviews (see also Berk-Seligson 2002b, 2007, 2009, referred to in Section 6 of Chapter 7 and Section 2.1 of Chapter 8).

Butters (2007) reports that sociolinguistic expert evidence is sometimes used in trademark cases: that is, disputes in civil courts over the registration of a trademark name for a company. He refers to cases where complaints have been made about trademarks being obscene or derogatory, as in the name of a football team ('The Redskins') and a women's motorcycle group ('Dykes on Bikes'). Other trademark cases often involve phonetic or morphological linguistic evidence, for example in relation to whether two similar trademark names are pronounced sufficiently differently that consumers will not confuse them.

Recently, sociolinguists and phoneticians have become involved in providing expert evidence in cases in which an asylum seeker's speech is analysed in order to assist governments in verifying the person's claims about their origin. This is being referred to as LADO, an acronym for 'language analysis in the determination of origins'. The initial expert advice to governments is often provided by phoneticians – who analyse the accent found in the sample audiorecorded speech of the asylum seeker, and who then assess the extent to which it is representative of the speech of people with the origin (national, regional or ethnic) claimed by the asylum seeker. But this assessment is not always done by trained linguists – some governments use 'native speakers' of the language in question, who assess the asylum seeker's speech in order to judge whether they are telling the truth about their origins. Several sociolinguists have given evidence in appeals against decisions made on the basis of LADO reports (Blommaert 2009; Corcoran 2004; Maryns 2004, 2006). And, as we will see in Section 4.4 below, these and other sociolinguists have raised questions about the assumptions about language use and language contact which underlie much of the LADO work (see for example Eades 2005, 2009, 2010; Fraser 2009; and Singler 2004 in addition to the references above).

Conley and O'Barr (2005) raise an important issue about the relationship between linguistic research and linguistic expertise in courts. (These issues, as explained above, apply equally to sociolinguistics and to linguistics.) Discussing US examples, Conley and O'Barr argue that linguistic expert evidence is typically available either to people who can afford to hire an expert, or to people whose cases have been taken up by scholars who have 'donated their services in pursuit of equity and fairness' (p. 162). (However, I believe it is not common for sociolinguists to provide expert opinions without charge, a practice which might be argued to compromise the neutrality of experts.) My experience suggests a third category, at least in Australia, where legal aid financial support can be available to people who cannot afford an expert. Like several other Australian linguists I have been hired by legal aid lawyers in cases where defendants would not have been able to afford an expert, but where modest legal aid funding was allocated for experts, not only in sociolinguistics, because of the issues of equity and fairness involved. Perhaps Australia is unusual in resourcing such options? Conley and O'Barr's view is that there is some kind of rationing in the way in which linguistic expertise is used – either according to who can afford an expert, or 'along political lines' (2005: 162–163). They further argue that 'a vast amount of research time and energy is devoted to pursuing an agenda set by the law'. While many linguists are professionally interested in 'answering questions posed by the law' (p. 174), Conley and O'Barr ask whether 'the legal tail [is] wagging the scientific dog'. In this discussion, they draw a distinction between linguistics applied to the law (where linguists pursue scholarly research in legal contexts) and linguistics responding to the law (where linguistic work responds to concerns within the law, for example those that arise from particular cases). We will see in this section that this distinction is not always tenable when examining the relationship between sociolinguistics and its applications to the law.

Interestingly, in some of the cases I've been involved in it is hard to see that the sociolinguistic research time and energy involved was 'pursuing an agenda set by law'. On the other hand, it could be seen as an agenda 'along political lines' – the cases were seen by the lawyers who called for expert evidence as test cases about the inequality experienced by Aboriginal Australians in the legal system (see Eades 2008a). One of these cases (*R v Condren*, see below and Section 7.1 of Chapter 7) involved a man whose murder conviction rested on a 'confession' which was alleged to have been fabricated by the police – in other words, a verbal. Police verballing (see Section 7.1 of Chapter 7) was seen as a major problem in the functioning of the criminal justice system in the 1980s, when this case took place. Legal aid lawyers working on Condren's case saw it as an important one for exposing this issue, and they allocated considerable funds to the running of this case, for example hiring one of the state's most senior barristers. The case had a complex trajectory through the legal system, reaching as far as the highest court in the country. Condren eventually succeeded, and his case played a role in the recognition of the problem of police verballing, and the establishment of mandatory electronic recording of police interviews with suspects (see CJC 1992: 90–91; Eades 1993, 1995a, 1997).[64] In another case (*R v Kina*), I presented sociolinguistic evidence about Aboriginal ways of using English, which directly resulted in widespread legal education on this topic, as well as the state Attorney-General's call for the legal system 'to have knowledge of and ... be sensitive to the problem of cross-cultural communication' (see Eades 1996a, 2003, 2007b, 2008a: 77–79). Thus, both of these cases illustrate a more complex situation than linguistics responding to the law. In both of these cases, existing sociolinguistic research on Aboriginal ways of speaking English was part of the 'response' in a particular case which had been identified by legal aid as representing wider failures of the criminal justice system. The explanatory power of sociolinguistic analysis then contributed not only to the success of the cases of two individuals, but more broadly to change in the way that the legal system operates, and in this way we see that sociolinguistic research can be applied to the law at the same time as it responds to the law (in Conley and O'Barr's 2005 terms).

But there are also other relationships between expert evidence and other sociolinguistic work. The questions put to experts in the course of their involvement in a case (whether in discussions with the lawyer, or in court, or in the US in depositions) can range widely. While some of these questions are clarification requests from a non-linguist lawyer trying to understand the linguist's expert report, others can be challenging and thought-provoking. Such questions can then influence future research directions, presumably an example of Conley and O'Barr's legal tail wagging the scientific dog. On the other hand, questions and judicial decisions about sociolinguistic expert evidence can sometimes reveal the extent to which the linguist's basic assumptions about how language works are not shared or understood outside of the discipline, as we will see in Section 4 below. This can lead to a second level of application in one or both of the ways to be considered below, namely legal education (Section 3) and addressing inequality (Section 4). I will illustrate these connections from my own experiences.

My written evidence in the Condren case, mentioned above, took the form of an 84-page report in which I analysed differences in Condren's ways of answering questions between his allegedly verbatim confession on the one hand, and two audiorecorded interviews with him on the other hand. I also wrote about the differences between the answers attributed to him in the so-called confession, and what was known about Aboriginal English ways of answering questions, more generally. I have written about this expertise and the judicial reactions to it in Eades (1993, 1995a, 1997). The judges refused to accept that there could be a specialised field of knowledge that could analyse the English of Aboriginal people: it is not uncommon for linguistic expertise about the use of English to be ruled as inadmissible, because of the view that the jurors all speak English, and they don't need an expert to tell them about their own language.

But I want to focus here on just one of the reactions from the three appeal judges in the case, namely the decision that evidence about Aboriginal English was not relevant to the speech of an individual, namely the appellant Condren. In the words of one of the judges, 'characteristics commonly found within a category of persons described as Aboriginal' were not relevant to the 'alleged responses of the applicant' (*R v Condren*: p. 296). But the way in which any person speaks is surely connected to 'the verbal response characteristics of a class'. The use of Russian interpreters in court for example, is founded on the view that any individual speaker of Russian shares a considerable amount of their speech with other speakers of that language. Similarly, where it is dialect or culture which most accounts for distinctive features in the way an individual person speaks, then what is at issue are features of language use which are shared with other people in the speaker's sociocultural group or community of practice. However, the judgment in Condren's case also appeared to assume that language use is determined by biology and that it can be understood by isolating a speaker from their sociocultural group. So, for example, one of the judges commented that, having observed Condren's mother giving evidence, he 'certainly formed the impression that she was of only partly Aboriginal extraction and indeed that part was not predominant' (p. 275). In other words, Condren's mother didn't look very Aboriginal. But it is socialisation – how a person grows up in a sociocultural environment – which most affects the way in which the person uses language. Skin colour is of no direct relevance, and can only play a small indirect role, if any at all.

This reaction in the judgment revealed that the judges were using a folk view of the way that language is learned that is at odds with the findings of linguistic and anthropological research. Perhaps it should not be surprising: why should judges be expected to know about research findings in any particular field, if these findings are not presented in evidence? Arguably, the lawyers who called me as a witness should have begun their questioning of me with these basic issues about language learning, biology and socialisation. However, from reading the judgments in this case, I learned something important about assumptions about language learning and use, a topic we will come back to in Section 4 below. And I realised that there are much more extensive implications for the justice system beyond a single case, when judges believe that an Aboriginal person whose mother doesn't look dark-skinned would not be using Aboriginal ways of communicating. In a legal system which had – and still has – serious failures in its delivery of justice to Aboriginal Australians, the way that Aboriginal people communicate goes far beyond the issue of verballing. These concerns, revealed so sharply in the Condren judgments, got me talking to lawyers and thinking about legal education, the topic of the next section. Thus, expert evidence can be the starting point for other applied sociolinguistic work, leading to both legal education and to changes which address inequalities in the legal system.

Students often ask how they can become a forensic (socio)linguist. In my view you should not set out to become a forensic (socio)linguist, in the narrow sense of the term. Experts give evidence in court because of their expertise, and there is a wide range of legal questions about which (socio)linguistic expertise can be sought. The most important prerequisite to becoming an expert (socio)linguistic witness is that a person is a sound scholar, with a PhD and a good scholarly publication record. The fact that you have studied the use of language in the legal system may well be relevant to some topics, and irrelevant to others. So, if you are interested in giving expert evidence in court, you must first become an expert. If you want to become an expert in language use in the legal system, this will not necessarily lead directly to expert evidence work. But it can enable you to have an impact on language use in the legal process, as we will see in the next two sections.

3. Legal education

Several sociolinguists who have worked in forensic linguistics in its narrow and/or broad definition, have applied aspects of their work to legal education. This can involve presenting invited talks to police officers, or to members of the legal profession or the judiciary. Or it can involve writing about language in the legal process, specifically for some or all of these groups who work in the legal process. Examples of such writings are found in Aldridge and Wood (1998), Eades (1992) and Walker (1999). Walker (1999) is a handbook which provides advice for legal professionals questioning children, especially in court, which we discussed in Section 2 of Chapter 5. Aldridge and Wood (1998) is a sociolinguistic study of 100 videorecorded police interviews with children, written with police officers as part of the intended audience, which we discussed in Section 5 of Chapter 8. Eades (1992) is a handbook for lawyers interviewing speakers of (Australian) Aboriginal English. The direct catalyst for the writing of this book was the problematic assumptions about language learning and use generally, and Aboriginal English specifically, which were revealed in the judgments in the Condren case (discussed in Section 2 above). But the handbook also had a broader and practical aim: to help lawyers to communicate more effectively with Aboriginal English speakers, and so it deals with some of the issues discussed in Section 3 of Chapter 5 above. In Eades (2004, 2008a) I have written about how the handbook appeared to be used in misconstruing the evidence of Aboriginal witnesses in the Pinkenba case, which we discussed in Section 5 of Chapter 6. I have learned that making a tool does not necessarily mean that people will use it as intended. You might like to discuss whether it is better never to make such a tool, and whether or not you agree with my conclusions about this issue (as explained in Eades 2004, 2008a).

In Section 2 above, we saw that linguists have sometimes been involved as expert witnesses in cases where the speech of an asylum seeker is analysed as part of the determination of their origins. This application of linguistics has been of particular concern to sociolinguists, because of the problematic assumptions about language use that are often involved, to be discussed in Section 4.4 below. Section 2 above provides some references to scholarly publications about this work. But a group of linguists, of whom many are sociolinguists, also engaged in legal and government education with the release of a set of guidelines about using linguistic analysis in the determination of the origin of asylum seekers (Language and National Origin Group 2004; for discussion of the guidelines see Eades and Arends 2004; Eades 2005, 2009, 2010; Fraser 2009). These guidelines present introductory information about such topics as language choice in multilingual societies, code-switching, language change and diffusion. The guidelines aim to provide general sociolinguistic expertise to governments, lawyers, refugee advocates and judicial decision-makers, both about the ways in which linguistic analysis can shed light on questions about speakers' origins and about limits to the ways in which it can be used.

Like the expert evidence discussed above which was given in legal cases testing major issues about inequality in the legal system, the application of sociolinguistics to legal education cannot always been seen as either sociolinguistics applied to the law, or sociolinguistics responding to the law (in Conley and O'Barr's 2005 terms, discussed above). Rather, sociolinguistic involvement in legal education – such as the examples discussed above – often appears to be motivated as much (or more) by concerns about how language use reproduces inequality as it is by any other concerns.

4. Investigating inequality

There are many ways in which the law can fail to deliver justice, or can fail to treat all people equally. For example, at the time of writing, the Australian *Racial Discrimination Act 1975*, is explicitly suspended in the Northern Territory as a result of 'emergency' legislation enacted in 2007 (NTER Review Board 2008). So the law which prohibits governments from treating a group of people differently from the rest of the population on the basis of their race no longer applies to many Aboriginal people in this Australian territory. In practice, this means that Aboriginal people in the Northern Territory are subject to greater governments control – for example over how they can spend welfare payments – than other Australians. This is an example of legislation which treats people unequally, and thus perpetuates inequality (and which presumably would not be allowed in a country with a constitutional or legislative bill of rights).

But the reproduction of inequality in and through the legal system typically originates not through legislation, but through situated processes and practices, that is through the ways that individuals treat other individuals in the legal process. Sometimes this inequality may arise because of blatant abuses of power, whether individual, or systemic such as Leo (2008) documents in his study of US police interrogations. On other occasions this inequality may arise from inadequate resources, such as when courts are unable to provide trained or accredited interpreters for speakers of particular languages. But the areas of greatest sociolinguistic interest are those where language use is directly involved in the failure of the legal system to treat people fairly. For example, in Section 7 of Chapter 8 we saw Jones's (2008a) finding that Jamaican suspects were not given the same chance to tell their version of events in police interviews as White British suspects. As we saw, Jones makes no connection between the language practices revealed in her study and the intentions of individual police officers. But her study raises important questions about how the language use she documents is connected to wider societal issues of racism and inequality. However, the role of language use in the failure to deliver justice is often more subtle.

4.1. Language ideologies and inequality

In this section we bring together a number of the specific findings of sociolinguistic research in the legal process through a consideration of some of the assumptions about language which permeate the legal process. These assumptions are taken-for-granted 'commonsense knowledge' which underpin language use in the legal process, and which often enable specific practices which can contribute to, or lead to, the unequal or unfair treatment of some people within the law. For example, in Section 2 of Chapter 4 we saw that it is typically taken for granted that if a witness needs an interpreter then this means they cannot use English for any of their evidence. This all-or-nothing view is based on assumptions about language learning and bilingualism that are at odds with sociolinguistic and applied linguistic findings, for example the findings about different kinds of language proficiency discussed in Section 2 of Chapter 4. Many individual legal professionals would be astonished to hear that sociolinguists (e.g. Angermeyer 2008) find a connection between this all-or-nothing view and related practices in the legal process on the one hand, and the unequal treatment of second language speakers on the other hand. When we examine the provision of interpreter services in courts, we do not see an oppressor or an oppressive structure bearing down on the liberties of individuals. But power relations are complex, and can often involve influences over the way people think (as we saw in Section 2 of Chapter 6). This is not to claim that lawyers, judges or court interpreter programmes are deliberately treating second language speakers unfairly. But the effects of problematic assumptions about bilingualism and language learning can be shown to involve just this: unfair treatment of second language speakers, as we will see in Section 4.4 below. So, taken-for-granted assumptions are of particular interest to scholars who study power relations and power struggles, and who seek to uncover the complex relationships between structures (such as the legal system) and the agency of individuals and groups. As we saw in Section 4 of Chapter 6, these assumptions are often called 'ideologies'. For explanation and discussion of the different uses of the word 'ideology', see Blommaert (2005: 158–202), Conley and O'Barr (2005: 143–145) and Woolard (1998).

Taken-for-granted assumptions about how language works are termed 'language ideologies' (also sometimes referred to as 'linguistic ideologies', e.g. Ainsworth 2008, see also Woolard 1998: 3; and also sometimes referred to as 'folk views' or 'folk linguistics'). A good working definition of 'language ideology' is provided by Blommaert (2005: 253): 'Socially, culturally and historically conditioned ideas, images and perceptions about language and communication'. Another definition is provided by Kroskrity (2004: 498): 'beliefs, or feelings about languages as used in their social worlds'. Sociolinguistics students who are not familiar with contemporary linguistic anthropology and sociolinguistic work on language ideologies should read some of the key work in this area, such as Blommaert (1999), Blommaert and Verschueren (1998), Kroskrity (2000, 2004), Schieffelin et al. (1998) and Woolard and Schieffelin (1994).

Central to the sociolinguistic work on language ideologies is the understanding that 'ideologies of language are not about language alone' (Woolard 1998: 3). Indeed, as Kroskrity (2004: 501) puts it, they often serve the interests of a specific social or cultural group. Thus, for example, many people believe that Standard English is the only 'correct' or 'proper' way to speak, and that to speak English in any other way indicates laziness, ignorance or lack of respect. This Standard English ideology serves the interests of educated people, and its pervasive belief throughout the education system continually serves to control the way that people think about English and its speakers (see for example Lippi-Green 1997; Silverstein 1996). One of the major contributions that sociolinguistics can make to the study of social life is to uncover the ways in which language ideologies 'serve to rationalise existing social structures, relationships and dominant linguistic habits' (Swann et al. 2004: 171). Thus, an examination of language ideologies about bilingualism and language learning can address the powerlessness of immigrants and indigenous people in the legal process (as Angermeyer 2008 shows). While there are often connections between language ideologies and the reproduction of inequality, linguistic anthropologists and sociolinguists use the term 'language ideology' about any socially, culturally and historically conditioned ideas about language, regardless of their connection to power relations. It is important, therefore, to remember that the term 'language ideology' is not used here with a Marxist-oriented interpretation. I will use it interchangeably with expressions like 'assumptions about how language works'. No society is ideology free, and not all ideologies are closely linked to the perpetuation of inequality.

As sociolinguists, we need to be sensitive to the danger of taking the high moral ground while ignoring the language ideologies within our own profession: for example, Woolard and

Schieffelin (1994: 59) point out that speech act theory is a way of looking at language use from a particular 'English linguistic ideology', which foregrounds the speaker's psychological state and backgrounds the social dimensions of language use.[65] At the same time, our work as sociolinguists revolves around studying how people use language, how people talk about language use, and what happens when people use language in particular ways. We are in a good position to uncover and reflect on disjunctions or contradictions between these three aspects of language use.

The connection between specific language ideologies and unequal treatment of particular people in the legal process can be complex. In Eades (2008a) I have examined in some detail certain assumptions about language use in cross-examination which are involved in continuing neocolonial control of the state over Aboriginal Australians. This is not the place for a detailed argument, but rather for an overview of some of the language ideologies which impact on the legal process. Some of these language ideologies are shared more widely in Anglo societies and are not just limited to the legal system, as we will see. It will not be possible in this chapter to address all of the language ideologies involved in ways in which the legal system fails to deliver justice. For example, we will not look at assumptions about deaf sign language or children's language (but see Section 7 of Chapter 4, Section 2 of Chapter 5, and Sections 3 and 5 of Chapter 8). And you will see that none of the alternative justice practices discussed in Chapter 10 will be discussed here. The focus of the rest of this chapter is on some of the areas where language ideologies are involved in the perpetuation of inequality in the legal system.

4.2. Language and understanding

Given the central importance of language to the legal process, it is not surprising that it rests on some strongly held and upheld assumptions about how language works. Three US scholars who combine legal and linguistic training and expertise have provided valuable discussions of some of these assumptions: Ainsworth (1993, 2008), Solan (1993), Tiersma (1999, 2001a) and Solan and Tiersma (2005). Arguably the most fundamental language ideology that pervades the legal system is one that is widely shared in western societies and is not restricted to the law. Ainsworth (2008: 14) calls this the 'correspondence theory of language', and she explains that this view holds that language 'is a medium that maps human thought onto an objective external reality and it does so transparently'. Several sociolinguists and linguistic anthropologists writing about language ideologies more generally have also discussed this view. Woolard and Schieffelin (1994: 71) refer to it as 'the tendency to see propositionality as the essence of language', Silverstein (1996: 287) talks about the 'plane of the functional utility of language as a means of representation or instrument of denotation', and Haviland (2003: 767) calls it the 'referential transparency' theory of language. This view that the essential function of language is to transparently express propositions, denotations or representations is so fundamental in western societies that we even find it prominently in dictionaries. For example, the *Macquarie Dictionary* of Australian English defines language in terms of communication, which in turn is defined as 'the imparting or interchange of thoughts, opinions, or information by speech, writing, or signs'. And the children's *Macquarie Junior Dictionary* defines language as 'any set of signs or symbols used to pass on information'. A sociolinguistic definition would not restrict definitions to this representational aspect: what about language being used for other aspects of communication, such as doing things with, to, or for people, for example joking, insulting, bargaining, arguing?

While sociolinguists approach language in terms of what people do with it, and how it works, within the legal system language is seen as 'an objective system of meaning' (Ainsworth 2008: 17), which can be transparently discovered, unequivocally understood and directly translated. But there are many ways in which language does not transparently correspond to some objective 'reality'. Consider the conversational use of questions. The most obvious function of questions is to find out information. But questions are often used with other functions, such as hinting (*Have you cleaned your room yet?*), complaining (*Why are you always running late?*) and requesting (*Could I have a cappuccino?*). Interlocutors can usually understand the function(s) of questions, because people take into account not just the transparent (semantic) meaning, but they also take account of contextual (pragmatic) features. But, as we saw in Section 2.6 of Chapter 7, US appeal courts, seeing language as an objective system of meaning, have taken the view that a literal interpretation of the semantic meaning of a sentence adequately and accurately conveys the speaker's meaning. Thus, courts have upheld decisions by police officers that suspects who say things like *Could I have a lawyer?* are not exercising their legal right to request a lawyer. Why do judges apply this language ideology in such seemingly absurd ways, when presumably these same judges would sometimes request coffee with the same formula, e.g. *Could I have a cappuccino?*

To answer this question, we need to go from language ideologies which are widely held in western societies to quite fundamental issues of legal interpretation. This book has not considered the area of forensic linguistic research and expert evidence which deals with statutory interpretation, as this area relies mainly on the linguistic specialisations of morpho-syntax and semantics (see for example Solan 1993). Linguists who work in statutory interpretation are concerned with how lawyers and judges interpret written law, and the theories of language involved when there is legal argument over meaning in a legal document (such as a statute or a contract). A central way in which the law approaches these arguments involves what is known as the 'plain meaning rule' (also referred to as 'the plain language rule' or 'the clear language rule').[66] The plain meaning rule is consistent with the correspondence theory of language, seeing legal documents as transparently representing objective meaning. This rule holds that 'when the language [in a legal document] is clear, courts have no authority to go beyond the words of the statute or contract, but must apply the clear language of the document to the facts before them' (Solan 1993: 93). Tiersma (1999: 126) explains that the effect of this rule is to focus the attention of courts 'on the meaning of words and sentences, rather than on the speaker's [or writer's] intent, even though that intent is legally what should decide the issue'. There has been much debate in US courts about the extent to which 'legislative intent' (or speakers'/writers' meaning) should be taken into account, and where and when the plain meaning rule should be invoked. And in recent years, there has been a strong 'revival of the traditional plain meaning rule' (p. 127), in the approach to statutory interpretation now referred to as 'textualism'. Textualism focuses on the actual words in the legal document (taken literally and in a decontextualised way; see Tiersma 2001a: 89), and thus privileges word and sentence meaning over speaker meaning.

It is hardly surprising then that judges use dictionaries so much in their legal interpretation work (Tiersma 1999: 127).

While this approach guides courts in their interpretation of legal documents, including judicial decisions and written laws, it seems to impact also on how courts deal with issues of the spoken language use of individuals who come before them. Thus, the seemingly absurd situation revealed by Ainsworth's study of judicial decisions about what suspects have to say in order to invoke their Miranda rights, make some kind of 'sense' when we understand the role of textualism in legal interpretation.

Parallel to the textualist (plain meaning) approach to legal texts is what we might call an 'ideology of literalism' approach to spoken language, that is that a literal interpretation of the semantic meaning of a sentence adequately conveys the speaker's meaning. As we saw, ignoring the pragmatic meaning of utterances like *Could I get a lawyer?*, police officers and courts have interpreted them as merely 'questions about the theoretical availability of counsel', rather than as requests for counsel (Ainsworth 2008: 8). Such an interpretation makes no sense in terms of ordinary conversation, except as some kind of (sick) joke. The effect of this ideology of literalism in the denial of justice is clear from Ainsworth's (2008) study: unless suspects share this ideology of literalism being used by the courts, and suspend their usual ways of talking, they are unable to exercise their rights in police interviews.

Another example of the ideology of literalism in the legal process is found in the way in which consent is defined in rape cases, as we saw in Section 4 of Chapter 6. Here we saw that a complainant can be taken to have consented to sexual activity if there is no proof of resistance. And in the abduction case in my (Eades 2008a) book, discussed in Section 5 of Chapter 6, there was a parallel situation: three young teenage Aboriginal boys were taken to have consented to going for a ride out of town with six armed police officers in the middle of the night, because they did not object. In these rape and abduction cases, the law seems to take the view that if a person does not want to do something, they say so. If they don't say or do something in resistance, they must have consented. Similarly, threats and force can be defined with no regard to context. As the cross-examination questions make clear in Extract 6–v, lawyers can argue that *no overt threat* was made, while Extract 6–x showed a lawyer defining *force* in a similar way, to dismiss the 13-year-old boy's claim that that he had been forced to get in the police car. As Ehrlich (2001) and Eades (2008a) point out, this approach completely ignores such contextual factors as the victim's fear of violence, unbalanced physical strength, experience and history of police violence against Aboriginal people. Thus, sociolinguistic research has exposed the ways in which a literal approach to the meaning of consent can be implicated in problems with the delivery of justice in rape and abduction cases. Exemplifying how sociolinguistics can go beyond descriptive and explanatory research, lawyer-linguist Tiersma (2007) has directly addressed this inequality with proposals for changes to the definition of the crime of rape. These changes would result in distinguishing between voluntary consent and consent because of 'threats, intimidation or fear caused by the defendant' (p. 96), as well as shifting the focus from the mental state of the complainant to that of the defendant (specifically to the defendant's knowledge about the complainant's mental state in relation to the question of consent).

We have seen how contextual factors, which seem to be common-sense issues in everyday interactions, are often ignored in the legal process – not just in cross-examination, but also in judicial decisions – consistent with the legal ideology of literalism. So, can we conclude that this ideology of literalism is something that laypeople should learn about in order to have the chance of a fairer hearing in the legal process? Not necessarily, according to Solan and Tiersma's (2005) study of how courts interpret speech acts (for example, whether *Could I get a lawyer?* is a theoretical query or a request). Their study concludes that the courts use 'selective literalism', sometimes interpreting speech acts literally, as direct speech acts, while at other times interpreting them non-literally, as indirect speech acts. An example of the former was the US Supreme Court case which revolved around a police officer who stopped a motorist late at night, and searched the trunk of the car, despite not having a search warrant, and not having grounds to search without a warrant. The officer's question *Does the trunk open?* was interpreted by the motorist as a request or command to open the trunk. But it was interpreted by the court as a question. Yet the contextual factors – particularly the power that the officer has over the driver in such situations – make it most likely that the officer's utterance *Does the trunk open?* was functioning as a command, and that the driver felt he had no choice, and thus did not 'freely and voluntarily' consent to open the trunk. This was consistent with the fact, ignored by the court, that indirect commands often take the form of a question.

But such literal interpretations are selective: Solan and Tiersma (2005: 200) point to the case of an 'impetuous youth' who sent a letter to President Reagan which contained the sentence: 'Resign or You'll Get Your Brains Blown Out'. The letter writer was convicted of threatening the life of the president: what is literally a prediction was given its indirect speech act interpretation as a threat. Eades (2006, 2008a: 324–326) discusses a parallel example of a court choosing a non-literal and indirect speech act reading of an utterance. In the abduction case discussed above, the utterance *Jump in the car* was interpreted non-literally, seemingly as the indirect speech act of an offer or suggestion. In this case the court seems to have accepted the opposite legal reasoning and understanding of how language works than in the US *Does the trunk open?* case. Solan and Tiersma (2005: 47–48) believe that 'it is hard to avoid the impression that courts have somewhat of a double standard when it comes to considering pragmatic information, such as specifics of context. They are significantly more likely to take it into account when it benefits the government, and less so when it helps the accused'.[67] In their study of selective literalism in the law, Solan and Tiersma found that the law 'is systematically more concerned with how a suspect asks to see a lawyer than it is with how a police officer asks to conduct a search' (p. 98). Thus, they conclude that suspects 'are held to a higher linguistic standard than the police' (p. 62).

We have seen that the correspondence theory of language assumes a transparent correspondence between language and objective meaning, and the ideology of literalism similarly assumes that the semantic meaning of an utterance adequately conveys the speaker's meaning, regardless of context. Closely linked to these two language ideologies is a well-known approach to communication known as the 'transmission' model. As Rock (2007: 15) explains, this theory views communication as a sender transmitting a message to a receiver, and it underlies much of the work on the comprehension of texts. It is also behind the practice in the legal system of reading scripted legal texts to laypeople, as we saw in the way judges give instructions to the jury (in Sections 6 and 7 of Chapter 3), and the way police deliver rights texts to suspects (in Section 2 of Chapter 7). The assumption is that meaning is in the text, and if the text is accurately read to laypeople – without any explanation, application or context – they are then able to make important legal decisions as a result. This includes jurors applying the law to a case to arrive at a decision about guilt or innocence, or suspects understanding their legal rights while in custody, and making decisions about whether or not to invoke them. We saw that the work of Heffer (e.g. 2005) and Rock (e.g. 2007) problematises this transmission model of communication and the related language practices. Sociolinguistic approaches see comprehension as an interactive social process rather than an individual cognitive ability. As Rock (2007: 22) explains, understanding is what people do rather than what people have.

The dominant legal approaches to language and understanding also assume that spoken and written language are effectively the same. We saw in Sections 1 and 5 of Chapter 9, and Section 7 of Chapter 7 that it is common for written documents to be treated as a transparent representation of spoken interaction. But there are important implications for the legal process which arise from ways in which spoken and written texts differ, as we will see in the next section, which deals with assumptions and practices associated with storytelling.

4.3. Storytelling and retelling

Storytelling and retelling are central to the legal process, as we have seen. In lawyer interviews, police interviews, courtroom hearings and informal and alternative legal processes, laypeople are required to tell their side of the story. Often these stories have to be retold at a later stage in the legal process, sometimes by the original teller, and at other times by an officer within the legal process. The process of recontextualisation – taking a story from one context and retelling it in a new context – can involve significant transformations. We have seen examples of this with summaries of interviewees' stories carried out by police officers (in Section 7.2 of Chapter 7 and Section 4.2 of Chapter 8), and lawyers or paralegals (in Section 5 of Chapter 9). And, as we saw in Sections 4 and 5 of Chapter 6, cross-examination involves lawyers summarising witnesses' stories in the propositions of questions. Further, many legal decisions involve the evaluation of individuals' stories, in terms of such features as consistency, accuracy, reliability and honesty. In the evaluation and assessment of people's stories and their recontextualisations, there are some recurring language ideologies.

First, a witness's or interviewee's story is assumed to be solely their own account, and the role of interviewer questions in the shaping of the story is typically ignored – in Trinch's (2003: 49–50) terms, this is the 'ideology of narrator authorship' (see also Eades 2008a: 322–323). But sociolinguistic research has shown that stories are often co-constructed by the storyteller and the other participants in the interaction (see Trinch 2003: 5). And when an interviewee tells their story in an interview, the interviewer's questions structure the story and influence the way it is told, for example what is included, and what is left out. Specifically within the legal system, several researchers have shown the role of interviewer questions in the way in which an interviewee tells their story: as we saw for example in Section 7.2 of Chapter 7, in the work of Rock (2001); Jönsson and Linell (1991) and Komter (2002, 2006b) in police interviews; and in Section 5 of Chapter 9 in the work of Trinch (e.g. 2003) in lawyer interviews.

Trinch (2003: 49–50) argues that the ideology of narrator authorship is found not just in the culture of the law, but more generally in western culture. This ideology relies on the 'prevalent' and 'tenacious' cultural notion of the 'true story', but ignores the collaborative and situated nature of storytelling. Treating co-constructed stories as the production of a single author is common in the legal process. For example, we saw in Section 4 of Chapter 9 how a defendant's instructions to his lawyer were produced from his answers to police questions. As Trinch points out, there can be problematic consequences from this ideology when the credibility of the narrator is challenged in cross-examination, which can result in the decision that a witness is a liar. For example, in Section 5 of Chapter 9, we saw the way in which a paralegal made subtle changes in her written summary of a client's story (see Extracts 9–ii and 9–iii). But this written summary (the affidavit) was produced with the client as sole author, and no indication of what exactly were the client's words, and what parts came from the paralegal's questions (thus blurring the source distinctions, see Section 7.2 of Chapter 7). Thus, no recognition was given of either the interactional nature of the story's production during the interview, or the paralegal's contribution to the written version of the story. Under later courtroom cross-examination the woman can be questioned on her written affidavit as if she is its sole author. Any inconsistency between her evidence in court and her written affidavit can be used to accuse her of lying, even if the inconsistency is in fact due to the paralegal's contributions to the story, either in the paralegal's questions or recontextualisation of her client's story in the written summary.

Another important finding of sociolinguistic research on storytelling is that there can be subtle variations in the ways in which a person retells the same story on different occasions (Norrick e.g. 1998; Schiffrin e.g. 2006).[68] This is not surprising, when you consider that the way in which a person tells a story depends, to varying degrees, on listeners' responses. The recontextualisation involved in a person retelling their own story may involve different emphases for different audiences, and it may result in some important changes. For example, it may involve the omission of details from the original telling of the story, or inclusion of details not found in its original telling, or a different choice of some of the words and expressions used. These changes, often quite subtle, are typically taken in the legal process to be inconsistencies which indicate that the person is not being truthful or reliable.

The central role of beliefs about inconsistency between different tellings of a story has been discussed by Matoesian (2000: 895; 2001: 68) as the 'linguistic ideology of inconsistency'. Matoesian points out that in assessing inconsistencies between different tellings of a person's story at different stages in the legal process, the legal system conceptualises inconsistency as 'logical' incongruity (2001: 37–38). In the language ideology underpinning the adversarial cross-examination process, the interactional nature of inconsistency is not considered – such as the influence of interviewers' questions on the way the story is told on different occasions, or the way in which an interviewer has summarised the interviewee's story in writing. Rather, inconsistency between different tellings of a person's story is typically seen as the failing of individual witnesses or interviewees, who can be therefore deemed to be lacking reliability and truthfulness. For exemplification of this ideology of inconsistency, tracing an example of recontextualisation of part of a witness's story from police interview to cross-examination and its evaluation in closing arguments and judicial decision, and then finally the print media, see Eades (2008a: 103–105, 222–223, 228–230, 271–273, 276, 279–282, 284, 319–321). This specific and damning example shows how inconsistency is achieved through the interactional work which is done at various stages of the legal process.

Both the ideology of narrator authorship and the ideology of inconsistency erase the interactional nature of storytelling and retelling. This is consistent with the central role in the legal process of decontextualised legally proven 'facts', discussed in Section 4 of Chapter 2. Just as the correspondence theory of language and the ideology of literalism both work on the basis of objective meanings which can be transparently expressed and understood, in recontextualisation practices representations of meanings and facts are seen as uniquely owned, and transparently and automatically repeatable from one context to another. These ways of thinking about language do not in themselves reproduce inequalities, but rather these 'commonsense' ways of understanding language enable actions which do. Thus, sociolinguistics also plays an important role in revealing the actual linguistic mechanisms which mediate between these ideologies and the reproduction of inequalities. In Section 4.3 of Chapter 3 and Sections 4 and 5 of Chapter 6, we saw how recontextualisation in cross-examination can involve subtle substitution of lexical items, or contests over the choice of lexical items. In Section 4 of Chapter 6, we saw how grammatical mechanisms – such as the grammar of non-agency – can be used in recontextualisation in cross-examination. And Section 5 of Chapter 6 showed the use of presuppositions in questions (see also Eades 2008a for examples of more linguistic mechanisms). While these cross-examination examples highlight the adversarial nature of courtroom talk, in Section 4.2 of Chapter 8 we saw the (probably unintentional) substitution of Standard English lexical items, which resulted in the misrepresentation of an Aboriginal English-speaking suspect's story. And in Section 5 of Chapter 9, we saw a paralegal's subtle changes to her client's story in the interviewer's written recontextualisation of it. Regardless of the legal strategy involved in these examples, they all show how recontextualisation which ignores the interactional production of stories and which blurs original source distinctions in this story production can be used against individuals as they work to have their story heard and believed. In this way, following Briggs (1993: 408), we can see that decontextualisation and recontextualisation play 'a crucial role in infusing texts with power'.[69]

Another linguistic mechanism which mediates between language ideology and power relations involves the ways in which earlier interviews (for example with police, or in examination-in-chief) are excerpted and read into cross-examination questions. This particular recontexualisation practice is typically done as a way of showing inconsistencies between different occasions on which the witness has told their story, or part of it. Given that these excerpted readings take only part of the earlier interview, then they necessarily involve decontextualisation – for example removing the excerpted fragment from what was said before and after it. But there are also problems with reading from transcripts, which present propositional content and do not record many important elements of the talk, such as emphasis, intonation, volume and pauses (see Eades 1996b). It is impossible to read out a transcript without making (often subconscious) choices about these aspects of speech. And these choices can make a fundamental difference in meaning. For example, a question such as *You were there, weren't you?* can be uttered with different word stress (or emphasis), intonation, volume and pauses to convey a range of meanings and attitudes, from bullying coercion, to uncertainty, to supportive reassurance. And the simplest monosyllabic answer *Yes* can be read from a transcript to convey confident agreement, when it may have been uttered after a lengthy pause in a tentative and barely audible voice. Thus the decontextualised fragment of a witness's earlier telling of their story can be presented by a lawyer in cross-examination in such a way as to convey a rather different version of the story or part(s) of it. As Matoesian (2000: 884) sees it 'direct quotes do not represent an exact wording of prior speech inasmuch as they refer to a form of constructed speech in which the reporting voice subtly penetrates into the reported utterance to strategically manipulate the audience's impression of the quoted speaker'. The subtlety of this recontextualisation, combined with the rules of evidence which control courtroom talk, make it difficult for even the most analytical of witnesses to present a meta-commentary on such a transformation of their story.

You might think these problems with reading from a transcript can be addressed by playing tape recordings of previous interviews instead. But Matoesian (2000: 888) argues that 'tapes never just speak for themselves'. He illustrates this by analysing how a defence lawyer cross-examining a rape complainant used the tape recording of her interview with police (p. 897):

… although the tape appears to speak for itself and although its meaning appears transparent, it only obtains such a quality because the defense attorney possesses the power to contextualize it, instruct the jury of its significance, and suggest how it should be interpreted and evaluated. He selects which texts to play, what the voices on the tape will say, and how to interpret those voices. He has the power to select which historical utterances to extract and how to juxtapose these in the current sequential context for persuasive effect, controlling the decontextualization and recontextualization of discourse. There is no opportunity for the witness to collaborate in choosing what to play, how much to play, and when to play it.

Matoesian goes on to explain that the power which lawyers have in such recontextualisation of earlier tape recordings is made possible because of what he calls 'a linguistic ideology of pure reference' (2000: 910), which we have seen referred to as the 'refererential transparency' theory of language, and the 'correspondence theory of language', in Section 4.2 above. That is, the way in which tape recordings are used in cross-examining witnesses about earlier versions of their story relies on matching of propositional content, completely removed from contexts.

But, not all recontextualisation of stories in the legal process takes place within adversarial struggles. In several chapters we have seen how the legal system privileges certain ways of presenting stories – ways that focus on 'facts' rather than experiences. Thus we saw in Sections 2, 3 and 5 of Chapter 9 that lawyers interviewing their clients steer them to produce a particular kind of story, one which focuses on specific incidents rather than experiences, and on rational aspects rather than emotional and social aspects of their story. And in Section 6 of Chapter 9, we saw that in their training as lawyers, law students have to learn to view people who are involved in legal matters in terms of how they argue and strategise, and in terms of the law. To do this, they have to ignore any emotional or moral concerns relating to these people. But this is not just the way that lawyers work – it is part of the larger agenda of the way in which the legal process works. When people go to lower courts without a lawyer they are more likely to have their story heard and believed, if they too can set aside moral or emotional concerns and present their story in terms of legal rules rather than their experiences in social relationships (Conley & O'Barr 2005: 73, see Section 2 of Chapter 10 above). Something very similar is happening too with what jurors are required to do, as we saw in the discussion in Section 7 of Chapter 3 of the narrative and paradigmatic modes of reasoning. Jurors are supposed to bring their layperson's approach to legal decision-making – is the defendant guilty? or, has the defendant wronged the complainant? But they are also supposed to apply the law logically and not view the events from a moral or emotional perspective. The work of jurors is another legal context in which everyday stories must be filtered through legal rules.

Almost all of the legal contexts where laypeople are asked to tell or retell their story or assess the stories of others provide opportunities for everyday ways of storytelling to be either thwarted or judged as unacceptable. As many people may not be skilled in legally acceptable ways of storytelling, language ideologies and practices involved in recontextualisation in the legal process can be involved in unequal delivery of justice and the perpetuation of inequality in the legal system.

4.4. Linguistic and cultural difference

In the two previous sections, we have seen a number of assumptions about how language works in monolingual interactions. Where speakers of second languages or dialects or from different cultural backgrounds are involved, these language ideologies can be compounded by assumptions about language and cultural difference, resulting in many challenges and compromises for the delivery of justice to immigrants and indigenous people. The most basic of these language ideologies, introduced in Section 1 of Chapter 4, is that monolingualism is the norm in society. This assumption is at odds with the evidence that multilingualism is more prevalent in societies around the world than monolingualism (Edwards 2004: 5; see also Auer and Wei 2007: 1). This 'myth of monolingualism' is part of the ideology termed by Blommaert and Verschueren (1998: 117) 'homogeneism', which holds that the most normal and also the ideal human society is 'as uniform and homogeneous as possible' (see also Blommaert 2005: 252).

It is important to point out that homogeneism is not restricted to the norm or desired ideal for a society, but is also projected onto individuals: thus each individual is seen as 'normally' monolingual and a member of one culture (Blommaert 1999: 428). This basic assumption can be seen to relate to widely held ideological positions about the relationship between individuals, language, culture and nation, which have been analysed in recent sociolinguistic and linguistic anthropology literature by a number of scholars including Blackledge (2005), Blommaert (1999), Blommaert and Verschueren (1998), Eades and Arends (2004), Hymes (1996), Piller (2001) and Silverstein (1996, 1998). There are many manifestations of this ideology of homogeneism, such as the view that diversity is 'pollution' and that migrants are problems (see Blommaert & Verschueren 1998). Our interest is in the related language ideologies in the legal system, particularly the monolingual language ideology (e.g. Angermeyer 2008): this is the view that monolingualism is both the norm in society and the best way for the operation of society generally, and the legal system specifically.

There are important ways in which the assumption that society is monolingual can result in unequal treatment for people who are not monolingual. We saw in Section 1 of Chapter 4 that people who give evidence in court through an interpreter do not have their own words recorded as official evidence, but rather the English words of the interpreter. There are clearly practical reasons for this, but it can disadvantage the second language speaker in later appeal proceedings. For example, what happens when such L2 speakers are cross-examined on details of their answers given in an earlier hearing? When they are told *In your trial you said XYZ*, it is not the witness's own words that will be read to them from the official transcript, but the rendition in this later hearing by the interpreter on that occasion of the English words of the interpreter in the earlier hearing (in technical terms this is a back-translation). There can be more than one way of interpreting many utterances, and thus there may be slight differences between the two different interpreted versions. We have seen, however, how these slight differences can assume great importance in the context of adversarial cross-examination (see Section 5.2 of Chapter 4, for example). And on a related issue, Walsh (1995, 1999, 2008) discusses the 'tyranny of the transcript' in Aboriginal land claim hearings in Australia. Whatever is recorded on the transcript becomes authoritative, despite any misrepresentations which might result from how the transcriber's best efforts to represent the evidence of L2 speakers of English can misrepresent what a speaker has said (such as we saw in Section 3 of Chapter 5).

Another problematic assumption related to the monolingual language ideology is that the only people who need interpreters for the language of the court (e.g. English) are those who have no fluency at all in this language. Thus, Angermeyer (2008: 391) found that the courts he studied worked on the frequently mistaken assumption 'that interpreters translate between two monolingual people'. The corollary is the assumption that bilingualism is the same as parallel monolingualisms. But as we saw in Sections 1 and 2 of Chapter 4, many people may have different kinds of fluency in the two or more languages they speak. As Blommaert *et al.* (2005: 199) explain, the 'phenomenon of "truncated multilingualism" – linguistic competencies which are organised topically, on the basis of domains or specific activities – is extremely widespread'. And people who speak more than one language may typically use their different languages within a single conversation (Wei 2000). The widespread use of code-switching in bilingual (and multilingual) conversations is not recognised within legal contexts (or in many other formal and informal contexts) by monolingual members of dominant societies. Thus, the legal system treats bilingual people with the taken-for-granted assumption that we have referred to in Chapter 4 as the 'all-or-nothing' view of language: a person needs an interpreter for all of their evidence or for none of their evidence. This language ideology thus forces people with degrees of bilingual fluency to act as monolinguals, as Angermeyer (2008) has shown. In such situations, people who do not hide the fact that they have some bilingual fluency run the risk of being seen as misrepresenting their need for an interpreter. In legal contexts which do not adhere to this language ideology, the rights to justice of bilingual people are arguably better served, as we saw in Section 2 of Chapter 4 with Cooke's (1996) example of the Djamparpuyngu and English-speaking defendant from northern Australia.

But it is not only witnesses in court who may have some bilingual fluency. Some judicial officers, lawyers or jurors may have fluency in the language of witnesses, and sometimes this fluency may be considerable. But so strong is the monolingual language ideology in the legal system, that these language skills typically have no place, and they can even be seen as a hindrance to the delivery of justice. Do you remember the discussion in Section 4.1 of Chapter 5 of the US case where bilingual English–Spanish speakers were not allowed to serve as jurors in a case in which evidence was to be given in Spanish and interpreted into English?

The lack of understanding of bilingualism and language learning also leads to several problems with the delivery of justice in the ways that interpreters are expected to work, as we saw in Chapters 4 and 8. Some of the taken-for-granted assumptions about language which we saw in monolingual situations in Section 2 above, are also relevant here. For example, the correspondence theory of language is found in the widespread view of interpreters as language conduits, or machines that take utterances in one language and transform them somehow automatically into utterances in another (Haviland 2003: 768 refers to this as the view of interpreters as 'transparent filters'). If, on the other hand, language is seen in social and interactional ways, then interpreters are treated as participants in the conversation, whose bilingual expertise and training in interpreting enable them to facilitate communication between speakers of two different languages (see Wadensjö 1998). Further, replacing the conduit or machine view of interpreters with one that sees them as participants in the conversation would result in more meaning-based approaches to interpreting. This should address a number of the ways in which second language speakers and interpreters suffer injustices in the legal system. For example, such a change should result in interpreters having more support for their work, such as being provided with contextual information relevant to their understanding of the specific utterances which they have to interpret. It should also focus greater awareness by monolingual participants of what is involved in interpreting, including their need to pay attention to the impact of their turn constructions and turn boundaries on the effectiveness of the interpreter's work (see Section 2.2 of Chapter 8).

At the same time, replacing an ideology which sees language as a transparent and objective medium of communication with one which also sees the social, interactional and cultural contexts could also have positive effects on the quality of interpretation. A legal system that acknowledges the importance of speaker meaning as well as utterance meaning (pragmatics as well as semantics) would encourage interpreters to pay attention to the 'little words' they often leave out. As we saw in Section 5.3 of Chapter 4, discourse markers like *well* and *so* might seem like optional extras, but they can play a vital role in signalling the speaker's pragmatic meaning or illocutionary force.

Another problematic assumption often made in the legal system relates to differences and similarities between languages. The correspondence view of language also tends to see different languages as comparable versions of identical propositions, a view which gives rise to the impractical expectation of word-for-word translation, discussed in Section 4 of Chapter 4. But such a conceptualisation of language ignores the ways in which languages are shaped by their speakers, and are both influenced by and have an impact on their speakers' world views, cultures and experiences. In Section 5 of Chapter 4, we saw a number of challenges for interpreters who are expected to provide equivalent utterances in different languages, typically with no scope for attention to the impact of cultural and linguistic difference. Scholars such as Cooke (1995b, 2004), Lee (2009a, 2009b) and Mikkelson (1998) have pointed out that these expectations on interpreters to translate without explanation of important cultural and linguistic differences do not serve the delivery of equal treatment within the law (see also Morphy 2007; Walsh 2008).

The correspondence approach to language also leads to some linguistically bizarre practices in immigration department interviews of asylum seekers in some countries. Although these practices do not originate in the legal process, they are relevant here because of the way that these cases often progress to the legal system, as mentioned above. Corcoran (2004) and Maryns (2004, 2006) discuss examples of immigration department interviewers – in the Netherlands and Belgium, respectively – assessing the genuineness of asylum seekers' claims to have come from Sierra Leone, by testing their performance in providing the Krio equivalent of isolated English lexical items, and counting from one to twenty in Krio.[70] This rudimentary kind of 'translation test' in LADO interviews is based on a number of problematic assumptions about linguistic difference.

First, it assumes that there is a discrete boundary between the creole language Krio and its lexifier language, English. However, these language names are a reification of complex overlapping and interrelated speech practices. The ideology of discrete, nameable languages is central to linguistics, and it is also found more widely in many societies. While it provides a useful way of thinking about speech practices and social groups, and plays an important role in language policy applications, it is a conventionally accepted ideology, a way of thinking about observable speech practices. But not all societies share this ideology, and within linguistics it is also increasingly being problematised (see Makoni & Pennycook 2007). In the case of asylum seekers from West Africa, this language ideology can be involved in unfair ways of disbelieving a person's claims about their origins, as Corcoran (2004) and Maryns (2004, 2006) have shown.

Second, these translation tests assume that speakers make the same distinction between Krio and English that the interviewer (or linguists) make. But the distinction between creole languages and their lexifiers is complex, and typically there is no simple way of distinguishing for many utterances or lexical items whether they are in the creole language or the lexifier language, or both. Thus in Corcoran's (2004) study, the interviewee's answers suggest that he does speak Krio, but at the same time they show the problems in assuming that he is making a distinction between Krio and English in the same metalinguistic way in which the interviewer does. Thus, for example, in answers to questions requiring him to translate the English words *green* and *sheep* in Krio, he says *green na green* (meaning *green* in English is *green* in Krio), and *ship na ship* (meaning *ship* in English is *ship* in Krio[71]). These examples and the numbers from one to twenty also reveal the problems of bivalency, that is the use of words that could simultaneously belong to both codes (Maryns 2006: 257, citing Woolard 1999). Bivalency such as this further calls into question the validity of using any kind of translation test between two closely related language varieties.

Third, the use of these problematic translation tests also highlights dimensions of the monolingual language ideology, in that these tests presuppose that the asylum seeker will have the same proficiency in both or all of the languages they speak (see Maryns 2005). And the monolingual language ideology has a wider effect on asylum seeker cases than these translation tests. As Eades *et al.* (2003) found, the basic premise of much LADO work is that asylum seekers will use just one language in their interview, and that any use of even one word from another language can be evidence that the interviewee is being dishonest about their origins (for specific examples see Eades 2005: 511, 2009: 34; see also Language and National Origin Group 2004). This expectation that people will speak only one language variety during an interview denies the realities of multilingualism and code-switching discussed above. It also denies other realities of 21st century language use by many people. As Blommaert *et al.* (2005: 205) remind us, 'how people use language is strongly influenced by the situation in which they find themselves'. Since leaving their place of origin, there may be many places where an asylum seeker stays for varying amounts of time, such as different locations in their own country, as well as in neighbouring countries, including multilingual refugee camps, and various other countries through which they travel before arriving in the country in which they seek asylum. In each of these locations, asylum seekers are communicating with others, and this can involve picking up new words, new ways of speaking, new language varieties. Blommaert (2009: 416, emphasis in original) shows that the sociolinguistic repertoires of asylum seekers – that is the language varieties in which they have some competence – are 'indicative of *time*, not just *space*' and that they 'index full histories of people and of places'. Therefore, for many asylum seekers it is unrealistic to expect an analysis of their speech to provide a fair way of isolating their place of origin from the rest of their personal history. Thus, the monolingual language ideology supports a number of problematic assumptions about language practices which appear to drive the assessment of the origin claims of asylum seekers. Discussion of these assumptions, practices and their consequences can be found in Corcoran (2004), Eades (2005, 2009, 2010), Fraser (2009) and Maryns (2004, 2005, 2006). A damning case study of the consequences of these 'anomalous frames for interpreting human behaviour' for the denial of justice to an asylum seeker is presented in Blommaert (2009).

Moving away from bilingual and multilingual people to speakers of non-standard dialects and people from diverse cultural backgrounds, we see much evidence (again) of assumptions of the correspondence theory of language, compounded by lack of awareness of variation within languages. Some of the effects of this have been discussed in Section 6 of Chapter 4, Sections 3 and 4 of Chapter 5, and Chapter 8. In Section 3 of Chapter 5 we saw that legal officers' ignorance about dialectal difference can lead to assessments of dishonesty – as in the lawyer who suggested that the Aboriginal witness who said there had been a *half moon* on a particular night was *making it up*. Such ignorance can also lead to misrepresentations of the witness's interview answers in the official record – as in the witness whose assertion that *Charcoal Jack was properly his father* was recorded as saying that *Charcoal Jack* was *probably his father*. And in Section 4.2 of Chapter 8, we saw that police officers' apparent ignorance about the meaning of *carrying on silly* in Aboriginal English, combined with their lack of attention to how the suspect was exemplifying this term in his police interview, led to misrepresentation of the suspect's interview answers in the written summary on which the murder charge was based.

Sociolinguistic research and legal education has a role to play in exposing problematic views about language and variation so that second dialect speakers can access equality in the law. The same applies for people from different cultural backgrounds whose different ways of communicating can directly impact on the ways in which they are assessed within the legal system (for example with people who use and interpret silence differently from the mainstream Anglo cultures which dominate the legal system, as we saw in Section 3 of Chapter 5). (See Eades 2008b for a discussion of some of the implications for Australian Aboriginal witnesses from cultural differences in assumptions about storytelling and retelling in court.)

5. Conclusion

Enacted in 1948 and now translated into more than 360 languages, the Universal Declaration of Human Rights declares that 'all people are equal before the law and are entitled without any discrimination to equal protection of the law' (Article 7). But we know that there are many ways in which the experiences of individuals in countries throughout the world fall short of this fundamental human right. The sociolinguistic study of language use can play a valuable role in explaining how language works and doesn't work in the legal process, and in contributing to the understanding of how the law delivers justice and fails to deliver justice. We have seen some of the ways in which these explanations and contributions have begun in research in common law countries, and we have seen many remaining questions and gaps. Now, over to you!

Assignments and further research

1. Examine the role of language ideologies in judicial decisions in your country relating to the voluntariness of confessions and related issues such as suspects' invocation of their rights. Using the work of Ainsworth, Solan and Tiersma discussed in this chapter as a starting point, consider to what extent the textualism of US law is found in other common law countries.

2. Examine the role of language ideologies in the unequal treatment of a particular minority group, for example deaf sign language users, children, or people with intellectual disabilities. A literature-based investigation of this topic could be suitable for an essay/term paper. An empirical study – which would start with a literature-based investigation – could be suitable for a thesis/dissertation.

3. Blommaert (2009: 415) says that the 'realities of "modern" reactions to postmodern phenomena, especially in the field of language, must be taken into account as part of the postmodern phenomenology of language in society'. Explain his argument as it relates to language ideology in the processing of asylum seekers, and discuss to what extent the general assertion is relevant to other language ideologies in the legal process.

Notes

1. Note that in Australia magistrates are appointed full time, and have legal qualifications and experience, corresponding to stipendiary magistrates in England and Wales and lower court judges in the US.

2. The overview information in this section is drawn from Dadomo and Farran (1996); David and Brierley (1985); Jackson and Kovalev (2006/2007); Powles and Pulea (1988); Tan (1997).

3. This is a court investigation by a coroner into a death which was not the result of natural causes. A coronial inquiry can result in criminal charges being laid against a person in relation to the death investigated.

4. However, in some jurisdictions, jurors are allowed to formulate written questions which are passed to the judge. Typically the judge then has a sidebar conversation with lawyers for both sides to make sure there is no objection to the jury question(s) being asked. If there is no objection, the judge then reads these question(s) to the witness.

5. Note that this rule, which is commonly found in Evidence Acts in Australia, is not found in the UK, where unfavourable inferences may be drawn from a defendant's failure to answer a question or questions in court (UK Criminal Justice and Public Order Act 1994, s35).

6. Videorecordings would be often preferable to audiorecordings (see Matoesian 2005a, 2008). But it is generally impossible for researchers to gain permission to make such videorecordings, and they are not usually carried out for the court's records.

7. In terms of the ethnography of speaking, these events could be termed 'speech events' (see Hymes 1974; Holmes 2008; and Assignment 6 at the end of this chapter).

8. See Cotterill (2003: 13–17) for a discussion of an initial questionnaire sent to 1000 prospective jurors in the O.J. Simpson case.

9. Danet *et al.* say that requestions and imperatives are less coercive than WH-questions, defining coercion as the degree to which question forms 'constrain or limit the witness' (1980: 226).

10. A wealth of empirical sociolinguistic research since then has pointed to a number of problems with Lakoff's assertions (see, for example Cameron *et al.* 1988).

11. Note that Lakoff called this feature 'speaking in italics'.

12. See Cotterill (2001) on relexicalisation, (2003) on lexicalisation, (2004) on lexical negotiation; Drew (1985, 1992) on alternative description; Eades (2006, 2008a) on lexical struggle, lexical perversion, overt correction and covert substitution; Ehrlich (2001, 2002) on (re)formulation; Ehrlich (2002) on recontextualisation.

13. In England and Wales and in Australia, the judge's summary for the jury is called the 'Summing up', while in the US it is referred to as the 'Charge'. In England and Wales and in Australia it occurs after the closing argument by the lawyer for each side. In the US the

'Charge' can refer to jury instructions given at the end of the case, as well as any given during the course of the trial. And in the US, the term 'Summing up' is an alternative name for the lawyers' closing arguments (as is 'summation', see Section 5 above).

14. http://www.kathlangcentre.org.au/services.htm accessed May 5, 2009.

15. Australian linguists use the terms 'light' and 'heavy' to correspond to the general linguistic terms 'acrolectal' and 'basilectal', which have been argued to be evaluative terms.

16. This example and the discussion of it are taken from Eades (2000).

17. That is, the Evidence Acts which apply in the Commonwealth (or Federal) jurisdiction, as well as the states of New South Wales and Tasmania.

18. Insightful reviews can be found in Blommaert (2005), Blommaert and Bulcaen (2000), Blommaert et al. (2001), Kress (2001), Pennycook (2001), Rampton (2001, 2006) and contributions to the 2001 special issue of Critique of Anthropology, including those by Blommaert, Bucholtz, Collins, Heller, Rampton, Slembrouck and Verschueren.

19. The term 'repair slot' indicates places in the structure of the guilty plea event where a judge or lawyer might either make a correction or ask for clarification on some point.

20. Legally, a rape case involves a defendant (= accused person) and a complainant (= person allegedly raped). Until and unless the defendant is found guilty, it is legally inaccurate to refer to the complainant as the victim. Also note that while most research on rape cases has examined women complainants, in a very small number of cases the complainant is male.

21. It is also reported in other parts of Australia; and in Saskatchewan, Canada it is such a well-recognised action that is has been lexicalised. There the label 'drop-off' refers to police taking someone – often an Aboriginal person – out of town and abandoning them there (see Eades 2008a: 306–307).

22. The relevant definitions from the Macquarie Dictionary of Australian English give walk as '1) to go or travel on foot at a moderate pace', and wander as '1) to ramble without any certain course or object on view, roam, rove, or stray; 2) to go aimlessly or casually'.

23. Elsewhere (Eades 2006, 2008a) I have discussed this strategy in more depth, using the term 'lexical perversion' to describe the substitution of words and phrases such as this, where this substitution distorts (or perverts) the way in which a person reports their own experiences.

24. Note that in some jurisdictions the term 'caution' is also used to refer to a warning given by police, formally or informally, about illegal actions. This type of police caution – used mostly with young people – is often referred to as diversionary action because it is used by police as a less serious alternative to arrest or charge (Cunneen & White 2002: 370–371). It has received little attention in the (socio)linguistic literature, but see Halldorsdottir (2006).

25. Section 4 of Chapter 11 will focus on language ideologies (also referred to as linguistic ideologies) in the legal process.

26. 'Conversational implicature' refers to the ways in which the context of a conversation is taken into account when speakers determine meaning. For example, if someone says *Could I get a lawyer?* it conversationally implies that the speaker wants a lawyer. Compare a customer in a coffee shop saying *Could I get a cappuccino?* This would be taken to conversationally imply that the person is ordering a cappuccino.

27. As we saw in Section 4 of Chapter 1, 'register' refers to the language variety used by a particular group of people or context. For example, suspects in the asymmetrical context of police interviews may be reluctant to use a bald imperative such as *Get me a lawyer*, instead using a less direct form such as *Could I get a lawyer*.

28. Leo (2008: 295) reports that at the time of writing, only eight US states and the District of Columbia had mandated electronic recording of interrogations in some or all types of criminal cases (see also Leo & Richman 2007).

29. See Milne and Bull (1999: Chapter 5) for an overview of several other studies of police interviews in England and Wales carried out between the introduction of the PACE Act in 1984 and national police interview training in 1992. This training is known as PEACE, which is an acronym standing for Planning and Preparation, Engage and Explain, Account, Closure and Evaluation.

30. Milne and Bull (1999: 39–47) provide a good account of some additions to the original cognitive interview and details of the structure of 'the enhanced cognitive interview'. See also Ord *et al.* (2004) and Schollum (2005: 58–60).

31. See Oxburgh *et al.* (forthcoming) for a review of literature on types of questioning in police interviews.

32. http://news.bbc.co.uk/2/hi/in_depth/uk/2000/the_shipman_murders/the_shipman_files/613627.stm

33. There are some parallels here with Matoesian's (2001: 171–173) analysis of the defendant in a rape trial constructing his professional identity as a medical doctor, and in effect answering some questions like an expert witness, rather than as a defendant.

34. At the beginning of 2009, this corpus now has more than 500 million words.

35. Gibbons (2003: 85) points out that the distinctive way in which police officers talk is sometimes also referred to as 'copspeak'.

36. While this has been introduced in Australia beginning in the early 1990s, and in England and Wales from the mid-1980s (Rock 2007: 142), in the US this development has been much slower, as we saw in Section 3 above.

37. I use the term 'members of minority groups' with some discomfort here, as I do not wish to marginalise anyone with this label. However, it is less cumbersome that the alternative expressions such as 'people who aren't members of the dominant group'. It is also more suitable to this chapter than the term 'vulnerable interviewees' which might at first seem appropriate, given its usage in Chapter 5. However, the term 'vulnerable' does not adequately convey the situation with interviewees discussed in

Section 7 of this chapter. Indeed, a more thorough discussion of the terminology would problematise the disempowering nature of the term 'vulnerable'. However, while most of the social groups discussed in this chapter are vulnerable, all of them are members of minority groups.

38. Berk-Seligson (2009: 180–182) examines a faulty Spanish translation of the US Miranda rights used in one particular case, and argues for the introduction of a standardised version.

39. But see Cooke (2002: 32–34) for a pilot programme in which an interview test was designed for lawyers to assess a person's need for an interpreter in police interviews or courtroom hearings.

40. We saw in Chapter 7 that police often view the purpose of an interview with a suspect as eliciting information required to make a charge. And the most widely used manual of police interrogation in the US (Inbau *et al.* 2001) sees the assessment of a suspect's behaviour as central. Note however, that an influential review of psychological research warns that making decisions about interviewees' guilt on 'the basis of their observable interview behaviour is a decision that is fraught with error, bias and overconfidence' (Kassin & Gudjonsson 2004: 39).

41. Cooke (1998: 147) explains that *skinship* is an English–Yolngu Matha interlanguage word which results from the fusion of the English word *kinship* and the Aboriginal English word *skin* which is used to refer to the social classification within an Aboriginal clan group which is known by anthropologists as 'subsection'.

42. See Evans (2002: 87–92) on a similar problem arising from misinterpretation of English modal *can* used by an Aboriginal speaker of English as a second language giving important evidence in a land claim hearing in the Northern Territory.

43. Also note that the interpreter used the French word *caution* to translate English *caution*. But this is an inaccurate translation – an example of a 'false friend' in translation, as it is more accurately seen as the equivalent of the English word *guarantee*.

44. After the conclusion of the trial in the New South Wales Supreme Court in 2005, the defendant gave me permission to write about my report on condition that I give no identifying details of the case. Quotations from the police interview are based on my transcription of the official audiorecording. In this case, the question of police verballing was irrelevant, as the interview was audiorecorded.

45. The other meanings which do not appear to be relevant in this interview are 'a. to manage; conduct', 'b. to continue; keep up without stopping', and 'e. to dally amorously; flirt'.

46. But note that in some jurisdictions in the US investigative interviews with child abuse victims are not done by police officers but by qualified experts, while police officers observe from another room (Anderson *et al.* 2002: 14).

47. M. Powell (2008: 193) explains that Australian investigative authorities have developed their own protocols involving various combinations of elements from other protocols.

48. This chapter will not deal with public interactions between lawyers and their clients in courtroom examination-in-chief, which have been discussed in Chapter 3.

49. As an aside, from my long experience with cane toads, I find the thought of devouring a cane toad, with or without toast, quite repulsive!

50. Bogoch only gives the English translations of conversations, and not the original Hebrew talk.

51. In England (and other countries such as Australia), legal work on cases is often shared between solicitors and barristers. Solicitors do the legal preparation of the case, which is then 'briefed' or handed over to a barrister, who takes the case to court. In complex cases, the solicitor sits with the barrister and assists, but does not speak in court. In summary (lower court) cases, often solicitors do all the work and barristers are not used.

52. This is an example of a formal legal word that dates from French influence on early Middle English, where it meant a letter, despatch or note. Note that the word 'brief' in US legal contexts has a slightly different meaning, namely an argument for the court (Tiersma 1999: 134).

53. 'Instructions' in this context refers to the client's version of their story, as well as what they want the lawyer to do on their behalf.

54. Trinch (2003: 205–206) points out that this specific assertion *This went on for about three hours* might give rise to problems in any further court case. Here in the affidavit it reads as if the struggle between the client and the abuser lasted *about three hours*. But in the interview, the client had reported that during the incident she had fallen asleep for a while, an incident which was omitted in the affidavit (and is not given in Extract 9–ii, which is excerpted from the complete interview). We saw in Turns 5–6 of that extract that the client estimated the time of *probably about three hours* in answer to the vague question *Do you know about how long this took?* Under cross-examination, she might be asked many more specific questions about the timing, and she may reveal that for part of the *three hours* she was asleep. The fact that this is not mentioned in the affidavit could then be used to accuse her of lying in the affidavit.

55. This paragraph draws heavily on the work of the Australian National Alternative Dispute Resolution Advisory Council, especially NADRAC (2003), http://www.nadrac.gov.au/.

56. This label also seems to fit the approach taken by Sarat and Felstiner (1995), which we discussed in Section 2 of Chapter 9.

57. An example of mediator impartiality that is not (primarily) achieved through talk is not accepting 'advances, offers or gifts' from parties (NADRAC 2001: 113).

58. Note, however, that we do not know how similar youth justice conferencing might be to hearings in childrens courts. As these are closed courts, there is no sociolinguistic research on interactions in childrens court.

59. Marchetti and Daly (2007: 427) point out that therapeutic courts are different from specialist courts, such as some child sexual assault courts. This is because specialist

courts deal only with a specialised area of the law, but they do not necessarily take a therapeutic approach.

60. Given that drug offences often have no victim (apart from the offender in some situations?), it is hard to see how a drugs court could work within a restorative justice approach.

61. Like Marchetti and Daly, I follow the Australian convention of using Indigenous (with capital 'I') to refer to Aboriginal and Torres Strait Islander people. But where referring more generally to indigenous people in other countries, I follow the international convention of using indigenous (with a lower case 'i').

62. At the time of writing in 2009, this transcript is still available online: http://www.abc. net.au/4corners/content/2005/s1478921.htm

63. The Federal Court of Australia has also issued guidelines for expert witnesses, available online: http://www.fedcourt.gov.au/how/prac_direction.html

64. One of the other important factors was the evidence of senior police officers to the Queensland Fitzgerald Inquiry into Police Corruption in 1988 that police regularly fabricated confessions for suspects whom they believed to be guilty (Eades 2008a: 28–29).

65. See also Conley and O'Barr (2005: 155–156) on a related issue, namely linguists' ideologies of law.

66. I will use the term 'plain meaning rule', following Tiersma (1999: 126), to avoid confusing this with plain English or plain language, which simply refers to ordinary English with no specialised register (as referred to in Section 2.2 of Chapter 7 and Section 2.3 of Chapter 8).

67. The abduction case complicates this issue as the accused in that case were the six police officers – i.e. the government – while the complainants were the three Aboriginal boys (see Eades 2008a: 7). Despite this complication, this case bears out Solan and Tiersma's general point.

68. Also relevant to the issue of inconsistency in story retelling are important cognitive aspects of memory which combine with interactional aspects of remembering (see Eades 2008b).

69. Maryns (2006) also shows with detailed analysis of several cases, how recontextualisation assumptions and practices can impact on asylum seekers' access to a fair hearing. Interviewers in the asylum process deal with interviewee stories in similar ways as police officers and lawyers do (see Section 7 of Chapter 7 and Section 5 of Chapter 9). Maryns (p. 316) summarises this in the asylum process with her finding that 'the asylum application procedure is constrained by a highly culture-specific linguistic-communicative ideology according to which the written word and its ensuing criteria of textuality – consistency, clarity and detail expressed in a monolingual standard code – are considered the most reliable means of expressing truth'.

70. Maryns (2006: 254) reports that this kind of translation test is used 'by several asylum agencies in Europe'.

71. In this example the asylum seeker had heard the interviewer's request to translate the word *sheep* as a request for *ship* (Corcoran 2004: 214).

Legal glossary

As indicated in Section 12 of Chapter 1, some legal terms vary in meaning between different countries using the common law system. This short glossary provides meanings of legal terms for the jurisdiction or country in which they are used in this book, and in some instances it also notes alternative meanings in other countries. Unless otherwise indicated, most of the definitions in this glossary draw on *Butterworths Concise Australian Legal Dictionary* (3rd edition). You are encouraged to consult law dictionaries relevant to your country, and to the country relevant to any study you are reading. The meanings provided here are intended only as introductory explanations.

ADR
An umbrella term for processes, other than judicial determination, in which an impartial person assists those in a dispute to resolve the issues between them. Typically stands for alternative dispute resolution, but also appropriate dispute resolution or assisted dispute resolution (NADRAC 2003: 4).

Affidavit
A written statement which may be used to support a legal application or as a substitute for oral testimony in court proceedings. The statement writer has to swear an oath or affirm (in front of an authorised official) that the contents of the statement are true.

Antecedent
In criminal law: the background and prior convictions of an offender considered for the purposes of sentencing. In the US it can also refer to the background of a witness.

Appellant
A party who appeals against a judicial decision.

Apprehended violence order – *see Protective order*

Arbitration
A process in which the parties to a dispute present arguments and evidence to a dispute resolution practitioner (the arbitrator) who makes a determination which is enforceable by the authority of the adjudicator (NADRAC 2003: 4).

Arraignment
The stage in or before a criminal trial in which the indictment is read to an accused person who is asked how they plead.

Authority
(1) A case, statute or other highly regarded legal text relied on and cited as a foundation for legal principles or for an exposition of the law; (2) a government or semi-government body with powers and responsibilities over designated areas.

Barrister
In Australia and the UK: a class of legal practitioner who is, by law or custom, limited to advocacy and advisory work. A barrister is similar to a trial lawyer in the US, except that a barrister does not prepare the case from the beginning – this work is done by a solicitor. In Canada, a barrister is not limited to advocacy and advisory work.

Brief
In Australia and the UK: (1) a set of papers given to a barrister retained to appear, advise or draft documents in a matter; (2) to retain a barrister to represent a client in a matter. In the US: a written argument, concentrating on legal points and authorities, which is used by the lawyer to convey to the court the essential facts of the client's case.

Caution
(1) The advice that police give suspects in some countries (including England, Wales and Australia) about their rights while they are being held in police custody; (2) a warning given by a police officer, often to a juvenile offender, as an alternative to prosecution.

Complainant

A person, not necessarily the victim, who commences criminal proceedings by lodging a complaint.

Conciliation

A process in which the parties to a dispute, with the assistance of the dispute resolution practitioner (the conciliator), identify the issues in dispute, develop options, consider alternatives and endeavour to reach an agreement (NADRAC 2003: 5).

Court

(1) A place where justice is administered; (2) the decision-maker(s) who sit(s) in a court.

Cross-examination

Questions in court addressed to a witness by a party other than the party who called the witness to give evidence.

Decision

A concluded opinion or determination.

Defendant

Any person against whom relief is sought in a matter, or who is required to attend proceedings in a matter as a party to the proceedings (civil or criminal). Specifically in criminal law a defendant is an accused person in a trial.

Deliberation

The process by which a jury reaches a verdict, through analysing, discussing and weighing the evidence (*Black's Law Dictionary*).

Deposition

In the US: a witness's out-of-court testimony that is reduced to writing (usually by a court reporter) for later use in court or for discovery purposes; the session at which this testimony is recorded (*Black's Law Dictionary*).

Direct examination – *see Examination-in-chief*

District Attorney (DA)

In the US: prosecutor (employed by government).

Evidence

Any object or information, other than legal submissions, which is used to prove or disprove the existence of a fact in issue.

Examination-in-chief

Questioning of a witness in court by the party who called that witness.

Exhibit

An object (such as a document, or photograph or weapon) received in evidence when tendered by one of the parties to a case.

Fact

Any act, occurrence or situation that has been legally proved, through evidence accepted in a trial.

Grand Jury

In the US: a body of (often 23) people who are chosen to sit permanently for at least a month – and sometimes a year – and who decide whether to issue indictments (*Black's Law Dictionary*).

Indictment

A formal written accusation charging a person with an offence.

Instruct, to

To retain or brief a legal practitioner to provide a legal service.

Instructions

(1) Directions given by the judge to the jury on points of law before their deliberation; (2) the information and directions that a client gives to their lawyer about their case.

Judgment

Determination of a court in legal proceedings.

Judicial officer

Judge or magistrate.

Judiciary

People who adjudicate legal disputes in courts of law.

Jurisdiction

The scope of a court's power to examine, determine facts, interpret and apply the law, make orders and declare judgments. It may be limited by geographical area, the type of parties who appear, the type of relief that can be sought and the point to be decided.

Jurisprudence

The theory of law.

Leading question

In court proceedings, a question to a witness that directly or indirectly suggests a particular answer, or that assumes the existence of a disputed fact, in relation to which the witness has not given evidence before the question is asked.

'Learned friend'

The traditional way in which barristers engaged in advocacy refer to each other in court. It is typically used instead of names.

Mediation

A process in which the participants to a dispute, with the assistance of a dispute resolution practitioner (the mediator), identify the disputed issues, develop options, consider alternatives and endeavour to reach an agreement (NADRAC 2003: 9).

Party

A person or an entity that enters into an agreement with another person or entity; a participant in a transaction or in legal actions or proceedings.

Plain meaning rule

The rule that if a writing, or a provision in a writing, appears to be unambiguous on its face, the meaning must be determined from the writing itself without resort to any extrinsic evidence (*Black's Law Dictionary*).

Plea

In criminal law, an accused person's answer to a charge when it is read to them in court (usually 'guilty' or 'not guilty'; but in some jurisdictions there is also the option of 'no contest').

Plea bargain

In criminal law, negotiations between prosecution and defence by which the accused agrees to plead guilty to an offence on condition that the prosecution not proceed with a more serious charge.

Probative value

The extent to which evidence should rationally affect the assessment of the probability of the existence of a fact in issue.

Protective/protection order

A court order prohibiting or restricting a person from harassing, threatening, and sometimes even contacting or approaching another specific person.

Rebuttal evidence

Information tendered to disprove an assertion made in evidence earlier in the proceedings.

Relief

Remedy sought by a plaintiff in a court action.

Remedy

The means available in the law or in equity by which a right is enforced or the infringement of a right is prevented, redressed or compensated.

Restraining order – *see Protective/protection order*

Self-incrimination privilege

The right of a person not to answer questions or produce material which may tend to implicate the person in a criminal offence or expose the person to a civil penalty. In Australia and the UK this is a common law right; in the US it is a constitutional right, provided for by the Fifth and Fourteenth Amendments.

Sidebar

A position at the side of the judge's bench where counsel can confer with the judge beyond the jury's earshot (*Black's Law Dictionary*).

Solicitor

A class of legal practitioner who is generally responsible for advising clients on legal matters, preparing legal documents, representing clients in summary matters and instructing barristers in relation to more complex advocacy work.

Statute

An act passed by a parliament, i.e. a written law.

Statutory rape

Sexual intercourse with a person under a certain age, determined by statute.

Verbal

(1) The colloquial term in Australia for a practice in which police fabricate a 'confession' or a statement which might be used to inculpate a person in an offence; (2) a fabricated confession.

Voir dire

In the US: examination by the judge or the attorneys of prospective jurors, to determine if any should be excluded, for example because of a particular bias. In Australia, the UK and other countries, including the US: a trial within a trial: a hearing where the admissibility of evidence, or the competency of a witness or juror is examined in the absence of the jury.

Sociolinguistic glossary

Many of the definitions given in this glossary draw, with permission, on Swann *et al.* (2004), to which readers are referred for excellent discussions and further elaborations.

Acrolectal

Originally used to refer to the variety of a creole language that is closest to the lexifier language. Now also used for a variety of language closest to the standard.

Addressee

The person addressed by a speaker or writer.

Address terms

The words used to address a speaker, such as title plus last name (*Dr Smith*), kinship terms (*mother*), terms of endearment (*sweetie*).

Back-translation

The process by which a text which has been translated by one person from language A to language B is translated by another person back from language B to language A; often used to expose translation problems, and as a check on accuracy.

Coda (in narrative analysis)

The end part of the narrative, where the speaker returns to the current conversation.

Community of practice

A social group that comprises people who interact in some common activity/activities (or practice/s).

Conversational implicature

The ways in which the context of a conversation is taken into account when speakers determine meaning.

Creole language

A new language that develops in a language contact situation – often from a pidgin language – because of a need for communication between people who do not have a language in common. A creole language is more fully developed than a pidgin language, and it is the first language of at least some of its speakers.

Dialects

Varieties of a language which are generally mutually intelligible, and which differ from each other in systematic ways, such as in accent, grammar, words and their meaning, and communication patterns.

Directive

An utterance designed to get someone to do something.

Discourse marker

A lexical item – e.g. *well* or *you know* – which typically doesn't have any propositional meaning independent from its context of use. Discourse markers are syntactically independent from the utterance, so that if you repeat the utterance without the discourse marker it still makes sense, although it does not convey the original pragmatic force. They often come at the beginning of an utterance, and are often essential in conveying pragmatic force.

Dyadic

Refers to conversation or interaction involving two people.

Ethnography

The systematic study of the beliefs and practices of a community or social group, usually based on close observation (often participant-observation) of activities.

Face-threatening act

Any action which damages or threatens another person's want to be liked and appreciated by others (their positive face) or their want to be left free of imposition (their negative face). For example an accusation is a threat to a person's positive face, and a request is a threat to a person's negative face.

Folk linguistics

Popular beliefs about language, many of which differ from (professional) linguistic understandings.

Front-translation

The process by which a text which is to be translated from language A to language B is first 'translated' into a plainer or clearer text in language A; particularly useful for complex legal texts.

Gratuitous concurrence

The action of a speaker freely saying *yes* in answer to a Yes/No-question (or *no* to a negative Yes/No-question), regardless of either the speaker's understanding of the question, or their belief about the truth or falsity of the proposition being questioned.

Interlanguage

The unstable but continually developing version of a language produced by a second or foreign language learner.

Language ideology

Socially, culturally and historically conditioned ideas, images and perceptions about language and communication (Blommaert (2005: 253); sometimes also termed 'linguistic ideology'.

Latching

The situation in conversational turn-taking when one speaker's turn follows on immediately from the previous speaker's turn, with no perceptible gap.

Lexical item

A unit of vocabulary, that is a word or phrase.

Lexifier language

The language that contributes most of the lexical items to a pidgin or creole language.

Lexis

The vocabulary system of a language.

Linguistic ideology – *see Language ideology*

Linguistic repertoire

The set of language varieties spoken (often, to varying degrees of fluency) by an individual or a group of people.

Modality

The way in which speakers and writers express attitudes to, beliefs about and degrees of certainty about what they are saying or writing.

Morphology

Study of the structure of words.

Open-ended questions

The term widely used in a range of disciplines and professions to refer to 'questions that encourage elaborate responses without dictating what specific information is required' (Powell 2008: 191).

Paralinguistic

Describes vocal features – such as laughter, sighing, giggling – which accompany speech but are not considered to be part of verbal language, although they do contribute to the meaning of what is said.

Passive

A grammatical term which refers to a sentence where the grammatical subject is the recipient or goal of the action, as in *She was noticed (by him)*. It contrasts with active voice where the grammatical subject is the agent of the action, as in *He noticed her*.

Phonetics

The study of speech sounds.

Phonetician

A linguist who specialises in the study of speech sounds.

Pragmatics

Broadly it refers to the study of how language is used in context; more narrowly, it contrasts with semantics, so that semantics studies the meanings of utterances, while pragmatics studies the meanings of speakers' utterances in their contexts of use.

Prosody

Aspects of intonation such as speech rate, pause structure, variation in loudness and pitch range.

Recontextualisation

Taking a text (spoken or written) from one context and reproducing it in a different context.

Register

A language variety used in a particular context, or by a particular group of people, usually sharing the same occupation or the same interests.

Repertoire – *see Linguistic repertoire*

Scaffold

Helpful interactions between an adult and child (or teacher and learner) that enable the child or learner to do something beyond their independent efforts.

Semantics

The study of linguistic meaning.

Socialisation

The process by which people learn the culture and language of their society, primarily via the family and peer group during childhood, and via school and the workplace later on.

Speech act

The act that is performed by an utterance (such as a threat, request or explanation).

Speech event

A culturally recognised activity associated with particular rules or norms for the use of speech.

Standby interpreting

The mode of interpreting for which an interpreter is present with a second language speaker, who chooses how much to use the dominant language (such as English), and when to use their first language. The interpreter does not need to interpret every utterance (because some utterances are in the dominant language), but is 'standing by' to interpret whatever the speaker says in their first language.

Syntax

The study of clause and sentence structure.

WH-questions

Questions which begin with one of the question words, such as *who, why, where, when, what, how, which.*

Yes/No-questions

Questions which can logically be answered by *yes* or *no*, although in practice they are not always answered in this way.

References

Abel, Richard L. (1981) Conservative conflict and the reproduction of capitalism: The role of informal justice. *International Journal of the Sociology of Law* 9, 245–267.

Ainsworth, Janet (1993) In a different register: The pragmatics of powerlessness in a police interview. *Yale Law Journal* 103, 259–322.

Ainsworth, Janet (2008) 'You have the right to remain silent … But only if you ask for it just so': The role of linguistic ideology in American police interrogation law. *International Journal of Speech, Language and the Law* 15 (1), 1–22.

Ainsworth, Janet (forthcoming). A lawyer's perspective: Ethical, technical and practical considerations in the use of linguistic expert witnesses. *International Journal of Speech, Language and the Law* 16 (2).

Aldridge, Michelle (2007) The questioning of child witnesses by the police and in court: A linguistic comparison. In Cotterill (ed.) (pp. 63–82).

Aldridge, Michelle and Joanne Wood (1998) *Interviewing Children: A Guide for Child Care and Forensic Practitioners.* Chichester: John Wiley and Sons.

ALRC (Australian Law Reform Commission) (1997) *Seen and Heard: Priority for Children in the Legal Process* (ALRC Report 84). Canberra: Australian Law Reform Commission.

ALRC (Australian Law Reform Commission) (2005) *Uniform Evidence Law* (ALRC Report 102). Canberra: Australian Law Reform Commission.

Anderson, Michelle Chernikoff, Thomas Knutson, Howard Giles and MaryLinda Arroyo (2002) Revoking our right to remain silent: Law enforcement communication in the 21st century. In Howard Giles (ed.) *Law Enforcement, Communication and Community* (pp. 1–32). Amsterdam: John Benjamins.

Angermeyer, Philipp Sebastian (2008) Creating monolingualism in the multilingual courtroom. *Sociolinguistic Studies* 2 (3), 385–403.

Angermeyer, Philipp Sebastian (2009) Translation style and participant roles in court interpreting. *Journal of Sociolinguistics* 13 (1), 3–28.

ARDS (Aboriginal Resource and Development Services Inc.) (2008) *An Absence of Mutual Respect: Bäynu Nayanu-Dapmaranhamirr Rom ga Norra.* Winnellie, Northern Territory: Aboriginal Resource and Development Services Inc. Retrieved on 31 August 2009 from www.ards.com.au

Arenson, Kenneth J. and Mirko Bagaric (2007) *Rules of Evidence in Australia: Texts and Cases.* Sydney: LexisNexis Butterworths.

Arthur, Jay M. (1996) *Aboriginal English: A Cultural Study.* Oxford: Oxford University Press.

Atkinson, J. Maxwell (1992) Displaying neutrality: Formal aspects of informal court proceedings. In Drew and Heritage (eds) (pp. 199–211).

Atkinson, J. Maxwell and Paul Drew (1979) *Order in Court: The Organisation of Verbal Interaction in Judicial Settings.* London: Macmillan.

Auburn, Timothy, Sue Drake and Carla Willig (1995) 'You punched him, didn't you?': Versions of violence in accusatory interviews. *Discourse and Society* 6 (3), 353–386.

Auer, Peter (ed.) (1998) *Code-Switching in Conversation: Language, Interaction and Identity*. London: Routledge.

Auer, Peter (1999) From codeswitching via language mixing to fused lects: Towards a dynamic typology of bilingual speech. *International Journal of Bilingualism* 3 (4), 309–332.

Auer, Peter and Li Wei (2007) Introduction: Multilingualism as a problem? In Peter Auer and Li Wei (eds) *Handbook of Multilingualism and Multilingual Communication* (pp. 1–14). Berlin: Mouton de Gruyter.

AUSIT (Australian Institute of Interpreters and Translators Inc) *Code of Ethics*. Retrieved on 8 May 2009 from http://www.ausit.org/eng/showpage.php3?id=650

Auty, Kate and Daniel Briggs (2004) Koori Court Victoria: *Magistrates Court (Koori Court) Act 2002*. *Law/Text/Culture* 8, 7–38.

Baldwin, John (1993) Police interview techniques: Establishing truth or proof? *British Journal of Criminology* 33, 325–352.

Basso, Keith H. (1970) 'To give up on words': Silence in Apache culture. *Southwestern Journal of Anthropology* 26 (3), 213–230.

Bauer, Janet (1999) Speaking of culture: Immigrants in the American legal system. In Moore (ed.) (pp. 8–28).

Berk-Seligson, Susan (2002a) *The Bilingual Courtroom: Court Interpreters in the Judicial Process: With a New Chapter*. Chicago: The University of Chicago Press. First published in 1990.

Berk-Seligson, Susan (1999) The impact of court interpreting on the coerciveness of leading questions. *Forensic Linguistics* 6 (1), 30–56.

Berk-Seligson, Susan (2000) Interpreting for the police: Issues in pre-trial phases of the judicial process. *Forensic Linguistics* 7 (2), 212–235.

Berk-Seligson, Susan (2002b) The Miranda warnings and linguistic coercion: The role of footing in the interrogation of a limited-English speaking murder suspect. In Cotterill (ed.), pp. 127–143.

Berk-Seligson, Susan (2007) The elicitation of a confession: Admitting murder but resisting an accusation of an attempted rape. In Cotterill (ed.) (pp. 16–41).

Berk-Seligson, Susan (2009) *Coerced Confessions*. Berlin: Mouton de Gruyter.

Blackledge, Adrian (2005) *Discourse and Power in a Multilingual World*. Amsterdam: John Benjamins.

Black's Law Dictionary (2004) 8th edition. St Paul, MN: West.

Blommaert, Jan (ed.) (1999) *Language Ideological Debates*. Berlin: Mouton de Gruyter.

Blommaert, Jan (2005) *Discourse*. Cambridge: Cambridge University Press.

Blommaert, Jan (2009) Language, asylum, and the national order. *Current Anthropology* 50 (4), 415–425.

Blommaert, Jan and Chris Bulcaen (2000) Critical Discourse Analysis. *Annual Review of Anthropology* 29, 447–466.

Blommaert, Jan and Jef Verschueren (1998) *Debating Diversity: Analysing the Discourse of Tolerance*. London: Routledge.

Blommaert, Jan, James Collins and Stef Slembrouck (2005) Spaces of multilingualism. *Language and Communication* 25, 197–216.

Blommaert, Jan, James Collins, Monica Heller, Ben Rampton, Stef Slembrouck and Jef Verschueren (2001) Discourse and critique: Part One, Introduction. *Critique of Anthropology* 21 (1), 5–12.

Bogoch, Bryna (1994) Power, distance and solidarity: Models of professional–client interaction in an Israeli legal aid setting. *Discourse and Society* 5 (1), 65–88.

Bogoch, Bryna (1997) Gendered lawyering: Difference and dominance in lawyer–client interaction. *Law and Society Review* 31 (4), 677–712.

Bogoch, Bryna and Brenda Danet (1984) Challenge and control in lawyer–client interaction: A case study in an Israeli legal aid office. *Text* 4 (1–3), 249–275.

Braithwaite, John (1989) *Crime, Shame and Reintegration*. Cambridge: Cambridge University Press.

Braithwaite, John (2002) *Restorative Justice and Responsive Regulation*. Oxford: Oxford University Press.

Brennan, Mark (1994) Cross-examining children in criminal courts: Child welfare under attack. In Gibbons (ed.) (pp. 199–216).

Brennan, Mark (1995) The discourse of denial: Cross-examining child victim witnesses. *Journal of Pragmatics* 23, 71–91.

Brennan, Mark and Roslin Brennan (1988) *Strange Language: Child Victims under Cross-examination*. 2nd edition. Wagga Wagga: Charles Sturt University.

Brennan, Mark and Roslin Brennan (1994) *Cleartalk: Police Responding to Intellectual Disability*. Wagga Wagga: Charles Sturt University.

Brennan, Mary (1999) Signs of injustice. *The Translator* 5 (2), 221–246.

Brennan, Mary and Richard Brown (1997) *Equality before the Law: Deaf People's Access to Justice*. Durham: Deaf Studies Research Unit, University of Durham.

Brière, Eugene (1978) Limited English speakers and the Miranda rights. *TESOL Quarterly* 12 (3), 235–245.

Briggs, Charles L. (1993) Metadiscursive practices and scholarly authority in folkloristics. *The Journal of American Folklore* 106 (422), 387–434.

Brown-Blake, Celia and Paul Chambers (2007) The Jamaican Creole speaker in the UK criminal justice system. *International Journal of Speech Language and the Law* 14 (2), 269–294.

Bucholtz, Mary (2000) The politics of transcription. *Journal of Pragmatics* 32, 1439–1465.

Bucholtz, Mary (2007) Variation in transcription. *Discourse Studies* 9, 784–808.

Bucholtz, Mary (2009) Captured on tape: Professional hearing and competing entextualizations in the criminal justice system. *Text and Talk* 29 (5), 503–523.

Butters, Ronald (2007) Sociolinguistic variation and the law. In Robert Bayley and Ceil Lucas (eds) *Sociolinguistic Variation: Theories, Methods and Applications* (pp. 318–337). Cambridge: Cambridge University Press.

Butterworth's Concise Australian Legal Dictionary (2004) Sydney: LexisNexis Butterworths.

Cameron, Deborah, Fiona McAlinden and Kathy O'Leary (1988) Lakoff in context: The social and linguistic functions of tag questions. In Jennifer Coates and Deborah Cameron (eds) *Women in their Speech Communities* (pp. 74–93). London: Longman.

Candlin, Chris and Yon Maley (1997) Intertextuality and interdiscursivity in the discourse of alternative dispute resolution. In Britt-Louise Gunnarson, Per Linell and Bengt Nordberg (eds) *The Construction of Professional Discourse* (pp. 200–222). London: Longman.

Carranza, Isolda E. (2003) Genre and institution: Narrative temporality in final arguments. *Narrative Inquiry* 13 (1), 41–69.

Castelle, George (2003) Misunderstanding, wrongful convictions and Deaf people. In Lucas (ed.) (pp. 168–176).

Ceci, Stephen J. and Maggie Bruck (1993) Suggestibility of the child witness: A historical review and synthesis. *Psychological Bulletin* 113, 403–439.

Ceci, Stephen J. and Maggie Bruck (1995) *Jeopardy in the Courtroom: A Scientific Analysis of Children's Testimony.* Washington DC: American Psychological Association.

CEOKR (Catholic Education Office Kimberley Region) (1994) *Fostering English Language in Kimberley Schools (FELIKS) Professional Development Course for Primary Schools.* Broome, Western Australia: Catholic Education Office Kimberley Region.

Chang, Yanrong (2004) Courtroom questioning as a culturally situated persuasive genre of talk. *Discourse and Society* 15 (6), 705–722.

Charrow, Robert P. and Veda R. Charrow (1979) Making legal language understandable: A psycholinguistic study of jury instructions. *Columbia Law Review* 79, 1306–1374.

Chaski, Carole (2001) Empirical evaluations of language-based author identification techniques. *Forensic Linguistics* 8 (1), 1–65.

Chesterman, Michael (2000) Criminal trial juries in Australia: From penal colonies to a federal democracy. In Vidmar (ed.) (pp. 125–166).

Chisholm, Richard and Garth Nettheim (2007) *Understanding Law: An Introduction to Australia's Legal System.* 7th edition. Sydney: LexisNexis Butterworths.

CJC (Criminal Justice Commission) (1992) *Report on the Investigation into the Complaints of Kelvin Ronald Condren and Others.* Brisbane: Criminal Justice Commission.

Clare, Isabel C.H. (2004) 'Psychological vulnerabilities' of adults with mild learning disabilities: Implications for suspects during police detention and interviewing. *International Journal of Speech Language and the Law* 11 (1), 159–162.

Cobb, Sara and Janet Rifkin (1991) Practice and paradox: Deconstructing neutrality in mediation. *Law and Social Inquiry* 16, 35–62.

Coleman, Hylwel (ed.) (1989) *Working with Language: A Multidisciplinary Consideration of Language Use in Work Contexts.* Berlin: Mouton de Gruyter.

Colin, Joan and Ruth Morris (1996) *Interpreters and the Legal Process.* Winchester, UK: Waterside Press.

Colvin, Eric, Suzie Linden and John McKechnie (2005) *Criminal Law in Queensland and Western Australia.* 4th edition. Sydney: LexisNexis Butterworths.

Conley, John M. and O'Barr, William M. (1990) *Rules versus Relationships.* Chicago: University of Chicago Press.

Conley, John M. and William M. O'Barr (2005) *Just Words: Law, Language and Power.* 2nd edition. Chicago: University of Chicago Press. First published in 1998.

Conley, John M., William M. O'Barr and E. Allan Lind (1978) The power of language: Presentational style in the courtroom. *Duke Law Journal* 1978, 1375–1399.

Cooke, Michael (1995a) Aboriginal evidence in the cross-cultural courtroom. In Eades (ed.) (pp. 55–96).

Cooke, Michael. (1995b) Understood by all concerned? Anglo/Aboriginal legal translation. In Marshall Morris (ed.) *Translation and the Law* (pp. 37–66). Amsterdam/Philadelphia: John Benjamins Publishing Company.

Cooke, Michael (1996) A different story: Narrative versus 'question and answer' in Aboriginal evidence. *Forensic Linguistics* 3 (2), 273–288.

Cooke, Michael (1998) Anglo/Yolngu Communication in the Criminal Justice System. PhD Thesis, University of New England, Australia. [available from author: *intercult@netspeed.com.au*]

Cooke, Michael (2002) *Indigenous Interpreting Issues for the Courts*. Carlton, Victoria: Australian Institute of Judicial Administration Incorporated.

Cooke, Michael (2004) *Caught in the Middle: Indigenous Interpreters and Customary Law*. Project 94, Background Paper No 2. Law Reform Commission of Western Australia. Retrieved on 8 May 2009 from http://www.lrc.justice.wa.gov.au/094-BP.html

Cooke, Michael (2009) Anglo/Aboriginal communication in the criminal justice process: A collective responsibility. *Journal of Judicial Administration* 19, 26–35.

Corcoran, Chris (2004) A critical examination of the use of language analysis interviews in asylum proceedings: A case study of a West African seeking asylum in the Netherlands. *International Journal of Speech, Language and the Law* 11 (2), 200–221.

Cotterill, Janet (2000) Reading the rights: A cautionary tale of comprehension and comprehensibility. *Forensic Linguistics* 7 (1), 4–25.

Cotterill, Janet (2001) Domestic discord, rocky relationships: Semantic prosodies in representations of marital violence in the O.J. Simpson trial. *Discourse and Society* 12 (3), 291–312.

Cotterill, Janet (ed.) (2002) *Language in the Legal Process*. Houndmills: Palgrave Macmillan.

Cotterill, Janet (2003) *Language and Power in Court: A Linguistic Analysis of the O. J. Simpson Trial*. Basingstoke: Palgrave Macmillan.

Cotterill, Janet (2004) Collocation, connotation, and courtroom semantics: Lawyers' control of witness testimony through lexical negotiation. *Applied Linguistics* 25 (4), 513–537.

Cotterill, Janet (ed.) (2007) *The Language of Sexual Crime*. Basingstoke: Palgrave Macmillan.

Coulthard, Malcolm (1994a) On the use of corpora in the study of forensic texts. *Forensic Linguistics* 1 (1), 27–33.

Coulthard, Malcolm (1994b) *Powerful* evidence for the defence: An exercise in forensic discourse analysis. In Gibbons (ed.) (pp. 414–427).

Coulthard, Malcolm (2000) Whose text is it: On the linguistic investigation of authorship. In Srikant Sarangi and Malcolm Coulthard (eds) *Discourse and Social Life* (pp. 270–287). Harlow, Essex: Pearson Education.

Coulthard, Malcolm (2004) Author identification, idiolect and linguistic uniqueness. *Applied Linguistics* 25 (4), 431–447.

Coulthard, Malcolm and Alison Johnson (2007) *An Introduction to Forensic Linguistics: Language in Evidence*. London: Routledge.

Coulthard, Malcolm and Alison Johnson (eds) (2010) *The Routledge Handbook of Forensic Linguistics*. London: Routledge.

Cummins, Jim (2000) *Language, Power and Pedagogy: Bilingual Children in the Crossfire*. Clevedon: Multilingual Matters.

Cunneen, Chris (2007) Reviving restorative justice traditions? In Johnstone and Van Ness (eds) (pp. 113–131).

Cunneen, Chris (2008) Understanding restorative justice through the lens of critical criminology. In Thalia Anthony and Chris Cunneen (eds) *The Critical Criminology Companion* (pp. 290–302). Sydney: Hawkins Press.

Cunneen, Chris and Rob White (2002) *Juvenile Justice: Youth and Crime in Australia*. Oxford: Oxford University Press.

Cunningham, Clark D. (1992) The lawyer as translator, representation as text: Towards an ethnography of legal discourse. *Cornell Law Review* 77 (6), 1298–1387.

Dadomo, Christian and Susan Farran (1996) *The French Legal System*. 2nd edition. London: Sweet and Maxwell.

Danet, Brenda (1980) 'Baby' or 'fetus'?: Language and the construction of reality in a manslaughter trial. *Semiotica* 32 (3/4), 187–219.

Danet, Brenda (1985) Legal discourse. In Teun A. Van Dijk (ed.) *Handbook of Discourse Analysis Vol 1. Disciplines of Discourse* (pp. 273–291). London: Academic Press.

Danet, Brenda and Bryna Bogoch (1980) Fixed fight or free-for-all? An empirical study of combativeness in the adversary system of justice. *British Journal of Law and Society* 7, 36–60.

Danet, Brenda, Kenneth Hoffman, Nicole Kermish, Jeffrey Rahn and Deborah Stayman (1980) An ethnography of questioning in the courtroom. In Roger Shuy and Anna Shnukal (eds) *Language Use and the Uses of Language* (pp. 222–234). Washington, DC: Georgetown University Press.

David, René and John E.C. Brierley (1985) *Major Legal Systems in the World Today: An Introduction to the Comparative Study of Law*. 3rd edition. London: Stevens and Sons.

Dingwall, Robert (1988) Empowerment or enforcement? Some questions about power and control in divorce mediation. In Robert Dingwall and John Eekelaar (eds) *Divorce Mediation and the Legal Process* (pp. 150–167). Oxford: Oxford University Press.

Drew, Paul (1985) Analyzing the use of language in courtroom interaction. In Teun A. Van Dijk (ed.) *Handbook of Discourse Analysis Volume 3: Discourse and Dialogue* (pp. 133–147). London: Academic Press.

Drew, Paul (1990) Strategies in the contest between lawyer and witness in cross-examination. In Levi and Walker (eds) (pp. 39–64).

Drew, Paul (1992) Contested evidence in courtroom cross-examination: The case of a trial for rape. In Drew and Heritage (eds) (pp. 470–520).

Drew, Paul and John Heritage (eds) (1992) *Talk at Work: Interaction in Institutional Settings*. Cambridge: Cambridge University Press.

Drizin, Steven and Richard A. Leo (2004) The problem of false confessions in the post-DNA world. *North Carolina Law Review* 82, 891–1007.

Dumas, Bethany (2000) US pattern jury instructions: Problems and proposals. *Forensic Linguistics* 7 (1), 49–71.

Dunstan, R. (1980) Context for coercion: Analyzing properties of courtroom 'questions'. *British Journal of Law and Society* 7, 61–77.

Eades, Diana (1988) 'They don't speak an Aboriginal language, or do they?'. In Keen (ed.) (97–117).

Eades, Diana (1992) *Aboriginal English and the Law: Communicating with Aboriginal English Speaking Clients: A Handbook for Legal Practitioners.* Brisbane: Queensland Law Society.

Eades, Diana (1993) The case for Condren: Aboriginal English, pragmatics and the law. *Journal of Pragmatics* 20 (2), 141–162.

Eades, Diana (1994) A case of communicative clash: Aboriginal English and the legal system. In Gibbons (ed.) (pp. 234–264).

Eades, Diana (1995a) Aboriginal English on trial: The case for Stuart and Condren. In Eades (ed.) (pp. 147–174).

Eades, Diana (ed.) (1995b) *Language in Evidence: Issues Confronting Aboriginal and Multicultural Australia.* Sydney: University of New South Wales Press.

Eades, Diana (1996a) Legal recognition of cultural differences in communication: The case of Robyn Kina. *Language and Communication* 16 (3), 215–227.

Eades, Diana (1996b) Verbatim courtroom transcripts and discourse analysis. In Hannes Kniffka (ed.) *Recent Developments in Forensic Linguistics* (pp. 241–254). Frankfurt: Peter Lang.

Eades, Diana (1997) The acceptance of linguistic evidence about indigenous Australians. *Australian Aboriginal Studies* 1997 (1), 15–27.

Eades, Diana (2000) 'I don't think it's an answer to the question': Silencing Aboriginal witnesses in court. *Language in Society* 29 (2), 161–196.

Eades, Diana (2003) 'I don't think the lawyers were communicating with me': Misunderstanding cultural differences in communicative style. *Emory Law Journal* 52, 1109–1134.

Eades, Diana (2004) Understanding Aboriginal English in the legal system: A critical sociolinguistics approach. *Applied Linguistics* 25 (4), 491–512.

Eades, Diana (2005) Applied linguistics and language analysis in asylum seeker cases. *Applied Linguistics* 26 (4), 503–526.

Eades, Diana (2006) Lexical struggle in court: Aboriginal Australians vs the state. *Journal of Sociolinguistics* 10 (2), 153–181.

Eades, Diana (2007a) Understanding Aboriginal silence in legal contexts. In Helga Kotthoff and Helen Spencer-Oatey (eds) *Handbook of Intercultural Communication* (pp. 285–301). Berlin: Mouton de Gruyter.

Eades, Diana (2007b) Aboriginal English in the criminal justice system. In Gerhard Leitner and Ian Malcolm (eds) *The Habitat of Australia's Aboriginal Languages: Past, Present, and Future* (pp. 299–326). Berlin: Mouton de Gruyter.

Eades, Diana (2008a) *Courtroom Talk and Neocolonial Control.* Berlin: Mouton de Gruyter.

Eades, Diana (2008b) Telling and retelling your story in court: Questions, assumptions and intercultural implications. *Current Issues in Criminal Justice* 20 (2), 209–230.

Eades, Diana (2009) Testing the claims of asylum seekers: The role of language analysis. *Language Assessment Quarterly* 6 (1), 30–40.

Eades, Diana (2010) Language analysis and asylum cases. In Coulthard and Johnson (eds) (pp. 411–422).

Eades, Diana and Jacques Arends (2004) Using language analysis in the determination of national origin of asylum seekers: An introduction. *International Journal of Speech, Language and the Law* 11 (2), 179–199.

Eades, Diana, Helen Fraser, Jeff Siegel, Tim McNamara and Brett Baker (2003) Linguistic identification in the determination of nationality: A preliminary report. *Language Policy* 2 (2), 179–199.

Edwards, Derek and Jonathan Potter (1992) *Discursive Psychology*. London: Sage.

Edwards, Jane (2001) The transcription of discourse. In Deborah Schiffrin, Deborah Tannen and Heidi E. Hamilton (eds) *The Handbook of Discourse Analysis* (pp. 321–348). Oxford: Blackwell.

Edwards, Viv (2004) *Multilingualism in the English-speaking World*. Oxford: Blackwell.

Ehrlich, Susan (2001) *Representing Rape: Language and Sexual Consent*. London: Routledge.

Ehrlich, Susan (2002) (Re)contextualizing accounts of sexual assault. *Forensic Linguistics* 9 (2), 193–212.

Ehrlich, Susan (2007) Normative discourses and representations of coerced sex. In Cotterill (ed.) (pp. 126–138).

Ehrlich, Susan and Jack Sidnell (2006) 'I think that's not an assumption you ought to make': Challenging presuppositions in inquiry testimony. *Language in Society* 35 (5), 655–676.

Eisen, Mitchell L., Jodi A. Quas and Gail S. Goodman (eds) (2002) *Memory and Suggestibility in the Forensic Interview*. Mahwah, NJ: Lawrence Erlbaum Assoc.

Enninger, Werner (1987) What interactants do with non-talk across cultures. In Karlfried Knapp, Werner Enninger and Annelie Knapp-Pothoff (eds) *Analyzing Intercultural Communication* (pp. 269–302). Berlin: Mouton de Gruyter.

Erickson, Bonnie, E. Allan Lind, Bruce C. Johnson and William M. O'Barr (1978) Speech style and impression formation in a court setting: The effects of 'powerful' and 'powerless' speech. *Journal of Experimental Social Psychology* 14, 266–279.

Evans, Nicholas (2002) Country and the word: Linguistic evidence in the Croker sea claim. In Henderson and Nash (eds) (pp. 53–100).

Fadden, Lorna (2007) Quantitative and qualitative analyses of police interviews with Canadian Aboriginal and non Aboriginal Suspects. In Krzysztof Kredens and Stanislaw Goźdź-Roszkowski (eds) *Language and the Law: International Outlooks* (pp. 305–322). Frankfurt am Main: Peter Lang GmbH.

Fairclough, Norman (1989) *Language and Power*. London: Longman.

Felton Rosulek, Laura (2008) Manipulative silence and social representation in the closing arguments of a child sexual abuse case. *Text and Talk* 28 (4), 529–550.

Felton Rosulek, Laura (2009) The sociolinguistic creation of opposing representations of defendants and victims. *International Journal of Speech, Language and the Law* 16 (1), 1–30.

Filipovic, Luna (2007) Language as a witness: Insights from cognitive linguistics. *International Journal of Speech, Language and the Law* 14 (2), 245–268.

Fisher, Ronald P. and R. Edward Geiselman (1992) *Memory-Enhancing Techniques for Investigative Interviewing: The Cognitive Interview*. Springfield, IL: Charles C. Thomas.

Fisher, Ronald P., Kendra H. Brennan and Michelle R. McCauley (2002) The cognitive interview method to enhance eyewitness recall. In Eisen *et al.* (eds.) (pp. 265–286).

Fivush, Robyn, Carole Peterson and April Schwarzmueller (2002) Questions and answers: The credibility of child witnesses in the context of specific questioning techniques. In Eisen *et al.* (eds.) (pp. 331–354).

Fox, Gwyneth (1993) A comparison of 'policespeak' and 'normalspeak': A preliminary study. In John Sinclair, Michael Hoey and Gwyneth Fox (eds) *Techniques of Description: Written and Spoken Discourse* (pp. 183–195). London: Routledge.

Fraser, Helen (2009) The role of 'educated native speakers' in providing language analysis for the determination of the origin of asylum seekers. *International Journal of Speech Language and the Law* 16 (1), 113–138.

Fuller, Janet (1993) Hearing between the lines: Style switching in a courtroom setting. *Pragmatics* 3 (1), 29–43.

Garcia, Angela (1991) Dispute resolution without disputing: How the interactional organization of mediation hearings minimizes argument. *American Sociological Review* 56, 818–835.

Garcia, Angela (1997) Interactional constraints on proposal generation in mediation hearings: A preliminary investigation. *Discourse and Society* 8 (2), 219–249.

Garcia, Angela (2000) Negotiating negotiation: The collaborative production of resolution in small claims mediation hearings. *Discourse and Society* 11 (3), 315–343.

Geiselman, R. Edward, Ronald P. Fisher, Iris Firstenberg, Lisa A. Hutton, Steven J. Sullivan, Ivan V. Avetissian and Allan L. Prosk (1984) Enhancement of eyewitness memory: An empirical evaluation of the cognitive interview. *Journal of Police Science and Administration* 12 (1), 74–80.

Gibbons, John (1990) Applied linguistics in court. *Applied Linguistics* 11 (3), 229–237.

Gibbons, John (ed.) (1994) *Language and the Law*. London: Longman.

Gibbons, John (1995) What got lost?: The place of electronic recording and interpreting in police interviews. In Eades (ed.) (pp. 175–186).

Gibbons, John (2001) Revising the language of New South Wales police procedures: Applied Linguistics in action. *Applied Linguistics* 22 (4), 439–469.

Gibbons, John (2003) *Forensic Linguistics* Oxford: Blackwell.

Gibbons, John and M. Teresa Turell (eds) (2008) *Dimensions of Forensic Linguistics*. Amsterdam: John Benjamins.

Giles, Peter and Peter F. Powlesland (1975) *Speech Style and Social Evaluation*. London: Academic Press.

Goffman, Erving (1974) *Frame Analysis*. New York: Harper and Row.

Gramsci, Antonio (1971) *Selections from the Prison Notebooks of Antonio Gramsci* (edited and translated by Quentin Hoare and Geoffrey Nowell Smith). London: Laurence and Wishart.

Grant, Tim (2007) Quantifying evidence in forensic authorship analysis. *The International Journal of Speech, Language and the Law* 14 (1), 1–26.

Grant, Tim (2008) Approaching questions in forensic authorship analysis. In Gibbons and Turell (eds) (pp. 215–230).

Gray, Peter R.A. (2000) Do the walls have ears? Indigenous title and courts in Australia. *International Journal of Legal Information* 28, 185–211.

Gray, Peter R.A. (2010) The future for forensic linguistics in the courtroom: Cross-cultural communication. In Coulthard and Johnson (eds) (pp. 591–601).

Greatbatch, David and Robert Dingwall (1989) Selective facilitation: Some preliminary observations on a strategy used by divorce mediators. *Law and Society Review* 23, 613–641.

Greatbatch, David and Robert Dingwall (1994) The interactive construction of interventions by divorce mediators. In Joseph P. Folger and Tricia S. Jones (eds) *New Directions in Mediation: Communication Research and Perspectives* (pp. 84–109). Thousand Oaks, CA: Sage.

Greatbatch, David and Robert Dingwall (1997) Argumentative talk in divorce mediation sessions. *American Sociological Review* 62 (1), 151–170.

Greatbatch, David and Robert Dingwall (1998) Talk and identity in divorce mediation. In Charles Antaki and Sue Winnicombe (eds) *Identities in Talk* (pp. 121–132). London: Sage.

Greatbatch, David and Robert Dingwall (1999) Professional neutralism in family mediation. In Srikant Sarangi and Celia Roberts (eds) *Talk, Work and Institutional Order: Discourse in Medical, Mediation and Management Settings* (pp. 271–292). Berlin: Mouton de Gruyter.

Green, Lisa J. (2002) *African American English: A Linguistic Introduction*. Cambridge: Cambridge University Press.

Grillo, Tina (1991) The mediation alternative: Process dangers for women. *Yale Law Journal* 100, 1545–1610.

Gumperz, John J. (2001) Contextualization and ideology in intercultural communication. In Aldo Di Luzio, Susanne Günther and Franca Orletti (eds) *Culture in Communication: Analyses of Intercultural Situations* (pp. 35–53). Amsterdam: John Benjamins.

Hale, Sandra (1999) Interpreters' treatment of discourse markers in courtroom questions. *Forensic Linguistics* 6 (1), 57–82.

Hale, Sandra (2002) How faithfully do court interpreters render the style of non-English speaking witnesses' testimonies? A data-based study of Spanish–English bilingual proceedings. *Discourse Studies* 4 (1), 25–47.

Hale, Sandra (2004) *The Discourse of Court Interpreting: Discourse Practices of the Law, the Witness and the Interpreter*. Amsterdam: John Benjamins.

Hale, Sandra and Gibbons, John (1999) Varying realities: Patterned changes in the interpreter's representation of courtroom and external realities. *Applied Linguistics* 20 (2), 203–220.

Hall, Phil (2008) Policespeak. In Gibbons and Turell (eds) (pp. 68–94).

Halldorsdottir, Iris (2006) Orientations to law, guidelines and codes in lawyer–client interaction. *Research on Language and Social Interaction* 39 (3), 263–301.

Harris, Sandra (1984) Questions as a mode of control in magistrates' courts. *International Journal of the Sociology of Language* 49, 5–28.

Harris, Sandra (1989) Defendant resistance to power and control in court. In Coleman (ed.) (pp. 132–164).

Haviland, John B. (2003) Ideologies of language: Some reflections of language and U.S. law. *American Anthropologist* 105 (4), 764–774.

Haworth, Kate (2006) The dynamics of power and resistance in police interview discourse. *Discourse and Society* 17 (6), 739–759.

Hayes, Hennessey (2006) Apologies and accounts in youth justice conferencing: Reinterpreting research outcomes. *Contemporary Justice Review* 9 (4), 369–385.

Heffer, Chris (2005) *The Language of Jury Trial: A Corpus-Aided Analysis of Legal–Lay Discourse*. Basingstoke: Palgrave Macmillan.

Heffer, Chris (2006) Beyond 'reasonable doubt': The criminal standard of proof instruction as communicative act. *International Journal of Speech, Language and the Law* 13 (2), 159–188.

Heffer, Chris (2007) The language of conviction and the convictions of certainty: Is *sure* an impossible standard of proof? *International Commentary on Evidence* 5 (1) Art.5. 1554–4567.

Heffer, Chris (2008) The language and communication of jury instructions. In Gibbons and Turell (eds) (pp. 47–66).

Heisterkamp, Brian L. (2006) Conversational displays of mediator neutrality in a court-based program. *Journal of Pragmatics* 38, 2051–2064.

Henderson, John and David Nash (eds) (2002) *Language in Native Title*. Canberra: Australian Institute of Aboriginal and Torres Straight Islander Studies.

Heydon, Georgina (2004) Establishing the structure of police evidentiary interviews with suspects. *International Journal of Speech, Language and the Law* 11 (1), 27–49.

Heydon, Georgina (2005) *The Language of Police Interviewing: A Critical Analysis*. Basingstoke: Palgrave Macmillan.

Hobbs, Pamela (2003a) 'Is that what we're here about': A lawyer's use of impression management in a closing argument at trial. *Discourse and Society* 14 (3), 273–290.

Hobbs, Pamela (2003b) 'You must say it for him': Reformulating a witness's testimony on cross-examination at trial. *Text* 23 (4), 477–511.

Holmes Janet (2008) *An Introduction to Sociolinguistics*. London: Longman.

Holmes, Janet and Miriam Meyerhoff (eds) (2003) *The Handbook of Language and Gender*. Oxford: Blackwell.

Home Office, United Kingdom. (1992) *Memorandum of Good Practice on Video Recorded Interviews for Child Witnesses in Criminal Proceedings*.

Home Office, United Kingdom. (2000) *Achieving Best Evidence in Criminal Proceedings: Guidance for Vulnerable or Intimidated Witnesses, Including Children*. Retrieved on 8 May 2009 from http://www.homeoffice.gov.uk/documents/ach-bect-evidence

Home Office, United Kingdom. (2007) *National Agreement on Arrangements for the Use of Interpreters, Translators and Language Service Professionals in Investigations and Proceedings within the Criminal Justice System*. Retrieved on 31 August 2009 from http://police.homeoffice.gov.uk/news-and-publications/publication/operational-policing/national-agreement-interpret.pdf?view=Standard&pubID=441359

Hoopes, Rob (2003) Trampling *Miranda*: Interrogating Deaf suspects. In Lucas (ed.) (pp. 21–59).

Howald, Blake (2008) Authorship attribution under the Rules of Evidence: Empirical approaches in a layperson's legal system. *The International Journal of Speech, Language and the Law* 15 (2), 219–247.

Hymes, Dell (1974) *Foundations in Sociolinguistics: An Ethnographic Approach.* Philadelphia: University of Pennsylvania Press.

Hymes, Dell (1996) *Ethnography, Linguistics, Narrative Inequality: Towards an Understanding of Voice.* London: Taylor and Francis.

Inbau, Fred E., John E. Reid, Joseph P. Buckley, and Brian C. Jayne (2001) *Criminal Interrogation and Confessions.* 4th edition. Gaithersberg, MD: Aspen.

Jackson, John D. and Nikolay P. Kovalev (2006/2007) Lay adjudication and human rights in Europe. *The Columbia Journal of European Law* 13 (1), 83–123.

Jacobs, Scott (2002) Maintaining neutrality in dispute mediation: Managing disagreement while managing not to disagree. *Journal of Pragmatics* 34, 1403–1426.

Jacquemet, Marco (1992) 'If he speaks Italian it's better': Metapragmatics in court. *Pragmatics* 2 (2), 111–126.

Jacquemet, Marco (1996) *Credibility in Court: Communicative Practices in the Camorra Trials.* Cambridge: Cambridge University Press.

Jakubowicz, Andrew, Heather Goodall, Jeannie Martin, Tony Mitchell, Lois Randall and Kalinga Seneviratne (1994) *Racism, Ethnicity and the Media.* Sydney: Allen and Unwin.

Jefferson, Gail (1989) Preliminary notes on a possible metric which provides for a 'Standard Maximum' silence of approximately one second in a conversation. In Derek Roger and Peter Bull (eds) *Conversation: An Interdisciplinary Perspective* (pp. 166–196). Clevedon: Multilingual Matters.

Jensen, Marie-Thérèse (1995) Linguistic evidence accepted in the case of a non-native speaker of English. In Eades (ed.) (pp. 127–146).

Johnson, Alison J. (2002) So? Pragmatic implications of so-prefaced questions in formal police interviews. In Cotterill (ed.) (pp. 91–110).

Johnstone, Gerry (2003a) Introduction. In Johnstone (ed.) (pp. 1–18).

Johnstone, Gerry (ed.) (2003b) *A Restorative Justice Reader: Texts, Sources Context.* Cullompton, UK: Willan Publishing.

Johnstone, Gerry and Daniel W. Van Ness (eds) (2007) *Handbook of Restorative Justice.* Cullompton, UK : Willan Publishing.

Jones, Claire (2008a) UK Police Interviews: A Linguistic Analysis of Afro-Caribbean and White British Suspect Interviews. Unpublished PhD thesis, University of Essex.

Jones, Claire (2008b) UK police interviews: A linguistic analysis of Afro-Caribbean and White British suspect interviews. *International Journal of Speech, Language and the Law* 15 (2), 271–274.

Jönsson, Linda and Per Linell (1991) Story generations: From dialogical interviews to written reports in police interrogations. *Text* 11 (3), 419–440.

Kandel, Randy (1994) Power plays: A sociolinguistic study of inequality in child custody mediation and a hearsay analog solution. *Arizona Law Review* 36, 879–972.

Kassin, Saul M. and Gisli H. Gudjonsson (2004) The psychology of confessions: A review of the literature and issues. *Psychological Science in the Public Interest* 5 (2), 33–67.

Keen, Ian (ed.) (1988) *Being Black: Aboriginal Cultures in 'Settled' Australia*. Canberra: Aboriginal Studies Press.

Koch, Harold (1985) Nonstandard English in an Aboriginal land claim. In John Pride (ed.) *Cross-cultural Encounters: Communication and Miscommunication* (pp. 176–195). Melbourne: River Seine Publications.

Komter, Martha (1994) Accusations and defences in courtroom interaction. *Discourse and Society* 5 (2), 165–187.

Komter, Martha (1998) *Dilemmas in the Courtroom: A Study of Trials of Violent Crime in the Netherlands*. Mahwah, NJ: Lawrence Erlbaum.

Komter, Martha (2002) The suspect's own words: The treatment of written statements in Dutch courtrooms. *Forensic Linguistics* 9 (2), 168–192.

Komter, Martha (2006a) Introduction. *Research on Language and Social Interaction* 39 (3), 195–200.

Komter, Martha (2006b) From talk to text: The interactional construction of a police record. *Research on Language in Social Interaction* 39 (3), 201–228.

Kress, Gunther (2001) Critical sociolinguistics. In Rajend Mesthrie (ed.) *Concise Encyclopedia of Sociolinguistics* (pp. 542–545). Oxford: Elsevier Science.

Kroskrity, Paul V. (2000) *Regimes of Language: Ideologies, Politics, and Identities*. Sante Fe, NM: School of American Research Press.

Kroskrity, Paul V. (2004) Language ideologies. In Alessandro Duranti (ed.) *A Companion to Linguistic Anthropology* (pp. 496–517). Oxford: Blackwell.

Kurzon, Dennis (1995) The right of silence: A socio-pragmatic model of interpretation. *Journal of Pragmatics* 23, 55–69.

Lakoff, Robin (1975) *Language and Woman's Place*. New York: Harper and Row.

Lane, Chris (1990) The sociolinguistics of questioning in District Court trials. In Allan Bell and Janet Holmes (eds.) *New Zealand Ways of Speaking English* (pp. 221–251). Clevedon: Multilingual Matters.

Lane, Chris, Katherine McKenzie-Bridle and Lucille Curtis (1999) The right to interpreting and translation services in New Zealand courts. *Forensic Linguistics* 6 (1), 115–136.

Langton, Marcia (1988) Medicine Square. In Keen (ed.) (pp. 201–226).

Language and National Origin Group (2004) Guidelines for the use of language analysis in relation to questions of national origin in refugee cases. *International Journal of Speech, Language and the Law* 11 (2), 261–266.

Laster, Kathy and Veronica Taylor (1994) *Interpreters and the Legal System*. Sydney: The Federation Press.

Law Society of the Northern Territory (2004) *Indigenous Protocols for Lawyers in the Northern Territory*. Retrieved on 8 May 2009 from http://www.lawsocnt.asn.au/fmi/xsl/lsnt/lsnt_publications.xsl

Lebra, Takie Sugiyama (1987) The cultural significance of silence in Japanese communication. *Multilingua* 6 (4), 343–357.

Lee, Jieun (2009a) Interpreting inexplicit language during courtroom examination. *Applied Linguistics* 30 (1), 93–114.

Lee, Jieun (2009b) When linguistic and cultural differences are not disclosed in court interpreting. *Multilingua* 28(4), 379–401.

Lee, Jieun (2010) Interpreting reported speech in witnesses' evidence. *Interpreting* 12 (1), 60–82.

Leo, Richard (1996a) Inside the interrogation room. *Journal of Criminal Law and Criminology* 86, 266–303.

Leo, Richard (1996b) The impact of *Miranda* revisited. *Journal of Criminal Law and Criminology* 86, 621–692.

Leo, Richard (1996c) *Miranda*'s revenge: Police interrogation as a confidence game. *Law and Society Review* 30 (2), 259–288.

Leo, Richard (2008) *Police Interrogation and American Justice*. Cambridge, MA: Harvard University Press.

Leo, Richard and Kimberly Richman (2007) Mandate the electronic recording of police interrogations. *Criminology and Public Policy* 6 (4), 791–798.

Levi, Judith N. and Anne Graffam Walker (eds) (1990) *Language in the Judicial Process*. New York: Plenum Press.

Liberman, Kenneth (1981) Understanding Aborigines in Australian courts of law. *Human Organization* 40, 247–255.

Lippi-Green, Rosina (1997) *English with an Accent: Language, Ideology, and Discrimination in the United States*. London: Routledge.

Loftus, Elizabeth F. (1979) *Eyewitness Testimony*. Cambridge, MA: Harvard University Press.

Lucas, Ceil (ed.) (2003) *Language and the Law in Deaf Communities*. Washington, DC: Gallaudet University Press.

Luchjenbroers, June and Michelle Aldridge (2008) Language and vulnerable witnesses across legal contexts: Introduction to the special issue. *Journal of English Linguistics* 36 (3), 191–194.

Macdonald, Gaynor (1988) A Wiradjuri fight story. In Keen (ed.) (pp. 179–200).

Macquarie Dictionary. Retrieved on 23 March 2008 from http://www.macquarieonline.com.au/dictionary.html

Macquarie Junior Dictionary. (1992) Milton, Qld: Jacaranda Press.

McElhinny, Bonnie (1995) Challenging hegemonic masculinities: Female and male police officers handling domestic violence. In Kira Hall and Mary Bucholtz (eds) *Gender Articulated: Language and the Socially Constructed Self* (pp. 217–243). New York: Routledge.

McElhinny, Bonnie (2003) Fearful, forceful agents of the law: Ideologies about language and gender in police officers' narratives about the use of physical force. *Pragmatics* 13 (2), 253–284.

McKee, Rachel (2001) *People of the Eye: Stories from the Deaf World*. Wellington: Bridget Williams Books.

MCQ (Magistrates Court of Queensland) (2008) *Annual Report 2007–2008*. Brisbane: Queensland Courts.

Makoni, Sinfree and Alastair Pennycook (eds) (2007) *Disinventing and Reconstituting Languages*. Clevedon: Multilingual Matters.

Maley, Yon (1995) From adjudication to mediation: Third party discourse in conflict resolution. *Journal of Pragmatics* 23, 93–110.

Maley, Yon, Christopher Candlin, Jonathan Crichton and Pieter Koster (1995) Orientations in lawyer–client interviews. *Forensic Linguistics* 2 (1), 42–55.

Marchetti, Elena and Kathleen Daly (2007) Indigenous sentencing courts: Towards a theoretical and jurisprudential model. *Sydney Law Review* 29 (3), 415–443.

Martin, J.R., Michele Zappavigna and Paul Dwyer (2009) Negotiating shame: Exchange and genre structure in Youth Justice Conferencing. In Ahmar Mahboob and Caroline Lipovsky (eds) *Studies in Applied Linguistics and Language Learning*. (pp. 41–72). Newcastle: Cambridge Scholars Press.

Martin, J.R., Michele Zappavigna and Paul Dwyer (forthcoming) Negotiating evaluation: Story structure and appraisal in youth justice conferencing. In Ahmar Mahboob and Naomi Knight (eds) *Directions in Appliable Linguistics*. London: Continuum.

Maryns, Katrijn (2004) Identifying the asylum speaker: Reflections on the pitfalls of language analysis in the determination of national origin. *International Journal of Speech, Language and the Law* 11 (2), 240–260.

Maryns, Katrijn (2005) Monolingual language ideologies and code choice in the Belgian asylum procedure. *Language and Communication* 25, 299–314.

Maryns, Katrijn (2006) *The Asylum Speaker: Language in the Belgian Asylum Procedure*. Manchester, UK: St Jerome Press.

Mather, Susan and Robert Mather (2003) Court interpreting for signing jurors: Just transmitting or interpreting? In Lucas (ed.) (pp. 60–81).

Matoesian, Gregory (1993) *Reproducing Rape: Domination through Talk in the Courtroom*. Chicago: University of Chicago Press.

Matoesian, Gregory (1995) Language, law, and society: Policy implications of the Kennedy Smith rape trial. *Law and Society Review* 29 (4), 669–701.

Matoesian, Gregory (2000) Intertextual authority in reported speech: Production media in the Kennedy Smith rape trial. *Journal of Pragmatics* 32, 879–914.

Matoesian, Gregory (2001) *Law and the Language of Identity: Discourse in the William Kennedy Smith Rape Trial*. Oxford: Oxford University Press.

Matoesian, Gregory (2005a) Struck by speech revisited: Embodied stance in jurisdictional discourse. *Journal of Sociolinguistics* 9 (2), 167–193.

Matoesian, Gregory (2005b) Nailing down an answer: Participations of power in trial talk. *Discourse Studies* 7 (6), 733–759.

Matoesian, Gregory (2008) You might win the battle but lose the war: Multimodal, interactive, and extralinguistic aspects of witness resistance. *Journal of English Linguistics* 36 (3), 195–219.

Mauet, Thomas A. (2000) *Trial Techniques*. 5th edition. Gaithersburg, MD: Aspen Publishers, Inc.

Mauet, Thomas A. and Les A. McCrimmon (2001) *Fundamentals of Trial Techniques*. 2nd Australian edition. Sydney: LBC Information Services.

Maynard, Douglas W. (1984) *Inside Plea Bargaining: The Language of Negotiation*. New York: Plenum Press.

Mellinkoff, David (1963) *The Language of the Law*. Boston: Little, Brown and Company.

Merry, Sally Engle (1990) *Getting Justice and Getting Even: Legal Consciousness among Working-Class Americans*. Chicago: University of Chicago Press.

Mertz, Elizabeth (2007) *The Language of Law School: Learning to Think like a Lawyer*. Oxford: Oxford University Press.

Middleton, David and Derek Edwards (1990) Conversational remembering: A social psychological approach. In David Middleton and Derek Edwards (eds) *Collective Remembering* (pp. 23–45). London: Sage.

Mikkelson, Holly (1998) Towards a redefinition of the role of the court interpreter. *Interpreting* 31 (1), 21–45.

Mildren, Dean (1999) Redressing the imbalance: Aboriginal people in the criminal justice system. *Forensic Linguistics* 6 (1), 137–160.

Milne, Rebecca and Ray Bull (1999) *Investigative Interviewing: Psychology and Practice*. Chichester: John Wiley & Sons.

Moeketsi, Rosemary (1999) *Discourse in a Multilingual and Multicultural Courtroom: A Court Interpreter's Guide*. Pretoria: J. L. Van Schaik.

Montalvo, Margarita (2001) Interpreting for non-English-speaking jurors: Analysis of a new and complex responsibility. *ATA Proceedings for the 42nd Annual Conference*, 167–176.

Montoya, Margaret (2000) Silence and silencing: Their centripetal and centrifugal forces in legal communication, pedagogy and discourse. *Michigan Journal of Race and Law* 5, 847–941.

Moore, Joanne (ed.) (1999) *Immigrants in court*. Seattle: University of Washington Press.

Morphy, Frances (2007) Performing law: The Yolngu of Blue Mud Bay meet the native title process. In Benjamin Smith and Frances Morphy (eds) *The Social Effects of Native Title: Recognition, Translation, Coexistence* (pp. 31–57). Canberra: ANU E Press.

Morris, Ruth. (1999) The gum syndrome: Predicaments in court interpreting. *Forensic Linguistics* 6 (1), 6–29.

Morrow, Phyllis (1993) A sociolinguistic mismatch: Central Alaskan Yup'iks and the legal system. *Alaska Justice Forum* 10 (2), 4–8.

Morrow, Phyllis (1996) Yup'ik Eskimo agents and American legal agencies: Perspectives on compliance and resistance. *Journal of the Royal Anthropological Institute* 2, 405–423.

Mufwene, Salikoko S., John R. Rickford, Guy Bailey and John Baugh (1998) (eds) *African-American English: Structure, History and Use*. London: Routledge.

Muysken, Pieter (2000) *Bilingual Speech: A Typology of Code-mixing*. Cambridge: Cambridge University Press.

NADRAC (National Alternative Dispute Resolution Advisory Council) (1997) *Issues of Fairness and Justice in Alternative Dispute Resolution*. Canberra: Commonwealth of Australia. Retrieved on 23 March 2009 from http://www.nadrac.gov.au/

NADRAC (National Alternative Dispute Resolution Advisory Council) (2001) *A Framework for ADR Standards*. Canberra: Commonwealth of Australia. Retrieved on 23 March 2009 from http://www.nadrac.gov.au/

NADRAC (National Alternative Dispute Resolution Advisory Council) (2003) *Dispute Resolution Terms.* Canberra: Commonwealth of Australia. Retrieved on 23 March 2009 from http://www.nadrac.gov.au/

Nakane, Ikuko (2007) Problems in communicating the suspect's rights in interpreted police interviews. *Applied Linguistics* 28 (1), 87–112.

Napier, Jemima, Rachel McKee and Della Goswell (2006) *Sign Language Interpreting: Theory and Practice in Australia and New Zealand.* Sydney: Federation Press.

Napier, Jemina, David Spencer and Joseph Sabolcec (2007) *Deaf Jurors' Access to Court Proceedings via Sign Language Interpreting: An Investigation.* New South Wales Law Reform Commission Research Report 14. Retrieved on 23 March 2009 http://www.lawlink.nsw.gov.au/lawlink/lrc/ll_lrc.nsf/pages/LRC_rrs

Neate, Graeme (2003) Land, law and language: Some issues in the resolution of Indigenous land claims in Australia. Paper delivered to the conference of the International Association of Forensic Linguists, Sydney. Retrieved on 1 July 2009 http://www.nntt.gov.au/News-and-Communications/Speeches-and-papers/Pages/Land_law_and_language.aspx

Newbury, Phillip and Alison Johnson (2006) Suspects' resistance to constraining and coercive questioning strategies in the police interview. *The International Journal of Speech, Language and the Law* 13 (2), 213–240.

New South Wales Police Service (1998) *Code of Practice for CRIME: (Custody, Rights, Investigation, Management and Evidence)* Updated 2008. Sydney: New South Wales Police Force.

Norrick Neal R. (1998) Retelling stories in spontaneous conversation. *Discourse Processes* 25 (1), 75–97.

Norrick, Neal R. (2005) Interactional remembering in conversational narrative. *Journal of Pragmatics* 37, 1819–1844.

NTER Review Board (2008) *Northern Territory Emergency Response: Report.* Canberra: Commonwealth of Australia.

O'Barr, William M. (1982) *Linguistic Evidence: Power and Strategy in the Courtroom.* New York: Academic Press.

O'Barr, William M. and Bowman K. Atkins (1980) 'Women's language' or 'powerless language'? In Sally McConnell-Ginet, Ruth Borker and Nelly Furman (eds) *Women in Language and Society* (pp. 93–109). New York: Praeger.

O'Connell, Daniel C. and Sabine Kowal (2000) Are transcripts reproducible? *Pragmatics* 10 (2), 247–269.

Ord, Brian, Gary Shaw and Tracey Green (2004) *Investigative Interviewing Explained.* Chatswood, NSW: LexisNexis Butterworths.

Ostermann, Ana Cristina (2003a) Communities of practice at work: Gender, facework, and the power of habitus at an all-female police station and a feminist crisis intervention center in Brazil. *Discourse and Society* 14 (4), 473–505.

Ostermann, Ana Cristina (2003b) Localizing power and solidarity: Pronoun alteration at an all-female police station and a feminist crisis intervention center in Brazil. *Language in Society* 32 (3), 351–381.

Oxburgh, Gavin Eric, Trond Myklebust and Tim Grant (forthcoming) The question of question types in police interviews: A review of the literature from a psychological and linguistic perspective. *International Journal of Speech Language and the Law.*

Palerm, Juan-Vicente, Bobby R. Vincent and Kathryn Vincent (1999) Mexican immigrants in court. In Moore (ed.) (pp. 73–97).

Pennycook, Alastair (2001) *Critical Applied Linguistics: A Critical Introduction.* Mahwah, NJ: Lawrence Erlbaum.

Philips, Susan U. (1986) Some functions of spatial positioning and alignment in the organization of courtroom discourse. In Sue Fisher and Alexandra Dundas Todd (eds) *Discourse and Institutional Authority: Medicine, Education and Law* (pp. 223–233). Norwood, NJ: Ablex.

Philips, Susan U. (1993) *The Invisible Culture: Communication in Classroom and Community on the Warm Springs Indian Reservation.* 2nd edition. New York: Longman.

Philips, Susan U. (1998) *Ideology in the Language of Judges: How Judges Practice Law, Politics and Courtroom Control.* New York: Oxford University Press.

Piller, Ingrid (2001) Naturalization language testing and its basis in ideologies of national identity and citizenship. *International Journal of Bilingualism* 5 (3), 259–277.

Poole, Debra Ann and D. Stephen Lindsay (2002) Children's suggestibility in the forensic context. In Eisen *et al.* (eds) (pp. 355–381).

Potas, Ivan, Jane Smart, Georgia Brignell, Brendan Thomas and Rowena Lawrie (2003) *Circle Sentencing in New South Wales: A Review and Evaluation.* Sydney: Judicial Commission of New South Wales.

Powell, Martine B. (2005) Contemporary comments. *Current Issues in Criminal Justice* 17 (1), 137–143.

Powell, Martine B. (2008) Designing effective training programs for investigative interviews of children. *Current Issues in Criminal Justice* 20 (2), 189–208.

Powell, Martine B., Ronald P. Fisher and Rebecca Wright (2005) Investigative interviewing. In Neil Brewer and Kipling D. Williams (eds) *Psychology and Law: An Empirical Perspective* (pp. 11–42). New York: The Guilford Press.

Powell, Richard (2008) Bilingual courtrooms: In the interests of justice? In Gibbons and Turell (eds) (pp. 131–160).

Powles, Guy and Mere Pulea (eds) (1988) *Pacific Courts and Legal Systems.* Suva: University of the South Pacific.

R v Condren (1987) *Australian Criminal Reports* 28, 261–299 (Queensland Court of Criminal Appeal).

R v Kina (1993) Unreported, Queensland Court of Appeal, 29 November.

Rampton, Ben (2001) Language crossing, cross-talk and cross-disciplinarity in sociolinguistics. In Nikolas Coupland, Srikant Sarangi and Christopher N. Candlin (eds) *Sociolinguistics and Social Theory* (pp. 261–296). London: Pearson Education.

Rampton, Ben (2006) *Language in Late Modernity: Interaction in an Urban School.* Cambridge: Cambridge University Press.

Reed, Maureen, Graham H. Turner and Caroline Taylor (2001) Working paper on access to justice for Deaf people. In Frank J. Harrington and Graham H. Turner (eds) *Interpreting Interpreting: Studies and Reflections on Sign Language Interpreting* (pp. 168–216). Coleford, UK: Douglas McLean.

Rigney, Azucena C. (1999) Questioning in interpreted testimony. *Forensic Linguistics* 6 (1), 83–108.

Roche, Declan (2007) Retribution and restorative justice. In Johnstone and Van Ness (eds) (pp. 75–90).

Rock, Frances (2001) The genesis of a witness statement. *Forensic Linguistics* 8 (2), 44–72.

Rock, Frances (2007) *Communicating Rights: The Language of Arrest and Detention*. Basingstoke: Palgrave Macmillan.

Roy, John (1990) The difficulties of limited-English-proficient individuals in the legal setting. In Robert Rieber and William Stewart (eds) *The Language Scientist as Expert in the Legal Setting* (pp. 73–84). New York: New York Academy of Sciences.

Russell, Debra (2002) *Interpreting in Legal Contexts: Consecutive and Simultaneous Interpretation*. Burtonsville, MD: Linstok Press.

Russell, Sonia (2000) 'Let me put it simply': The case for a standard translation of the police caution and its explanation. *Forensic Linguistics* 7 (1), 26–48.

Sarat, Austin and William Felstiner (1990) Legal realism in lawyer–client communication. In Levi and Walker (eds) (pp. 133–151).

Sarat, Austin and William Felstiner (1995) *Divorce Lawyers and Their Clients*. London: Oxford University Press.

Scheffer, Thomas (2006) The microformation of criminal defense: On the lawyer's notes, speech production, and a field of presence. *Research on Language and Social Interaction* 39 (3), 303–342.

Schieffelin, Bambi B., Kathryn A. Woolard and Paul V. Kroskrity (eds) (1998) *Language Ideologies: Practice and Theory*. Oxford: Oxford University Press.

Schiffrin, Deborah (1994) *Approaches to Discourse*. Oxford: Blackwell.

Schiffrin, Deborah (2006) *In Other Words: Variation in Reference and Narrative*. Cambridge: Cambridge University Press.

Schollum, Mary (2005) *Investigative Interviewing: The Literature*. Wellington: Office of the Commissioner of Police, New Zealand. Retrieved on 1 February 2009 from http://www.police. govt.nz/resources/2005/investigative-interviewing/

Schwartz, Melanie (2004) Opening a circle of hope: The NSW government review of circle sentencing. *Indigenous Law Bulletin* 5 (29), 4.

Shepherd, Eric (2007) *Investigative Interviewing: The Conversation Management Approach*. Oxford: Oxford University Press.

Shuy, Roger W. (1990) Evidence of cooperation in conversation: Topic-type in a solicitation to murder case. In Robert Rieder and William Stewart (eds) *The Language Scientist as Expert in the Legal Setting* (pp. 85–105). New York: The New York Academy of Science.

Shuy, Roger W. (1993) *Language Crimes: The Use and Abuse of Language Evidence in the Courtroom*. Oxford: Blackwell.

Shuy, Roger W. (1995) How a judge's *voir dire* can teach a jury what to say. *Discourse and Society* 6 (2), 207–222.

Shuy, Roger W. (1997) Ten unanswered language questions about Miranda. *Forensic Linguistics* 4 (2), 175–196.

Shuy, Roger W. (1998) *The Language of Confession, Interrogation, and Deception*. Thousand Oaks, CA: Sage.

Shuy, Roger W. (2005) *Creating Language Crimes: How Law Enforcement Uses and Abuses Language*. Oxford: Oxford University Press.

Shuy, Roger W. (2006) *Linguistics in the Courtroom: A Practical Guide*. Oxford: Oxford University Press.

Silbey, Susan S. and Sally E. Merry (1986) Mediator settlement strategies. *Law and Policy* 8, 7–32.

Silverstein, Michael (1996) Monoglot 'standard' in America: Standardization and metaphors of linguistic hegemony. In Donald Brenneis and Ronald K.S. Macaulay (eds) *The Matrix of Language: Contemporary Linguistic Anthropology* (pp. 284–306). Boulder, C.: Westview Press.

Silverstein, Michael (1998) Contemporary transformations of local linguistic communities. *Annual Review of Anthropology* 27, 401–426.

Singler, John V. (2004) The 'linguistic' asylum interview and the linguist's evaluation of it, with special reference to applicants for Liberian political asylum in Switzerland. *International Journal of Speech, Language and the Law* 11 (2), 222–239.

Solan, Lawrence M. (1993) *The Language of Judges*. Chicago: The University of Chicago Press.

Solan, Lawrence M. and Peter M. Tiersma (2005) *Speaking of Crime: The Language of Criminal Justice.* Chicago: University of Chicago Press.

Sourdin, Tania (2008) *Alternative Dispute Resolution*. 3rd edition. Sydney: Law Book Company.

Stern, Ludmila (1995) Non-English speaking witnesses in the Australian legal context: The War Crimes Prosecution as a case study. *Law/Text/Culture* 2, 6–31.

Sternberg, Kathleen J., Michael E. Lamb, Phillip W. Esplin, Yael Orbach and Irit Hershkowitz (2002) Using a structured interview protocol to improve the quality of investigative interviews. In Eisen *et al.* (eds) (pp. 409–436).

Stygall, Gail (1994) *Trial Language: Differential Discourse Processing and Discursive Formation.* Amsterdam: John Benjamins.

Stygall, Gail (2001) A different class of witnesses: Experts in the courtroom. *Discourse Studies* 3 (3), 327–349.

Stygall, Gail (2008) 'Did they *really* say that?': The women of Wenatchee: Vulnerability, confessions and linguistic analysis. *Journal of English Linguistics* 36 (3), 220–238.

Sutton, Peter (2003) *Native Title in Australia: An Ethnographic Perspective*. Cambridge: Cambridge University Press.

Swann, Joan, Ana Deumert, Theresa Lillis and Rajend Mesthrie (2004) *A Dictionary of Sociolinguistics.* Edinburgh: Edinburgh University Press.

Ta, Tai Van (1999) Vietnamese immigrants in American courts. In Moore (ed.) (pp. 140–157).

Tan, Poh-Ling (ed.) (1997) *Asian Legal Systems: Law, Society and Pluralism in East Asia*. Sydney: Butterworths.

Tannen, Deborah (1989) *Talking Voices: Repetition, Dialogue, and Imagery in Conversational Discourse.* Cambridge: Cambridge University Press.

Tiersma, Peter M. (1993) Reforming the language of jury instructions. *Hofstra Law Review* 22, 37–78.

Tiersma, Peter M. (1999) *Legal Language*. Chicago: University of Chicago Press.

Tiersma, Peter M. (2001a) Textualizing the law. *Forensic Linguistics* 8 (2), 73–92.

Tiersma, Peter M. (2001b) The rocky road to legal reform: Improving the language of jury instructions. *Brooklyn Law Review* 66 (4), 1081–1118.

Tiersma, Peter M. (2006) *Communicating with Juries: How to Draft More Understandable Jury Instructions*. Williamsburg, VA: National Centre for State Courts.

Tiersma, Peter M. (2007) The language of consent in rape law. In Cotterill (ed.) (pp. 83–103).

Tracy, Karen and Anna Spradlin (1994) Talking like a mediator. In Joseph Folger and Tricia Jones (eds) *New Directions in Mediation: Communication Research and Perspectives* (pp. 110–132). Thousand Oaks, CA: Sage.

Trezise, Patricia (1996) Use of language and the Anunga Rules: R v Jean Denise Izumi. *Aboriginal Law Bulletin* 79 (3), 17–18.

Trinch, Shonna (2001) The advocate as gatekeeper: The limits of politeness in protective order interviews with Latina survivors of domestic abuse. *Journal of Sociolinguistics* 5 (4), 475–506.

Trinch, Shonna (2003) *Latinas' Narratives of Domestic Abuse: Discrepant Versions of Violence.* Amsterdam: John Benjamins.

Trinch, Shonna (2005) Acquiring authority through the acquisition of genre: Latinas, intertextuality and violence. *International Journal of Speech, Language and the Law* 12 (1), 19–48.

Trinch, Shonna (2006) Bilingualism and representation: Locating Spanish–English contact in legal institutional memory. *Language in Society* 35 (4), 559–593.

Trinch, Shonna (2007) Deconstructing the 'stakes' in high stakes gatekeeping interviews: Battered women and narration. *Journal of Pragmatics* 39, 1895–1918.

Turner, Graham H. (1995) The bilingual, bimodal courtroom: A first glance. *Journal of Interpretation* 7 (1), 3–34.

Uehara, Randal J.K. and Christopher N. Candlin (1989) The structure and discoursal characteristics of *voir dire.* In Coleman (ed.) (pp. 453–473).

Van Dijk, Teun A. (1993) Principles of critical discourse analysis. *Discourse and Society* 4 (2), 249–283.

Vertes, John (2002) Jury trials in Inuit and other Aboriginal communities. Paper presented to the Joint Meeting of the Canadian Law and Society Association and the Law and Society Association in Vancouver.

Vidmar, Neil (ed.) (2000a) *World Jury Systems.* Oxford: Oxford University Press.

Vidmar, Neil (2000b) The Canadian criminal jury: Searching for a middle ground. In Vidmar (ed.) (pp. 211–248).

Wadensjö, Cecilia (1998) *Interpreting as Interaction.* London: Longman.

Wakefield, Hollida (2006) Guidelines on investigatory interviewing of children: What is the consensus in the scientific community? *American Journal of Forensic Psychology* 24 (3), 57–74.

Walker, Anne Graffam (1987) Linguistic manipulation, power, and the legal setting. In Leah Kedar (ed.) *Power through Discourse* (pp. 57–80). Norwood, NJ: Ablex Publishing Corporation.

Walker, Anne Graffam (1993) Questioning young children in court. *Law and Human Behaviour* 17 (1), 59–81.

Walker, Anne Graffam (1999) *Handbook on Questioning Children: A Linguistic Perspective.* 2nd edition. Washington, DC: ABA Center on Children and the Law.

Walker, Samuel, Cassia Spohn and Miriam DeLone (1996) *The Color of Justice: Race, Ethnicity and Crime in America.* Belmont, CA: Wadsworth Publishing Company.

Walsh, Michael (1994) Interactional styles in the courtroom: An example from northern Australia. In Gibbons (ed.) (pp. 217–233).

Walsh, Michael (1995) Tainted evidence: Literacy and traditional knowledge in an Aboriginal land claim. In Eades (ed.) (pp. 97–124).

Walsh, Michael (1999) Interpreting for the transcript: Problems in recording Aboriginal land claim proceedings in northern Australia. *Forensic Linguistics* 6 (1), 161–195.

Walsh, Michael (2008) 'Which way?' Difficult options for vulnerable witnesses in Australian Aboriginal land claim and native title cases. *Journal of English Linguistics* 36 (3), 239–265.

Walter, Bettyruth (1988) *The Jury Summation as Speech Genre*. Amsterdam: John Benjamins.

Wei, Li (2000) Dimensions of bilingualism. In Li Wei (ed.) *The Bilingualism Reader* (pp. 3–25). London: Routledge.

Wei, Li (2005) 'How can you tell?' Towards a common sense explanation of conversational code-switching. *Journal of Pragmatics* 37, 375–389.

Winiecki, Don (2008) The expert witnesses and courtroom discourse: Applying micro and macro forms of discourse analysis to study process and the 'doings of doings' for individuals and for society. *Discourse and Society* 19 (6), 756–781.

Wierzbicka, Anna (2003) 'Reasonable man' and 'reasonable doubt': The English language, Anglo culture and Anglo-American culture. *International Journal of Speech Language and the Law* 10 (1), 1–22.

Wilson, Claire and Martine Powell (2001) *A Guide to Interviewing Children: Essential Skills for Counsellors, Police, Lawyers and Social Workers*. Sydney: Allen and Unwin.

Wood, James (2007) Jury directions. *Journal of Judicial Administration* 16, 151–164.

Woodbury, Hanni (1984) The strategic use of questions in court. *Semiotica* 48 (3/4), 197–228.

Woolard, Kathryn A. (1998) Introduction: Language ideology as a field of inquiry. In Bambi B. Schieffelin, Kathryn A. Woolard and Paul V. Kroskrity (eds) *Language Ideologies: Practice and Theory* (pp. 3–47). Oxford: Oxford University Press.

Woolard, Kathryn A. (1999) Simultaneity and bivalency as strategies in bilingualism. *Journal of Linguistic Anthropology* 8 (1), 3–29.

Woolard, Kathryn A. (2004) Codeswitching. In Alessandro Duranti (ed.) *A Companion to Linguistic Anthropology* (pp. 73–94). Oxford: Blackwell.

Woolard, Kathryn A. and Bambi B. Schieffelin (1994) Language ideology. *Annual Review of Anthropology* 23, 55–82.

Woolls, David (2003) Better tools for the trade and how to use them. *International Journal of Speech Language and the Law* 10 (1), 102–112.

Woolls, David and Malcolm Coulthard (1998) Tools for the trade. *Forensic Linguistics* 5 (1), 33–57.

Young, Linda (1994) *Crosstalk and Culture in Sino-American Communication*. Cambridge: Cambridge University Press.

Yuille, John C., Robin Hunter, Risha Joffe and Judy Zaparniuk (1993) Interviewing children in sexual abuse cases. In Gail S. Goodman and Bette L. Bottoms (eds) *Child Victims, Child Witnesses: Understanding and Improving Children's Testimony* (pp. 95–115). New York: Guilford Press.

Zappavigna, Michele, Paul Dwyer and James Martin (2008) Syndromes of meaning: Exploring patterned coupling in a NSW Youth Justice Conference. In Ahmar Mahboob and Naomi Knight (eds) *Questioning Linguistics* (pp. 165–187). Newcastle: Cambridge Scholars Publishing.

Subject index

abduction, 13, 47, 108, 116–122, 125, 245–246, 264n67
Aboriginal Australians, 241, 264n61
  courtroom hearings, 93–99, 115–122, 225–227, 245, 255
  land claims, 30, 235, 252, 262n42,
  mediation, 216
  native title, 95
  police interviews 138–140, 153, 167–170, 173–175, 237–240, 249, 255
  worldview and culture, 93–99, 256
  see also Aboriginal English, Aboriginal languages, indigenous courts.
Aboriginal English
  Australia, 36, 89–92, 116, 153, 173–175, 226, 238, 240, 249, 255
  Canada, 172–173
Aboriginal languages, Australia, 68, 76, 77, 162–163, see also Djamparpuyngu, Kriol, Yolngu Matha.
abortion, 49
accusation sequence, 50
address terms, 193, 269
ADR. See alternative dispute resolution.
advocacy, 71, 101, 125, 163, 191, 197, 200, 218, 234, 240, 265, 267
affidavit, 7, 189, 196–201, 211, 248, 263n54, 265
African Americans. See African American (Vernacular) English.
African American (Vernacular) English, 53, 89
Afro–Caribbean people, 146, 181–183
agency, 5, 42, 108, 113–114, 116, 122–123, 199–200, 242, see also grammar of non-agency.
alcohol courts. See therapeutic courts.
alternative dispute resolution, 206–207, 217–218, 263n55, 265, see also mediation.
American Sign Language, 78, 171
antecedent form, 8, 10
apology, 91, 223–224
arbitration, 206, 212–213, 265
Arnhem Land. See Australia, Northern Territory.
articles (definite and indefinite), 72–73
assault, 35, 45, 72, 79–80, 91, 96–98, 106, 168, 172, 195, 200, 212, 227, see also sexual assault.
asylum seekers. See LADO.
AUSIT (Australian Institute of Interpreters and Translators Inc), 69
Auslan, 79

Australia 4, 10, 13, 18, 21, 30, 31, 35, 36, 40, 41, 42, 55, 72, 79, 84, 90, 92, 95, 98–100, 115, 118, 132, 133, 134, 145–146, 150, 153, 155, 156, 166, 180, 189, 190, 210, 216–220, 225–227, 235, 237, 240, 259n11, n5, n13, 260n15, n21, 261n36, 262n47, 263n51, n55, 264n61, n63,
  New South Wales, 22, 30, 31, 41, 96, 100, 125, 133, 162, 190, 222, 227, 260
  Northern Territory, 66, 68, 77, 89, 93, 162–164, 241, 262n42
  Queensland, 14, 22, 92, 102, 115, 153, 224, 264n64
  Victoria, 100, 227
  Western Australia, 163, 190
  see also Aboriginal Australians, Aboriginal English
Australian Law Reform Commission, 100, 102, 180

back translation, 252, 269
bail, 30
balance of probabilities, 29
Bank of English, 42, 154, see also Cobuild Corpus of Spoken English.
barrister, 118, 185–196, 237, 263n51, 265, 267
Basic Interpersonal Communication Skills (BICS), 67
Belgium, 254
Bentley case (UK), 153–154
beyond reasonable doubt, 28–29, 34, 55–57
BICS. See Basic Interpersonal Communication Skills.
Birmingham Six case (UK), 153
bivalency, 254
bomb threat, 235
Brazil, 204
bribery, 236
Bridgewater Four case (UK), 153
brief, 195–196, 263n51, n52, 265
British Sign Language, 80
burden of proof, 29, 56
burglary, 195, 197

CALP. See Cognitive Academic Language Proficiency.
can, 262n42
Canada, 4, 21, 41
  Northwest Territories and Nunavut, 65, 76, 88, 92, 107, 127, 151, 176, 220, 225, 265

Quebec, 18

Saskatchewan, 260n21

carry on, 173–175

caution. *See* police caution.

challenge (in jury selection), 40–41

children

in court, 11, 84–88, 99, 101, 234, 240

in police interviews, 11, 176–179, 234, 240

see also youth justice conferencing

childrens court, 35, 118, 263n58, *see also* juvenile court.

China, 47

Chinese language, 65, 92

circle sentencing, 226–227

civil law, 18, 28–31, 34, 64, 115, 123–125, 206, 210, 212, 220–221, 236, 266–267 *see also* continental law, small claims courts.

closing address. *See* closing argument.

closing argument, 40, 52–54, 196, 249, 259n13

Cobuild Corpus of Spoken English, 37, 153

see also Bank of English.

code-switching, 61, 102, 197, 213, 240, 252, 255

coercion, 108

in court, 44, 109, 111–112, 123, 250

in police interviews, 132, 139, 145, 150, 152–153, 155, 165, 170, 176, 180–181, 183, 236, 259n9

Cognitive Academic Language Proficiency, 67

cognitive interviewing, 132, 146, 147–149, 177, 180, 261n30

common law, 4, 18–19, 21–22, 28, 30–31, 40, 220, 225, 234, 256

comprehension, 13, 89, 109, 134–141, 167–168, 175, 179, 246–247, *see also* understanding.

conciliation, 206–207

Condren case (Australia), 237–240

confession, 47, 132–133, 142, 144–146, 152, 153–155, 165, 168, 172, 180, 235, 237–238, *see also* fabricated confession, false confession.

consent, 72, 108, 113–116, 123, 201, 211, 245–246

constructed dialogue, 215

contempt of court, 32–33

continental law, 18, 28, 30, 41

contrast device (in cross–examination), 51–52, 112

Conversation Analysis (CA), 15–16, 50, 112, 182, 206, 213–218

conversation management, 146, 149

conversational implicature, 143, 261n26, 269

copspeak. *See* policespeak.

coronial inquiry, 30, 76, 89, 93, 95, 259n3

corpus linguistics, 22, 37, 42, 153–154, 261n34

could, 143, 244–246, 261n26, 27

court TV, 37

creole languages, 77, 89, 172, 181, 254, 269, 270, *see also* Krio, Kriol, Jamaican Creole, Torres Strait Creole.

Criminal Justice Commission, Queensland, Australia, 92

Critical Discourse Analysis (CDA), 15

critical sociolinguistics, 12, 15

critical turn, 12, 108

culture, 5, 11, 15, 47, 53, 65, 76, 84, 90–101, 115, 118, 125, 138, 142, 168, 194, 201–202, 209–216, 222, 226, 238–239, 242, 248, 251–256, 270, 271

cultural presuppositions, 92–99

customary law, 4, 18, 95

Cyprus, 18

deaf sign language, 11, 65, 78–80, 82, 170–171, 204, 243, 257, *see also* American Sign Language, Auslan, British Sign Language.

decontextualisation, 249, *see also* entextualisation, recontextualisation.

demeanour of witnesses, 53, 93

descriptive linguistics, 15

dialect, 7–8, 48, 238–239, 255–256, 269, *see also* eye dialect, second dialect speakers.

directions, jury. *See* jury instructions.

disability, 65, 88, 99, 101, 180

discourse analysis, 14–15, 54, 108, 194, 202

discourse markers, 74, 76, 181, 253, 269, *see also so, well.*

disintegrative shaming, 221–222

divorce, 31, 188–193, 198, 215, 217, 220

Djamparpuyngu language, 68, 76, 253

do you remember?, 85–87

do you understand?, 135, 137–141

domestic violence, 42, 189, 197–201

don't have to. See have to.

drug courts. *See* therapeutic courts.

Duke study, 47–49, 107, 142, 194, 207

electronic recording of police interviews, 134, 139, 143, 146, 155–156, 179, 237, 261n28

England and Wales, 4, 10, 18, 21, 29, 33, 37, 55, 57–58, 84, 88, 106, 132–138, 142, 145–147, 153, 156, 162, 165, 176, 180–182, 194–195, 259n1, n13, 261n29, n31, 263n51

emphasis. *See* prosody.

entextualisation, *See* decontextualisation, recontextualisation.

ethnography of discourse, 207, 210

ethnography of speaking/communication, 14, 194, 259n7
European Convention on Human Rights, 64
evidence. *See* rules of evidence.
exhibit (in court), 35, 73, 195, 266
expert witnesses, 48, 92, 95, 134, 137, 153–155, 167, 172, 180, 234–240, 244, 261n33, 264n63
eye contact, 79, 93
eye dialect, 16

fabricated confession, 153–155, 172, 235, 237–239, 264n64, 268
fact (legal concept), 34–35, 43, 266
false confession, 144–145, 180
family group conferencing, 221
family law, 31, 190, 206, 220, *see also* divorce.
family violence courts. *See* therapeutic courts.
fear, 113–114, 124, 245
feedback markers. *See* minimal responses.
Fifth Amendment, 13, 267
forensic linguistics, definition, 234
forgiveness, 221, 224
formalism approach to law, 191
French language, 165–170, 262n43, 263n52
front-translation, 169, 270

gendered language use, 15, 47–48, 191–194, 209
gist (in *so*-prefaced questions), 182
grammar of non–agency, 42, 114–116, 249
gratuitous concurrence, 91, 138, 170, 270
guilty plea, 31, 34, 108–112, 123, 139, 142, 203, 260n19

handling stolen goods, 58–59
have to 167–170
hearsay, 43, 215
Hebrew language, 263n50
hedges, 47–48, 142, 173, 194
Hernandez case (US), 92–93
Hindu law, 18
homogeneism. *See* language ideology, monolingual language ideology.
Hong Kong, 65
"hot–tubbing", 235

ideology, 110–111, 113–114, 189, 192, 264n65, n69, 270, *see also* language ideology.
impartiality, 41, 69, 164, 206, 213–219, 234–235, 263n57, 265, *see also* neutrality.
implicature. *See* conversational implicature.
"improper" questions in cross-examination, 99–101, 125–126

indigenous courts, 11, 225–228
informal courts. *See* small claims courts.
instructions, jury. *See* jury instructions.
instructions to lawyer, 195–196, 248, 263n53, 266
intellectually disabled people, 99, 101, 180
intensifiers, 47–48, 194
interactional sociolinguistics, 15, 108
International Covenant on Civil and Political Rights 64
interpreters
    assessing the need for, 66–69, 162–163
    court, 7, 64–80, 252–253
    jurors, 65
    lawyer interviews 197
    linguistic challenges for, 72–77, 165–170, 254
    objections to, 69–70
    police interviews, 162–172, 262n39
    professional ethics, 69, 164
    rights to, 64, 162
    role, 70–71, 84, 164–165, 238, 241
    small claims courts 213
    see also deaf sign language, police officers as interpreters, stand-by interpreting, translation.
interrogation. *See* police interview with suspect.
intonation. *See* prosody.
Israel, 18
Italian language, 89

Jamaican Creole, 77, 172
Japanese language, 78, 92, 166
Jewish law, 18
judicial decision. *See* decision.
jury selection, 40–42
jury instructions, 54–57, 136, 188, 247, 259–260n13, 266
juvenile court, 210, *see also* childrens court.

Kina case (Australia), 237–238
Koori Court, 227
Korean language, 72–73
Krio language (Sierra Leone), 254
Kriol language (Australia), 77, 89, 172

LADO (language analysis in the determination of origin of asylum seekers), 236–237, 240, 254–255, 264n69, n70
land claims. *See* Aboriginal Australians, land claims.
landlord-tenant disputes, 210–211
Language and National Origin Group, 240, 255

language ideology, 142, 241–256
  correspondence theory of language, 142,
    243–247, 253
  inconsistency, 248–251
  literalism, 245–247
  monolingual language ideology, 68, 213,
    251–256
  narrator authorship, 247–251
  Standard English ideology, 242
  see also ideology, selective literalism, textualism,
    transmission model of communication.
Language Intricacies and Manipulation
  Proficiency (LIMP), 67–68
Language Intricacies and Mental States (LIMS), 68
law school, 201–203
leading questions, 35, 43–44, 87–88, 97, 146, 267
legal education, 237, 239–240, 256
legal register, 8–11, 58, 141–143, 192, 261n27,
  264n66, 270–271, see also policespeak.
legalese. See legal register.
lexical perversion, 259n12
LIMP. See Language Intricacies and Manipulation
  Proficiency.
LIMS. See Language Intricacies and Mental
  States.
linguistic anthropology, 108, 202, 242, 251
linguistic ideology. See language ideology.

magistrates court, 106, 150, 225–227
Malay language, 65
Malaysia, 65
Malta, 18
manual, trial, 40, 43, 195
Māori, 29–30, 69, 225
Márquez case (US), 164
matched guise technique, 48
mediation, 11, 31, 206–207, 210–221, 263n57, 267
mediator. See mediation.
memory, 85–88, 119, 147–149, 176, 264n68
mental health courts. See therapeutic courts.
minimal responses, 236
Miranda warning, 132–135, 141–145, 162, 171, 245,
  262n38
monolingual language ideology, 68, 213, 251–256
monolingualism, 65–66, see also monolingual
  language ideology.
morphosyntax, 11, 15, 58, 236, 244, 270, see also
  articles (definite and indefinite), grammar of
  non-agency, nominalisation, passive voice,
  prepositions, pronouns, unaccusative
  construction.

multilingualism, 213, 251–256, see also
  monolingual language ideology,
  monolingualism.
murder, 28, 34, 42, 68, 80, 86, 137, 139, 150–153,
  172, 173–175, 180, 236, 237, 256

NADRAC (National Alternative Dispute
  Resolution Advisory Council, Australia),
  216–219, 263n55, n57, 265–267
narrative, 40, 49, 58–59, 68, 97–98, 145, 147–148,
  153–157, 176–177, 196, 198, 200–201, 223, 251,
  269, see also language ideology, narrator
  authorship, storytelling.
Native Americans, 92, 225
native title. See Aboriginal Australians, native title.
neighbourhood disputes, 207–210, 211–212
neocolonialism, 115–123, 243
Netherlands, 18, 51, 156–157, 254
neutrality, 214, 216, see also impartiality.
New Zealand, 21, 29–30, 65, 68–69, 79, 84, 147,
  220, 225
Nigeria, 18
nominalisation, 85, 114
Northern Ireland, 50, 133
Norway, 73

open-ended questions, 88, 145, 147–148, 177, 270
opening statement (in court), 42

PACE (Police and Criminal Evidence Act, UK
  1984), 261n29
Papua New Guinea, 18
paradigmatic approach, 58–59, 98, 209, 251
paralegal, 189, 197–201, 211, 247–249
participation framework, 146–147, 214
passive voice, 11, 42, 55, 85, 154, 270
patriarchy, 60, 112–115, 123–124, 209, 220
PEACE (training for police interviews in UK),
  261n29
peremptory challenge. See challenge (in jury
  selection).
perjury, 236
Philippines, 18
Pinkenba case (Australia), 115–122
plain English, 55, 169–170
plain meaning rule, 244–245, 264n66, see also
  textualism.
plea. See guilty plea.
police,
  accused, 13, 47, 116
  interpreters, 164–165

interviews, 7, 8, 10, 11, 12, 13, 66, 90–92,
132–183, 235–237, 241, 244–250, 261n27,
n29, n31, 262n40, n44
statements, 153–157
witnesses in court, 7, 8–10, 50
see also Afro-Caribbean people, children,
coercion, cognitive interviewing,
confession, conversation management,
creole languages, deaf sign language,
intellectually disabled people,
interpreters, Miranda warning, PEACE,
Pinkenba case, police caution,
policespeak, resistance, second dialect
speakers, second language speakers,
youth justice conferences.
police caution, 260n24, 265
diversionary, 115, 195, 196
in suspect interview, 132–142, 162, 163, 165–167,
170, see also Miranda warning.
policespeak, 10, 153–155
position reports (in mediation), 218–219
poststructuralism, 122
powerful/powerless speech, 48–49, 107, 209
pragmatics, 11, 73–76, 90–92, 142–143, 170,
244–246, 253, 269, 270, see also address
terms, discourse markers, gratuitous
concurrence, hedges, silence.
prepositions, 11, 77, 168, 178
prescriptivism, 6–7
presuppositions in questions, 10, 52, 67, 107, 118,
124, 151, 193, 249, see also cultural
presuppositions.
prisoner's friend (in police interviews), 163–164,
168
problem-oriented courts. See therapeutic courts.
procedure-oriented judge, 110–112
pronouns, 13, 21
proof. See burden of proof, standard of proof.
proposals (in mediation), 218
prosodic questions, 44
prosody, 16, 36, 74, 270
protective order, 197–200, 211–212, 227, 267
psycholinguistic research, 85, 134–135, 142, 234

quoted speech. See constructed dialogue.

rape, 50–51, 107–108, 112–115, 123–125, 152,
199–200, 211, 245, 250, 260n20, 261n33,
267, see also sexual assault.
rape shield laws, 112
realism approach to law, 191

recontextualisation, 116, 117, 123, 156, 174, 197, 200,
247–251, 259n12, 264n69, 270, see also
decontextualisation, entextualisation.
record-oriented judge, 110–111
recross-examination, 43
re-examination, 43
reformulation, see recontextualisation.
refugees. See asylum seekers.
register. See legal register.
reintegrative shaming, 221–223, 225
relational approach to litigation, 208–209, 211
repetition, 53, 100, 112–113, 181, 191, 196, 227
requestions, 44, 87, 259n9
resistance
of suspects in police interviews, 144, 149–153
of witnesses in court, 51, 79, 106–107, 119–122
restorative justice, 207, 220–224, 225–226
restraining order. See protective order.
retributive justice, 221
rule-oriented approach to litigation, 208–209,
211
rules of evidence, 33, 34–35, 37, 43, 68, 85,
100–101, 118, 125, 207, 215, 217, 221, 234–235,
250, 259n5
Russian language, 68, 72, 238

scaffolding, 224, 271
Scotland, 18
second dialect speakers, 84, 88–92, 153, 172–175,
181, 256
second language speakers, 11, 64–80, 153, 162–172,
181, 224, 234, 242, 251–254
selective facilitation, 217, 219
selective literalism, 246
self-incrimination privilege, 13–14, 55, 59, 267
semantics, 11, 15, 72, 89–90, 170, 192, 244–246,
253, 270, 271
Sesotho language, 72
sexual assault 35, 72, 84, 99, 101, 112–115, 123–124,
168, 263n59, see also rape.
Shari'a law, 18
shoplifting, 195
Sierra Leone, 254
sign language. See deaf sign language.
silence,
in interaction, 36, 52, 79, 90–93, 112, 113, 178,
191, 236, 256
right to silence, 13, 132–136, 163, 165–170, 180
silly, 174–175, 255
Sinhala language, 65
small claims court, 30, 65, 68–69, 115, 207–214

so, 181–183, 253
sociolegal research, 5, 12, 22, 107–108, 111–112, 115,
    182, 207, 209, 219, 224
sociology of language, 15
Socratic method, 202
solicits (in mediation), 218–219
South Africa, 18
Spanish language, 65, 73–76, 93, 145, 155, 164,
    170, 197, 253, 262n38
speech act theory, 243
Sri Lanka, 65
standard of proof, 55–56
stand-by interpreting, 68, 90, 94, 271
statutory interpretation, 244
storytelling, 34, 40, 67, 68, 86, 116, 149, 156, 198,
    207–209, 247–251, 256, 264n68, *see also*
    narrative.
suggestibility, 87–88
suicide, 155, 235
summary for jury 40, 54–57, 259n13
summation. *See* closing argument.
summing up. See summary for jury.
Sweden, 156–157
systemic functional linguistics, 223
syntax. *See* morphosyntax.

tag questions, 44, 47, 75–76
Tamil language, 65
television,
    closed-circuit television in trials, 88
    televised trials (*see also* court TV), 37
    television police/courtroom dramas, 13, 19, 133
textualism, 244–245, *see also* plain meaning rule.
theft, 58–59, 195, 223
therapeutic courts, 220, 224–226, 263n59
topic analysis, 236
Torres Strait Creole, 172
trademark cases, 236
transcript, 9, 31, 65, 72, 86, 156, 172, 188–189,
    249–250, 252
transcription, xii–xiii, 16–17
transmission model of communication,
    246–247
translation, 14, 22, 64, 72–73, 76, 162, 169, 172,
    175, 244, 254–255
    see also back-translation, front-translation,
        interpreting.
trial manual. *See* manual, trial

unaccusative construction, 114
understanding, 58, 66, 73, 74, 77, 78, 85, 90–93,
    95, 99, 101, 109, 112, 123, 135–141, 162, 167,
    171–172, 175, 178, 202, 243–247, 249, 253,
    270, *see also* comprehension.
United Kingdom, 21, 132, 172, 210, 215, 259n5
    Home Office, 69, 176
    see also England and Wales.
United States, 30, 49, 53, 54, 55, 65, 71, 79, 84, 89,
    92, 110, 132–134, 137, 142–145, 147, 155, 156, 165,
    170–171, 180, 189–191, 202–203, 207, 210, 212,
    214–215, 220, 224, 237–238, 241, 243, 244,
    246, 253, 259n13, 261n28, 262n38, n40, n46
    Arizona, 109–112, 195
    California, 28, 55, 164
    Florida, 164
    Hispanic/Latino people, 91, 145, 152, 155,
        164–165, 170, 197
    Louisiana, 18
    New Mexico, 65
    New York, 68, 164, 212–213
    see also Native Americans.
Universal Declaration of Human Rights, 256
upshot (in *so*-prefaced questions), 182

vagrancy, 117, 122
variationist sociolinguistics, 15, 48
verbal. *See* fabricated confession.
victim-offender mediation, 221
voir dire, 21, 41–42, 268
volume (of speech). *See* prosody.
vulnerable witnesses, 83–101, 106, 125, 176, 261n37

well, 74–75, 253
Welsh language, 69
West Africa, 254
WH-questions, 43–44, 87, 98, 149, 171, 181, 271
Whorfian hypothesis, 5
written legal texts, 6–7, 9, 12–14, 18, 28, 35, 54–56,
    58, 67, 70, 76, 109, 135–136, 141–142, 153–157,
    162, 173–175, 188–190, 194–201, 202,
    244–245, 248–249, 259n4, 265, 266, 267

Yes/No-questions, 43–44, 77–78, 87, 91, 98, 171,
    181, 198, 213, 259n9, 270, 271
Yolngu Matha language, 168, 262n41
youth justice conferences, 221–224, 263n58
Yup'ik Eskimo people, 91, 99

Author index

Abel, Richard L, 219
Ainsworth, Janet, 142–143, 173, 235, 242–245
Aldridge, Michelle, 99, 177–179, 240
Angermeyer, Philipp Sebastian, 65, 68–69, 165, 212–213, 241–242, 252
Arends, Jacques, 240, 251
Atkinson, J. Maxwell, 50, 212–213
Auburn, Timothy, 132
Auty, Kate, 227

Baldwin, John, 146
Berk-Seligson, Susan, 69, 71, 76, 80, 91, 133–134, 145, 152, 155, 162, 164–165, 167, 170–171, 236, 262n38
Blommaert, Jan, 12, 122, 242, 251, 252, 260n18, 270
Bogoch, Bryna, 40, 191–194, 198
Braithwaite, John, 221–222, 224
Brennan, Roslin, 84, 180
Brennan, Mark, 66, 84–85, 179, 180
Brennan, Mary, 78–80
Brière, Eugene, 134, 162
Briggs, Daniel, 227
Brown-Blake, Celia, 172, 181
Bruck, Maggie, 87, 176
Bucholtz, Mary, 16
Bull, Ray, 146–149, 180, 261n29, n30
Butters, Ronald, 236

Candlin, Chris, 41, 229
Carranza, Isolda E, 53–54
Castelle, George, 171
Ceci, Stephen J, 87, 176
Chambers, Paul, 172, 181
Chang, Yanrong, 47
Charrow, Robert P and Veda R, 55, 135
Chaski, Carole, 155, 235
Clare, Isabel C H, 180
Cobb, Sara, 216, 220
Colin, Joan, 69, 70
Conley, John M, 5, 12, 16, 47–49, 107–108, 111, 115, 122, 125, 188, 206–211, 220, 237–240, 242, 251
Cooke, Michael, 67, 69, 76, 77–78, 89, 93–95, 162–163, 167–170, 172, 253–254, 262n39, n41
Corcoran, Chris, 236, 254–255
Cotterill, Janet, 37, 42, 53, 107, 119, 141–142
Coulthard, Malcolm, 12, 153–155, 235
Cunneen, Chris, 222, 225–226
Cunningham, Clark D, 188

Daly, Kathleen, 220, 225–226
Danet, Brenda, 40, 44, 49, 87, 193, 259n9
Dingwall, Robert, 215–220
Drew, Paul, 31, 50–51, 107, 119, 259n12
Drizin, Steven, 180
Dumas, Bethany, 55
Dunstan, R 46

Eades, Diana, 12, 14, 36, 46, 90–93, 95–99, 107, 115–122, 125, 153, 162, 183, 237–240, 243, 245–249, 251, 255, 256, 259n12, 260n23
Edwards, Derek, 149
Edwards, Viv, 65, 76, 251
Ehrlich, Susan, 42, 107, 112–115, 119, 123–124, 151, 245, 259n12
Evans, Nicholas, 262n42

Fadden, Lorna 172
Felstiner, William, 189–194, 198, 201, 209
Felton Rosulek, Laura, 54
Filipovic, Luna, 73
Fisher, Ronald P, 147–148, 180
Fivush, Robyn, 88
Fox, Gwyneth, 154
Fraser, Helen, 237, 240, 255
Fuller, Janet, 53, 89

Garcia, Angela, 213–218
Geiselman, R. Edward, 147–148
Gibbons, John, 12, 67, 76, 91, 134–135, 137, 139, 153–154, 162–163, 181
Grant, Tim, 155, 235
Gray, Peter R A, 95, 235
Greatbatch, David, 215–219
Grillo, Tina, 220
Gudjonsson, Gisli H, 132, 180, 262n40
Gumperz, John J, 92

Hale, Sandra, 70–71, 74–76
Hall, Phil, 154
Halldorsdottir, Iris, 194–196
Harris, Sandra, 44, 46, 47, 106–107, 150
Haviland, John B, 243, 253
Haworth, Kate, 150, 152
Hayes, Hennessey, 224
Heffer, Chris, 10, 33, 36–37, 40, 54–59, 70, 98, 209, 247
Heisterkamp, Brian L, 216

Henderson, John, 95
Heydon, Georgina, 132, 146–147
Hobbs, Pamela, 53, 89
Holmes, Janet, 4
Hoopes, Rob, 79, 171
Howald, Blake, 155, 235

Inbau, Fred E, 171, 262n40

Jacobs, Scott, 216, 218
Jacquemet, Marco, 89
Jensen, Marie-Thérèse, 153
Johnson, Alison, 12, 150–152, 154, 179, 181, 235
Johnstone, Gerry, 221, 224
Jones, Claire, 146, 181–183, 241
Jönsson, Linda, 156–157, 174, 247

Kandel, Randy, 215, 219–220
Kassin, Saul M, 132, 180, 262n40
Koch, Harold, 90
Komter, Martha, 18, 51, 156–157, 174, 188, 247
Kroskrity, Paul V, 242
Kurzon, Dennis, 90

Lakoff, Robin, 47, 142, 194, 259n10
Lane, Chris, 46, 68–69
Laster, Kathy, 71
Lee, Jieun, 72–73, 254
Leo, Richard, 133–134, 143–145, 155, 180, 241, 261n28
Liberman, Kenneth, 91
Lindsay, D Stephen, 87
Linell, Per, 156–157, 174, 247
Lippi-Green, Rosina 6, 242
Loftus, Elizabeth F, 49
Luchjenbroers, June, 99

McCrimmon, Les A, 40, 86
McElhinny, Bonnie, 158
Maley, Yon, 188, 190
Marchetti, Elena, 220, 225–226
Martin, JR, 222–224
Maryns, Katrijn, 236, 254–255, 264n69, n70
Mather, Susan and Robert, 79
Matoesian, Gregory, 16, 51, 107, 112–113, 118–119, 248, 250, 261n33
Mauet, Thomas, 40, 49, 86
Maynard, Douglas W, 218
Mellinkoff, David, 12, 58
Merry, Sally Engle, 209–213, 220
Mertz, Elizabeth, 34, 201–203, 209
Mikkelson, Holly 7, 73, 76, 254

Mildren, Dean, 164
Milne, Rebecca, 146–149, 180, 261n29, n30
Moeketsi, Rosemary, 72
Montalvo, Margarita, 65
Montoya, Margaret, 93
Morphy, Frances 76, 95, 254
Morris, Ruth, 69–71
Morrow, Phyllis, 91, 99

Nakane, Ikuko, 165–167
Napier, Jemina, 65, 79–80, 82
Nash, David, 95
Neate, Graeme, 95
Newbury, Philip, 150–152, 181
Norrick, Neal R, 149, 248

O'Barr, William M, 5, 12, 16, 47–49, 107–108, 111, 115, 122, 125, 188, 206–211, 220, 237–240, 242, 251
Ord, Brian, 133, 148–149
Ostermann, Ana Cristina, 158, 204

Philips, Susan U, 33, 51, 92, 108–112, 123, 139, 142, 203
Poole, Debra Ann, 87
Potas, Ivan, 226
Potter, Jonathan, 149,
Powell, Martine B, 148–149, 176–177, 262n47
Powell, Richard, 65–66

Reed, Maureen, 80
Rifkin, Janet, 216, 220
Rigney, Azucena C, 76
Roche, Declan, 221
Rock, Frances, 133–138, 141–142, 156–157, 162, 174, 246–247
Roy, John, 162
Russell, Debra 79
Russell, Sonia, 141–142, 165, 167, 170

Sarat, Austin 189–194, 198, 201, 209
Scheffer, Thomas, 194–196
Schieffelin, Bambi B, 242–243
Schiffrin, Deborah, 16, 149, 248
Schollum, Mary 132–133, 145, 147, 261n30
Schwartz, Melanie, 226
Shepherd, Eric, 149
Shuy, Roger W, 41, 132, 137, 139, 155, 157, 180, 236
Sidnell, Jack, 107, 151
Silbey, Susan S, 229
Silverstein, Michael, 242–243, 251

Singler, John V, 237
Solan, Lawrence M, 141, 179, 180, 236, 243–246
Sourdin, Tania, 206, 216, 219
Spradlin, Anna, 229
Stygall, Gail, 41, 53, 155
Swann, Joan, 14, 74, 242, 269

Tannen, Deborah 215
Taylor, Veronica, 71
Tiersma, Peter M, 10, 12, 40, 53, 55–56, 58, 135, 141, 170, 179, 180, 236, 243–246, 263n52, 264n66
Tracy, Karen, 229
Trezise, Patricia, 172
Trinch, Shonna L, 197–201, 211–212, 247–248
Turner, Graham H, 79

Uehara, Randal K, 41

Van Ness, Daniel W, 221, 224
Verschueren, Jef, 242, 251

Vertes, John, 65
Vidmar, Neil, 22, 41

Wakefield, Hollida, 176
Walker, Ann Graffam, 44, 84–87, 179, 240
Walsh, Michael, 90, 95, 252, 254
Walter, Bettyruth, 53–54
Wierzbicka, Anna, 55
Wilson, Claire, 177
Winiecki, Don, 62
Wood, James, 55
Wood, Joanne, 176, 177–178, 240
Woodbury, Hanni, 44
Woolard, Kathryn A, 61, 242–243, 254
Woolls, David, 155

Yuille, John C, 176

Zappavigna, Michele, 223